"O _____ have
see _____ war."

GENER _____ cARTHUR

"Duty—Hon _____ hallowed words
reverently di _____ be, what you can
be, what you _____ llying points. . . .
You now fac _____ of change . . . of
such dreams _____ ke life the most
exciting of a _____ h all this welter
of change, y _____ , determined, in-
violable—it _____

"A masterly _____ ly warlord, this
fact-filled de _____ glas MacArthur
matches the _____ ashing the myth
behind the m _____ l intact. Moving
at breathtaki _____ ent—from mile-
stones, indee _____ *hur* gives us the
missing link _____ g of two world
wars and the _____ ught them."

_____ *urago*, Author of *Patton*

GREGORY PECK

as

MacARTHUR

A RICHARD D. ZANUCK/DAVID BROWN PRODUCTION

ED FLANDERS

DAN O'HERLIHY

Written by **HAL BARWOOD & MATTHEW ROBBINS**

Music by **JERRY GOLDSMITH**

Directed by **JOSEPH SARGENT**

Produced by **FRANK McCARTHY**

A UNIVERSAL PICTURE

TECHNICOLOR

PG PARENTAL GUIDANCE SUGGESTED

SOME MATERIAL MAY NOT BE SUITABLE FOR PRE-TEENAGERS

★ ★ ★ ★ ★

MacArthur

Clay Blair, Jr.

★ ★ ★ ★ ★

PUBLISHED BY POCKET BOOKS NEW YORK

Another *Original* publication of POCKET BOOKS

POCKET BOOKS, a Simon & Schuster division of
GULF & WESTERN CORPORATION
1230 Avenue of the Americas, New York, N.Y. 10020

ISBN: 0-671-81200-9

First Pocket Books printing July, 1977

4th printing

Trademarks registered in the United States and other countries.

Printed in the U.S.A.

MacArthur

★ ★ ★ ★ ★

CHAPTER ONE

★ ★ ★ ★ ★

IN THE EARLY morning hours of December 8, 1941, the telephone rang in the master bedroom of a lavish penthouse atop the Manila Hotel. Lieutenant General Douglas MacArthur, United States Army, commanding the land and air forces in the Philippines, answered. The caller informed the general that the Japanese had launched a surprise attack against the principal U.S. Navy base in the Pacific, Pearl Harbor.

MacArthur left no document revealing his immediate personal reaction to this momentous news. No doubt, like all Americans, he was shocked and stunned. He dressed quickly and called for his car, a brand-new black 1941 Cadillac sedan. The driver threaded through Manila's dark, deserted streets to the massive stone walls of the Old City, then through a shield-emblazoned gate. Winding through the narrow streets of Old City, the Cadillac pulled to a stop at No. 1 Calle Victoria. This was MacArthur's general headquarters (GHQ), a series of interconnected and unattractive barrackslike structures built atop the massive Old City wall. The lights were on; MacArthur's staff was gathering.

MacArthur's private office was large and spacious,

aired by big windows and ceiling fans. It seemed more like a formal drawing room than a military headquarters. It was furnished elegantly: old books and pictures, inlaid cabinets dating back to Spanish colonial days, a deep sofa, comfortable chairs, a beautiful Chinese screen, and a huge Chippendale desk. Going immediately to this desk, MacArthur called a staff conference with a half dozen of his closest advisers.

Douglas MacArthur was a remarkable man to behold. He was lean and handsome, every inch the soldier. At sixty-one, he looked a full twenty years younger. He stood five feet eleven inches and carried himself "as if he had a flagpole for a spine." His eyes and hair were dark brown—some said the hair was dyed. He smoked heavily—pipes, cigars, cigarettes—but he did not drink. His uniform was immaculately neat and well-tailored. There was almost a theatrical air about him, as though every gesture and word he spoke had been rehearsed, that every moment of his waking life were being recorded or filmed for history. His ego and vanity were large and evident.

MacArthur was extraordinarily quick, well-trained, and highly disciplined. One distinguished officer who served under him, Matthew B. Ridgway, thought MacArthur was an authentic "genius." Another, Dwight D. Eisenhower, wrote that he had a "phenomenal memory, without parallel in my knowledge." He had read widely in history, biography, philosophy, science, law. He evidently forgot little of what he read. Ike wrote that after "reading through a draft of a speech or a paper, he could immediately repeat whole chunks of it verbatim." He constantly astounded visitors by reciting obscure details of a previous meeting ten, twenty, or even forty years past.

MacArthur appeared to be driven by a compulsion to talk. Anyone with two or three questions to ask usually found himself deluged by a monologue that might go on for an hour and a half. It was an unforgettable experience. Whatever the subject, MacArthur could expound on it brilliantly and eloquently, always to the point, never pausing to grope for a word or idea—but at great length. During these monologues, the general invariably paced the floor (he seemed incapable of talking while seated; one aide estimated he paced five miles a day), holding a pipe in his thin, delicate hands, lighting and relighting it, using up endless matches. He was hypnotic, persuasive, vital. Those who met him in these sessions were overwhelmed, but had a profound and boundless admiration for him.

Curiously, this ability to spellbind extemporaneously in private did not carry over to public life. MacArthur's public speeches, always carefully drafted, were exceedingly long and windy, often turgid and cluttered with baroque, purple, or quaintly classical language. His delivery was dull, monotonous, uninspiring, overly serious. For those who did not know MacArthur personally, he was wrongly perceived as bombastic, pedantic, humorless, and unimaginative.

There were real weaknesses, of course. He had a slavish hunger for praise that, as Ridgway put it, "led him on some occasions to claim or accept credit for deeds he had not performed." HQ press releases mentioned only MacArthur by name, and in these, he invariably referred to "my army" or "my navy" or "my air force." He was impulsive, driven by an idealistic optimism and a feeling of infallibility that often led him to pass over or discount more realistic staff appraisals. Once he set his mind on a course of action, he wouldn't take no or maybe for an answer. Inevitably this led to winnowing out of strong men on the staff, leaving yes-men and sycophants. He had a tendency to withdraw, to remain aloof from day-to-day operations, confining himself to his inner office or his penthouse. This denied him the benefits of personal contact and give-and-take with his men in the field or Manila society. He had not the slightest ability to brook criticism or admit error. He would go to extraordinary lengths to conceal an error—even to official lies.

No one recorded what was said at this fateful staff meeting in Manila. No doubt most of the men were bewildered. In public and in private, MacArthur had belittled the Japanese military machine. He believed the Japanese Army had spent itself in various bloody excursions in China. He had optimistically told the staff he did not believe the Japanese would initiate an overt military move against the United States until at least April 1942, if then. If there was such an overt move, he as-

sumed that it would be preceded by a formal declaration
of hostilities.

He was wrong, seriously wrong, in his estimates of
Japanese capabilities and intentions. In fact, the Japanese
were now embarked on one of the boldest, most efficient
and productive military operations in the history of man-
kind. The overall goal was nothing less than the military
subjugation of the entire western Pacific, the Far East,
and all of China; the ejection of the white man from those
areas; and, ultimately, the creation of an interdependent
economic system, euphemistically termed the Greater
East Asia Co-Prosperity Sphere. It was to be a "quick
war" that would so dishearten and weaken the United
States and her allies that they would literally give up and
leave to Japan what she had conquered.

The Japanese war plan that was now unfolding with
machinelike precision envisioned the following: 1) destruction of the U.S. Pacific Fleet at Pearl Harbor; 2)
the capture of Wake Island; 3) simultaneous strikes
against MacArthur's air and sea power in the Philippines
and the British base at Hong Kong; 4) an invasion of
Thailand and the Malay Peninsula aimed at the capture
of Singapore. After MacArthur's air and sea power had
been destroyed, Japanese troops would invade and conquer the Philippines and then push southward to capture
Borneo, the Celebes, Java, Timor, New Guinea, and—
perhaps—Australia.

A key element of the Japanese strategy was to quickly
overwhelm the Philippines, then a commonwealth under
the direct protection of the U.S. government. The Philippines then, as now, had no glittering economic resources
to offer (other than copper deposits), but this immense
island land mass with its seventeen million mostly pro-
Western inhabitants lay between Japan and the strategic
oil- and rice-rich lands to the south. A hostile military
presence in the Philippines would be a thorn in the flank
of the onrushing conquerors. In Japanese hands, the
Philippines would provide air and sea bases from which
to launch attacks to the south and, later, to protect her
extended lines of communication and supply.

No one at the staff meeting was remotely aware of this
plan, least of all that the Philippines was high on the list
of Japanese objectives. The speculation was just the
opposite. The Japanese had attacked the Pacific Fleet at

Pearl Harbor, but that did not necessarily mean the Japanese would attack the Philippines, a commonwealth with its own government, without at least a declaration of war. Besides that, MacArthur recalled in his memoirs *Reminiscences* the initial reports from Pearl Harbor were misleading. They indicated the Japanese had suffered a "setback." Surely they would not attack the Philippines any time soon if that were true. Thus, at a time when MacArthur and his staff should have been most alert for Japanese treachery, seeking every scrap of information that could be had, a dangerous indecisiveness and complacency settled in. Within a few hours, disaster would strike. The fate of the Philippine Islands would be tragically determined for the next four years.

CHAPTER
TWO

★ ★ ★ ★ ★

THE DAYS, MONTHS and years immediately ahead would be a time of testing for Douglas MacArthur. The supreme test. He would suffer humiliating, professional defeat. He would plunge into deepest despair and paranoia. But eventually the tide of war would turn. On the road back he would engineer one smashing victory after another. He would soar to giddy professional heights. His name would become a household word. He would seriously be proposed as a presidential candidate—long before Dwight D. Eisenhower. He would emerge from World War II with a reputation as one of the greatest generals in American history, a living legend. In the post war years he would rise to even greater reknown and power as absolute ruler of a defeated Japanese nation. He would end his professional career with another severe testing—the Korean war. That testing would lead to a historic personal confrontation with President Harry S Truman in one of the most controversial episodes in United States military history.

Before turning to these events let us look more closely at the character and background of the man himself. To begin at the beginning: Douglas MacArthur's parents were extraordinary people. They exerted a profound influence on their son. More than most parents, they shaped his character, his choice of careers, and, as he grew to manhood, sustained him with love and counsel in difficult moments.

His father, Arthur MacArthur, was first and foremost a soldier. He was born in Chicopee, Massachusetts, in 1845, son of a Scottish immigrant he moved the family to Milwaukee, Wisconsin, when Arthur was four years old. The senior MacArthur became a lawyer, politician, and, in later years, a distinguished federal judge in Washington, D.C.

In 1862, when Arthur was but seventeen years old, he joined the 24th Wisconsin Voluntary Infantry, a Milwaukee outfit. For the next two and a half years, Arthur MacArthur fought with awesome courage and tenacity. Perryville. Murfreesboro. Missionary Ridge. Atlanta. Nashville. He was wounded several times. He won the nation's highest award for valor, the Medal of Honor. At age nineteen he rose to the rank of colonel, and command of the regiment, the youngest colonel in the Union Army. In June 1865, age twenty, he returned the regiment to Milwaukee for demobilization and took up the study of law.

But soldiering was his first love. After one year as a civilian, Arthur MacArthur was back in uniform in the Regular Army with the rank of captain. For the next twenty-three years he remained a captain, serving in various Army posts, mostly grim frontier encampments in the West and Southwest, subduing Indians. In 1889 he was promoted to major and served a four-year stint in Army headquarters in Washington, D.C. There, he won a Doctor of Laws degree from the National Law School. Then came another promotion—to lieutenant colonel—and a four-year tour in Houston, Texas. In 1897, age fifty-two, he was sent to St. Paul, Minnesota, where he might have served out his twilight years in peaceful obscurity but for the onset of the Spanish-American War.

When war was declared in April 1898, Arthur Mac-

Arthur was promoted to brigadier general, and command of an infantry brigade that was shipped to the Philippines. He bravely led his brigade in the brief battle of Manila. But real fame came to him from another quarter. After the Spanish capitulated, the United States obtained possession of the Philippines in return for $15 million. The Filipinos took a dim view of this transaction. They wanted total freedom. The fiery insurgent Emilio Aguinaldo declared himself a dictator and launched a bloody war against the U.S. occupation troops. General MacArthur, now commanding a division, was the principal field commander in this unpopular war against Aguinaldo and his rebels. MacArthur's feats, which included a dozen bloody battles and finally the capture of Aguinaldo, were prominently reported in American newspapers. He soon rose to command of all U.S. forces in the Philippines and was named military governor of the islands as well. This was Arthur MacArthur's finest hour as a soldier.

During his fourteen months as military governor, MacArthur ruled with a firm but humane hand. He instituted many liberal reforms. He created a free public school system. Drawing on his law experience, he revamped the archaic and repressive judicial system. He launched an ambitious economic program. He laid the groundwork for a military establishment. But he was soon upstaged by a civilian governing commission headed by William Howard Taft. MacArthur and Taft almost immediately fell into dispute, firing off testy letters to Washington. MacArthur was relieved and sent home; Taft became civilian governor.

It is fair to assume that Arthur MacArthur should have been named to the Army's top job, the newly created post of Chief of Staff. But his feud with Taft and his testy letters to Washington probably cost him that honor. In the ensuing years he served in various obscure posts, was an official Army observer in Japan during the Russo-Japanese War, received an honorary promotion to lieutenant general (with no specified duties); and in 1909, after forty-six years in the Army, he retired. Three years later, while addressing a Civil War veterans group, he died at age sixty-seven.

Douglas MacArthur's mother, Mary Pinkney Hardey, was born in Norfolk, Virginia, in 1852, one of fourteen children of a wealthy and aristocratic cotton merchant. She was nine years old when the Civil War began, and her brothers and relatives went off to fight for the Confederacy. She and her sisters soon left Norfolk, safe from the war in a summer home in North Carolina. After the war, Pinky, as she was nicknamed, graduated with honors from a Baltimore finishing school Mount de Sales Academy. In the winter of 1874–75, then aged twenty-two, she went to New Orleans for the social season. At a Mardi Gras ball she met the thirty-year-old bachelor Captain Arthur MacArthur, then stationed in New Orleans. They were married on May 19, 1875, at Riveredge, the Hardy plantation in Norfolk.

Within the next four and a half years the MacArthurs had three children, all boys: Arthur, Malcolm, and Douglas, who was born at the Army post in Little Rock, Arkansas, January 26, 1880. Shortly after, the family was moved to Fort Wingate, New Mexico (outside Gallup), where in 1883, age six, Malcolm died of measles. In his memoirs, Douglas MacArthur wrote: "His loss was a terrible blow to my mother, but it seemed only to increase her devotion to Arthur and myself. This tie was to become one of the dominant factors of my life."

When Douglas was four, the family moved to Fort Selden, a tiny, desolate outpost on the Rio Grande, a few miles north of Las Cruces, New Mexico. MacArthur recalled: "It was here I learned to ride and shoot even before I could walk and talk. My mother, with some help from my father, began the education of her two boys. Our teaching included not only the simple rudiments but above all else a sense of obligation. We were told to do what was right no matter what the personal sacrifice might be. Our country was always to come first. Two things we must never do: never lie, never tattle."

By all accounts Douglas got much from his mother in these crucial, formative years. She was an aristocrat, descended on both sides of her family from early and distinguished pre-Revolutionary stock. She made certain, in the fine old Southern tradition, that Douglas had a firm sense of family and a responsibility to uphold its reputation. She encouraged him to read and study history and the biographies of famous world leaders. An Episcopalian, she instilled in him a strong sense of religion. She insisted on neatness. From an early age Douglas, like his mother, was fastidious in his dress. (He was kept in curls and skirts until the age of eight.) She repeatedly told him that some day he would be a great man like his father, thus implanting a strong sense of destiny.

Douglas began his formal education, age six, at Fort Leavenworth, Kansas, in 1886. MacArthur recalled his three years of education there: "I was a poor student." He was not much better during his four years at the Force Public School in Washington, D.C., where, he recalled, his grades were only "average." But in 1893, when his family moved to Houston and Douglas, then thirteen, entered the West Texas Military Academy for his four years of high school, he began to shine both scholastically and athletically. He stood at the top of his class all through school (his senior year average was 97.33) and, on graduation in June 1897, was valedictorian. Athletically, he was a tennis champion, played baseball (shortstop) and football. In his senior year, he quarterbacked the football team to a perfect season—none of the opposing teams scored a single point against West Texas. Recalling those days, MacArthur said: "This is where I started."

By now there was no doubt about what Douglas MacArthur wanted in life: to be a soldier like his father. (His older brother, Arthur, had entered the U.S. Naval Academy, graduating in 1896.) Soldiering was in his blood. The first step was the United States Military Academy at West Point. After failing to obtain a presidential appointment, he and his mother returned to the MacArthur "hometown" of Milwaukee, where they had political pull with a local congressman. For the next year and a half, Douglas and his mother lived in a hotel while Douglas prepped for the competitive examination at a high school and under tutors.

He took the exam in the spring of 1898. The night before, he could not sleep. He felt nauseous. He recalled: "But the cool words of my mother brought me around. 'Doug,' she said, 'you'll win if you don't lose your nerve. You must believe in yourself, my son, or no one else will believe in you. Be self-confident, self-reliant, and even if you don't make it, you will know you have done your best. Now, go to it.' " When the exam scores were posted, Douglas MacArthur stood at the top.

CHAPTER
THREE

★ ★ ★ ★ ★

DOUGLAS MACARTHUR ENTERED West Point on June 13, 1899, age nineteen. His physical report declared that he was in "normal condition." It gave his height as five feet, ten-and-a-half inches, his weight as one hundred thirty-five pounds. He had his mother's coloring: dark hair (almost black), dark eyes. One of his classmates, Hugh S. Johnson, recalled that Douglas was the handsomest young man he had ever seen. Douglas was inordinately proud to be there. Years later he wrote that it was "the fulfillment of all my boyish dreams . . . the pride and thrill of being a West Pointer has never diminished . . . I can still say 'That is my greatest honor.' "

At that time his father was in the Philippines, now a famous general-governor. Douglas's older brother, Arthur, was at sea on a naval vessel. His mother, left alone, had no real roots in Milwaukee, so she decided to join her son at West Point. She moved to Craney's Hotel on the edge of The Plain. For the next two years—until General MacArthur came home in 1901—Douglas saw his mother each evening for a half hour or so. A close relationship between mother and son became even closer, giving rise to the joking legend that Douglas was the

11

only cadet whose mother went through West Point with him.

That summer, as was the tradition during the plebes' summer camp, Douglas underwent hazing, which in those days was brutal exercises. Because his father was famous, and perhaps because it was known that his mother was living at Craney's Hotel, the upperclassmen gave Douglas an exceptionally difficult hazing, so much so that one night he collapsed in his tent with convulsions. As it happened, a few months later a court of inquiry was appointed to investigate this despicable practice at West Point, and young Douglas, under duress, was a principal witness. He testified freely about the details of the hazing, but when asked to identify the upperclassmen who inflicted it, he hesitated. He recalled: "If the court insisted and ordered me to reveal the names, and I refused to obey the order, it would in all likelihood mean my dismissal and the end of all my hopes and dreams. It would be so easy and expedient to yield, to tell, and who would blame me?"

His mother was close by during this first professional crisis in the life of the youthful cadet. She sent him this extraordinary message:

Do you know that your soul is of my soul such a part
That you seem to be fiber and core of my heart?
None other can pain me as you, son, can do;
None other can please me or praise me as you.
Remember the world will be quick with its blame
If shadow or shame ever darken your name.
Like mother, like son, is saying so true
The world will judge largely of mother by you.
Be this then your task, if task it shall be,
To force this proud world to do homage to me.
Be sure it will say, when its verdict you've won,
She reaps as she sowed: "This man is her son!"

MacArthur added: "I knew then what to do. Come what may, I would be no tattletale." And for his decision, in one stroke, young Douglas won the admiration of the entire Corps of Cadets.

In his four years at West Point, Douglas MacArthur made a remarkable impression and record of achievement. He was a dedicated—even dazzling—scholar and soldier, a handsome general's son with an aristocratic bearing and a fierce determination to uphold the family's proud military tradition. On the scholastic side he stood first in his class three out of four years. (He dropped to fourth place in his third year.) On the military side he won outstanding honors: in his second year he was named Company A corporal; in his third Company B first sergeant. In his senior year he won the most coveted military honor of all: first captain of the Corps of Cadets. In addition, he won his "A" in athletics as a shortstop on the varsity baseball team. On June 11, 1903, age twenty-three, he graduated with a cumulative grade of 98.14, said to be the highest achieved by any cadet in twenty-five years.

In those days the U.S. Army numbered but 100,000 men. Following in the tradition of West Point's high-standees, Douglas chose the Engineer Corps, considered *the* elite outfit. For the next nine years he served in the field at various posts in the shadow of his illustrious father. It was a curiously uneven nine years.

In his first assignment Douglas was sent to the Philippines with the 3rd Engineer Battalion. His father—something of a folk hero in Manila—had only recently left that place after his rift with Taft. In routine assignments, Douglas toured the island of Luzon, where his father had achieved fame. One of these assignments was to help survey the Bataan Peninsula. On another assignment the young lieutenant was waylaid by two guerrillas. One of them shot at MacArthur with an antiquated rifle. The slug tore through MacArthur's campaign hat and slammed into a tree. MacArthur recalled: "Like all frontiersmen, I was expert with a pistol. I dropped them both dead in their tracks. . . ." During the tour—cut short when he came down with malaria—MacArthur met and became friends with two young Filipinos, recent law school graduates, Manuel Quezon and Sergio Osmena. Years later, both would become presidents of the Philippine commonwealth.

After a year in San Francisco, spent largely in recovering from the malaria, MacArthur received a dream assignment. In October 1905, he was ordered to become aide to his father, who was in Japan (with Mrs. MacArthur) as an official observer of the Russo-Japanese War. MacArthur hastened to Japan. The fighting was over. The task father and son faced was to evaluate the

Japanese military. Young MacArthur met the top brass
—those "grim, taciturn, aloof men of iron chartacter and
unshakable purpose"—and was impressed by the "bold-
ness and courage" of the ordinary Japanese soldiers. He
was likewise impressed by the Japanese urge to expand
beyond their teeming borders. He wrote: "Having conquered Korea and Formosa, it was more than evident
that they would eventually strike out for control of the
Pacific and domination of the Far East."

. Thereafter, father and son were ordered to expand
their intelligence-gathering mission to the whole of the
Far East, India and the Chinese mainland. For the next
nine months, they traveled (and compiled reports) in
Hong Kong, Singapore, Rangoon, Calcutta, Bombay, then
back to Java, Siam (now Thailand), Indochina (now
Vietnam) to Shanghai. It was an unparalleled opportunity
for a young officer to see and learn. And it was love at
first sight. The Far East, MacArthur recalled, came to
have a "mystic hold" on him. The lands he saw "became part of me." They "were to color and influence
all the days of my life." He concluded: "It was crystal
clear to me that the future, indeed, the very existence of
America, were irrevocably entwined with Asia and its
island outposts."

After that trip his next assignments were bound to be
anticlimactic—and they were. At times the young Mac-
Arthur behaved like a spoiled, overly sensitive brat. In
fact, his Army career went into a dangerous slump.

In the fall of 1906, MacArthur reported to an advanced engineering school in Washington, D.C. A few
months later, as additional duty, he was appointed a
junior military aide to President Theodore Roosevelt,
whom he greatly admired, and with whom, MacArthur
recalled, he had many long and private discussions about
the Far East. The glitter and pomp of the White House
social season may have distracted MacArthur from his
studies. The final report of the commandant, Major E.
Eveleth Winslow, was professionally devastating: I am
sorry to have to report that . . . Lieutenant MacArthur
. . . displayed, on the whole, but little professional zeal,
and his work was far inferior to that which his West
Point records show him to be capable of."

By that time, General and Mrs. MacArthur were living in Milwaukee, the general in semiretirement with no

real duties. For his next tour, probably at his own request, Douglas was assigned to that city to serve as assistant to West Pointer Major William V. Judson. Perhaps this time he spent too much time with his parents, or too much time with correspondence courses, taking him away from his duties. Again the summation of MacArthur was professionally devastating. Judson wrote: "I am of the opinion that Lieutenant MacArthur, while on duty under my immediate orders, did not conduct himself in a way to meet commendation and that his duties were not performed in a satisfactory manner."

MacArthur's career now reached its nadir. He was next assigned to his old outfit, the 3rd Engineer Battalion, then stationed at Fort Leavenworth. His job was to command Company K, the "lowest rated of the twenty-one companies on the post." Shortly after this, his mother—without her son's knowledge—sought to find him a job in civilian life. In his magisterial biography of MacArthur, Dr. D. Clayton James writes that Mrs. MacArthur sent a letter directly to none other than Edward H. Harriman, the Union Pacific railroad tycoon, proposing that he hire her son. Some of Harriman's lieutenants actually investigated MacArthur. When one of them came to Fort Leavenworth for a personal interview, MacArthur was astonished. He immediately scotched the whole project. Of Mrs. MacArthur, Dr. James writes: "So far she had proven to be a mixed blessing to his career, ambitiously driving him to succeed and giving him love which he needed, but also interfering with his duties and trying his loyalty to his chosen profession."

MacArthur spent four and a half long years at Fort Leavenworth in various duties. Perhaps as a reaction to his mother's vote of no confidence in his Army career, he tackled his duties with the zeal and professionalism he had displayed at West Point. He transformed Company K into the champion outfit on the post. He proudly recalled: "I could not have been happier if they had made me a general." He exuberantly joined in athletic activities, playing on the baseball and polo teams. His superiors now rated him excellent in all categories. He was promoted to captain and given additional responsibilities.

Family tragedy struck when Douglas was thirty. His

mother became "seriously ill" in about 1910. The nature of the illness has never been discovered, even in the exhaustive research of Dr. James; but it was enough to cause Douglas and his older brother, Arthur, constant worry. Then in 1912, General MacArthur died, leaving Mrs. MacArthur alone and ill in Milwaukee. The decision was made that once again she should live with Douglas. He requested duty in Milwaukee. When that was denied, he asked for the Washington area, near Johns Hopkins Hospital; and after having his mother in his crowded, totally unsuitable quarters at Fort Leavenworth for a brief time, his request was granted. He was assigned to the War Department in Washington. MacArthur and his mother found a comfortable house in a fashionable Washington neighborhood.

For both mother and son, life in the nation's capital was far more interesting and challenging. For MacArthur professionally, it was the beginning of a long, steady climb that would lead him to the pinnacle of the Army.

CHAPTER
FOUR

★ ★ ★ ★ ★

IN 1912, ARMY Headquarters in Washington—the Chief of Staff's Office—was a very small outfit, deliberately limited by a Congress fearful of, and often hostile to, the military establishment. The handsome, debonair Captain Douglas MacArthur, son of the famous general, soon came to the attention of the Chief of Staff, Major General Leonard Wood. The following year, Wood appointed MacArthur to the General Staff, then considered the "brains" of the U.S. Army. This appointment, a singular honor, brought MacArthur into intimate working and social contact with the great and near-great of Washington. His duties—planning for mobilization and war and preparing presentations of these plans to Congress—broadened his vision and outlook considerably. He gained a reputation as a forthright, sometimes outspoken staff officer who was not afraid to say no if he believed no was the answer.

While serving in this job, relations between the United States and Mexico took a sudden, drastic turn. General Victoriano Huerta took the Mexican government by force and launched a vicious anti-American purge below the border. To protect the rights and property of Amer-

17

ican citizens in Mexico, President Woodrow Wilson ordered the Navy, Marines, and a brigade of U.S. Army infantry to Vera Cruz. U.S. forces seized the city on April 21, 1914. Chief of Staff Wood began organizing a larger Army force—a Field Army, should it be necessary.

Douglas MacArthur was soon an on-the-scene participant in this tense crisis. On May 1, 1914, General Wood ordered him to Vera Cruz to serve as his personal eyes and ears, reporting back the "lay of the land" and anything else that might be "useful." On arrival, MacArthur was appalled to see that there was no mechanized transport. If the Field Army did come, it would be entirely dependent on animals. Hearing that there were some railroad locomotives hidden behind enemy lines, MacArthur found a guide and promptly slipped behind those lines to verify the rumors. In a hair-raising adventure in which MacArthur was forced to kill about seven of the enemy who surprised and chased him, he brought back the valuable news that there were indeed five locomotives, three useful to the Field Army.

For this exploit, General Wood recommended MacArthur for the Medal of Honor. But the War Department turned it down. When he received the news, MacArthur was incensed and hurt. In a brazen letter, he challenged the War Department brass who had disapproved his medal and asked for a review. Again the medal was denied. One of MacArthur's biographers Frazier Hunt, a close friend, writes: "To many in the Army inner circles this protest seemed rash and impertinent; to others it was courageous and commendable . . . ." But there was "no question" that Mrs. MacArthur approved, Hunt adds. She may even have prompted him to write the letter.

Momentous events now shook the world. On July 28, 1914, Europe exploded into a fearful, bloody war that was soon to drag in all of the major powers of the world. Japan, now a formidable Far East power, joined the Allies against Germany. As the ground fighting intensified and a frightful new menace, the German U-boat, scorched the high seas the United States—slowly at first, then rapidly—mobilized its military might. For the next two years, as a member of the General Staff, MacArthur, now promoted to major, helped shape the expansion of the U.S. Army, working closely with the Chief of Staff and the Secretary of War, Newton D. Baker, whom he served as aide. As an additional duty, Baker appointed MacArthur "press censor," actually the public relations or publicity man of the War Department. In that capacity, MacArthur was to explain the Army's mobilization policies to the press, and through it to the nation, and to manipulate the press into supporting the Army. By all accounts, including the recollections of the reporters he dealt with, MacArthur performed brilliantly, making contacts in the Fourth Estate that would be valuable to his professional career.

In April 1917, the United States declared war on Germany. Like most West Pointers, Douglas MacArthur was eager to go with the troops to France. His opportunity soon came. The War Department activated a division of the National Guard composed of units from twenty-six states—the 42nd "Rainbow" Division. On August 1, MacArthur was promoted to full colonel and named Chief of Staff of the division. The division commander, William A. Mann, was an older man who would shortly retire. He gave MacArthur plenty of chance to be in charge, and MacArthur was clearly the dominant personality in the division. After two and a half months of intense training, the 27,000 men of the Rainbow Division embarked for France, in the forefront of General John J. Pershing's American Expeditionary Force (AEF). After further training and shaking down, in mid-February 1918, the division was moved into the trenches in a "quiet sector," Luneville, in southern Lorraine. It was the coldest winter in decades.

Douglas MacArthur at once established himself as one of the most colorful and fearless officers in the AEF. His dress was distinctive: a floppy cap (he refused to wear a metal helmet or gas mask), bright turtleneck sweater, gleaming puttees, and a riding crop. The press soon tagged him "the Beau Brummell of the AEF." He first demonstrated his extraordinary courage on the night of February 26, when he voluntarily joined a French raiding party. To his delight, the fighting was "savage and merciless." About six hundred Germans were captured. For his role, MacArthur won his first decoration, the Croix de guerre. Later, the U.S. Army awarded him the Silver Star for this action.

The 42nd Rainbow Division was on the front in the Lorraine sector for about four months. During that time, it was almost continuously in combat, and MacArthur, although technically a staff officer, was continuously out front, leading and exhorting the troops like his father had done in the Civil War. He won a Distinguished Service Cross for valor. He was "slightly gassed" and, for that, awarded the Purple Heart. When the division was finally withdrawn from the front lines on June 21, the corps commander, a French general, praised MacArthur for his brilliant direction of the 42nd Division staff. By then the division was a tough, battlewise outfit; MacArthur, one of the best-known American soldiers in France.

Back in the States, Mrs. MacArthur was still attempting to guide—and advance—her son's professional career. As Dr. James wrote, on June 11 she wrote General Pershing a personal, "heart-to-heart" letter, imploring the general to promote Douglas to a general officer. She reminded Pershing of their old friendship, of her friendship with Secretary of War Baker, and ticked off her son's record of achievement at West Point. She pointed out that in April, three officers junior to her son had been promoted to general, including classmate Hugh S. Johnson, who "stood far below my son in the class of 1903," and who was a year younger than Douglas, then thirty-nine.

Whether or not this letter influenced Pershing is not known. Relations between MacArthur and Pershing and his staff were cool. By then MacArthur had clashed with members of Pershing's staff, whom he considered mediocre, and on at least one occasion the general had royally chewed out MacArthur. Nonetheless, on June 26, MacArthur was promoted to brigadier general. As Dr. James wrote, Mrs. MacArthur wrote Pershing a letter of thanks, stating: "You will *not* find our Boy wanting."

How true those words! After a brief rest, the division returned to the trenches on July 4, assigned to the French Fourth Army on the Champagne front, near Rheims. The Germans had massed their elite divisions in that area for a final, all-out attempt to seize Paris and win the war. The savage battle commenced on July 15. The 42nd Division fought with awesome tenacity and professionalism. In his floppy hat and riding crop—and his always neat khakis and puttees—Brigadier General MacArthur was usually first over the top, leading his men into hand-to-hand combat. For his heroism in this fight which stopped the German juggernaut in its tracks, MacArthur won a second and third Silver Star.

The Allies now opened an all-out offensive against the Germans. The 42nd Division was transferred to the French Sixth Army at Chateau Thierry. On July 25, it went into action. Again, the fighting was savage and merciless, hand-to-hand, seesawing back and forth. The division suffered appalling losses—nearly fifty percent. For four days and nights, MacArthur recalled, he did not sleep. The Allies overran the German positions, thrusting deep into German territory. For his heroism in this action, MacArthur won his fourth Silver Star. The French gave him a second Croix de guerre and made him a Commander in the Legion of Honor.

After that, the division was withdrawn for rest and rebuilding. During the lull, MacArthur was shifted from Chief of Staff of the division to command of its 84th Infantry Brigade. By September 10, the division was back in the line on the Saint-Mihiel front as part of Army Corps, First American Army. The objective this time was to wipe out a German salient at Saint-Mihiel, captured by the Germans at the beginning of the war in 1914. The 84th Brigade—with MacArthur out front—was a leading element in the assault. The brigade achieved its objective, and more. During this and subsequent fighting, MacArthur won his fifth and sixth Silver Stars for gallantry.

In late September, the Allies began the massive Meuse-Argonne offensive, the last great battle of the war. The 42nd Division, attached to the U.S. V Corps, was assigned to capture the enemy stronghold Côte de Châtillon. On the night of October 11, MacArthur was severely gassed and almost blinded. But he refused to be hospitalized. He continued to work and lead his troops. The fighting at Châtillon was ghastly, but the brigade achieved its objective. For this action MacArthur (for the second time in three years) was recommended for the Medal of Honor and promotion to major general. Both the medal and the promotion were denied. In place of the Medal of Honor, MacArthur received a second Distinguished Service Cross, and a second Purple Heart for the gassing.

After a brief rest, the division was back in the line on

November 4, advancing toward Sedan. The following night, owing to an ambiguous movement order from headquarters, the U.S. troops became involved in a colossal and dangerous foul-up. One U.S. division crossed ahead of two others, and the troops became unknowingly intermingled. During the foul-up, a patrol from another brigade came upon Brigadier General Douglas MacArthur wearing his nonregulation outfit. Thinking he was a German, an officer drew his pistol and brought MacArthur back to his headquarters at gunpoint. Luckily, there had been no firing. MacArthur was soon identified and released with many apologies. He returned to combat —and yet another Silver Star, his seventh. Soon after that, November 11, the war ended, and MacArthur was promoted to command the division. Pershing had selected him as a major general, but owing to a new War Department rule limiting the number of generals, the promotion had to be denied.

The 42nd Rainbow Division had performed well. It served at the front for 224 days, in actual combat 162 days. It suffered a total of 14,683 casualties, 2,713 dead. Beyond any question or doubt, its finest West Pointer was Douglas MacArthur, one of the most highly decorated officers to emerge from the war: two Distinguished Service Crosses, seven Silver Stars, two Purple Hearts, and several French and other foreign decorations. Secretary of War Newton Baker called MacArthur "the greatest frontier general" of World War I. Few could challenge that professional appraisal.

CHAPTER
FIVE

★ ★ ★ ★ ★

WHEN DOUGLAS MACARTHUR returned from Europe, April 1919, still holding the temporary rank of brigadier general, he met a cold reception. The nation had fought and won "the war to end wars." Now it was sick of war. It was demobilizing the military establishment, placing its faith in the diplomats who were, it was believed, structuring a peace at Versailles that would last forever. Battlefield heros like MacArthur were no longer needed and soon forgotten.

The new Army Chief of Staff—Peyton C. March, Pershing's chief artillery officer in France—assigned MacArthur to a job that would tax his leadership skills to the utmost: superintendent of the Military Academy at West Point. At that time West Point was in a chaotic mess. In order to produce officers for the trenches in France, the course of instruction had been reduced to one year. Five classes had graduated in 1917–18, leaving only the fourth classmen. Some cadets who had graduated and been commissioned were being ordered back for further training. Some elements in Congress wanted to abolish West Point outright; others wanted to set the term at two years. Peyton March was dissatisfied with the hidebound and narrow curriculum, the silly empphasis on hazing. "West Point is forty years behind the times," he told MacArthur. "Revitalize and revamp the academy." MacArthur tried to beg off; he was a soldier, not an educator. But he had no choice. Reluctantly he entrained for West Point, bringing his mother, who was now sixty-seven and again seriously ill.

MacArthur, the liberal reformer, spent three years as superintendent of West Point—June 1919 to June 1922. During the whole of that time he was locked in deadly political battles with various factions which had a vested interest in the school. The Congress. The War Department. The alumni. The faculty. The Corps of Cadets. In spite of the obstacles thrown in his path, he succeeded magnificently in this assignment. His biographer Dr. James sums it up thusly: "Many aspects of MacArthur's long career are still controversial, but in the Long Gray Line, there is general agreement that he, more than any other man, led West Point across the threshold into the rapidly changing world of modern military education. Indeed, his pioneering efforts at the United States Military Academy rank as one of his most important contributions to the development of the modern Army."

While he was superintendent of West Point, MacArthur's personal life took an unexpected and hugely complicated turn. For the first time, so far as is known, he fell seriously in love. The woman was Louise Brooks, then in her middle thirties, a fabulously wealthy divorcee.

Her biography to that point is rather complex. She was born in New York, daughter of Oliver E. Cromwell, a rich attorney and yachtsman. Cromwell died when Louise was quite young. Her mother then married Edward T. Stotesbury, a Philadelphia banker who was reputed to be worth over a hundred million dollars. In 1908, Louise married Walter D. Brooks, Jr., a wealthy Baltimore contractor. They had two children. During the war, Louise and Walter, and Louise's brother James (who later married the tobacco heiress Doris Duke), lived very well in Paris, members of the international set. They became very good friends with General Pershing and members of his staff. The gossips whispered that Pershing and Louise had had an affair; but in fact, as Frazier Hunt discloses in his biography of MacArthur, Louise was deeply infatuated with one of Pershing's aides, a bachelor named John G. Quekemeyer. In 1919, in Paris, Louise and Walter Brooks were divorced. When Pershing returned to Washington after the war she also went there to serve as Pershing's official Washington hostess, and perhaps to pursue her affair with Quekemeyer. A year or so later, she and MacArthur met.

Meanwhile, in the summer of 1921, General Pershing was named to succeed Peyton March as Chief of Staff of the Army. Pershing, never one of MacArthur's most ardent admirers, was one of those conservative West Point alumni who disagreed with the liberal reforms MacArthur was energetically pushing through. After he had been Chief of Staff only a few months, he decided enough was enough: MacArthur had to go. In November 1921, Pershing informed MacArthur that at the close of the academic year, June 1922, MacArthur would be detached and sent to overseas duty in the Philippines. In his place, Pershing would appoint a far more conservative superintendent.

This news was released to the public in January 1922, about the same time that MacArthur and Louise announced their engagement. The press had a field day. It revived the old gossip linking General Pershing and Louise and speculated that Pershing had kicked MacArthur out of West Point to overseas "exile" because MacArthur had won the girl. There was so much publicity that General Pershing himself was finally forced to publicly deny that he was involved in a love triangle with one of his junior generals. "It's all damn poppycock," he told the *New York Times*. "General MacArthur is being ordered to the Philippines because he stands at the top of the list of officers due for foreign service . . . I know General MacArthur well. He is one of the most splendid types of soldier I have ever met and all this stuff is idle nonsense."

MacArthur and Louise were married on Valentine's Day, February 14, 1922, at the Stotesbury Palm Beach mansion El Mirasol. MacArthur completed the academic year at West Point, and then later in the year, they sailed for routine garrison in Manila, bringing along Louise's young daughter and son. Douglas's mother, still frail and sickly, returned to Washington to live with her older son, Arthur. Although the job he held in Manila

must have seemed mundane after West Point, Mac-
Arthur was happy to be back in Manila after eighteen
years. The current governor general, with whom he
worked in tandem, was his old and revered boss retired
Army Chief of Staff Leonard Wood. But Louise was
bored. She missed the social swirl of New York and
Washington and resented MacArthur's spartan life-style,
the long hours he gave to his work. Dr. James presents
evidence that Louise still had "deep feelings" for Pershing's aide Quekemeyer and says she seemed to regret
not having married him.

They had only been in Manila about four months
when a cable came from Arthur's wife, Mary, that Mrs.
MacArthur was again desperately ill and not expected to
live. Douglas, Louise, and the two children sailed home,
arriving in March 1923. By the time they got to Washington, Mrs. MacArthur was much improved. Louise and
Douglas turned around and sailed back to Manila. This
was Douglas's last meeting with Arthur, who died later
in the year of appendicitis.

In the year following, 1924, Mrs. MacArthur was well
enough to again begin lobbying for a promotion for her
son Douglas. Dr. James again presents one of her gush-
ing, fawning, "heart-to-heart" letters to General Pershing.
In it, she unabashedly pleads that Pershing give her son a
promotion to major general. "You could give him his
promotion by the stroke of your pen." Whether or not
this letter influenced Pershing is not known. However, as
one of his last acts in office, Pershing promoted Mac-
Arthur to major general, effective January 15, 1925. At
age forty-five, he would be the youngest major general
in the Army.

Coincident with the promotion, MacArthur was
ordered back to the States to command the III Corps
area, with headquarters near Baltimore where Louise had
a magnificent estate, Rainbow Hill. Back in the social
swirl, entertaining political stars and business tycoons,
Louise was happy again—at least temporarily. But it was
a grim time for Douglas MacArthur professionally.
Shortly after he assumed his new duties, he was appointed a judge in the famous court-martial of the air
power zealot Brigadier General William "Billy" Mitchell.
In his memoirs, MacArthur remarked that this assignment
was "one of the most distasteful orders I ever received."

Billy Mitchell was a good friend; both he and MacArthur claimed Milwaukee as their hometown. There were close family ties. Mitchell's father had served with MacArthur's father in the 24th Wisconsin Infantry during the Civil War.

For some years the brilliant, outspoken Billy Mitchell had been urging the Army (and the Navy) to wholeheartedly embrace the aircraft as a weapons system and establish a separate arm to oversee its development. By 1925 he had become more than a gadfly; he repeatedly denounced the Army and Navy high commands in public, almost as though he were seeking martyrdom in a courtmartial. In September 1925, he was ordered to Washington to stand trial for, in effect, insubordination.

Mitchell was so clearly guilty that it was expected the trial would last no more than a week. But Mitchell turned the occasion into a forum for his views on air power, highly publicized by the media. The trial dragged on for seven long weeks, in an atmosphere that was circuslike. Mitchell's biographer Burke Davis reports that MacArthur was "uncharacteristically silent" during the trial and that he spent most of his time staring at Louise, who attended every open session. It was a shrewd political stance for MacArthur to take. He was a rising star in the Army, near the pinnacle, often mentioned in the press as a likely bet to be Chief of Staff. The Billy Mitchell trial was political dynamite. If MacArthur showed a bias, for or against Mitchell, he was bound to alienate either the foot soldiers or the aviators in the Army and, likewise, the highly partisan members of Congress who might someday help boost his appointment to Chief of Staff.

The thin evidence indicates that MacArthur indeed continued a middle-of-the-road stance when it came time for the secret ballot and thereafter obscured his actual vote with elusive statements. Dr. James concludes that what probably happened was that MacArthur voted guilty (as Mitchell surely was), but then may have argued for clemency—that Mitchell not be dismissed from the service. This recommendation—if there was such a recommendation from MacArthur—was adopted. Mitchell was found guilty, and suspended for five years. He resigned from the Army two months later. In later years, Mitchell and his family, in public statements, expressed gratitude for MacArthur's role in the trial. But the very fact that MacArthur was a member of the court that "persecuted" Mitchell turned many aviators against him. The animosity would linger on into World War II.

Meanwhile, all was not serene in the MacArthur household. Louise had become utterly disenchanted with Army life. (She may have been influenced by the sudden death of Quekemeyer in 1926, which left her devastated.) She urged her husband to retire, enter private business, and make big money. This course had no appeal for the general, who probably had his cap set for Chief of Staff. Whatever the cause of the friction, by August 1927, Dr. James reports, they had separated, Louise living in New York, MacArthur remaining in her Baltimore mansion, Rainbow Hill. On June 18, 1929, Louise was granted a divorce in Reno. In later years Louise blamed the divorce on "an interfering mother-in-law." She went on to two more marriages, both of which ended in divorce.

In the summer of 1928, Douglas MacArthur was again assigned to Manila, this time in the top military job: Commander of the Department of the Philippines. "No assignment could have pleased me more," he wrote in his memoirs. He found Manila "bright and lively as ever." He spent his time with some staff officers who "formed a gay and lively group." He also saw a great deal of his very old Filipino friend Manuel Quézon, who was now "the undisputed leader of the Filipinos," and the new governor general, Henry L. Stimson, who had replaced Leonard Wood. MacArthur and Stimson developed a warm and lasting friendship.

In the fall of 1928, Republican Herbert Hoover was elected President. He appointed the Oklahoma oil tycoon Patrick J. Hurley as his secretary of war, and Stimson was appointed secretary of state. MacArthur was well-known to both Hoover and Hurley, who had served under Pershing in France. Six months after Hoover was inaugurated, July 1929, MacArthur received a cable from Army Chief of Staff General Charles P. Summerall: "The President desires to appoint you as Chief of Engineers." This cable precipitated a professional crisis for MacArthur, catapulting him into a high-stakes political poker game.

As MacArthur knew well, Summerall was due to step down as Army Chief of Staff in about one year. Summerall was a MacArthur admirer and had probably hinted

in private conversation that he would recommend Mac-
Arthur as his successor. By Army tradition, MacArthur
had the inside track. He was the senior ranking major
general with four years or more of service before retirement. He was the most decorated, the best known to the
Congress and the public. He was still very young—and
President Hoover had made it known that he preferred a
younger man with no ties or obligations to the entrenched Army bureaucracy. There was competition, of
course. General Pershing, who still carried much weight
in Washington, was lobbying for at least two other candi-
dates. And still other names had been thrown in the pot
by other factions.

MacArthur knew that if he accepted the job of Chief of
Engineers—a powerful fiefdom within the War Department—his chances of moving up, or over, to Chief of
Staff would be slim indeed. For one thing, it would
return him to the Engineers; Chiefs of Staff were invariably selected from the "line." No Chief of Engineers
had ever gone on to be Chief of Staff—the top Engineer
job was considered honor enough. But MacArthur had
to weigh the fact that President Hoover and War Secretary
Hurley had not offered the Engineers job without considerable thought. It could mean that they had already
considered him for the upcoming Chief of Staff job and
passed him over. If he turned the job down, it might be
considered an act of disloyalty, spoiling any chance he
might have had for consideration as Chief of Staff.

MacArthur gambled. He turned the offer down. But
in the long run, he won. Powerful men in Washington
were lobbying for his appointment to Chief of Staff.
These included, in addition to Summerall, MacArthur's ex-
father-in-law, Edward Stotesbury (who contributed heavily
to Hoover's campaign), and Secretary of War Hurley.
Hurley was cool at first because of MacArthur's divorce.
(He said, "In Oklahoma, any man who cain't hold his
woman isn't considered worth much.") But in time Hurley
came around and stood toe-to-toe against the Pershing
group.

On August 5, 1930, as his tour in Manila was coming
to a close, MacArthur received a cable from the War
Department: "President has just announced your detail
as Chief of Staff to succeed General Summerall." In his
memoirs, MacArthur claims he had second thoughts

about wanting the job—even though it meant four stars. The Nation had plunged into the Great Depression. Pacifist sentiment was running high. It would mean a mighty political struggle to keep the Army budget from being decimated. He wrote: "I knew the dreadful ordeal that faced the new Chief of Staff and I shrank from it." But along came a prescient cable from his mother urging him to accept the job. MacArthur recalled: "She said my father would be ashamed if I showed timidity. That settled it."

CHAPTER
SIX

★ ★ ★ ★ ★

MacARTHUR WAS SWORN in as Chief of Staff on November 21, 1930. He was fifty years old, the youngest Chief of Staff in the Army's history. He moved into the luxurious Chief of Staff's home, Quarters Number One at Fort Myer. His frail and aging mother—she was in her seventy-eighth year—who had been living with her widowed daughter-in-law, Mary MacArthur, now moved in with her son at Fort Myer. To make her life more comfortable, the Army added an elevator and a second-floor sun porch to Quarters Number One. Then, as MacArthur wrote, he prepared to "face the music."

It was strong music indeed. The economy was a shambles. More than eight million people were out of work, many in desperate financial straits, living in shanty towns and begging on the streets. Herbert Hoover was a cautious conservative, who lived by a simple philosophy of rugged individualism, which MacArthur also embraced wholeheartedly. The President believed that man should—and could—succeed in life without welfare assistance from the government. Consequently, he had taken only a few tentative and largely unsuccessful measures to manipulate the economy and provide jobs. From coast to

coast there were reports that Communists (and their bed-
fellow Pacifists) were infiltrating unions, schools, churches,
and the media, with the aim of revolution. The Hoover
administration fell into a paranoid state, not unlike that of
the Nixon administration of the 1970s.

In such times the Army was a logical target for the
economizers. Everyone, it seemed, was bent on cutting
down its expenditures. The authorized strength of the
Army had been set at 18,000 officers and 285,000 men.
But during the Jazz Age of the 1920s, Congress, by with-
holding funds, had gradually whittled it down to a pitiful
force of 12,000 officers and 125,000 men (including 6,000
Filipino Scouts), ranking it in size sixteenth among the
armies of the world. The current War Department budget
amounted to a mere $350 million. Even so, Hoover
demanded further economies—closing down bases, forcing early retirements. A congressman introduced a bill
to cut the officer corps from 12,000 to 10,000. And so
the music went, month after month.

The Army could not have found a better champion
than Douglas MacArthur to steer it through this dark
period. He worked tirelessly and shrewdly to protect it
from decimation. He spent a large part of his time in the
halls of Congress, earnestly and eloquently (and sometimes arrogantly) lashing out at the Pacifists and pleading the Army's cause. "Any nation that would keep its
self-respect must be prepared to defend itself," he said
in a typical defense. "History has proved that nations
once great that neglected their national defense are dust
and ashes. Where are Rome and Carthage? Where Byzan-
tium? Where Egypt, once so great a state? Where Korea,
whose death cries were unheard by the world?" He might
have added, where Manchuria? It was not long after
MacArthur took office that it fell to the Japanese General
Hideki Tojo. Even so, MacArthur managed to get his
budget through Congress and stave off the cut in the
officer corps—only by a whisker vote.

As the Great Depression spread across the land like a
deadening flow of lava, more and more families went
under. By an act of Congress passed in 1924, veterans of
World War I were due a bonus in 1945. Some of these
veterans began to agitate for an immediate bonus, and
Congressman Wright Patman introduced a bill to that
effect in late 1931. In May 1932, penniless and hungry

veterans began to descend on the capital in ever increasing hordes, living in squalid camps, to help lobby passage of the Patman bill. The media labeled the influx the Bonus March.

Although there was no proof, President Hoover and General MacArthur became convinced that the Bonus Army was part of a Communist conspiracy. It was a chilling moment. This raged, Red-led mob infiltrating the nation's capital might touch off a revolution that could overthrow the government. Behind the scenes, Hoover ordered MacArthur to alert Army troops in the Washington area. Tanks and tear gas were made ready.

The Patman bill passed in the House but failed in the Senate, perhaps because Hoover had coldly declared he would veto it. Some of the Bonus Army gave up and went home, but about 10,000 remained in the capital, each day becoming angrier and more vociferous. Finally on July 28, in a tense and confused confrontation, Washington police fired on the mob, killing two veterans and injuring many others. Feeling the situation was getting out of hand, the Washington police appealed to Hoover, and Hoover instantly called Secretary of War Hurley. Hurley promptly gave MacArthur a written order to have Army troops disperse the mob. The order concluded: "Use all humanity consistent with the due execution of this order."

MacArthur firmly believed the government to be in real peril, vulnerable to a Red takeover. He decided that he, personally, would lead the Army troops into the streets of Washington. He changed from business suit into Army uniform bedecked with rows of fruit salad. This impulsive decision was unwise politically. It was command overkill, like smashing a thumbtack with a sledgehammer. (Among the officers accompanying MacArthur were Majors Dwight D. Eisenhower and George S. Patton.) Using tear gas—but not pistols or rifles—the Army troops easily dispersed the mob, fortunately without a serious injury to either side. But it was not a pretty picture: beribboned MacArthur routing the hapless veterans, some of whom had fought with him in France.

When the dubious enterprise was finished, MacArthur's considerable ego got in the way of his common sense. Against the advice of Eisenhower, for one, he took it upon himself to meet with the media. (Eisenhower thought that

MacArthur should have laid low and let the civilian authorities, Hoover and Hurley, who had ordered the eviction confront the media.) During this conference, MacArthur boastfully gave the wrong impression that he had taken it upon himself to save the government by driving the veterans out of Washington. Inevitably he became the object of awesome abuse from coast-to-coast. Liberals, New York Governor Franklin D. Roosevelt among them, saw him as a very dangerous man, a fascist demagogue who might arouse a swing to the right and win control of the government—as Hitler had recently done in Germany. MacArthur was convinced to his dying day that the Bonus March had been a Red conspiracy and that because he broke it up, the Kremlin marked him as a man to be destroyed.

In January 1933, Franklin Roosevelt was inaugurated President. Out went Hoover, Secretary of War Hurley, and MacArthur's other conservative friends and associates in Washington. In came that strange band of New Dealers with a host of socialistic welfare schemes that MacArthur found alien—even threatening—to his own philosophy. MacArthur and Roosevelt had met years before when Roosevelt was in the Navy Department. Now, renewing the old acquaintanceship, they regarded each other warily but with mutual respect. Other New Dealers did not share Roosevelt's admiration for MacArthur. The caustic Secretary of the Interior Harold L. Ickes wrote: "MacArthur is the type of man who thinks that when he gets to heaven, God will step down from the great white throne and bow him into His vacant seat. . . ."

What was to be Navy-man Roosevelt's attitude toward the Army? MacArthur soon found out. First Roosevelt used it as a vehicle to establish the Civilian Conservation Corps, a massive operation that inducted 275,000 recruits in a month and a half. Then the other shoe fell. Roosevelt ordered MacArthur to cut the Army budget by a crippling fifty-one percent, with comparable slashes in the National Guard and reserves.

MacArthur was appalled. He went at once to the White House and made his case in blunt barracks-room language. In response, as MacArthur wrote, Roosevelt, "turned the full vials of his sarcasm upon me." MacArthur felt a paralyzing nausea, as he had when he took his West Point exams. The debate grew more intense. Finally, storming for the door, MacArthur resigned orally. At that, Roosevelt backed down and said, "Don't be foolish, Douglas; you and the budget must get together on this." MacArthur wrote that when he left the Oval Office, Roosevelt's Secretary of War, George H. Dern, cheered him: "You've saved the Army." But MacArthur was so wrought up he vomited on the White House steps.

MacArthur wrote that after that meeting Roosevelt was on the Army's side. But was he? The final War Department budget that year was $277 million—down from the crippling $304-million Hoover budget of the previous year. In the following year it rose, but only slightly, to $284 million. In truth, the Army had to make do on a shoestring, slashing every unnecessary dime. Most glamorous new weapons (such as aircraft and tanks) had to be denied or postponed, much to the fury of the airmen and tankers, who passionately and wrongly blamed their misfortunes on MacArthur. And all this was in the face of Japanese aggression in the Far East and the rapid buildup of Hitler's army and air force.

The traditional term for the Chief of Staff was four years. Accordingly, MacArthur was due to step down in the fall of 1934. In January 1934, after Roosevelt had been in office one year, he began to consider reappointing MacArthur to a second term, possibly as a gesture to the conservative elements in the nation. When that word leaked out, Roosevelt was deluged with advice, pro and con, from powerful men in and out of government. In the end, he compromised. On December 12, 1934, he announced that he would reappoint MacArthur, not for four more years, but long enough for him to shepherd the War Department's fiscal 1936 budget through Congress. And that budget, influenced by darkening horizons around the world, was a substantial increase: $355 million.

While MacArthur was serving as Chief of Staff, the United States government took certain steps to divest itself of the Philippine Islands. In 1934, Congress passed the Tydings-McDuffie Act, authorizing commonwealth status for the Philippines in 1935 and complete independence by July 4, 1946. This action forced MacArthur and war planners in the Army and Navy departments to reexamine U.S. military policy with respect to the Philippines.

Ever since the United States took possession of the Philippines in 1898 following the Spanish-American War, there had been a plan of sorts to defend that place from a potential enemy, usually assumed to be Japan. The plan was called Orange. It was essentially a Navy plan, evolved from the theories of the Navy's nineteenth century strategist Alfred Thayer Mahan. The plan was this. A small garrison of U.S. troops, supported by a limited naval force, known rather grandiosely as the Asiastic Fleet, would be stationed on the main Philippine island, Luzon, in close proximity to Manila and its magnificent harbor. If Luzon were attacked by a hostile sea power, the garrison and its supporting naval force would fight a six-month delaying action, falling back to the mountainous Bataan Peninsula and the island citadel of Corregidor at the mouth of Manila Bay, above all denying Manila Bay to the enemy. In the meantime, the U.S. Fleet would mobilize and steam to the rescue, engage the hostile naval force in a decisive all-out sea battle, and destroy it.

Plan Orange was never very realistic, but for decades it remained firm U. S. military policy. Naval officers studied it and rehearsed many of its features in annual exercises. It dictated the characteristics of naval vessels, such as speed. It led in part to the construction of the Panama Canal, which would enable the fleet to get there faster. It was vastly complicated and weakened after World War I, when the Japanese were mandated numerous islands in the Pacific (such as the Carolines and Gilberts) which lay directly along the track the U.S. Fleet would have to take, and by the introduction of the aircraft into naval warfare. Hardheaded analysts pointed out that the fleet would now have to fight its way across the Pacific in the face of hostile land-based aircraft on the mandated islands. Nonetheless naval planners clung to the concept through years and decades.

But now that the Tydings-McDuffie Act was law, what was to happen? No one was quite sure. The best solution seemed to be to encourage the Philippines (with American help) to build up gradually a military force, reaching a point of self-sufficiency by the time independence was granted in 1946. Until that time, Plan Orange would more or less remain in effect. integrating whatever Philippine defense forces were available at any given time.

Every officer who studied Plan Orange saw its weaknesses. One, Brigadier General Stanley D. Embrich, expressed the view that it would "literally be an act of madness" to send the U.S. Fleet to the Philippines in face of a Japanese attack. But in November 1934, when the War Department plans division recommended a gradual evacuation of all U.S. troops to be completed by 1946, MacArthur replied curtly, "Not approved." Yet MacArthur himself had no faith in Plan Orange. It was, he wrote later, "a completely useless document." He expressed the view that if hostilities with Japan broke out, he would send two divisions to the Philippines—not with the idea of withdrawing to Bataan and Corregidor á la Plan Orange, but with the idea of defending "every inch" of the archipelago. However, in his last year as Chief of Staff, MacArthur had little or no success in persuading a pinch-penny Congress to authorize aid for the Philippines. Thus it can truly be said that during his tour as Chief of Staff, MacArthur himself failed to take a realistic view of Philippine defense policy and left standing the ambiguous and realistic Plan Orange.

CHAPTER
SEVEN

★ ★ ★ ★ ★

IN THE SUMMER of 1935, as MacArthur's tour as Chief of
Staff was coming to a close, he faced the not inconsider-
able question of what he would do next. He was fifty-five
years old, nine years shy of the normal retirement age of
sixty-four. He had held the Army's top post; to step down
to a lesser command, a corps for example, would be
demeaning for him and awkward for his successor. It
would, in effect, be a repetition of the last unhappy nine
years of his father's Army career. MacArthur was not
one who could find fulfillment in a sinecure. He required
a challenging executive position in an enterprise of weight
and significance.

The problem was fortuitously solved by the change in
the status of the Philippines. MacArthur's old friend
Manuel Quezon was then the preeminent politician in the
Philippines, certain to be elected first president of the
newly emerging commonwealth. On a trip to Washington,
Quezon invited MacArthur to come to the Philippines to
help him guide the commonwealth to maturity and plan
its military defenses. MacArthur was enthusiastic about
the offer. He loved the Philippines. The MacArthur name
was legendary there. Ten years of commonwealth status,

culminating in independence, almost exactly coincided with the number of years of active service he had remaining. What better way to spend them than helping to launch a new nation?

President Roosevelt was quick to give his blessing to the scheme. But a knotty problem arose. Exactly what title and official status was MacArthur to enjoy? Under the new law, the United States governor-generalship had been abolished, replaced by the less portentous office of high commissioner. Roosevelt, MacArthur, and Quezon thought MacArthur should be appointed high commissioner. But when MacArthur discovered he would have to resign from active service (and receive smaller retirement pay), he demurred. It was finally decided that he would go as a "military adviser" to Quezon, remaining on active duty in the U.S. Army. In addition to his army pay, he would receive the munificent sum of $33,000 a year salary and expenses from the Philippine government.

The exact timing of his relief from the office of Chief of Staff became a somewhat complicated and delicate matter and led to another famous Roosevelt-MacArthur contretemps. The root of the problem was probably MacArthur's formidable ego. He wished to defer his relief—the naming of his successor—until he arrived in Manila. His reasoning was that if he came on the Philippine scene still wearing the four stars of Chief of Staff of the U.S. Army, it would be much more impressive to the Filipinos. Roosevelt agreed to this—to postpone any announcement until December 15, 1935—but on October 1, while MacArthur and his entourage were still en route to Manila, Roosevelt broke the agreement and named Malin Craig as Chief of Staff, effective immediately. This action automatically demoted MacArthur to the rank of a two-star major general. He was shocked and dismayed. He denounced Roosevelt in salty language. No researcher has ever satisfactorily explained Roosevelt's motives. Perhaps it was one of his typically cunning and spiteful thrusts designed to deflate the MacArthur ego.

The entourage that departed San Francisco, appropriately enough on the liner *President Hoover*, was of considerable size. It included MacArthur; his mother, now eighty-three and in very poor health; the widow Mary MacArthur, who would help care for Mrs. MacArthur; an Army physician, Dr. Howard J. Hutter, who had been ministering to Mrs. MacArthur for a dozen years, and who had become virtually a private family doctor; Major Dwight D. Eisenhower, forty-five, who had been Mac-Arthur's aide in Washington for over two years and now would be his chief of staff in the Philippines; a Spanish-speaking West Point classmate Ike had recruited for his assistant, Major James B. Ord; MacArthur's personal aide, Captain Thomas J. Davis; and one or two clerks. During a shipboard cocktail party in honor of Boston's notorious politician James M. Curley, MacArthur met a young lady named Jean Marie Faircloth, who was bound for Shanghai. She shortly became an unofficial, though ever-present, member of the entourage.

It was not an altogether pleasant passage. Mrs. Mac-Arthur became progressively worse. On arrival in Manila, MacArthur was forced to cancel social engagements; his triumphant return to that city was darkened by the realization that his mother was slipping away. He, Mary Mac-Arthur, and his mother moved into the Manila Hotel. On December 3, less than two months after their arrival, Mrs. MacArthur died of cerebral thrombosis (a blood clot in the brain). A sorrowful MacArthur buried her temporarily in a Manila cemetery, intending to rebury her in Arlington National Cemetery alongside his father. He wrote in his memoirs: "Our devoted comradeship of so many years came to an end."

In those days, Miss Faircloth, then thirty-seven and un-married, was described by those who knew her well as a petite (barely five feet tall), dark-haired, vivacious lady. It is perhaps not coincidental that in background and personality she greatly resembled MacArthur's mother. She was a Southerner, born December 28, 1898, in Nashville, Tennessee, and raised in nearby Murfreesboro. (In his memoirs, MacArthur wrote: "She was a rebel . . . and still is.") Daughter of a wealthy, aristocratic flour mill owner, Jean Faircloth, like MacArthur's mother, was descended from pre-Revolutionary stock. Her grandfather Richard Beard, a captain in the Confederate Army, fought opposite MacArthur's father at Missionary Ridge and Stone River. He became prominent in Tennessee politics. Four of her great uncles were in the Confederate Army; one of them became a chief justice of the Tennessee supreme court. She grew up enthralled by tales of Civil War battles, infatuated with any and all things military.

She attended private schools in Murfreesboro and then, for one year, a private college Ward-Belmont in Nashville. Her father died in 1929, leaving her a great deal of money. Since then, she had traveled to many parts of the world. She was bright, witty, and knowledgeable.

It was evidently love at first sight. Jean cancelled her planned trip to Shanghai and followed the MacArthur party to Manila. She was by MacArthur's side through the trauma of his mother's death and thereafter. Because MacArthur was officially in mourning, it was a quiet courtship. But since Jean was constantly in his company, Manila society could not fail to notice and to wonder where it might finally lead.

Quezon was inaugurated president of the Philippine Commonwealth on November 15, 1935. Almost immediately MacArthur—assisted by Eisenhower, Ord, and others in the Army at Manila—began implementing the plans for building a Filipino military establishment that they had begun in Washington and worked on en route to Manila. The plan was based loosely on the Swiss military establishment. The Army would consist of a small permanent cadre of professional soldiers (drawn mostly from the constabulary), who would train 40,000 citizen-soldiers a year at one hundred camps throughout the islands. In addition, there would be a West Point type academy for officer training. By 1946 MacArthur would have fully trained forty divisions—a force of 400,000 men. In addition, there was to be an air force of two hundred fifty planes and a navy composed of fifty PT boats armed with torpedoes. The cost of all this—$8 million a year—would be borne by the Filipino government. The United States would provide military equipment on loan or sold at cost. The ambitious long-term goal was to make the Philippines entirely self-sufficient militarily by 1946. Until that day, Plan Orange would remain in effect.

Publicly MacArthur boasted: "By 1946 I will make the islands a Pacific Switzerland that would cost any invader 500,000 men, three years, and more than five billion dollars to conquer. . . . These islands must and will be defended. I am here by the Grace of God. This is my destiny."

On paper, the plan for a Filipino army seemed logical and straightforward enough. But in reality, it became ex-

ceedingly difficult to execute. MacArthur met opposition
on every front. Many Filipinos resented the high cost of
the program. Many resented the imposition of conscrip-
tion. Washington was skeptical and unhelpful for several
reasons. Some feared that the militarization of the Philippines would gravely antagonize the Japanese. Some felt it
would be dangerous to train and arm Filipino natives; it
could lead to an armed insurrection, a repeat of the bloody
insurrection of 1899. In the War Department, Chief of
Staff Malin Craig, operating on a shoestring, pronounced
the plan militarily unrealistic. As a consequence, the War
Department provided only a thin trickle of arms and supplies, and these were obsolete.

Not the least of MacArthur's problems was President
Quezon, a volatile chameleonlike politician with grandiose
dreams of his own. In late 1936, after a mere year in
office, he proposed that Washington grant full independence to the Philippines by December 31, 1938—two years
away. He had some support for this proposal in the U.S.
Congress, but Roosevelt and his New Dealers were
adamantly opposed. Quezon kept pushing; and with each
push, he antagonized New Deal Washington all the more.
His campaign for independence further complicated the
problem of obtaining military aid for the embryonic
Filipino army.

In early 1937, Quezon and MacArthur went to Washington to drum up support for their various ideas. By that
time, Roosevelt and the New Dealers were so miffed at
Quezon that Roosevelt refused to invite him to the White
House. MacArthur called on Roosevelt. There ensued
another famous Roosevelt-MacArthur brouhaha. In the
end, Roosevelt agreed to see Quezon. In this meeting,
Quezon further antagonized Roosevelt by demanding that
he give his support to immediate independence. While
that was going on, MacArthur tried to wheedle military
supplies out of the War Department. But, as he wrote,
"My request . . . went unheeded."

MacArthur took the occasion of this visit to see to some
important personal matters. He interred his mother's body
in Arlington National Cemetery. Then, on April 30, in a
quiet civil ceremony in the New York City Municipal
Building, he married Jean Faircloth. His aide Major Davis
and the faithful Dr. Hutter served as witnesses. Soon
afterwards, MacArthur and Jean and his party returned to

Manila; Quezon went on to tour Europe. This was the last time MacArthur and Jean would set foot in the United States until 1951.

In Manila, the newlyweds moved into an air-conditioned penthouse atop a new five-story wing of the Manila Hotel. It was a lavish home, with sweeping views of Manila Bay, a library containing MacArthur's eight thousand books, and several bedrooms and baths. Jean soon became pregnant, and on February 21, 1938, the child, a boy they named Arthur, was born.

In the wake of this troublesome and wholly fruitless visit to Washington, a movement was launched to fire MacArthur. Just *who* launched it has never been discovered. No doubt it had Roosevelt's blessing. On August 6, 1937, Chief of Staff Craig informed MacArthur by confidential letter that upon completion of two years service in Manila (October 1937), he would return to the United States for other duty. MacArthur was stunned and shocked, as was Quezon. The latter offered MacArthur a job as military adviser to the Philippine government with the rank of field marshal of the as yet nonexistent Philippine Army. MacArthur gratefully accepted, and on December 31, 1937, he officially retired from the U.S. Army after thirty-eight years of service. The loss of official status with the War Department meant that MacArthur's repeated requests for military supplies for the Philippines no longer carried official weight.

This new appointment drew fire from several quarters. MacArthur appeared in public in a ridiculous new field marshal uniform of his own design that gave him the appearance of a banana-republic dictator. Made of sharkskin, it was white, with a red ribbon at the base of the lapels, and adorned with four stars. He also carried a gold baton. His liberal critics in the United States leaped on this, ridiculing him as the "Napoleon of Luzon." Philippine critics deplored his salary ($16,500) and emoluments (free penthouse), which were paid by the already overburdened Filipino taxpayers.

In the next two years, as Japan consolidated its position in Manchuria and invaded mainland China to battle Chiang Kai-shek, the Filipino military establishment wobbled along indecisively. Quezon, who was secretly dickering with the Japanese to arrange a hands-off-the-Philippines pact, blew hot and cold as the political situation dictated. The Na-

tional Assembly held MacArthur's budget to $8 million,
about half what was needed. As a consequence, Mac-
Arthur was unable to maintain the goal of training 40,000
men a year. But he came remarkably close: By the end of
1940, about 135,000 had completed six months active duty
and training and returned to civilian life. The Filipino Air
Force and Navy fared less well. By the end of 1940, the
Air Force consisted of forty obsolete planes and one
hundred pilots; the Navy had two PT boats purchased
from the British. To make matters worse, Quezon and
MacArthur fell into dispute. The quicksilverish Quezon
became temporarily disillusioned with the program, forced
a further cut in the budget, and went so far as to say
publicly: "The Philippines could not be defended even if
every last Filipino were armed with modern weapons."

The amiable chief of staff, Dwight Eisenhower, worked
long and hard for MacArthur to help make the Filipino
Army a success. In December 1939, after four years on
the job, he was transferred back to duty in the States,
ending six consecutive years of duty under MacArthur.
Later, when Ike rose to great prominence in Europe, and
still later when partisan politics intruded, Ike and Mac-
Arthur would have a falling out. Ike would say of this
tour that he "spent four years studying dramatics under
MacArthur." MacArthur would describe Ike as "the best
clerk I ever had." But when Ike left Manila in 1939, the
two men were on the best of terms. In his book *At Ease*,
published in 1967, Ike was complimentary to MacArthur
and wrote that "working with him brought an additional
dimension to my experience."

Ike was replaced as chief of staff by a man of far different temperament: Colonel Richard K. Sutherland. A
handsome Yale graduate, Sutherland had entered the Army
in 1916 as a commissioned officer and had fought with the
AEF in France. For the twenty-three years of peace, he
had served in the usual routine Army garrison or school
assignments in the States and abroad, joining the Philippine contingent in 1938. He was bright, brittle, aloof,
arrogant, and a tenaciously hard worker. MacArthur admired his organizational and executive skills. But Sutherland had one large failing: an obsession for shielding his
boss, of assuming responsibilities and making decisions
that should have been made by MacArthur himself. Even
the most senior generals in Luzon found it tough to get by

Sutherland for a direct word with MacArthur. Thus, with Sutherland in harness, MacArthur became even more isolated from his men and the military realities in the Philippines.

It was a pleasant time for the MacArthurs personally. Although he visited his office seven days a week, the general spent a great deal of time at the penthouse with Jean and little Arthur, nicknamed Sergeant, or reading or pacing the terrace overlooking beautiful Manila Bay. He was an inordinately proud and doting father. He expressed his feelings eloquently in a prayer:

Build me a son, O Lord, who will be strong enough to know when he is weak, and brave enough to face himself when he is afraid; one who will be proud and unbending in honest defeat, and humble and gentle in victory.

Build me a son whose wishes will not take the place of deeds; a son who will know Thee—and that to know himself is the foundation stone of knowledge.

Lead him, I pray, not in the path of ease and comfort, but under the stress and spur of difficulties and challenge. Here let him learn to stand up in the storm; here let him learn compassion for those who fail.

Build me a son whose heart will be clear, whose goal will be high; a son who will master himself before he seeks to master other men; one who will reach into the future, yet never forget the past.

And after all these things are his, add, I pray, enough of a sense of humor, so that he may always be serious, yet never take himself too seriously. Give him humility, so that he may always remember the simplicity of true greatness, the open mind of true wisdom, and the meekness of true strength.

Then, I, his father, will dare to whisper, "I have not lived in vain."

CHAPTER
EIGHT

★ ★ ★ ★ ★

IN 1941 THERE was a sharp turnabout in the Filipino attitude toward defense. Japan, having entered into a Tripartite Pact with Germany and Italy, seized Hainan Island off Indochina. In the spring and summer of 1941, having bullied a weak Vichy government into submission, Japan occupied Indochina in force.

It was a moment of high drama. In retaliation, President Roosevelt took harshly provocative steps. He froze all Japanese assets in the United States. He forbade further trade of any kind with Japan. He closed the Panama Canal to Japanese shipping. For a few weeks that summer U.S. military leaders, convinced that war with Japan was imminent, put all forces in the Pacific on full alert. But the moment passed, tensions eased, and the United States entered into extensive diplomatic negotiations with Japan.

These events, together with Hitler's smashing military successes in Europe, led Washington to take a hardheaded look at the world situation and formulate sweeping new global military strategy. The most important feature to emerge from this new strategy was the decision that if the United States went to war against Germany or Japan or both, she would first dedicate her resources to the defeat of Hitler. The final war plan stated: "If Japan does enter the war, the military strategy in the Far East will be defensive." In sum: Crush Hitler first, then Japan.

This new policy also led the military planners to take a more realistic look at the situation in the Phillipines. It was now realized that the forces there—as MacArthur had insisted for years—were inadequate to execute Plan Orange. In July 1941, Washington took dramatic steps to rapidly expand those forces. It ordered the Filipino Army (twelve infantry regiments, on paper) mobilized and merged with the American garrison. On July 26, 1941, MacArthur was recalled to active duty with the rank of Lieutenant General and placed in command of all land and air—but not naval—forces in the Far East. The new Army Chief of Staff, George C. Marshall, significantly stepped up the trickle of infantry arms and supplies to the Philippines and promised much, much more. In addition, he promised a vast increase in air power: 340 bombers (brand-new B–17s and B–24s) and 130 fighters (brand new P–40s).

In addition, Washington ordered that the Asiatic Fleet be augmented. The mission of this small fleet, commanded by a feisty much-respected admiral Thomas C. Hart, was to do everything in its power to blunt a naval advance against the Philippines, pending the arrival of the U.S. Fleet in accordance with Plan Orange. The principal striking arm was a flotilla of submarines believed to be the best "coastal defense" weapons system. When MacArthur arrived in the Philippines, there were only six old World War I vintage S boats. But in 1939 and 1940, the force was increased by eleven new fleet submarines. In October 1941, the Navy sent another twelve new fleet boats and a tender. The Asiatic Fleet submarine arm then numbered six S boats and twenty-three fleet boats, by far the largest concentration of United States submarines anywhere.

Admiral Hart and General MacArthur set great store by this submarine force. One reason was that the fleet boats were equipped with torpedoes that was actuated by magnetic exploders which had been developed in greatest secrecy. It was believed that these torpedoes represented a quantum leap in the history of naval weapons. In theory, they could be set to explode beneath the keel of a naval vessel, breaking its back instantly. One such torpedo would be sufficient to sink a destroyer or light cruiser or a troop

transport. Two would be sufficient to sink a battleship or
aircraft carrier or heavy cruiser. If a hostile invasion force
approached the Philippines, the submarine force would put
to sea and annihilate it.

Admiral Hart had yet another secret weapon in the
Philippines: a skilled team of codebreakers and Japanese
linguists, one of three such units in the Navy. (The others
were in Washington and Pearl Harbor.) Army codebreakers had cracked an important Japanese diplomatic
code Purple. U.S. Navy codebreakers had broken an important Japanese Navy code JN–25. The Manila codebreaking unit was equipped with machines for reading
Purple and JN–25. It was believed that this unit, known
as Cast, would be of inestimable value in providing advance warning of Japanese ship movements in the Far
East. With advance warning from the codebreakers, Admiral Hart's submarines and General MacArthur's air
force could deploy to intercept on the high seas.

The rapid buildup of Philippine forces in the late summer and fall of 1941—with Washington's promises of
more to come—greatly encouraged General MacArthur.
He now uncorked on Washington a scheme he had been
working on for some months, a radical change in Plan
Orange, which had been renamed Rainbow 5. Instead of
fighting a delaying action on Luzon and withdrawing to
the Bataan Peninsula, MacArthur proposed that his forces
defend all of the Philippine archipelego. He argued that
with the impending arrival of additional supplies and aircraft, the rapid mobilization of the Filipino Army (planned
at 200,000 men by April 1942), and the arrival of additional promised U.S. troops, he could stop a Japanese
invasion cold by April 1942. He wanted to stand and
fight at the beaches. On November 21, Army Chief of
Staff Marshall, swayed by MacArthur's contagious enthusiasm, signaled his approval of the new policy.

A few days later, Washington became aware—through
its interception of secret Japanese diplomatic dispatches
on the Purple machine—that the talks with Japanese
diplomats had become a futile exercise. On November 27,
the Navy Department sent Admiral Hart the following
message:

This dispatch is to be considered a war warning.
Negotiations with Japan looking toward stabilization

of conditions in the Pacific have ceased. An aggressive move by Japan is expected within the next few days. The number and equipment of Japanese troops and the organization of naval task forces indicates an amphibious operation against either the Philippines, Thai or Kra Peninsula or possibly Borneo. Execute appropriate defensive deployment. . . .

On the same day, General Marshall sent MacArthur a similar warning:

Negotiations with Japanese appear to be terminated to all practical purposes, with only the barest possibility that the Japanese government might come back and offer to continue. Japanese future action unpredictable but hostile action possible at any moment. If hostilities cannot be avoided . . . the United States desires that Japan commit the first overt act.

These judgments had been reached largely on the basis of intercepts from the Purple codebreaking machine. War seemed certain to Washington, but where it would come was anybody's guess. As the Navy message to Hart said, the Navy believed it would come in the Philippines or farther south in the Far East. No one in Washington suspected Pearl Harbor. Inasmuch as the Japanese carrier fleet bearing down on Hawaii maintained strictest radio silence, the codebreakers had "no information" to report. They wrongly assumed and reported that the Japanese carrier forces were in "home ports."

Upon receipt of these messages, MacArthur and Hart conferred briefly, then both men placed their forces on full alert. MacArthur reported to Washington that he was ready for any eventuality. But, as he told his staff and visitors, he believed the Japanese, if they attacked at all, would not do so until April 1942. That was the date the Filipino Army would reach its full strength of 200,000 men. Here, it would seem, MacArthur allowed his optimism to cloud his judgment. It was really wishful thinking.

As it happened, at the time of the attack on Pearl Harbor, there were about 131,000 troops under MacArthur's command deployed for battle (19,000 U.S. troops; 12,000 Filipino Scouts; 100,000 Filipino citizen-soldiers organized into ten divisions). Most of the Filipinos were poorly equipped, for example, with obsolete World War I Enfield rifles. There was little artillery and a mere 108 light tanks. The planned buildup of the air forces was only partially complete. There were thirty-five B–17 bombers and seventy-two P–40 fighters, plus about forty obsolete planes of the Filipino air force.

That these forces were to prove woefully inadequate to the task was not the fault of Douglas MacArthur. Few men had fought more unrelentingly for the Philippines and the buildup of its military strength. Considering what he had had to work with—and until the summer of 1941, Washington's indifference to his pleas for help—he had accomplished a near-miracle. The ground and air forces now deployed were lucky to have as their commander one of the finest soldiers and field generals the Army had ever produced. But even he could not stave off the disaster which lay ahead.

CHAPTER
NINE

★ ★ ★ ★ ★

Now, IN THE early morning hours of December 8, 1941, Manila time, MacArthur's staff gathered in his office to ponder the news from Pearl Harbor. The overriding question was, what to do? The information from Washington and Pearl Harbor was still fragmentary. There was as yet no word from Washington to execute War Plan Rainbow 5. The November 27 war warning from Marshall had placed MacArthur under strict orders not to make an overt gesture of war against Japan. There were, to his knowledge, no Japanese forces attacking the Philippines. It may well have been, as others have suggested, that MacArthur held out hope that the Japanese would not attack the Philippines at all. Unfortunately, the Navy codebreakers, located inside Malinta Tunnel on Corregidor, had nothing useful to offer on Japanese intentions at this stage.

But there was a real disaster in the making: Before the day was half over, the Japanese would destroy over half of MacArthur's air forces on the ground, thereby dooming the Philippines. Just how this disgrace occurred has never been adequately explained. Congress investigated every facet of the Pearl Harbor disaster, but not this catastrophe. Therefore, in attempting to reconstruct the event, historians have had to reply on various unofficial (and unsworn) diaries, memoirs, and statements of the key men involved. The recollections are in sharp conflict on important points. As near as can be ascertained, this is about what happened.

The commander of the Far Eastern Air Force was Major General Lewis H. Brereton. He had arrived in early November, only a month past, with the vanguard of new aircraft. He maintained his headquarters at Nielson Field, well outside Manila. He was extremely busy organizing his force, building air fields, and supporting facilities (barracks, hangars, gasoline and ammo storage dumps, mess halls, etc.) to accommodate the huge numbers of planes and men on the way to the Philippines. He had some severe handicaps: little or no radar or anti-aircraft guns to protect his installations, very few spare parts or engines for the planes. There had been no time, really, to plan for war or to integrate his operations with the ground and naval forces.

That morning there were five fields that could handle Brereton's seventy-two new P–40s, but only two that could handle the thirty-five heavy B–17 bombers: Clark Field, about fifty miles northwest of Manila, and Dei Monte Field, on the island of Mindanao, far to the south. Several days prior, for safety's sake, MacArthur (or Sutherland in MacArthur's name) had ordered *all* thirty-five of the B–17s to Del Monte Field, believed to be beyond range of Japanese bombers on Formosa. But Brereton had sent only about half—seventeen—to Del Monte because he planned to base most of the soon-to-arrive B–17s at that place. Therefore, there would be no room in Del Monte for the eighteen planes he had left at Clark Field.

When news of the attack on Pearl Harbor reached Brereton (as he recalled it), he went immediately to MacArthur's office in Manila, arriving at about 5:00 A.M. He had a bold idea. He wanted to launch the eighteen B–17s at Clark Field against Japanese shipping on Formosa. Incredibly, he could not get past Sutherland to see MacArthur. Sutherland denied Brereton permission to make this raid—it would be an overt act—but told him to get the planes ready. Sutherland recalled that what he told Brereton was to get three B–17s ready for a photo mission to find out where the Japanese shipping might be. About a half hour after Brereton left, about 5:30 A.M., word came from Washington to execute War Plan Rainbow 5. But for about three hours (or perhaps longer) there was apparently no further exchange between Brereton and Sutherland. The B–17s remained on the ground at Clark Field—sitting ducks.

In later years, MacArthur wrote that he knew nothing of a proposal by Brereton to bomb Formosa that morning. He said that had the proposal been seriously meant, it should certainly have been made to him "in person." If it had been, MacArthur went on, he would have disapproved it. A small mission of fifteen or eighteen bombers with green pilots, against heavily fortified Formosa, without fighter support (Brereton's P–40s couldn't reach Formosa from existing fields) would have been "suicidal." He was certainly correct in this judgment; the Japanese had hundreds and hundreds of planes on Formosa, fully alerted, waiting to pounce. The B–17s would have been annihilated. He did not say so, but a flight of three unescorted B–17s on photo reconnaissance would also have been annihilated. If MacArthur's recollection is correct, it meant that his chief of staff was giving orders for an operation, or operations, that he, MacArthur, would have disapproved, an extraordinary assumption of power. And beyond that, Sutherland was indecisive. He kept Brereton waiting for hours with no final word one way or the other.

Given the factors involved and the uncertainly of the moment, neither Brereton nor Sutherland seems to have considered the most prudent course for the B–17s. That course surely was to immediately place the eighteen bombers at Clark Field beyond Japanese bomber range, send them to Del Monte Field on Mindanao. Later, when the situation clarified itself and cooler heads deemed feasible a mission against Formosa (or anywhere else), the bombers could have been launched from Del Monte, using Clark merely for refueling. The evacuation of these planes would have cleared Clark Field, reducing confusion and giving the P–40s more operating room.

Shortly after eight o'clock, five hours after the Pearl Harbor attack, a radar set at Iba (on the west coast of Luzon) picked up Japanese aircraft inbound for Luzon. No doubt the Japanese pilots were tense and fearful,

believing Luzon to be fully alerted just as Formosa was
alerted. They had planned to coordinate this attack with
the one on Pearl Harbor, but the weather on Formosa
that morning had been bad, delaying takeoff for hours.

When the alarm was given, Brereton scrambled his
fighters and ordered the eighteen B–17s at Clark Field
into the air to avoid destruction. They were merely to
orbit, not go to Del Monte, an indication Brereton was
still hell-bent on the suicidal mission to Formosa. The
Japanese planes attacked to the north and west of Clark
Field, but not Clark.

Brereton called Sutherland again, requesting permission
to launch the bombing raid against Formosa. Sutherland
again denied permission for this mission, but he okayed
the three-plane photo reconnaissance. Brereton had no
quarrel with this plan; but he told Sutherland that if the
photo planes failed to return, he would send his bombers
anyway, presumably that afternoon. In addition, Brereton
said, that night he would bring the seventeen bombers up
from Del Monte to Clark and launch them on a follow-up
Formosa raid the following morning.

Between about ten and eleven o'clock, the eighteen
orbiting B–17s were returned to Clark Field. Three were
chosen for the recon mission and prepared for cameras.
Meanwhile, the P–40s at Clark and Iba and other fields
had been busy on scrambles all morning. Now many were
earthbound, being refueled and repaired. Shortly after
noon, swarms of Japanese fighters and bombers struck
Clark and Iba Fields without warning. In a matter of
minutes the Japanese, unopposed in the air, destroyed
all eighteen B–17s at Clark and about fifty-five of the
seventy-two P–40s at Clark and Iba. It was a first-class
disaster. In one stroke the Japanese had virtually wiped
out MacArthur's air power in the Philippines and, with
it, his capability of bombing the invasion ships and providing air intelligence for the flotilla of submarines.

In the dark days that followed, the remaining handful
of fighters based on Luzon were gradually chewed up by
the Japanese. The seventeen B–17s at Del Monte made
some ineffectual attacks against the enemy, but without
fighter escort they were highly vulnerable. By the end of
the first week, there were only fourteen left. MacArthur
ordered that these be flown south to Australia to avoid
destruction. Major General Brereton soon followed, or-

dered out of Luzon by MacArthur himself in one of their
few face-to-face confrontations. MacArthur told Brereton:
"I hope that you will tell the people outside what we have
done and protect my reputation as a fighter."

In later years, MacArthur would have nothing unkind
to say about this disaster. In fact, he publicly defended
Brereton and praised the airmen under his command. But
in private, he had nothing but contempt for the air staff.
For their part, the airmen had little love or respect for
MacArthur. They recalled that he had served on Billy
Mitchell's court-martial, that he had not approved Air
Corps expenditures for new aircraft while Chief of Staff
of the Army. The old animosity welled. MacArthur did
not understand air power, they felt. He or Sutherland had
denied permission for an attack on Formosa. Because of
that, and other ambiguous and conflicitng orders that
morning, Brereton's planes had been caught on the ground.

Now, thirty-five years after the event, where to place
the blame? Without question or caveat, it must be laid
at MacArthur's feet. The newly arrived air power was
the single most important weapon at his disposal that
morning and Brereton his single most important subordinate commander. It is inexcusable, even inconceivable,
that MacArthur did not immediately confer with Brereton
face-to-face to at least discuss a matter of paramount importance: the protection of the bombers. That he apparently allowed Sutherland to manage, or mismanage,
this vital matter seems a lapse so great it was deserving
of immediate relief of command and perhaps even a court-
martial. He was probably lucky that the events which
followed precluded any immediate investigation. Otherwise, he might well have sunk from sight in disgrace, like
the Navy and Army commanders at Pearl Harbor, Admiral Husband E. Kimmel and General Walter C. Short.

CHAPTER
TEN

★ ★ ★ ★ ★

THE COMMANDER OF the Asiatic Fleet, Admiral Thomas C. Hart, had had a long and distinguished naval career. Born in 1877, he was a graduate of the Naval Academy class of 1897. He was three years older than MacArthur and in terms of military service senior by six years. Though he was required to coordinate his activities with MacArthur's headquarters, he was an independent military command, reporting directly to the Navy Department in Washington. Hart was aloof, proud, and a strict disciplinarian.

Unlike MacArthur, Hart had believed for months that a Japanese attack on the Philippines was imminent. Long ago he had taken harsh preparedness steps, such as sending Navy dependents back to the States and maintaining his forces on almost continuous alert. In accordance with a direct order from the Navy Department, he had sent the major surface ships of the Asiatic Fleet (the heavy cruiser *Houston*, two light cruisers *Marblehead* and *Boise*, thirteen destroyers) to bases far to the south in the Celebes and Borneo. This move was designed to protect them from Japanese air attack. If war came, these surface forces were to join up with British and Dutch naval forces in the Far

East for a coordinated attack against the Japanese. But the main striking arm of the Asiatic Fleet, the twenty-nine submarines and their three tenders, was kept in Manila Bay, together with a force of twenty-eight Navy patrol bombers.

There was little or no professional or personal contact between MacArthur and Hart. On the contrary, the available evidence suggests a strong personality clash. Even so, Hart was infected by MacArthur's contagious enthusiasm for the "stand and fight" policy. When Hart saw the rapid buildup of air power taking place, he rashly decided his puny Asiatic Fleet surface force (the three cruisers and thirteen destroyers) ought to be returned to Manila Bay, where—aided by MacArthur's air power, codebreaking, and the submarine force—they might give a good account of themselves against a Japanese naval force. The Navy Department denied Admiral Hart permission to do this. But, entirely on his own initiative, Hart continued to retain the submarine force at Manila Bay. As long as MacArthur's air could provide protection, they would operate from that place. Thus, the burden of the naval defense of the Philippines fell to the submarine force.

Because of all this, an extraordinary responsibility fell on the shoulders of Hart's submarine commander, John Wilkes, and his chief of staff, James Fife. Both men were tragically lacking in imagination, leadership, and resourcefulness. Wilkes was a lackadaisical administrator, bored with such vital matters as maintenance. Fife was an introverted, teetotaling martinet, widely disliked by the swashbuckling submarine skippers and crews. The Asiatic Fleet submarine force had not been properly trained for war; no simulated long-distance war patrols had been carried out, for example. When war did come, Wilkes and Fife insisted the skippers conduct themselves with extreme caution. They were to be frugal with the supersecret torpedoes.

The submarine war plan for the defense of the Philippines was, briefly, this. Upon the outbreak of hostilities, one third of the force, about eight boats, would be dispatched to distant enemy bastions such as Formosa, Indochina, Hainan, etc. Another one third would patrol close around the perimeter of Luzon, to scout for possible invading forces. The other third would be held in Manila Bay as a "strategic reserve." If a Japanese invasion force was discovered approaching Luzon, the strategic reserve would be concentrated immediately at the point of contact. In accordance with this plan, on December 8 and 9, following the attack on Clark and Iba Fields and the orders to execute War Plan Rainbow 5, eighteen submarines put to sea.

On December 9, after Admiral Hart had had a thorough briefing on the extent of aircraft losses at Clark and Iba Fields, he was appalled. He saw clearly that it would be impossible for his submarine force to operate from Manila Bay. The three large tenders would be sitting ducks. That night he ordered the newest tender, *Holland,* and one other, *Otus,* not fully operational, to pick up supplies and equipment at the Cavite Naval Station and flee south. The oldest tender, *Canopus,* would remain, camouflaged at the Manila docks, to service the submarines for as long as possible.

The next day, December 10, Japanese aircraft again appeared over Manila in force and virtually unopposed. The target that day was the large, vital Cavite Naval Station, where *Otus* was then taking on cargo. In a devastating attack, the Japanese airmen completely destroyed the base. *Otus* luckily escaped with minor damage and fled south. But the new fleet submarine *Sealion* was so badly damaged she had to be destroyed. A sister ship, *Seadragon,* was also damaged, but with temporary repairs from *Canopus* she was able to escape to the south. The Cavite submarine and torpedo repair facilities were wiped out along with two hundred thirty-three supersecret magnetic submarine torpedoes.

Following this attack, the submarine war plan was abandoned. The strategic reserve of submarines put to sea, joining the advance elements already on patrol. Altogether there were now twenty-two submarines at sea. The other five were in repair or held back. Of these twenty-two, five were sent to the east coast of Luzon, thirteen to the west coast of Luzon or to distant points such as Indochina, four were placed close in along the southern approaches to Luzon. Never in its history had the U.S. Navy deployed so large a submarine force for combat. None of the skippers or the crews had ever been in a war. They were naturally apprehensive and, following Wilkes's orders, cautious in the extreme.

The Japanese invasion forces designated for the capture

of the Philippines, in particular Luzon, were enormous. Then assembled in the Formosan ports of Takao and Keelung, in the Pescadores and in the Palaus, were well over one hundred troop transports. These would debark soldiers at the two principal invasion points: Lingayen Gulf on the west coast of Luzon (December 21) and Lamon Bay on the southeast coast (December 24). In addition there would be smaller landings at Aparri (December 10) and Vigan (December 11) and Legaspi (December 11). To support the troop transports, the Japanese Navy had mobilized a large force of men-of-war: one light aircraft carrier, two battleships, seven heavy cruisers, sixteen light cruisers, thirty-seven destroyers, and dozens of tenders, minesweepers and minelayers, gunboats, and so on. Soon these forces got under way and headed toward Luzon.

One by one the submarines, patrolling individually, began to make contact with the enemy naval forces. Off Formosa, *Sturgeon* and *Searaven* made cautious approaches, fired torpedoes, and missed. Off Indochina, *Pickerel, Spearfish,* and *Sargo* likewise found targets and fired. No hits. *Seawolf* found a seaplane tender at anchor in Aparri. She fired eight torpedoes. No explosions. Everywhere it was the same story. There seemed to be something wrong with the torpedoes. Baffled and discouraged, the skippers complained to the Manila-based commanders, Wilkes and Fife. Neither man investigated these complaints.

There was indeed something drastically wrong with the supersecret torpedo. In fact, it had *three* serious defects, each tending to conceal the other. It ran deeper than designed, too deep for the magnetic exploder to work. The magnetic exploder itself was defective as well as the standard contact exploder. But, in one of the most appalling scandals of any war in history, months and months would go by before these defects were isolated and corrected.

There was another, totally unexpected problem in the Asiatic submarine force. A high percentage of the skippers, all Naval Academy graduates trained to "go in harm's way," turned out to be overly cautious in combat. Instead of boldly attacking targets, these skippers delayed and procrastinated or even went deep and lay on the bottom or slipped away. The skipper of *Sailfish,* patrolling off Vigan, cracked up after a minor set-to with a Japanese destroyer, locked himself in his cabin, and demanded to be relieved. Others found minor excuses to terminate their war patrols prematurely and return to Manila Bay. It was a sorry chapter in the Navy's proud history.

For decades, most military experts and naval strategists had believed that if the Japanese attacked Luzon, the most logical place to strike would be Lingayen Gulf on the west coast. From that wide, shallow gulf the overland route to Manila lay across a broad, fertile plain, where tanks and other mechanized vehicles could maneuver most effectively. And so it developed. The major Japanese thrust of seventy-six transports carrying 80,000 combat soldiers of the Japanese 14th Army plus supporting units converged on that place December 21.

For reasons that have never been explained or fathomed, Wilkes and Fife left Lingayen Gulf virtually unguarded. Only one creaky World War I-vintage S boat was sent there. Her firepower consisted of twelve old torpedoes. Something went wrong with her radio, and fearing she might have met misfortune, on December 16 Wilkes ordered her back to Manila. In her place he sent the newer fleet boat *Stingray*. After a day or two, *Stingray*'s skipper complained of minor leaks and requested permission to return to Manila. It was granted.

Late on the afternoon of December 21, the skipper came to periscope depth preparatory to surfacing for the voyage to Manila. In his periscope he saw column upon column of smoke. It was the main Japanese invasion force, strung out for twenty miles, bearing down on Lingayen Gulf. But instead of attacking this submariners' dream (or nightmare), he scuttled out to sea to get off a "contact report" to Wilkes. Wilkes thereupon canceled the orders to return to Manila and told the skipper to attack. He did not follow these orders. He failed to fire a single torpedo. The whole force slipped by him into Lingayen Gulf. He was summarily relieved of command.

Upon receiving *Stingray*'s contact report, Wilkes rushed six boats to the gulf approaches. The skippers had specific orders to penetrate the gulf and attack. But by then the Japanese had stationed a strong destroyer screen at the entrance. Only one boat, an old S class, got inside. In a truly daring attack, her skipper sank a big transport, *Hayo Maru*. The fleet boat skippers outside attacked the destroyers but sank nothing. Slightly to the north, one of these fleet boats sank a very small transport off Vigan. These two transports were the only Japanese ships sunk by the Asiatic Fleet Submarine Force in Philippine waters. As the naval historian Samuel Eliot Morison wrote, "These casualties disturbed the enemy less than did the weather."

The failure of Wilkes and Fife to properly guard Lingayen Gulf was inexcusable. There had been plenty of time and resources. There were fourteen submarines in the vicinity of Lingayen Gulf between December 20 and 25. Had Wilkes and Fife placed these boats at sea on an arc along the approaches to Luzon, one or several of the boats would surely have picked up the invasion force where there was sea room to attack aggressively and repeatedly. Instead, they had sent boats to far-off places like Indochina, putting only one boat at Lingayen Gulf. This boat was very close in, too close to operate effectively. By the time it gave the alarm, it was too late.

All in all, the submarine defense of Luzon was a fiasco. There is no other word. Without doubt Wilkes and Fife themselves shoud have been relieved of command. However, as in MacArthur's case, unfolding events precluded investigation. Wilkes and Fife not only escaped reprimand, they were actually both decorated with important medals. Fife was promoted.

By Christmas Day it was clear that the Navy could do nothing of substance to assist MacArthur in the defense of the Philippines. Japanese airplanes swarmed over Manila all day long. Men on *Canopus* were so busy diving for cover they had no time to make submarine repairs. The submarine diesel oil stocks had inadvertently been destroyed. Admiral Hart left Manila by submarine to join his surface forces in the defense of Java. One by one the submarines were ordered to depart Manila and head south. In the latter days of December, Wilkes, Fife, and others of the submarine staff boarded submarines and abandoned Manila. The tender *Canopus,* moved under protection of the guns of Corregidor, was left behind with all her submarine technicians, torpedoes, and spare parts.

MacArthur was understandably enraged at Hart and the Asiatic Fleet for the submarine failure at Lingayen Gulf, for the wholesale bugging out of Manila. His fury soon enlarged to encompass the distant Navy Department and the frosty Chief of Naval Operations, Admiral Ernest J.

King. When the war broke, there was a very large convoy en route from Honolulu to Manila: eight ships escorted by the cruiser *Pensacola*. The ships carried vital replacement aircraft and war supplies for the Luzon garrison. Having regained the keys to the Japanese naval code JN-25, Admiral King knew the awesome power of the Japanese Navy in Philippine waters and concluded that to send the convoy through would be suicidal. He diverted it to Australia, intending that its aircraft should fly from there to Luzon. They never did. MacArthur, perhaps unaware of the overpowering Japanese naval strength in his area, believed the Navy should have ordered this convoy, and others, to fight its way to Manila, assisted by the ships that survived Pearl Harbor, notably the three aircraft carriers, and by Hart's U.S., British, and Dutch surface forces in the south.

These events led to icy feelings between MacArthur and the U.S. Navy. MacArthur believed, not without some justification in those dark days, the Navy lacked the will to fight, that its leaders were spineless. In several sharp cables to Washington, he implied as much. King, Hart, and the rest of the naval establishment naturally resented these implications. The hard feelings continued throughout the war, and the U.S. Navy became a prime source of anti-MacArthur propaganda.

CHAPTER
ELEVEN

★ ★ ★ ★ ★

MacArthur's ground troops were scattered all over the Philippine archipelago, ready to stop the Japanese at the beaches. The bulk of the best trained and most seasoned troops were on Luzon. These troops were divided into three principal groups: the North Luzon Force, the South Luzon Force, and a strategic reserve. The North and South Forces were composed of divisions and regiments of Filipino citizen-soldiers with a sprinkling of U.S. infantrymen in the key executive positions. The strategic reserve, bivouacked in the Manila area, was composed of two divisions.

With the loss of half his air power on December 8, MacArthur might well have reconsidered his bold plan to stand and fight, to meet the Japanese on the beaches. Indeed, in retrospect, some of his underlings have asserted that the *only* prudent course at that point was to abandon that grandiose scheme and revert to the old War Plan Rainbow 5: the immediate withdrawal to Bataan and Corregidor. Had MacArthur done so, there would have been ample time to execute two of the most complicated aspects of that plan: the stockpiling of food and ammunition on Bataan and the preparation of strong defensive positions. But MacArthur, perhaps still holding hope the submarines and their fabulous torpedoes would destroy an invasion force or some other miracle would occur, stuck by his guns. The stand and fight policy remained in force. The consequences of this utterly unrealistic decision would be tragic.

On December 22, the Japanese 14th Army, commanded by Lieutenant General Masaharu Homma, charged ashore on the eastern beaches of Lingayen Gulf, about one hundred ten miles northwest of Manila. The North Luzon Force, commanded by Major General Jonathan M. "Skinny" Wainwright, deployed for combat. Wainwright had about 28,000 men to oppose Homma's 80,000 shock troops. They were organized into four divisions of citizen-soldiers, a cavalry regiment of Philippine scouts, and a supporting group of light tanks.

Wainwright's men met the Japanese on the beaches. Almost instantly, disaster ensued. The ill-trained, ill-equipped 11th and 71st Filipino divisions collapsed as combat units. Thousands of Filipinos flung aside their old rifles and fled in terror for the hills. The other two divisions of Filipino citizen-soldiers held together as units, but they were no match for General Homma's battle-seasoned Regular Army troops. They fell back, some in confusion, all in desperate fear. The only consistently dependable outfit was the 26th Cavalry, composed of Philippine scouts.

It was much the same story in the south. On December 24, a force of some 7,000 Japanese troops plus supporting units landed at Lamon Bay (unseen by U.S. submarines in the area), about seventy miles southeast of Manila. The South Luzon Force, commanded by Brigadier General George M. Parker, Jr., deployed for combat. Parker had about 16,000 men, organized into two Filipino citizen-soldier divisions. These citizen-soldiers were no match for the Japanese either. They fell back, permitting the Japanese to make rapid advances toward Manila.

Homma's strategy was now clear. He had established two pincers, one at Lingayen Gulf, one at Lamon Bay. He would close those pincers, trapping MacArthur's forces between them, either in Manila or, more likely, on the flat open plain north of Manila. There was only one way to avoid the pincers and certain annihilation: a speedy withdrawal to Bataan and Corregidor. In other words, revert to the old War Plan Rainbow 5.

The execution of that plan now would be much more complex in every respect. Wainwright, facing the superior force in the north, would have to fight a difficult delaying action with green troops, obsolete weapons, and no air power, while Parker's southern force and the strategic reserve in Manila made their way to Bataan. In addition, supply troops would have to gather and ship to Bataan food and ammunition sufficient to sustain the garrison for months. This task would now have to be done in great haste under a rain of Japanese bombs.

The first part of the plan, the troop withdrawal, was executed with astonishing success. General Wainwright kept his surviving forces intact. They fell back in five stages, fighting gallantly, demolishing railroads and bridges behind them. In the south, General Parker turned over his command to Brigadier General Albert M. Jones, went to Bataan, and began the construction of defenses. Hard on his heels, Jones withdrew the South Luzon Force, plus some independent Filipino forces, in orderly fashion through Manila to Bataan. Lastly, Wainwright withdrew to Bataan. In all of this complex maneuvering, casualties had been light. Altogether, 80,000 U.S. and Filipinos made it to the Bataan perninsula. In addition, there were an unexpected 26,000 Filipino refugees.

The military historians who have studied this troop redeployment in detail have labeled it "brilliant," as indeed it was. Homma had expected to conquer Luzon in a month. As it turned out, it would take him about four months to dislodge the "Battling Bastards of Bataan." The delay may have upset the Japanese timetable for further conquests; certainly the long siege was a serious drain of manpower, shipping, and air power. It was also a stirring morale-builder on the home front in the States. In his memoirs, MacArthur, glossing over the delay in executing the plan, wrote: "I have always regarded my decision to withdraw to Bataan as not only my most vital one of the Philippine defense campaign, but in its corollary consequences one of the most decisive of the war."

The second part of the plan, the shipment of food and ammunition to Bataan, was not so well executed. In fact, it was a disaster. Precise and urgent orders from MacArthur's headquarters were not forthcoming. In the confusion of war, big army depots crammed with supplies and food were prematurely abandoned to the Japanese. Quixotic orders from President Quezon also hampered the operation. Quezon refused permission to MacArthur's supply troops to take over the railroads (deserted by the Filipinos) or to confiscate food in commercial warehouses or to take rice from the local provinces. One consequence of the latter order was that fifty million bushels of rice at Cabanatuan, enough to supply the Bataan troops for five years, had to be left behind, even though there was ample manpower and trucking to move it. Inexplicably, MacArthur seems to have done nothing to have these restrictive orders revoked. As a result, the Bataan defenders found very little food, ammunition, or medical supplies when they arrived. On January 5, MacArthur had to order all troops under his command to go on half-rations. In the end, it was the shortage of food and medicine as much as anything else that forced the Battling Bastards to give up.

During the early days of the war, MacArthur, Jean, and their son Arthur, now going on four, continued to live in the penthouse at the Manila Hotel. The immediate household now included Arthur's amah, a Chinese woman named Loh Cheu but called Ah Cheu, and MacArthur's new military aide Sidney L. Huff. Huff was a onetime naval officer who had retired in Manila after a heart attack. MacArthur had recruited Huff to build the Filipino PT boat navy. After war broke out, Sid Huff had been commissioned a lieutenant colonel in the U.S. Army. He was very close to the general and Jean and Arthur, always at hand, virtually a member of the family.

On Christmas Eve, as Homma's pincers closed in on Manila from the south and north, MacArthur called Huff (as Huff recalled in his memoirs) and said: "Sid, get Jean and Arthur. We're going to Corregidor." Huff found a truck and parked it at a rear door of the hotel. Jean packed a suitcase, mostly filled with food and clothes for Arthur and a few priceless family photographs. At the last minute she scooped MacArthur's decorations and medals from a glass case, wrapped them in a towel, and put them in the suitcase. Huff picked up Arthur's tricycle, and then they were off in the darkness to the Manila docks. Left behind in the penthouse were almost all of the MacArthur possessions: furniture, silver, china, clothing, and the eight thousand volumes in the library. (Huff later returned for MacArthur's Colt 45 pistol, his old floppy campaign hat, and a bottle of scotch.) They crossed Manila Bay to Corregidor on an inter-island steamer, the *Don Esteban*. Quezon and his family and his professional staff, and the U.S. High Commissioner Francis B. Sayre and his family, also withdrew to Corregidor.

Corregidor, known formally as Fort Mills and informally as "The Rock," is an island of about seventeen hundred acres in area. Its surface is irregular, with peaks ranging from 400 to 600 feet. It bristled with forty-two huge long-range guns and mortars covering the sea approaches to Manila Bay (but not Bataan at the rear). Inside, it was laced with tunnels branching off the main, fourteen-hundred-foot Malinta Tunnel. There were then about ten thousand people on Corregidor: four thousand soliders, four thousand military noncombatants, two thousand civilians. The men lived inside the tunnels or in barracks on the high ground of the west end of the island known as Topside or near the low dock area called Bottomside. They had been far better supplied with food and ammunition, per capita, than the men on Bataan.

The MacArthurs and Ah Cheu moved into a house located in the Topside compound, formerly the residence of the artillery commander. Huff and Sutherland and others of MacArthur's staff took over one end of a three-story barracks at Topside. Four days later, December 29, Japanese aircraft bombed Topside to smithereens.

As Huff recalled, when the air raid alarm sounded Jean grabbed Arthur and ran to a fortified shelter near the house. She and Arthur huddled there during the bombing. But MacArthur fearlessly stayed near the house, in the yard, "protected" by a hedge, counting the Jap planes (eighteen) and "building up a towering anger." His Filipino orderly, Sergeant Domingo Adversario, took off his own helmet and held it over MacArthur's bare head. A piece of flying shrapnel hit Adversario in the hand holding the helmet. Thereafter the MacArthurs moved to a house on Bottomside, about a mile from the entrance to Malinta Tunnel, where MacArthur and his staff had established a headquarters. During the many air raids to follow, Jean and Arthur were jeeped from the house to the protection of the tunnel.

In the days that followed, General Marshall in Washington suggested that Jean and Arthur be evacuated from Corregidor by submarine. MacArthur discussed this with Jean, but she refused to leave. MacArthur recalled that he cabled Marshall: "I and my family will share the fate of the garrison." A short time later, Huff recalled, MacArthur showed him a small pistol, no larger than his hand. It had been his father's pistol when he was in the Philippines. But it had no bullets. After scrounging all over Corregidor, Huff found two that would fit. "Thanks," MacArthur said to him. "They will never take *me* alive, Sid."

CHAPTER
TWELVE

★ ★ ★ ★ ★

BY NOW, ONE month into the war, the Japanese had achieved many of their objectives. They had shattered the U.S. Pacific Fleet at Pearl Harbor. They had captured Wake Island and Guam. They had sunk the main striking power of the British Far East naval forces, the capital ships *Prince of Wales* and *Repulse*. They had overrun Hong Kong, landed an invasion force on the Malay Peninsula, and were converging on Singapore, which would surrender in a few days. They had destroyed MacArthur's air power, isolated his ground forces on Bataan, and forced Hart's submarines to flee southward. Staging from Davao on Mindanao, they had launched invasion forces in Borneo, the Celebes, Ambon, and other islands to the south of the Philippines. Yet other forces prepared to invade Java and Sumatra.

What now was to become of the beleaguered forces on Bataan? Statements issued from Washington, perhaps in a misguided attempt to bolster morale, gave the very definite impression that help was on the way. In late December, President Roosevelt said: "The resources of the United States, of the British Empire, of the Netherlands East Indies, and of the Chinese Republic have been dedicated by their people to the utter and complete defeat of the Japanese war lords." That same day, the Navy Department said publicly: "The U.S. Navy is following an intensive and well planned campaign against the Japanese forces which will result in positive assistance to the defense of the Philippine Islands." A few days later, January 5, Marshall sent MacArthur an encouraging message reporting a "stream of four-engine bombers" on the way to the Far East and holding out hope that an "assault in the southern Philippines" might be staged. "Every day of time you gain," he told MacArthur, "is vital to the concentration of the overwhelming power necessary for our purpose." High Commissioner Sayre, in a radio broadcast to the Filipinos, said, "Help is surely coming, help of sufficient adequacy and power that the invader will be driven from our midst. . . ." Responding to these statements, which he fully believed, on January 10 MacArthur visited the troops on Bataan and told them: "Help is definitely on the way. We must hold out until it arrives."

These statements, together with MacArthur's erroneous belief that the Japanese had overextended themselves, led him to suggest to Washington several hopelessly unrealistic stratagems. He urged that Russia be persuaded to come into the war against Japan—attacking the home islands from the north, destroying her exposed oil reserves, and forcing her to curtail her southward expansion. Independent of that suggestion, he later proposed that the U.S. air power already in Australia and on the way (Brereton's force, augmented by the "streams" of reinforcements), plus the Navy's aircraft carriers, be concentrated against Mindanao, which was not yet completely occupied by the Japanese. When that place had been wiped out by Allied air power, he urged that an army corps (three divisions plus artillery, engineers, and other support) be landed there. With Mindanao in American hands, the air power could then be directed against Homma's forces on Luzon, so weakening them that U.S. troops could land and relieve the Bataan garrison. The latter was certainly a bold, aggressive plan, but it was dependent upon two key factors: a massive buildup of air power in Australia and a massive concentration of sea power in the western Pacific.

Unknown to MacArthur, according to his memoirs,

United States military planners had already adopted the smash-Hitler-first-Japan-second global strategy. Thus, in Washington, most eyes were on Europe and Britain, then nearly strangled by a U-boat blockade, and on Africa and the Mid-East. Most of the available air and sea power was being concentrated far-off from Bataan, in another sphere of the globe. As for Russia, she was already being drained in Europe; her inadequate Far East forces were entirely dependent on a single railroad, the Trans-Siberian, which could easily be cut by the Japanese. At that stage it would have been foolhardy for her to enter the war against Japan.

It would likewise have been foolhardy for the Navy to risk its three surviving Pearl Harbor-based carriers in the western Pacific. The codebreakers could help avoid a direct confrontation between the American carriers and the larger force of Japanese carriers, but the greater danger was Japanese land-based aircraft, impossible to track, or avoid, by codebreaking.

Actually, Washington had already mentally written off the Bataan garrisons. Short of shutting down operations in Europe and the Mideast and wholesale transfer of air and naval power to the Pacific, it tried every conceivable way to send help. But what actually got there was pitiful indeed. Three small freighters landed 10,000 tons of food on Cebu for transshipment to Corregidor. Two other ships were sunk in the attempt. But only 1,000 tons of this, a four-day food supply, reached Corregidor by surface craft. No amount of money could persuade commercial ship captains in Australia to make further trips. Admiral Hart's submarines made a token contribution. In four separate missions to Corregidor, they unloaded a limited quantity of small arms and antiaircraft ammunition and a total of twenty-seven tons of food from the Cebu stocks.

The Bataan defenders dug into hilly jungle terrain in the northern neck of the peninsula. They were divided into two basic forces: I Corps (23,000 men) on the west, commanded by General Wainwright, and II Corps (25,000 men) on the east, commanded by General Parker. On January 12, General Homma attacked Parker's troops in force. In the savage battle that ensued, the Filipino citizen-soldier 51st Division disintegrated and ceased to exist, but the other units held on gamely. A week later Homma's troops hit Wainwright's sector with equal fury.

One battalion of Filipinos disintegrated, but the other units remained intact, fighting gallantly. By January 22, when Sutherland visited the front, it was clear the Bataan force could not hold. He recommended a fallback to the Bagac-Orion line, about halfway down the peninsula. By January 26, this difficult maneuver was accomplished. When the line was manned, MacArthur wired Marshall that his forces would "fight it out to complete destruction."

The Japanese pressed forward, but not so vigorously. Homma had his problems, too. He had badly underestimated MacArthur's strength—and stubborn courage. His troops were near exhaustion from a month of intense fighting. Manila Bay was not yet in Homma's control. His supplies had to be laboriously unloaded on the beaches at Lingayen Gulf and transshipped to the front. He was, in fact, embarrassingly bogged down and even considered asking Tokyo for additional reinforcements. MacArthur, who interviewed Homma after the war, wrote that Homma was even thinking of giving up, bypassing the force on Bataan. He consolidated his line and, for the time being, limited his troops to patrol actions.

For the next eight weeks there was an eerie lull on the Bataan battlefields. The opposing forces clashed in minor patrol skirmishes and exchanged artillery salvos, but there were no major thrusts by either side. At first MacArthur was buoyed by this inactivity. He jubilantly claimed the Japanese attack had been stopped dead in its tracks. But the time dragging by was not on his side. The food was running out, with no hope of more arriving. His men were literally starving, driven to eating anything they could forage in the jungles and drinking polluted water. By mid-February only fifty-five percent of them were considered combat-efficient. Thousands were incapacitated by diseases: malaria, dysentery, beriberi, dengue.

Morale plummeted. Where was the help Washington had promised? And where was MacArthur? For reasons not clear, MacArthur had visited the troops on Bataan only once. It was not out of personal cowardice. He was a man without fear in combat; a fatalist who believed that when his time came, it would come. During these weeks he repeatedly and fearlessly exposed himself to enemy aerial bombs and artillery shells on Corregidor. "There was no bravado in this," he wrote in his memoirs. "It was simply my duty."

Whatever the reason, it was a grave mistake not to visit the troops. Fantastic rumors circulated to the effect that he was living in princely style on Corregidor, eating gourmet meals, while on Bataan they starved. There was some justification for this. MacArthur had ordered that some of the food stocks on Bataan be removed to Corregidor, probably anticipating a final withdrawal to the fortress. The food ration for the men on Corregidor was four times greater than that of the soldiers on the peninsula. This situation led to the composition of a ballad which was circulated on Bataan and bestowed on Mac-Arthur his infamous nickname. One verse suffices:

Dougout Doug MacArthur lies ashaking on the Rock
Safe from all the bombers and from any sudden shock
Dougout Doug is eating of the best food on Bataan
And his troops go starving on.

MacArthur did not help the morale situation by his public relations policy. He clamped a strict censorship on media reports from Corregidor. The only news out of Corregidor came from MacArthur's official war communiqués. These were often dishonest, vainglorious, self-serving, only rarely giving credit to deserving individuals or combat units. Dr. James reported that of one hundred forty-two such communiqués issued between December 8, 1941, and March 11, 1942, one hundred and nine mentioned only one individual—MacArthur. It would come as a surprise to many Ameicans to learn that the Fourth Marines were even on Bataan. This unfortunate censorship and communiqué policy, encouraged by sycophant press officers apparently bent on canonizing Mac-Arthur, would continue through the whole of World War II.

In Malinta Tunnel, Quezon, ill with tuberculosis and confined to a wheelchair, grew increasingly enraged with Roosevelt. Where was the help Roosevelt promised? Why should he countenance the killing of so many Filipinos if the cause were indeed a lost one? Finally, on February 8, he and his cabinet reached the end of their rope. They drafted and passed an extraordinary document. The gist of it was that Roosevelt should immediately grant

the Philippines full independence; the Philippines should
then be "neutralized" and a deal made with Japan for
quick withdrawal of both U.S. and Japanese forces; the
Filipino Army would be disbanded.

When MacArthur was handed this document, he conferred with High Commissioner Sayre. Sayre took the
position that if American help "cannot or will not arrive
here in time to be availing," then the Quezon proposal
"is the sound course to follow." MacArthur radioed the
Quezon proposal and Sayre's comment to Roosevelt,
along with a message of his own in which he outlined,
again, the grim situation on Bataan-Corregidor, and said:

> Since I have no air or sea protection, you must be
> prepared at any time to figure on complete destruc-
> tion of this command. You must determine whether
> the mission of delay would be better furthered by the
> temporizing plan of Quezon or by my continued
> battle effort. . . . So far as the military angle is
> concerned, the problem presents itself as to whether
> the plan of President Quezon might offer the best
> possible solution of what is about to be a disastrous
> debacle.

This message aroused much consternation in Washington. It *seemed* to be a MacArthur endorsement of the
Quezon plan; at any rate, he had not objected to it.
Roosevelt promptly replied to MacArthur and Quezon,
rejecting the scheme but authorizing surrender of Filipino
forces if it became necessary. To Quezon, Roosevelt said:
"So long as the flag of the United States flies on Filipino
soil as a pledge of our duty to your people, it will be
defended by our own men to the death." To MacArthur,
Roosevelt gave orders to uphold that pledge, not to surrender U.S. forces "as long as there remains any possibility of resistance." MacArthur replied that he had "not
the slightest intention in the world" of surrendering the
Filipino troops and that he and the Filipinos would fight
"to destruction."

MacArthur's critics would seize on this exchange of
messages to skewer him. To them, his stand smacked of
"moral abdication" or "appeasement" or "surrender" or
"a display of weakness." They would write, for example,
that "Roosevelt's staunchness saved MacArthur's reputa-

tion." MacArthur would explain it this way: By forwarding the Quezon message, and his own, he was merely making one more attempt to jar Washington out of its complacency and pressure it to send the necessary supplies.

By this time, there were several clear signs that Washington considered the situation on Bataan ultimately hopeless, merely a matter of time before the ax fell. The first of these was an order from Chief of Naval Operations, Admiral King, to dismantle the valuable Cast codebreaking unit and remove the entire outfit and its machines from Corregidor. On February 4, seventeen of the codebreakers, including the commanding officer of the unit, Rudolph Fabian, packed up the machines and left on the submarine *Seadragon*. The other codebreakers followed on other submarines. In all, seventy-five codebreakers were evacuated, the largest single contingent and the only complete outfit to leave the Rock.

The next was a series of suggestions from Washington that the military and civilians leaders (and families) be evacuated from Corregidor. MacArthur agreed to evacuate Quezon and Sayre and their parties, but he refused to leave himself. Nor would Jean or Arthur leave. MacArthur radioed: "I am deeply appreciative of the inclusion of my own family in this list, but they and I have decided that they will share the fate of this garrison." On February 22, Roosevelt sent him a direct, official order to evacuate Corregidor. At first, MacArthur considered resigning his commission and joining the Battling Bastards of Bataan as a "simple volunteer." But he decided to obey Roosevelt's order—in the hope of finding reinforcements and returning to Bataan. He would take some of his staff, a nucleus to form a new army.

The plan was that all the leaders would leave by submarine. On February 20, Quezon, his wife and three children, Vice-Preisdent Osmeña, and others—ten altogether—departed on the submarine *Swordfish*. It was a rough voyage for Quezon. *Swordfish* dropped the party at the island of Panay, from whence it made its way to Mindanao and freedom. Then *Swordfish* returned to Corregidor to embark High Commissioner Sayre, his wife and son, and seven members of his staff. *Swordfish* delivered the Sayre party to Australia without incident.

The Navy designated the submarine *Permit* to evacuate MacArthur and his party. *Permit* was now commanded by Wreford Chapple, the officer who had fearlessly charged his S boat into Lingayen Gulf and sunk the only Japanese ship of consequence during the invasion of the Philippines. Chapple was then patrolling off Java, which had been captured by the Japanese after a futile naval defense by Admiral Hart. He headed for Corregidor.

In the meantime, MacArthur had decided on another means of escape. Admiral Hart had left behind in Manila six PT boats, commanded by John D. Bulkeley. Bulkeley's little group had fought bravely (but ineffectually) against Japanese naval forces. MacArthur had come to like and admire Bulkeley. There were four PT boats left. MacArthur would run the Japanese naval blockade by PT boat. Some have speculated that the decision may have been conceived as a clever stunt to embarrass the U.S. Navy, to demonstrate how easily the "blockade" could be penetrated. But in his memoirs, Sid Huff implied that MacArthur had claustrophobia and couldn't stand being cooped up in a submarine. In any case, the staff was appalled, and tried to talk him out of it. But MacArthur could not be dissuaded.

CHAPTER THIRTEEN

★ ★ ★ ★ ★

THE ESCAPE PLAN was fairly complicated. The MacArthur party, twenty-two in all, would depart at night on Bulkeley's four surviving PT boats. MacArthur and his family would leave from Corregidor in one boat in order not to draw undue attention. The others would embark at Mariveles and Sisiman Cove on Bataan. The boats would then slip out through the U.S.-laid minefield at the mouth of the bay and rendezvous at about 10:00 P.M. The first night they would run to Tagauayan, a small deserted islet in the unoccupied Cuyo Islands, arriving about 7:30 A.M. The next day they would wait there, out of sight of Japanese aircraft. *Permit* would put into Tagauayan that night and, if MacArthur so desired, take him and his party on to Australia. Otherwise, the second night the four boats would leave at about 5:00 P.M. and run down to Cagayan, Mindanao, still in United States hands, arriving at about 7:00 A.M. There, at Del Monte Field, four B–17s from Australia would meet them and fly them out to Australia.

On the evening of March 11, Bulkeley brought his boat, *PT–41*, to the dock at Corregidor. The deck was piled high with extra drums of gasoline. Major General

Jonathan Wainwright, designated by MacArthur as commander of the Bataan and Corregidor forces, was on hand
to oversee the final preparations and say good-bye. Soon
MacArthur's limousine with its four-star insignia on the
license plate came into view. MacArthur, looking tired
and gaunt and down in weight twenty-five pounds, got
out of the car. Each member of the party was permitted
one suitcase. These were loaded on board together with
a duffle bag of canned food. (Earlier, MacArthur had
sent out a footlocker with Quezon containing personal
items such as his marriage license, Arthur's birth certif-
icate, family pictures, securities, his decorations, and
about $100 in cash.) At the last moment, MacArthur
directed Sid Huff to remove the four-star insignia from
his automobile and bring it along.

Now it was time to say good-bye to Wainwright, a
poignant moment. The two men shook hands. MacArthur
gave Wainwright a farewell present: a box of cigars
and two jars of shaving cream. He said, "If I get through
to Australia, you know I'll come back as soon as I can
with as much as I can. In the meantime, you've got to
hold." Then MacArthur, raising his floppy campaign hat
in a farewell gesture to Corregidor, boarded *PT-41*.

The passengers on Bulkeley's *PT-41* now settled into
crowded quarters. There were nine passengers: Mac-
Arthur, Jean, Arthur (carrying his favorite toy, a stuffed
rabbit), Ah Cheu, Sid Huff, Sutherland, and three other
officers. Bulkeley started the three Packard engines and
threaded carefully through the minefield at the mouth of
the bay. There he rendezvoused with the three other
boats (PTs *32*, *34*, *35*), whose decks were also piled
high with gasoline drums. These boats carried the other
thirteen passengers, including MacArthur's intelligence
chief, Charles A. Willoughby; his communications chief,
Spencer B. Akin; and Rear Admiral Francis W Rockwell, who had been senior naval commander since Hart's
departure.

It was a moonless night. Soon the boats were moving
along at high speed in mounting seas. MacArthur and
Jean sat on a mattress on the floor of the lower cockpit.
Arthur and Ah Cheu occupied bunks. The *41* bounced
"like a cork" (Huff recalled) or a "cement mixer" (Mac-
Arthur recalled). Soon all passengers except Jean and
ex-Navy-man Huff were miserably seasick. MacArthur

may have now regretted his decision to go by PT boat. At any rate he began seriously to consider boarding *Permit* on the morrow at Tagauayan.

The tactical plan was that the four boats would remain in a close "diamond" formation. If a Japanese vessel spotted them, Bulkeley would run away at high speed; the other three boats would turn and fight. But during the night all four boats became separated on the high seas. Each proceeded to the rendezvous alone. Fortunately none encountered any Japanese vessels. The first big hurdle was crossed with relative ease. Even so, few slept.

During the night one of the boats, *PT–32*, had gone ahead of Bulkeley's *PT–41*. In the early light of dawn, *32*'s skipper saw what he thought was a Japanese destroyer coming up astern very fast. Reacting hastily, the skipper ordered his decks cleared for combat. He jettisoned the extra gasoline drums and made ready the torpedo tubes. A couple of MacArthur's generals, including Spencer Akin, advised the skipper to hold fire until they could be absolutely sure it was the enemy. He did, and a good thing. They shortly identified the "destroyer" as Bulkeley's *PT–41*, "oddly magnified in the half-light of dawn."

During the night they had fallen behind schedule. Neither the *41* nor the *32*, which was having serious engine problems, could reach Tagauayan without a dangerous run in broad daylight. So Bulkeley led the two boats to another island in the Cuyo group. They anchored in a protected cove. They waited there—restlessly—until early afternoon. They saw no sign of Japanese air or sea patrols, so they decided it would be safe to proceed in daylight. At about 5:30 P.M. they reached Tagauayan. One other boat, *PT–34* (with Admiral Rockwell embarked), was there waiting. But there was no sign of the fourth boat, *PT–35*, on which Willoughby and others were embarked. It never did show up. It went on alone to the final destination, Cagayan, Mindanao.

The submarine *Permit* was scheduled to arrive that evening. MacArthur and the others discussed whether or not they should transfer to it. This time MacArthur was more favorably disposed, apparently believing he could tolerate claustrophobia better than seasickness. But when Admiral Rockwell predicted—wrongly, as it turned out—

the seas would be smoother this second night, it was decided to go on by PT boat.

This raised a bit of a problem. The *32* boat had jettisoned her extra fuel drums; she could not make it to Mindanao. It was therefore decided that her passengers would be transferred to the *34* and *41*. The *32* would wait for *Permit* to show up, inform her captain that all was well and that MacArthur had gone on to Mindanao by PT boat. After that the *32* was to go on to Iloilo, Panay (still in friendly hands), make repairs, take on fuel, and proceed to the south, rejoining the other boats at some future time and place. At about 6:30 P.M., the *34* and *41* departed Tagauayan.

As it turned out, this arrangement proved to be an unfortunate one for the crew of *32*. *Permit* arrived the following morning, March 13. By then the skipper of *32* had decided *32* could not make Iloilo; only one of its three engines was working properly. The hull was leaking. So *Permit* destroyed *32* with her deck gun, embarked her crew (fifteen men), and slipped out to sea. *Permit* was then ordered to Corregidor to evacuate a large contingent of codebreakers. As a consequence, the crew of *32* went back to the place from whence it had just escaped. Moreover, to make room for the thirty-eight codebreakers, eight of the *32* crew had to be put ashore on Corregidor. These eight men shared the fate of the garrison. After a harrowing voyage (including a nightmarish twenty-two-and-a-half-hour depth charge attack), *Permit* delivered the other seven crew of *PT–32* to Australia.

After leaving Tagauayan, the *34* and *41* boats set course for Cagayan. If the seas had been smoother as Rockwell predicted, it would have been an easy night's run. But the seas were fearfully rough. Again it was a wet, miserable night. And again MacArthur was seasick. This night they had a close call with the enemy. Not long after setting forth, while it was still daylight, Bulkeley spotted what he believed to be a Japanese cruiser. The two boats evaded at high speed. Apparently they were not seen. But until that fact was definitely established, tension ran high on the two boats.

Huff recalled that later that night he experienced the "strangest two hours" of his life. He had just dozed off when at about midnight MacArthur, who apparently did not sleep either night, woke him. The general wanted to talk. The aide listened dutifully. For two hours Mac-Arthur conducted a monologue, speaking in a "voice slow and deliberate and barely distinguishable above the high whine of the engines." He reviewed his recent six-year tour in the Philippines, his efforts to build an adequate defense, the outbreak of war, the campaigns on Luzon. Huff thought MacArthur was trying to "get it all straight in his mind." It was, Huff recalled, "a little uncanny" and "bitterly dramatic" and "gravely sad." Huff concluded: "He had been thrust downward from the crest as far as a man could go."

They fell behind schedule again that night. When dawn came, they were still about three hours short of Cagayan. It was three tense hours; all-hands alert for Jap air or sea patrols. As they approached the harbor they were not sure it might not already be in Japanese hands. Luckily it was not.

They put into the dock, congratulating Bulkeley on a job well-done. They had traveled 560 miles through enemy-held waters. A little later they were relieved to see PT-35 arrive with Willoughby and the others.

The U.S. Army commander in the area, Brigadier General William F. Sharp, had good news and bad. The good news was that although the Japanese forces were closing it, Del Monte Field was still operational. The bad news was that there were no B-17s waiting. Australia had sent three old crates, survivors of the fighting in Java. One had crashed into the sea; one had turned back with engine trouble; one limped into Del Monte, but Sharp (as he recalled) declared it unfit and sent it back to Australia.

The party was then forced to wait at Cagayan with the Japanese closing in until other aircraft could be found. MacArthur was furious. He fired off messages demanding safe air transportation for his party. They waited three and a half days. Finally a reluctant U.S. Navy in Australia, which had previously turned a deaf ear to MacArthur's requests, provided three brand-new B-17s. One turned back en route, but two arrived at Del Monte the evening of March 16. The pilots were exhausted after the nine-hundred-mile flight, but they drank "gallons of coffee" and soon took off with the entire MacArthur party. Bulkeley and his PT men stayed on another month fighting the Japanese at sea. In April, on MacArthur's orders, they were flown to Australia. For his heroism, Bulkeley was awarded the Medal of Honor.

The flight to Darwin, Australia, was uneventful—until the very end. Nearing Australia, they received word a Japanese air raid was in progress at Darwin. The two B–17s diverted to Batchelor Field, about fifty miles to the south of Darwin. They touched down at about 9:30 A.M., March 17. Getting off the plane, setting feet on the safe Australian soil, Sid Huff thought the five-day-escape saga had been "a kind of miracle."

The final destination in Australia was Melbourne, on the southern coast. An Air Corps C–47 carried the party from Batchelor Field to Alice Springs in central Australia. From there the group took a train to Melbourne. When it stopped at Adelaide, reporters asked MacArthur for a statement. His response would become one of the most famous in military annals:

> The President of the United States ordered me to break through the Japanese lines and proceed from Corregidor to Australia for the purpose, as I understand it, of organizing the American offensive against Japan, a primary object of which is the relief of the Philippines. I came through and *I shall return.*

MacArthur's escape from Corregidor instantly became one of the most talked about and inspiring tales of World War II. Coming as it did at that dark moment in U.S. history when nothing seemed to be going right for the military, it was a real shot in the arm. Mac had outtricked the wiley Japanese! President Roosevelt added luster to the deed by awarding him the Medal of Honor. Almost overnight General MacArthur, already the hero of Bataan, achieved mythic status. In some quarters he was being urged to look way ahead and run for the presidency in 1944. Republican ticket, of course.

CHAPTER
FOURTEEN

★ ★ ★ ★ ★

THE NEXT SIX weeks were among the most depressing in MacArthur's life. Although he now enjoyed the highest esteem of the Free World, had won a Medal of Honor like his father (the only father-son winners in history), and was a hugely popular hero in Australia, behind the scenes he suffered terrible anguish and pain. This was caused by a number of factors not evident to his admiring public. What he found, militarily, in Australia, the worsening situation on Bataan and Corregidor, and a feeling that Washington had deliberately betrayed him, all combined to deepen his depression. The betrayal by Washington he took either as a personal rebuke or a sinister plot to undermine or destroy him.

MacArthur had arrived in Australia fully expecting to find a large army and air force which he would lead to the Philippines to relieve the beleaguered forces on Bataan and Corregidor. What he found was something else again. In all Australia there were less than 25,000 army and air force personnel, mostly engineers and other support troops. There was not even one combat division. The aircraft strength totaled about 250 planes, but only a small percentage of these was operable. The Allied naval force consisted of about six heavy and light cruisers and twenty-five submarines of the U.S. Asiatic Fleet. The submarines were badly in need of overhaul; the skippers and crews were exhausted from four months of combat and demoralized by repeated torpedo failures.

Journalist Clark Lee, a close friend and confident of MacArthur's from Manila-Corregidor days, saw MacArthur in Australia about this time. Later, in his book *Douglas MacArthur*, he wrote that when MacArthur discovered how little military power there was in Australia, that there was no hope of rescuing his troops in the Philippines, he was "literally stunned." He quotes MacArthur as saying the discovery was the "greatest shock and surprise of the whole damn war." He wrote that MacArthur "turned deathly white, his knees buckled, his lips twitched. After a long silence, MacArthur whispered miserably, 'God have mercy on us.'"

Not only were there no military forces to lead back to the Philippines, Australia itself appeared to be in danger. In addition to overrunning Borneo, the Celebes, Ambon, Malay, Sumatra, Java, and Timor, the Japanese had captured the Australian territory of New Britain. Staging from a powerful base on New Britain, Rabaul, they were pushing southwestward and southeastward in force. They had established bases at Lae and Salamaua, New Guinea, and invaded the Solomon Islands at Bougainville. The New Guinea bases directly threatened the Australian outpost of Port Moresby in Papua, southeast New Guinea. The conquests in the Solomon Islands threatened the vital Allied sea lanes from Hawaii to Australia and supporting bases in the New Hebrides, New Caledonia, Fiji, and Samoa.

MacArthur found that Australia's seven million population fully expected a Japanese invasion at any moment. They were demoralized and afraid. The Australian military defenses were pitifully weak. The few scattered army units in Australia, mostly militia, could not repulse a determined Japanese assault. In fact, Australian military planners had already settled on what MacArthur believed to be a defeatist strategy of falling back to what was called the Brisbane Line, conceding to the invaders the entire northern half of Australia. Not only was there to be no rescue of the Bataan troops, MacArthur had now to face the discouraging fact that Australia itself might turn into another Bataan. He told the Australian public:

I am glad indeed to be in immediate cooperation with the Australian soldier. I know him well from World War days and admire him greatly. I have every confidence in the ultimate success of our joint cause; but success in modern war requires something more than courage and a willingness to die: it requires careful preparation. This means the furnishing of sufficient troops and sufficient material to meet the known strength of a potential enemy. No general can make something out of nothing. My success or failure will depend primarily upon the resources which the respective governments place at my disposal. My faith in them is complete. In any event I shall do my best. I shall keep the soldier's faith.

MacArthur still officially commanded the forces on Bataan and Corregidor, and elsewhere in the Philippines. He desired to retain that command for a very good reason: If he turned it over to Wainwright and Wainwright was overwhelmed or forced to surrender, Wainwright would then have the power to order the surrender of all U.S. troops throughout the Philippines. Should the Japanese insist Wainwright invoke that power in return for accepting his surrender, Wainwright would have no choice. But as long as MacArthur still held overall command, Wainwright could only legally surrender the troops on Bataan and Corregidor. The others could fight on.

Washington evidently did not appreciate this point, or else chose to ignore it. On March 20, Army Chief of Staff Marshall, without telling MacArthur, began sending messages to Wainwright addressed to "Commander in Chief, U.S. Army, Far East." When MacArthur learned of this, he fired off a protest to Marshall, explaining his reasoning. Marshall radioed he was "not impressed." It was unrealistic for MacArthur to think he could command U.S. forces in the Philippines from Australia. MacArthur diplomatically told Marshall he was "heartily in accord" with the new setup, but privately he (and GHQ) was furious. He did not really accept the new setup and continually interfered with it.

The situation on Bataan, meanwhile, was going from bad to worse. Two weeks after MacArthur landed in Australia, the Japanese launched a savage new offensive against the Bagac-Orion line. In three days the entire II Corps collapsed. Then came heavy pressure on I Corps' front. Wainwright's troop commander on Bataan, Major General Edward P. King, Jr., reported the situation was desperate: His starving troops could not hold out.

President Roosevelt's February "no surrender" edict had not been rescinded. From Australia, MacArthur radioed Wainwright that "under no conditions" should he surrender. "If food fails," MacArthur said, "you will prepare and execute an attack on the enemy." He included a detailed plan for the attack. To Marshall, MacArthur reported he was prepared to return to Bataan and lead the attack himself. Wainwright passed all this along to General King. But King had already made up his mind. On April 9, without Wainwright's knowledge, he surrendered the Bataan force, some 75,000 men, the largest army in American history to lay down its arms.

MacArthur was confused, angry, dismayed, but helpless. All he could do was issue a forlorn press release: "The Bataan force went out as it would have wished, fighting to the end of its flickering hope. No army has ever done so much with so little and nothing became it more than its last hour of trial and agony."

Corregidor, too, was now clearly doomed. But Homma was cautious in his approach, waiting until May 5 to land troops on it. By then Roosevelt had rescinded the "no surrender" policy. At noon on May 6, Wainwright ordered a white flag hoisted over Corregidor. Again MacArthur could only issue a press release:

> Corregidor needs no comment from me. It has sounded its own story at the mouth of its guns. It has scrolled its own epitaph on enemy tablets. But through the bloody haze of its last reverberating shot, I shall always see the visions of its grim, gaunt, and ghostly men, still unafraid.

As MacArthur had feared, Homma demanded that Wainwright order the surrender of all troops in the Philippines or else face the possibility that the eleven thousand men on Corregidor would be massacred. On May 7,

Wainwright, by radio, ordered the total capitulation of all U.S. forces throughout the Philippines. MacArthur was enraged. He wanted at all cost for whatever troops remained to fight on—organized into formal units or as guerrillas. He radioed Sharp on Mindanao: "Orders emanating from General Wainwright have no validity." To Marshall he said: "I believe Wainwright has temporarily become unbalanced and his condition renders him susceptible of enemy use." But all this was in vain. Sharp and others—fearing the Corregidor force would be massacred—surrendered.

Again MacArthur was furious, dismayed, and helpless. His Philippine force was gone. He never really forgave Wainwright for not at least attempting a final offensive. When Washington recommended Wainwright for a Medal of Honor, MacArthur opposed it, arguing that others were more deserving. Marshall and Secretary of War Stimson persevered, and after the war (when MacArthur had cooled and seemed to embrace Wainwright), Wainwright received the medal.

As if all this were not depressing enough, MacArthur now received a personal blow. He had assumed that he would be named supreme commander of the entire Pacific Theater, that he alone would command the war against Japan. But Admiral King, rightly believing that the Pacific war would be largely a naval war and having no faith in MacArthur, opposed the appointment. He believed the theater should be commanded by an admiral. The upshot was a compromise. The Anglo-American Joint Chiefs of Staff divided the enormous Pacific into two separate theaters: the Pacific Ocean Area (POA), commanded by Admiral Chester W. Nimitz in Pearl Harbor, and the Southwest Pacific Area (SWPA), commanded by MacArthur. With this stroke, MacArthur was reduced to a far lesser role than he had envisioned. He wrote bitterly:

> Of all the faulty decisions of the war perhaps the most inexplicable one was the failure to unify the command in the Pacific . . . [it] cannot be defended in logic, in theory or even in common sense. It resulted in divided effort, the waste of diffusion and duplication of force, undue extension of the war with added casualties and cost.

All these events cast MacArthur into the deepest fit of paranoia and gloom he had ever known. Washington had "tricked" him into leaving his men in the Philippines to go to Australia for help that was nonexistent. Washington had taken his Philippine command away from him, given it to Wainwright, who failed to attack, then abjectly surrendered. Washington had "led him to believe" he would command the Pacific Theater, then promptly divided it up between himself and Nimitz. All MacArthur really had left were a few untrained troops in Australia, and that continent itself was threatened. Even if he could save it, it would be years before he could fight his way back to the Philippines. Journalist Lee reported Mac-Arthur as saying that his worst enemies were "not in front, but behind me in Washington." Lee wrote:

> MacArthur soon became convinced that he was opposed by a powerful group of enemies in Washington whose considerations of both world strategy and Pacific strategy were influenced by their hatred of him. To intimates he named names. "George Marshall, who hates me . . . a Navy cabal . . . A New Deal cabal." He despised Harry Hopkins; had the utmost contempt for the British military leader in Washington, Sir John Dill, and wavered between including Roosevelt in his group of supposed enemies.

MacArthur settled in Melbourne, then the military command center of Australia. He, Jean, Arthur and Ah Cheu, and the staff moved into quarters on the sixth floor of the Menzies Hotel.

The MacArthurs were national heroes in Australia, much in demand socially and for public appearances and speeches. But aside from forming a close personal and working relationship with Australia's Prime Minister John Curtin, who admired MacArthur profoundly, by and large they kept to themselves. The ever-present aide Sid Huff recalled that Jean appeared to sublimate her own life to MacArthur's:

> . . . in these dark days Jean quit living her own life and began to center everything she did around the General, and, of course, around her son. I believe it was established in her mind that henceforth her duty

was to be solely concerned with bringing whatever help and comfort she could to her husband . . . indeed, he was a lonely, angry man who needed her help as never before.

MacArthur had always been the doting father to Arthur. During this period, he was even more solicitous. Sid Huff recalled that the general inaugurated the deplorable custom of giving Arthur a new present every morning—in fact, two identical presents so that Arthur could give one to his playmate. "We were hard pressed at times to find a variety of presents," Huff wrote. But Huff solved the problem by contacting an old Navy buddy in the States who operated a wholesale toy and sports company. "Not long afterwards," Huff recalled, "I received two big boxes that were filled with everything from toy airplanes to balloons and boxing gloves. And there were ten of each!" Huff and Jean hid the toys away and doled them out, two at a time, every day, except on Arthur's birthdays. On those occasions, MacArthur gave Arthur one present for each year of his age (carefully meted out every fifteen minutes), a practice he continued for years and years.

The protective shield Jean and Sid Huff wrapped around the general in these dark times was carried over to the office. Journalist Lee observed that the staff, which now proudly (but somewhat inaccurately) called itself the Bataan Gang, was troublesome—or worse. He wrote: "Some of them acted like men who had personally lifted him down from the cross after he had been crucified by Marshall/Admiral King/Harry Hopkins, and they determined that nothing again should ever hurt him. . . . They moved in an atmosphere of unreality. The world centered around MacArthur; nothing else was important. . . . They formed an exclusive group that resented and suspected 'outsiders'. . . ."

In spite of what MacArthur and his staff thought, Washington—Marshall in particular—was doing everything possible to send men and war material to MacArthur. Long before MacArthur arrived in Australia. Roosevelt and Britain's Prime Minister Winston Churchill had made the decision that Australia must be saved so that it could be employed as a key springboard in the ultimate counter-attack against Japan. About the time MacArthur arrived there, Roosevelt and Churchill had agreed to return to

Australia two of the three crack Australian Imperial Forces Army divisions that had been fighting in North Africa. In addition, General Marshall had ordered that the 32nd and 41st U.S. Army divisions (then in training in the States) be shipped forthwith to Australia, together with additional antiaircraft and engineer units and support forces, bringing the total U.S. troop strength to 100,000 men. Marshall likewise ordered a rapid buildup of the Australian-based air forces to about eight groups—535 first-line bombers and fighters. Admiral King sent a half-dozen destroyers, two additional submarine tenders, and six more old S-class submarines. He also began an "exchange program" to overhaul and modernize the twenty fleet submarines basing in Australia.

CHAPTER
FIFTEEN

★ ★ ★ ★ ★

MACARTHUR HAD BEEN named "Allied" commander of the Southwest Pacific because he would command Australian, Dutch, New Zealand, and other troops, as well as American. Accordingly, his staff should have had an "international" composition, made up of officers from all the nations under his command. But MacArthur mostly ignored this guideline from Washington. He named Australian General Thomas Blamey, a veteran of the Mideast War, to command the ground forces, but all the other key jobs went to Americans. Lieutenant General George H. Brett replaced Brereton as chief of the Allied Air Forces. His Allied naval commander was Vice Admiral Herbert F. Leary, USN. Sutherland remained as chief of staff. Others of the Bataan Gang, including Willoughby and Akin, were assigned to the remaining top jobs.

This was an unhappy staff indeed. MacArthur had little faith in his three top commanders. For some reason (perhaps the quick surrender at Singapore), MacArthur did not hold the Australian soldier in high regard. Blamey's post would turn out to be largely ceremonial; MacArthur and GHQ, by various headquarters subterfuges, would bypass him and actually command the ground forces. By now, MacArthur was deeply bitter at the U.S. Navy for failing to come to his rescue in the Philippines. He vented his ire on Leary, who was not a forceful personality. He

91

was likewise bitter at the Air Corps, both for the fiasco at Clark Field and for its failure at Java and elsewhere. Brereton's replacement, Brett, caught that ire. MacArthur refused to see him for eight days—then flayed him alive. Sutherland, more arrogant than ever, did little to mold this group into a smooth executive team. All shared Mac-Arthur's paranoia that Washington was bent on undermining or defeating them.

This pitiful, unhappy command was valuably assisted by a true secret weapon: Rudolph Fabian's codebreaking unit. It had survived the vicissitudes of war intact and now was housed in Melbourne's heavily guarded Monterey Building, home of the Royal Australian Navy's Intelligence Division. Administratively, it was still under U.S. Navy control, but its priceless product—an unending stream of decoded Japanese diplomatic and naval traffic—was delivered daily to MacArthur. These reports would shape MacArthur's forthcoming strategy for the military defeat of Japan. They would enable him to outsmart the Japanese at almost every turn. They would contribute enormously to his reputation as a brilliant field commander.

Not long after the codebreaking unit had established itself in Melbourne, it produced a galvanizing piece of intelligence, one of the most valuable of the war. It was an operational order precisely spelling out Japanese objectives for their forces based at Rabaul. In early May they would launch a twin-pronged invasion force. The bulk of it would be employed to capture, by amphibious assault, the Australian outpost in Papua, Port Moresby. A smaller element would land on Tulagi Island in the Solomons to build a seaplane base, designed to support the Port Moresby operation and to prepare the way for later invasions of New Caledonia, Fiji, and Samoa. The invasion forces would be supported by strong naval forces: the heavy carriers *Shokaku* and *Zuikaku*, the light carrier *Shoho*, plus many cruisers and destroyers.

The Port Moresby invasion force was a threat of grave proportions. Although the Japanese high command in Tokyo had decided against invading Australia itself (at least for the time being), MacArthur and his advisers did not know that. They had to assume that once the Japanese held Port Moresby, it would only be a matter of time before Australia itself was invaded. Only 270 miles of water separated Port Moresby from the beaches of the northernmost Australian territory, Queensland (less than two hours flying for a bomber). Based on past performance, that would be an easy amphibious jump for the Japanese.

The radios between Washington, Pearl Harbor, and Melbourne crackled with schemes and plans to blunt the Port Moresby invasion. With the incalculable advantage of the codebreaking intelligence, it seemed an ideal time to strike a decisive blow—in an area relatively safe for U.S. Navy carrier operations. What was finally decided upon was a joint effort by Nimitz and MacArthur. Nimitz would send two carriers, *Yorktown* and *Lexington* (his two other carriers, *Hornet* and *Enterprise,* were committed to Jimmy Doolittle's raid on Tokyo), and escorting cruisers and destroyers. MacArthur would send whatever surface naval forces and submarines he could put to sea. In addition, whatever land-based bombers MacArthur could muster would fly reconnaissance and bombing missions against Japanese bases and naval forces.

On May 4 to May 8 the Japanese and Allied forces met in what became known as the Battle of the Coral Sea. It was the first time in history that carriers had ever fought one another and the first time that opposing combatant ships never came within sight of each other. In the four-day melee, U.S. carrier aircraft sank the light carrier *Shoho* and one of the big Port Moresby invasion transports, and severely damaged the heavy carrier *Shokaku.* Japanese aircraft sank the U.S. destroyer *Sims,* a tanker *Neosho,* and damaged both *Yorktown* and *Lexington. Lexington,* soon swept by uncontrollable fires, was abandoned and sunk by U.S. destroyers. In a tactical sense, the United States lost the battle. But in the strategic sense, it won. The Port Moresby invasion force turned back. For the first time in the war, a Japanese military force had been denied its objective. For the moment, Australia was safe.

MacArthur's forces—air and sea—played only a minor role in the battle. Brett's handful of planes bombed bases at Lae, Rabaul, and Bougainville, and conducted photo reconnaissance missions. They found the Port Moresby invasion force at sea and attacked it, claiming several sinkings. These claims were not borne out in Japanese records examined after the war. By mistake, Brett's bombers attacked MacArthur's small American-Australian naval force (three cruisers, two destroyers) supporting

Nimitz, killing nine men but, fortunately, sinking no ships. Other planes of Brett's command found the Japanese going ashore at Tulagi but were not able to break up this invasion. Nor were the aircraft from the *Lexington* and *Enterprise* able to stop the Tulagi operation. The seaplane base was established.

Shortly after this battle, the codebreakers provided further valuable intelligence on overall Japanese operations. Something big was afoot in the Central Pacific area; just what was not clear. After that operation, whatever it was, the Japanese would extend the thrust in the Solomons beyond Tulagi to take New Caledonia, Fiji, and Samoa in order to cut the line of communication from the United States and Hawaii to Australia. In addition, the projected seizure of Port Moresby would remain on the program. But it would not be an amphibious operation. The Japanese would land at Buna and send troops overland—over the towering Owen Stanley Mountains—to attack Port Moresby from the rear. Significantly, this decision released Japanese carriers for other assignments.

The codebreakers now bent every effort to find out what the Japanese operation in the Central Pacific might be. After intensely hard work, the unit at Pearl Harbor figured it out beyond doubt. Japanese Admiral Isoroku Yamamoto had launched a massive invasion force against Midway Island (with a feint at Alaska), hoping to draw the U.S. Fleet into a decisive battle and annihilate it. The codebreakers provided an exact order of battle, even noting that *Shokaku*, damaged at Coral Sea, and *Zuikaku*, which had lost her aircraft in the same battle, would not be present in the carrier force.

To meet this grave threat, Nimitz mobilized every combatant ship and aircraft in his command. These were principally the carriers *Enterprise* and *Hornet* and *Yorktown* (hastened from the South Pacific to Pearl Harbor), supporting cruisers and destroyers, and about twenty submarines. These forces met the Japanese on June 3 to 6. United States naval aircraft sank all four big carriers supporting the invasion forces: *Akagi, Kaga, Soryu, Hiryu.* They also sank the heavy cruiser *Mikuma.* The United States lost the *Yorktown* and a destroyer, *Hammann.* It was, as has been described by the naval historian Walter Lord, "an incredible victory" for Nimitz and the U.S. Navy. In a single month—at Coral Sea and Midway—

Nimitz had dealt Japanese carrier aviation a blow from which it would never fully recover. This greatly curtailed Japan's ability to take the sea offensively at will. In fact, immediately after the battle, the plan to invade New Caledonia, Fiji, and Samoa was shelved indefinitely. The tide in the Pacific War had turned—thanks to the code-breakers.

The terrific destruction of Japanese carrier aviation in these two battles led to a momentous shift in American Pacific strategy. The global strategy was still Hitler-first-Japan-second, but the planners in Washington, Pearl Harbor, and Melbourne now began to think beyond the purely defensive posture imposed on the Pacific. Only seven months into the war and still hobbled by a shortage of everything (except codebreaking), they began to hatch plans to go on the offensive. Most of these plans centered on the same objective: the reduction or capture of the Japanese base on New Britain, Rabaul. It was the command center, the staging base for Japanese thrusts into New Guinea and the Solomons. Its capture would stop these thrusts at the source and force the Japanese back some seven hundred miles to their mid-Pacific base, Truk.

By now, MacArthur's military posture had improved considerably. The combat-hardened Australian 6th and 7th divisions had come home. Prime Minister John Curtin had inaugurated plans for an imposing Australian Army of ten divisions. The other eight were already in training. The two American divisions, the 32nd and 41st, had arrived. In spite of the combat attrition, the total air strength had risen steadily. MacArthur had built a network of new air fields in northeast Australia, placing his bombers much closer to the Japanese bases in the Solomons, New Britain, and New Guinea.

In early June, shortly after the smashing success at Midway, MacArthur proposed to Washington a daring plan: a direct amphibious assault on Rabaul. He believed that with the available forces under his command, plus the loan from Nimitz of one Marine amphibious division and carrier support, he could take Rabaul, then considered "lightly defended," in short order. Follow-up plans submitted to Washington, called Tulsa 1 and Tulsa 2, predicted that Rabaul could be captured in the astonishingly brief period of "two weeks" and "eighteen days," respectively.

General Marshall and his planners received these plans
with enthusiasm. But when Marshall laid them before the
Joint Chiefs of Staff, he met a frosty reception from the
Navy. Admiral King believed MacArthur's plan was
utterly unrealistic. By then the Japanese had half a dozen
air bases ringing Rabaul. How were they to be destroyed
in such short order? MacArthur's fighters could not reach
Rabaul from his existing bases; he would have to rely
solely on unescorted bombers. If the bases were not
destroyed, Japanese planes would surely attack the carrier
and invasion forces at sea. Even if the Australian and
U.S. troops got ashore, there was a monumental problem.
Rabaul was not lightly held by any means. The thousands
of crack troops of the "South Seas Detachment" that
turned back from the Port Moresby invasion were still in
Rabaul. Besides these objections, there was a critical
shortage of troop transport, far too little to lift Mac-
Arthur's three divisions from Australia, plus a Marine
division.

There was yet another problem. Admiral King still
wished the war in the Pacific to be primarily a Navy show,
with MacArthur and the U.S. Army reduced to a supporting role. During these prolonged and delicate negotiations
within the JCS, Admiral King made his position quite clear
by arrogantly ordering Nimitz to prepare a plan for the
capture of Rabaul by the Navy and the Marines. When
MacArthur got wind of this King-Nimitz exchange, he
was furious. After all, Rabaul did lie within his theater of
operations. On June 28, he fired off a famous message to
Marshall:

It is quite evident . . . that the Navy contemplates
assuming general command control of all operations
in the Pacific Theater, the role of the Army being
subsidiary and consisting largely of placing its forces
at the disposal and under command of Navy or
Marine officers. . . .

This angry message, and others, precipitated a political
crisis within the JCS, leading to further extended talks,
and to a resolution of the immediate offensive strategy
and command situation. The solution, sent to Nimitz and
MacArthur on July 2, was set forth in plain but firm
language. The main objective would be Rabaul. Its cap-

ture would be carried out not by a MacArthuresque quick thrust but in three gradual steps: the first by Nimitz, the second two by MacArthur. Step one would be the recapture of Tulagi and adjacent islands in the southeast Solomons. MacArthur would provide Nimitz land-based air and limited naval support during this operation. The second step would be to recapture Lae and Salamaua and northeast New Guinea, together with the rest of the islands in the upper Solomons (New Georgia, Bougainville). The third and final step would be the taking of Rabaul itself.

MacArthur was satisfied with this compromise. Perhaps on reflection and study he saw that Rabaul could not be easily seized in two weeks or eighteen days. It would have to be enveloped gradually, with one pincer moving up the Solomons, the other up through New Guinea. The advance would be controlled largely by the ability of the Allied forces to gain control of the air from Japanese advanced bases. In this plan, MacArthur had won the lion's share of the responsibility. Tulagi would surely fall quickly. Then it would be strictly his show.

In the ensuing days, the planners at Pearl Harbor and Melbourne drafted specific plans to implement the broad JCS directives. For step one, the capture of Tulagi, Nimitz appointed sub-Commander Vice Admiral Robert L. Ghormley, who set to work in feverish haste. On July 5, only three days after the JCS plan had been promulgated, the codebreakers reported to Nimitz the alarming news that the Japanese were landing Seabees on Guadalcanal, an island adjacent to Tulagi, and had started to build an airfield. To MacArthur (and Ghormley) this was ominous. MacArthur seized the opportunity to urge Washington to defer the Tulagi operation indefinitely, pleading a shortage of airfields, planes, and troops. In a message to Marshall, King noted haughtily: "Three weeks ago MacArthur stated that, if he could be furnished amphibious forces and two carriers, he could push through right to Rabaul. He now feels that he not only cannot undertake this extended operation but not even the Tulagi operation." King agreed to a one week postponement of the Tulagi operation, which would now include Guadalcanal, but no more. In overriding MacArthur's objections, and pushing ahead on Tulagi-Guadalcanal, Admiral King, in the words of the naval historian Samuel Eliot Morison, "made one of the great decisions of the war."

CHAPTER
SIXTEEN

★ ★ ★ ★ ★

IN THE MASTER plan for the reduction of Rabaul, the Joint Chiefs of Staff had assigned MacArthur responsibility for the next major step beyond Tulagi-Guadalcanal. This was the capture of the Japanese bases in New Guinea—Lae and Salamaua—and in the upper Solomon Islands. No timetable had been specified. The timing of the next step would depend on how fast Ghormley could secure Tulagi-Guadalcanal, and how fast MacArthur could prepare airfields and assault forces for the operations in New Guinea. These factors, in turn, would be influenced by Japanese plans or reactions to offensive moves by the Allies. In fact, Japanese plans would drastically impede the implementation of step two.

In spite of the setbacks at Coral Sea and Midway, the Japanese high command had not given up plans to seize Port Moresby in Papua, the southeastern territory of New Guinea. An airfield complex at that place, only 270 miles from Australian soil, would enable them to dominate the whole of northeastern Australia and the sea approaches. It would deny MacArthur an advance base from which to launch air or land thrusts toward Rabaul or the Philippines. It would secure the right flank of Japanese incursions into the Solomon Islands.

After the Battle of the Coral Sea—the failure to take Port Moresby by amphibious assault in early May—it will be recalled, the Melbourne codebreakers provided the intelligence that the Japanese were not giving up, and that the next attempt would be overland via Buna and the back-door trail over the Owen Stanley Mountains. It would appear that MacArthur's staff, notably his intelligence chief. Charles Willoughby, disbelieved the codebreakers. Willoughby did not think the Japanese could cross the rugged, near-impenetrable Owen Stanley range with sufficient force to pose a serious threat to Port Moresby.

The official Army historian of this campaign quotes several Willoughby statements to this effect. For example: "An overland advance in strength is discounted in view of logistic difficulties, poor communications, and difficult terrain." If the Japanese did land at Buna, Willoughby believed, it would be only for the purpose of building an airfield there. MacArthur evidently shared Willoughby's view. The Army historian reports that before Midway MacArthur believed that if there were to be a second Japanese thrust at Port Moresby, it would be made by Japanese amphibious forces backed up by carrier- and land-based aircraft. After Midway, he may have concluded that the danger of a carrier-based amphibious assault on Port Moresby was far less likely, even remote. In any case, a threat to Port Moresby by the back-door Owen Stanley Mountains was completely discredited.

Perhaps for these reasons the defenses at Port Moresby were seriously neglected. MacArthur reinforced it with one Australian brigade, but this unit was composed of green militia soldiers. In addition, he dispatched a few U.S. engineers and antiaircraft troops to build and guard a complex of ten airfields under construction there and at Milne Bay, on Port Moresby's right flank. These airfields were to serve as staging bases for the forthcoming assault on Lae and Salamaua. Nor was any serious effort made to reinforce the handful of Australian troops holding the territory near Buna, and between Buna and the Owen Stanley Mountains.

Meanwhile, in July MacArthur's planners concluded that in the forthcoming Lae-Salamaua assault, an advance airfield in the Buna area would be required. This was a delicate situation. Buna, plus the surrounding area, was still (lightly) held by the Australians. But if the Allies began construction of an airfield at Buna, it would almost certainly invite a Japanese reaction, either a strong air attack or an amphibious assault. Accordingly, in mid-July MacArthur approved a plan to build this field in greatest secrecy and very quietly send supporting troops (infantry as well as antiaircraft batteries) in four stages.

All the while, the Japanese were unfolding their Port Moresby operation exactly as forecast by the codebreakers. In July they massed troop transports and supply ships at Rabaul to lift the assault forces to Buna. The Australians sent to build the airfield near Buna got wind of the Japanese plan through unspecified intelligence sources and instantly notified GHQ. Headquarters was then in a state of confusion owing to the fact that MacArthur and GHQ were in the process of moving from Melbourne to Brisbane. The Australians urged that troops be immediately airlifted to Buna. But GHQ ho-hummed the threat. The original plan would be adhered to.

General Brett's B-17s had been making sporadic and largely ineffectual raids on Rabaul. His crews were tired and dispirited; the aircraft, in a poor state of readiness and repair In addition, relations between MacArthur and Brett had deteriorated to the point that MacArthur had asked for Brett's relief. His replacement had already been chosen and was on the way to Australia by air. For these and other reasons, Brett flew no bomber missions on July 18 and 19. On those days the Japanese assault forces moved out of Rabaul and headed for Buna.

The initial wave—three thousand shock troops—struck Buna on July 22. Too late, Brett's bombers took to the air. They sank one transport and a landing barge, but this was small potatoes. The Japanese suffered only minor casualties. They charged ashore, brushing aside the few Australians and native militia. A specially designated force headed immediately for the Kokoda Trail that led over the Owen Stanley Mountains to Port Moresby, scattering the handful of Australians and natives designated to block the trail. In the days following, another thirteen thousand Japanese troops landed at Buna.

This was a first-class military disaster. MacArthur had not only lost the opportunity to get to Buna first, he was now faced with dislodging sixteen thousand crack Japanese troops from Papua before he could even think of attacking Lae and Salamaua. Days and weeks passed before GHQ perceived the exact extent of the threat. For example, a full month after the invasion, Willoughby still refused to believe the Japanese would attempt the Kokoda Trail to Port Moresby. The Japanese objective, he insisted, was to build an airfield at Buna.

While this new disaster was unfolding in MacArthur's lap, on August 7, Admiral Ghormley landed the U.S. Marines on Tulagi and Guadalcanal. Both islands were overwhelmed and secured promptly. But, in reaction, Japanese naval forces surprised Ghormley's naval forces in a night battle at Savo Island. They delivered a devastating torpedo and gun attack, destroying four desperately needed heavy cruisers and killing a thousand U.S. and Australian sailors. Thereafter, the Japanese at Rabaul began sending reinforcements to Guadalcanal at night, by destroyers. The Japanese seriously underestimated the number of U.S. Marines on Guadalcanal, thinking it would be an easy matter to dislodge them. For that reason, the majority of the Japanese Rabaul ground forces remained committed to Buna. But they sent enough troops to Guadalcanal to throw the Allied operation into jeopardy.

Thus, by late August, both MacArthur and Ghormley found themselves in perilous circumstances. The Japanese on Rabaul—fighting on two fronts, Guadalcanal and Buna—proved to be far more aggressive and powerful than MacArthur had foreseen. It would take six months of bloody jungle fighting to win at Guadalcanal and Buna. The timetable for the reduction of Rabaul would be set back again and again.

CHAPTER SEVENTEEN

★ ★ ★ ★ ★

In his memoirs, MacArthur boasted grandly that rather than sit back on the Brisbane defensive line and await the Japanese, he decided to "make the fight for Australia beyond its own borders" in the Papua section of New Guinea. True, he had proposed an assault on Rabaul, with supportive landings at the Japanese bases at Lae and Salamaua, but these proposed New Guinea operations were minor in nature. Papua was no place to fight a war. The terrain is among the most formidable in the world. The truth seems to be that MacArthur got sucked into Papua against his will—because he and GHQ disbelieved the codebreakers and let the Japanese grab Buna first. They had now to be dislodged before MacArthur could begin the Lae-Salamaua operations. This would turn out to be an enormous chore. Buna would become as great a challenge as Bataan-Corregidor, and almost as ruinous.

When it finally dawned on GHQ that Buna was a perilous situation, MacArthur hastily took steps to counter the Japanese invasion. As soon as transportation could be found (seven troopships) he ordered the battle-hardened Australian 7th Infantry Division to Papua. Major General Sydney F. Rowell, an Australian, took command of all troops in Papua.

Now a new threat loomed. The codebreakers, listening intently to the flow of traffic from Rabaul, discovered that the Japanese were going to make a subsidiary landing at Milne Bay, on the right flank of Port Moresby. A successful occupation of Milne Bay would be disastrous, comparable to the loss of Port Moresby itself. It had a fine harbor—better than Port Moresby's. MacArthur had begun construction on three of his airfields there. If these fell into Japanese hands, Japanese bombers could threaten MacArthur's new air base system in northeastern Australia, Port Moresby, Guadalcanal, and even Brisbane itself. From Milne Bay it would be an easy amphibious step—230 air miles—to Port Moresby.

This time MacArthur believed the codebreakers and took appropriate defensive action. He ordered that one brigade of the Australian 7th Division—the 18th—be diverted to Milne Bay, along with support troops. This brought the total Milne Bay strength to about 9,500 men: 6,500 combat soldiers, 2,000 U.S. soldiers (engineers, antiaircraft, airmen, etc.), and 1,000 service troops. Major General Cyril A. Clowes, a tough, battle-wise Australian, took charge of this force, reporting to General Rowell, who had established his headquarters in Port Moresby. All this was done in greatest secrecy so as not to reveal to the Japanese that their codes were compromised.

The Japanese, thus outwitted, badly underestimated the defending force at Milne Bay. On August 25, they landed with only 1500 men. They encountered stiff ground resistance and (when the weather allowed) harassing air attacks. Four days later they landed 770 reinforcements. These didn't help much. After about a week of fierce fighting, the Japanese ordered a total withdrawal of surviving forces, leaving 600 dead behind.

This little-known battle was a milestone of sorts. It was the first time in the war that a Japanese amphibious force had been stopped on the beaches. The victory—as at Coral Sea and Midway—was essentially another codebreaking victory. But because of the total secrecy imposed on codebreaking, those who engineered this victory never received the credit.

Elsewhere in Papua, the picture was not so bright. Japanese General Tomitaro Horii took personal charge of the force embarked on the Kokoda Trail. In spite of the Australian troops rushed from Port Moresby to stop him,

and unimaginably tough terrain with all the attendant
supply problems, he made tremendous gains. Still dis-
believing Horii's attack was intended as the real one
against Port Moresby, and completely unaware of his
large strength, GHQ could not understand why the
Australian troops were repeatedly forced to fall back.
Around the Brisbane GHQ safely removed from the battle
scene and the facts, there was much unfortunate dis-
paragement of the fighting skill and courage of the Australian soldiers. By September 14, in an amazing feat,
Horii had reached Imita Ridge, only twenty miles above
Port Moresby.

Coincident with this troublesome turn in Papua, Mac-
Arthur made three major changes in the leadership of his
sea, air, and ground forces. One—the naval commander—
was of small consequence. But the other two men would
become vastly important figures in the general's personal
and professional life. They would remain by his side all
the way to the Japanese surrender in Tokyo Bay, becoming, in effect, his operational right and left hands.

MacArthur's naval commander, Vice Admiral Leary,
was replaced by Admiral Arthur S. "Chips" Carpender,
USN. He was a lackluster, meddlesome officer who himself would be replaced a year and a half later by a man
of far greater strength and imagination. Carpender could
not have been much of an inspiration to MacArthur. His
appointment was yet another indication of Admiral King's
contempt for MacArthur. The top-drawer naval officers
went to Nimitz or to the Atlantic Fleet. In those days,
"MacArthur's Navy" got the second-raters.

The principal naval force basing in Australia was still
the submarines, now grown to a fleet of about thirty-one
boats. Two new officers now commanded these submarines: Charles A. Lockwood, Jr., and Ralph W. Christie.
Lockwood ran the twenty fleet boats basing in Fremantle.
He was busy weeding out overly cautious skippers and
testing the defective torpedoes. (This led—six months into
the war—to the correction of one important defect.)
Lockwood was a Nimitz man who wound up in Mac-
Arthur's Navy by the luck of the draw. He was not happy.
He literally despised Carpender and vice versa, but fortunately they were separated by an entire continent. In six

months he would leave to run Nimitz's submarine force at Pearl Harbor.

Christie ran the eleven old S boats, basing at Brisbane, where MacArthur (and Carpender) had now established GHQ. Christie was more diplomatic than Lockwood. He got along fine with Carpender and developed a close professional relationship with MacArthur. He would become a star in MacArthur's Navy. After the war he said that MacArthur "was one of the truly great men in history."

Lockwood's long-range fleet submarines were deployed strategically against Japanese strongholds in vast areas of the Far East. Indochina. The Philippines. Java. Borneo. Their mission was to interdict the flow of raw material—oil, food, minerals, rubber—to the Japanese homeland. They were alerted and guided to most targets and convoys by codebreaking information relayed to them by Lockwood But the returns were still poor. Lockwood could only maintain a half-dozen boats on station at any given time. There were still too many overly cautious skippers. The torpedoes still had two major defects, as yet undetected, and being at the tail end of an enormous pipeline, Lockwood was hampered by a continuous shortage of torpedoes. In addition, the submarine force, still feeling its way, was loath to adopt the technique of wolf-packing then being utilized so successfully by the German U-boats in the Atlantic. In sum, Lockwood and his cohorts, however eager had much to learn about fighting a strategic submarine war.

Christie's old short-range S boats were operated more tactically than strategically. Also relying on codebreaking for information on enemy ship movements (as well as the famous Australian network of Coast Watchers and MacArthur's aircraft), they patrolled in the Solomons and near the southern approaches to Rabaul. (Nimitz's submarines were blockading Truk as well as attempting to cut the Truk-Rabaul supply lines. No submarines could work close to the Buna area because the water was too shallow and dangerous.) These S boats, which used a different kind of torpedo did fairly well, considering their age and chronic mechanical infirmities. One sank a big Japanese minelayer damaged by carrier air in the Battle of Coral Sea. Another sank the Japanese heavy cruiser *Kako*, one of those which had devastated Ghormley's forces at Savo Island. Yet another sank a big transport carrying troops to Guadalcanal.

The submarines had failed MacArthur at Lingayen Gulf, but now, in Australia, he seemed to be fascinated with their operations. In Brisbane he saw Ralph Christie almost daily, and he entered into S-boat deployment tactics. In time he would come to hold submariners in highest regard. He would utilize their boats more and more for secret missions, such as resupplying the guerrilla forces in the Philippines. He would urge decorations for submarine skippers far beyond what the Navy Department was willing to give.

A far more significant command change occurred in the Air Force. Brett was shipped home under a cloud. To replace him came fifty-one-year-old George S. Kenney. He arrived in late July to find MacArthur in the midst of the early stage of the Buna debacle. Kenney was a dynamic, take-charge fireball, equally gifted as a leader and administrator. The military historians are unanimous about Kenny. He was the best thing to happen to MacArthur in a long while. MacArthur's close friend Clark Lee wrote: "The importance of Kenney to MacArthur in the following three years cannot be overestimated." In MacArthur's tight little inner circle, Kenney would even displace Sutherland as the general's most trusted adviser and confidant. MacArthur wrote in his memoirs: "Of all the brilliant air commanders in the war, none surpassed him. . . ."

Kenney has told his story in two books, *General Kenney Reports* and *The MacArthur I Know*. As he relates it, when he arrived in Australia he walked into a buzz saw. In his first meeting with MacArthur, the general ("who was a little tired, drawn and nervous") spent a half-hour in nonstop denunciation of the Australian-based U.S. Air Force. "He had no use for anyone in the organization from Brett on down to and including the rank of colonel," Kenney wrote. MacArthur compared the airmen to an "inefficient rabble of boulevard shock troops whose contribution to the war effort was practically nil." Moreover, they were antagonistic to GHQ "to the point of disloyalty." Chief of Staff Sutherland had similar disparaging words.

Kenney was amazed and astonished at the bitterness and vituperation. He frankly pledged his loyalty to Mac-

Arthur and a clean sweep of the deadwood. At the end of the meeting, MacArthur put his arm around Kenney's shoulder and said, "George, I think we are going to get along together all right."

Leaving GHQ Kenney made a hurried inspection of his major installations. He found an "appalling" mess. Pilots and crews were disgruntled and disillusioned. Everywhere, planes were grounded for lack of minor spare parts; of sixty-two B–17s, only five could fly. The hidebound bureaucratic supply depot, far away in Melbourne, would not release spare parts without properly filled out paperwork—submitted with umpteen copies. Far too many aircraft were in leisurely overhaul. The actual number of missions flown and bombs dropped compared to aircraft in inventory was absurdly low. None of the crews knew very much about bombing technique. The few that did reach the designated targets did little or no damage.

Kenney hit his command like a tornado. In a matter of a few days he totally rearranged the Air Force. He sacked five generals and countless colonels and brought in new blood, notably his able second-in-command Brigadier Ennis C. Whitehead. He put a blowtorch to the hides of those in the supply and overhaul installations. He toured his combat bases at breakneck pace, inflaming the pilots and crews. He broke down the Sutherland barrier at GHQ, dealing directly with MacArthur himself. In a very short time he had MacArthur's complete confidence.

Kenney was in full control by the time of the Guadalcanal landings, August 7. His planes were operating out of northeast Australia, Port Moresby, and Milne Bay—bombing, strafing, and engaging enemy fighters in aerial dogfights. On August 7, he delivered a special present to MacArthur and Ghormley. By mounting a maximum effort, Kenney was able to put eighteen B–17s over Rabaul that morning, the largest single heavy bomber raid in the Pacific war to date. Kenney claimed his bombers destroyed seventy-five Jap fighters on the ground at Rabaul and eleven in the air. After the war, it was discovered Kenney's damage figures were uniformly far in excess of the reality. No matter. It was an aggressive effort, and there was more—much more—on the way. MacArthur was mightily pleased. He and Kenney rained medals on the airmen.

The second major command change came in the ground forces. The two American divisions in Australia—the 32nd and 41st—had been formed into I Corps, reporting to MacArthur's overall ground commander, the Australian General Thomas Blamey. In late August, command of this corps was assigned to fifty-six-year-old Major General Robert L. Eichelberger, a scholarly, much-liked, thoroughly competent West Pointer. He arrived in the midst of the Milne Bay fight.

General Eichelberger inspected the troops of the I Corps. They had now been in training in Australia since April and May—all summer. Eichelberger, too, found a mess. As he related in his book *Our Jungle Road to Tokyo*, he arrived expecting those divisions to be well-schooled in jungle warfare. But, he wrote, the "American troops were in no sense ready for jungle warfare." He gave the 32nd Division a "Barely Satisfactory" rating in "Combat Efficiency." One soldier in that division told him that in twenty months of training, he had been given only one night problem. GHQ was not pleased with Eichelberger's report. It was a reflection on GHQ—and MacArthur.

Japanese General Horii was now knocking at the back door of Port Moresby. It was still hard for GHQ to believe it, but there he was and something had to be done quickly to stop him. Kenney, who was commuting to Port Moresby, reported to MacArthur that the Australian commander there, Sydney Rowell, had a "defeatist attitude." Kenney wrote that this attitude "had permeated the whole Australian force in New Guinea." If something "drastic" were not done soon, he told MacArthur, "we would lose Port Moresby."

Whereupon, MacArthur and GHQ formulated a sweeping—and risky—military plan. They would reinforce the Kokoda Trail above Port Moresby with Australian troops. Then they would send a strong ground force overland, in a "wide turning movement." The force would cross the Owen Stanley range lower down the peninsula, over a steeper but shorter route, and attack Horii from the rear, forcing his withdrawal from the Kokoda Trail. It was risky for several reasons. It required passing through awesomely rugged and relatively unknown terrain. It required a very long supply line. If the Japanese won quickly at Guadalcanal, they might shift surplus troops to Buna, overwhelming this overextended force by amphibious assault.

General Blamey himself went to Port Moresby to take charge of this crucial maneuver, and to relieve Rowell and engender a positive spirit in the Australian troops. Behind Blamey came more troops from the veteran Australian 6th Division. By then, MacArthur had decided at least some of the green, ill-trained troops of the U.S. 32nd and 41st divisions must be utilized. Eichelberger chose the 126th and 128th regiments of the 32nd Division for the mission. Kenney proposed that he airlift some of these troops to Port Moresby. GHQ opposed the idea; but Kenney, as was his wont, ignored GHQ and got approval directly from MacArthur. It was the largest movement of troops by air in the war up to that time. The rest came by sea.

Meanwhile, things were not going well for the Japanese at Guadalcanal. The U.S. Marines were fighting with amazing tenacity and skill. The Japanese needed more troops, fast. General Horii was ordered to stop his advance on Port Moresby until Guadalcanal was secure. A short time later (as the situation on Guadalcanal deteriorated even further), he was ordered to withdraw from the Kokoda Trail and set up a strong perimeter defense on the Buna beaches. Horii must have been one of the most disappointed generals in history. His troops had achieved the impossible. They had Port Moresby in sight. Now he was told to give it all back, almost for free.

As Horii began his withdrawal General Blamey sent Australian troops in pursuit on the Kokoda Trail and launched MacArthur's "turning movement." The U.S. 126th Regiment led the turning movement forces: the first American ground forces under MacArthur to go on a real offensive against the Japanese. They crossed the Owen Stanley range through the near-impenetrable Kapa Kapa Trail.

As the situation now unfolded, it became clear that Horii was beating a hasty retreat to Buna. The game now was to try to catch him between giant pincers on the plains before he reached Buna. One pincer would be the Australian troops pursuing over the Kokoda Trail, the other, the 126th Regiment hacking and clawing over the Kapa Kapa Trail. And so the race was on.

Although his own troops were now committed to battle,

Eichelberger himself was left out in the cold. It was strictly a MacArthur-Blamey show, with Sutherland playing a strong supporting role at GHQ. It would appear from Eichelberger's book that he did not yet have MacArthur's confidence. He definitely did not have Sutherland's. When Eichelberger proposed that he and some of his staff go to Port Morseby to learn about jungle fighting to better teach his other troops, MacArthur "favored" the idea. But Sutherland disapproved, and Eichelberger wrote: "The answer was no and that was that." Eichelberger was permitted only one brief rear area "inspection trip" to Port Moresby, and that before American troops actually entered combat. Sutherland studiously kept Eichelberger's name out of MacArthur's communiqués. For many, many weeks, the American public knew nothing of Eichelberger.

CHAPTER
EIGHTEEN

★ ★ ★ ★ ★

HAVING ORDERED GENERAL HORII to withdraw to a defensive holding position on the Buna beachhead, Rabaul now concentrated its naval, air, and ground power against United States forces on Guadalcanal. So vast was this effort that, ultimately, the full weight of the Japanese Combined Fleet was committed. Nimitz, in turn, responded with all he had. From September to December, 1942, the fighting at sea and in the air and on the ground was furious and continuous, totally overshadowing the operation in Papua. United States and Japanese losses at sea were severe. In six major naval battles and related actions, both sides lost twenty-four major combatant vessels: the United States two carriers, eight cruisers, and fourteen destroyers; Japan one carrier, two battleships, four cruisers, eleven destroyers, and six submarines. Many ships were badly damaged. For a long while there was serious doubt that Nimitz could hold onto Guadalcanal. In the midst of the campaign, he relieved Ghormley, placing the legendary sailor Admiral William F. "Bull" Halsey in overall command of his South Pacific operations. After that, things got better. By January 1943, the United States had won a hard-earned victory. The surviving Japanese ground forces evacuated Guadalcanal.

MacArthur, hard-pressed in Buna, could contribute little to the Guadalcanal campaign. Other than Kenney's persistent B–17 bombing attacks on Rabaul, his principal contribution came in the form of submarines. Twelve of Lockwood's twenty Fremantle-based fleet boats and a tender were shifted to Christie's command in Brisbane. In addition to maintaining a submarine blockade of Truk, Nimitz rushed MacArthur thirteen fleet boats and two tenders from Pearl Harbor. This substantial concentration of fleet boats—about twenty-five in all—operated under Christie from Brisbane, with Christie delicately taking orders from both Halsey and MacArthur (or Carpender). But these submarines, deployed tactically in the New Britain-Solomons areas, like the old S boats which they replaced, turned in disappointing bags. The torpedoes were still defective; they were continuously harassed and bombed by Japanese aircraft (and on several occasions, Kenney's aircraft). It was not yet realized that submarines were virtually useless deployed tactically. They sank no Japanese ships worthy of note. At best, they were merely a psychological threat to the Japanese.

In Buna, the race was on to trap General Horii's forces (Horii drowned) between the Australian and U.S. pincers on the plain before they reached Buna. This effort failed. Both the Australians pursuing over Kokoda Trail and the U.S. forces making the turning movement farther south bogged down in hostile jungle and mountainous terrain. Supply trains could not keep pace. It became necessary for Kenney to air-drop supplies to the advancing troops. While this was a worthy and innovative enterprise, Kenney was hampered by bad weather. In the end, the Japanese slipped through the pincers and established the beachhead along a ten-mile stretch of the coast, Gona-Sanananda-Buna.

GHQ vastly underestimated Japanese strength at the beachhead. Willoughby, who had persistently downgraded Japanese force levels since early summer, believed the Japanese had suffered heavy losses on the Kokoda Trail and elsewhere. He, and others, guessed that there were no more than fifteen hundred to two thousand troops. The defenses would be slight. If further setbacks were incurred at Guadalcanal, Rabaul would probably order the troops to withdraw completely. In fact, there were about six thousand Japanese troops at Gona-Buna. They were stoutly dug in, in a series of defensive positions the official U.S. Army historian described as a "masterpiece."

On November 6, anticipating a quick victory in Gona-Buna, MacArthur and his principal staff officers (Sutherland, Kenney, Willoughby, et al.) left Brisbane and set up a forward headquarters in Port Moresby. The general moved into Government House, a rambling one-story structure on a hill overlooking the harbor. General Kenney and others also found rooms at Government House. As at Melbourne and Brisbane, MacArthur was reclusive. He did not often venture from the heavily guarded headquarters.

General Eichelberger, now the second-highest-ranking Army general in the Pacific after MacArthur, was still out in the cold. Although, he wrote, MacArthur had told him he would lead American troops into the forthcoming Gona-Buna battle, and Eichelberger flew to Port Moresby for that purpose, Sutherland scotched that plan. He ordered Eichelberger back to Australia to train U.S. troops, insultingly insisting that he return immediately in a frail and unreliable courier plane. Eichelberger was "a little incredulous," but he was a good soldier and obeyed orders. It would seem that the ever-protective Sutherland wanted MacArthur to get all the glory for the forthcoming Gona-Buna victory.

GHQ issued the battle plan on November 14. The Australian 7th Division (commanded by Major General George A. Vasey) on the left would attack and overrun Gona-Sanananda. The U.S. 32nd Division (commanded by Major General Edward F. Harding) on the right would attack and overrun Buna. These troops, fully believing the campaign would be a piece of cake, moved out on November 16, bursting with optimism. The terrain was mostly swampy and jungle. But everyone believed that in no time at all, victory would be in hand.

Both divisions immediately encountered fierce opposition from the tenacious, well-entrenched, and formidable Japanese defenders. Soon they were completely bogged down, bedeviled by torrential downpours, jungle diseases, and a critical shortage of supplies, especially food. Casualties were very heavy. In the green U.S. 32nd Division, leadership was wanting and morale dropped like a stone. The regrettable old GHQ talk about the unreliability and cowardice of the Australian troops was again revived.

The same charge was now leveled against Harding and
the 32nd Division. Once more in deep trouble, MacArthur
repeatedly called on the Navy—Admiral Halsey—for
carrier air and other naval support. But Halsey (quite
rightly) refused to risk his precious surviving ships in the
dangerous waters east of Papua.

Now, belatedly, MacArthur sent for Eichelberger. He
arrived in Port Moresby two weeks after the campaign
began, November 30. He had an extraordinary meeting
with MacArthur, Sutherland, and Kenney on the veranda
of Government House. He found MacArthur and Sutherland in a deep funk. MacArthur said at once, "Bob, I'm
putting you in command at Buna. Relieve Harding. I am
sending you in, Bob, and I want you to remove all officers
who won't fight. Relieve regimental and battalion commanders; if necessary, put sergeants in charge of battalions
and corporals in charge of companies—anyone who will
fight. Time is of the essence; the Japs may land reinforcements any night." He paused and added, "Bob, I want you
to take Buna or not come back alive."

The next day, Eichelberger flew to the Buna front. He
found the leadership in the 32nd Division "lacking." The
troops were in terrible physical shape—suffering from
malaria, dengue, dysentery, and jungle ulcers, slowly starving on one-third rations. He fired General Harding and
several colonels and majors. He took steps to greatly im-
prove the supply—and food—situation. He went to the
front lines and personally led a company into battle, shouting, "Lads, come along . . ." He was very nearly shot by
a concealed Japanese sniper. A general officer and Eichelberger's aide were hit and had to be evacuated. In time,
every American general officer except Eichelberger was
wounded and evacuated.

Swamped under by "prodigious rains" and egged on by
messages from MacArthur ("Strike!") and suffering appalling losses, Eichelberger led the division forward, inch
by bloody inch. General Vasey's Australian 7th Division
on the left also crawled ahead. By December 14, Eichelberger, in a truly remarkable performance, took Buna
Village. The Australians, in an equally remarkable performance and with equally heavy casualties, overran Gona.
Eichelberger received a congratulatory message from Mac-
Arthur, "A grand letter from the Big Chief." But, as

Eichelberger wrote, "the worst of the campaign still lay ahead of us."

They had taken Buna and Gona in name only. There were still thousands of Japanese dug into strong positions. The Australians had yet to close in on Sanananda. The U.S. forces faced strong Japanese positions on the right flank of Buna. These troops had to be rooted out. On December 18, after a brief pause, the U.S. forces, reinforced by fresh ground troops (and seven light Australian tanks), jumped off. Again the resistance was fanatical. "Every inch was sorely contested," Eichelberger wrote. By Christmas Day, the fighting in his sector "was desperate and the outcome of the whole, miserable, tortured campaign was in doubt." Eichelberger was astounded and incensed to read a GHQ communiqué: "On Christmas Day our activities were limited to routine safety precautions. Divine services were held."

The American advance bogged down critically. Eichelberger, a moody man, wrote MacArthur: "I think the low point of my life occurred yesterday." Was Buna to become "an American military disaster?" he asked himself. But a few days later the situation shifted in his favor. On January 3, the Japanese suddenly collapsed. At last, and at great cost, the U.S. Army had won its first victory against the Japanese. Considering the magnitude of this achievement, MacArthur's letter of congratulations to Eichelberger was lukewarm:

> I am so glad that you were not injured in the fighting. I always feared your incessant exposure might result fatally. With a hearty slap on the back.
>
> > Most cordially,
> > MacArthur

But GHQ made one concession. For the first time Eichelberger and the 32nd Division were mentioned in an official communiqué.

Following the Buna victory, MacArthur, Blamey, and the GHQ staff returned to Brisbane. To Eichelberger's total astonishment, MacArthur then released a statement clearly implying the Papuan campaign was finished, what was left was merely a "mopping up operation." The statement concluded: "One of the primary objects of the campaign was the annihilation of the Japanese Papuan

Army under Lieutenant General Horii. This can now be regarded as accomplished." But the important fortifications at Sanananda had not yet been conquered. The Australian forces were still bogged down there. There was seven thousand Japanese entrenched in Sanananda. Eichelberger believed it would be every bit as tough to defeat them as it had been at Buna.

On January 11, 1943, Eichelberger took command of all Allied troops in Papua and immediately commenced a joint Australia-United States attack on Sanananda. Again, the resistance was fanatical; the Allied casualties appalling. Fortunately for the Allies (and unknown to them), a day after this tough campaign began, Rabaul ordered the Japanese forces to withdraw by sea. During the next week, while this evacuation was in progress, the fighting was intense. But on January 22, the Australian-American pincers closed on Sanananda, and all Japanese resistance ceased. Allied casualties in this "mopping up operation" had been 3,500—700 more than in the Buna fight. Standing at the edge of the Buna military cemetery, Eichelberger could not stop the flow of tears.

But now, truly, the Papuan campaign was over. In a curiously dishonest communiqué of January 28 announcing its finish, MacArthur boasted that total Allied losses had been small because "the time element was in this case of little importance." Again Eichelberger was dumbfounded and incensed. Every foot of the way he had been harassed by a steady flow of personal messages from MacArthur stressing that time was of vital importance. In truth, the Allied losses had been very, very heavy. About 3,000 Americans and Australians had died from all causes in the overall Papuan campaign. Another 5,400 had been wounded. (Guadacanal cost 1600 killed and 4200 wounded.)

It was one of the costliest campaigns in the Pacific war. All that had been accomplished in six months of bloody fighting was to eject the Japanese who had been permitted to land at Buna in the first place because GHQ disbelieved the codebreakers. Fortunately for GHQ this blunder could be hidden behind the ultra-secret stamp of that enterprise, and MacArthur was free to crow that he had made the fight for Australia beyond its own borders.

CHAPTER
NINETEEN

★ ★ ★ ★ ★

THE WEARY ALLIED soldiers in Papua and Guadalcanal were withdrawn for R & R ("rest and recuperation") in Australia and New Zealand, replaced by fresh troops. The American ships damaged at Guadalcanal limped to Pearl Harbor and the States for repairs. A definite "lull" descended over the two military theaters. It would be a long pause, six months.

All hands had learned several lessons in these campaigns. The Japanese were skillful, well-trained fighters. The high command seemed determined to fanatically defend every inch of its conquests in the South and Southwest Pacific. There were not going to be any easy victories here. Any further Allied action would clearly require far more military strength than either MacArthur or Halsey possessed. There would have to be much closer coordination between the land, air, and sea forces, better planning and shrewder utilization of that priceless weapon—codebreaking.

Back in Brisbane after an absence of two months, MacArthur resumed his businessmanlike routine of Theater Commander. GHQ had established itself in the nine-story AMP (insurance) office building in downtown Brisbane.

MacArthur's office, one aide recalled, was plain, almost austere. There was a desk, usually uncluttered, a couch, one bookcase, and a few chairs. There were no maps on the wall, only pictures of George Washington and Abraham Lincoln. From this office, the sixty-three-year-old general presided over his far-flung forces in a calm and efficient manner, usually sitting at his desk, but often pacing as he thought through the unending flow of problems.

The MacArthurs had set up living quarters at Lennon's Hotel, a busy, air-conditioned establishment in downtown Brisbane, exclusively reserved for military VIPs. They had three adjoining suites, including a kitchen. Sid Huff recalled. They led the same monastic life they had in Melbourne. At first they took all their meals from the hotel dining room. But MacArthur soon tired of the limited menu and Jean, no great shakes as a cook, took over preparation of the meals in the suite. Each day she went off to the food markets and did the shopping. Huff remembered that at first, the experiment was something of a disaster, and he was pressed into service as an "adviser." (A hotel maid also advised.) Gradually Jean acquired a limited skill at the stove.

MacArthur's daily routine was rigid. He rose about seven. After his toilet, he played the gift-giving game with Arthur. Then he settled down in the suite to read dispatches and reports. He arrived at his office about ten o'clock. He worked at his desk (dictating to a "pool" secretary) or presided over meetings or took phone calls for several hours, then went home for lunch and a nap. (An office worker "alerted" Jean when he left so she could have lunch ready.) After the nap, he returned to the office for several more hours. Then home. Since returning to active duty in July 1941, MacArthur had given up his predinner cocktail—all alcohol, in fact. He ate a quiet dinner with Jean, then smoked a cigar. Then bed.

Few people dared to interrupt MacArthur in his home. An exception was the ebullient George Kenney, who lived two floors below. He recalled that he'd get some "bright idea" and pop up and knock on the door, pretending to have come for a decent cup of stateside coffee or whatever. Kenney would then broach his bright idea, sometimes going on until 2 A.M. He wrote: "Jean would sit down and listen till she finally would get sleepy and fall sound asleep."

MacArthur, these days, was in very fine spirits; the gloom and the depression swept away by the success in Papua. Courtney Whitney, an aide who would soon join GHQ wrote in his book *MacArthur:* "Those who had not been with him at Port Moresby naturally expected to see a weary figure bowed by the exhaustion of one of history's worst battles. Instead, MacArthur looked as if he had been vacationing. There was a sparkle in his eyes and a spring in his step. At a press conference he joked and laughed with correspondents."

Elsewhere, those with responsibility for setting the global war strategy began to take a second look at the Pacific. This began in January 1943, when Roosevelt and Churchill and the Combined Chiefs of Staff met in Casablanca. Admiral King, insisting that it was vital to keep mounting pressure on the Japanese, urged that the total Allied military power deployed against Japan be doubled —from the current fifteen percent to thirty percent. Churchill and his advisers, preoccupied with Europe and the Mediterranean, reluctantly agreed. Whereupon King pronounced, with no small optimism, that by May 1943, MacArthur and Halsey could seize Rabaul. He went on to propose that following the fall of Rabaul. Nimitz should be launched on a Central Pacific thrust, aimed at the early seizure of the Gilbert Islands (Tarawa-Makin). But a decision on this was deferred.

In March, at the invitation of the U.S. Joint Chiefs, MacArthur, Nimitz, and Halsey sent representatives to Washington to discuss specific tactical objectives for the Pacific campaign for 1943. Kenney and Sutherland represented MacArthur. Sutherland presented MacArthur's plan, called ELKTON. Essentially it was the same plan embodied in the July 2, 1942, JCS directive. But MacArthur had raised the ante considerably. In addition to forces in hand, he would need five more divisions, forty-five more air groups (twice the 1800 planes he and Halsey then had), and numerous naval vessels and landing craft. The delegates were astonished—and antagonized—by Sutherland's arrogance in his presentation. The pipe dream of seizing Rabaul by May was shattered. In the end—the conference dragged on for two weeks -the JCS agreed to send MacArthur limited reinforcements: two or three divisions, more planes and ships.

The new Pacific war plan that emerged from these talks was issued on March 28. It was a refined and slightly swollen version of the old Step Two. The main objective was still the reduction of Rabaul, the gradual moving forward of the Allied "bomber line." In the western section of the theater, MacArthur's immediate domain, it called for the seizing of Lae and Salamaua and nearby areas in New Guinea (plus two small unoccupied islands on the southeast coast of New Guinea: Woodlark and Kiriwina) and a landing on southern New Britain (the island on which Rabaul was located). In the eastern section of the theater—Halsey's immediate domain—it called for the seizure of the upper Solomon Islands of New Georgia and Bougainville. The timing and coordination of these mutually supporting operations would be left to MacArthur and Halsey. MacArthur would be the overall commander of the operation, although the naval forces in Halsey's theater would be controlled by Nimitz.

On April 15, Halsey flew to Brisbane to meet with MacArthur for the first time. It quickly turned into a mutual admiration society. In his memoir, *Admiral Halsey's Story*, the admiral recalled:

> Five minutes after I reported, I felt as if we were lifelong friends. I have seldom seen a man who makes a quicker, stronger, more favorable impression. He was then sixty-three years old, but he could have passed as fifty. His hair was jet black; his eyes were clear; his carriage erect. If he had been wearing civilian clothes, I still would have known at once that he was a soldier . . . We had arguments, but they always ended pleasantly. Not once did he, my superior officer, ever force his decisions on me. On the few occasions when I disagreed with him, I told him so, and we discussed the issue until one of us changed his mind. My mental picture poses him against the background of these discussions; he is pacing his office, almost wearing a groove between his large, bare desk and the portrait of George Washington that faced it; his corncob pipe is in his hand (I rarely saw him smoke it); and he is making his points in a diction I have never heard surpassed.

In his memoirs, MacArthur recalled:

William Halsey was one of our great sailors . . . of the same aggressive type as John Paul Jones, David Farragut, and George Dewey. His one thought was to close with the enemy and fight him to the death. The bugaboo of many sailors, the fear of losing ships, was completely alien to his conception of sea action. I liked him from the moment we met, and my respect and admiration increased with time. His loyalty was undeviating, and I placed the greatest confidence in his judgment. No name rates higher in the annals of our country's naval history.

The upshot of the MacArthur-Halsey conference was an intricate and detailed plan for the execution of ELKTON. Operations would begin in June. As a first step, Halsey's forces would attack New Georgia in the Solomons. Simultaneously, MacArthur's forces would invade the unoccupied Woodlark and Kiriwina islands, off the east coast of New Guinea. The combined operations were code-named CARTWHEEL.

In May, Roosevelt and Churchill met again, in Washington, at what was called the Trident Conference. It would prove to be a momentous turning point for the war in the Pacific. At issue again was the strategy conflict between MacArthur and King. MacArthur held that there should be only one road to Tokyo, his own; that is, a total concentration of forces in his theater, with the aim of a single thrust through New Guinea to the Philippines to Formosa to Japan. King flatly opposed this concept, believing the war could best be won by an island-hopping Navy-Marine thrust through the Central Pacific—Gilberts, Marshalls, Carolines, Marianas, Formosa, Japan.

In the end, Churchill and Roosevelt reached a compromise. There would be *two* roads to Tokyo, both the MacArthur road and the King road. In effect, this was a victory for King. It meant that at long last Nimitz could be launched on his Central Pacific thrust. King received specific approval for the first step, the invasion of the Gilberts (Tarawa-Makin) in November 1943.

MacArthur was not pleased with the decision one bit. In follow-up discussions with General Marshall by cable and radio, he continued to oppose the two-road concept, arguing that "no vital strategic objective" was gained by seizing the Central Pacific islands, that the division of

effort and command was wasteful and inefficient. (In his
memoirs, he wrote that he was even willing to take a
"subordinate" position in a unified command.) But these
arguments failed to sway the Joint Chiefs of Staff. The
decision had been made; there was no overturning it.

During this enforced six-month lull in ground operations, MacArthur's chief concern was to prevent the
Japanese from further reinforcing the garrisons in New
Guinea, principally Lae and Salamaua, soon to be invaded.
The responsibility for this effort fell to the Brisbane-based
fleet submarines and to Kenney's large—and growing—
air forces.

There had been a game of musical chairs in the submarine high command, occasioned by the death of
Nimitz's submarine boss. Charles Lockwood (in Fremantle) went to Pearl Harbor to run Nimitz's submarines.
Ralph Christie replaced Lockwood in Fremantle. James
Fife, one of those who planned the abortive submarine
"defense" of Lingayen Gulf, was named by MacArthur
and Carpender to command the Brisbane submarine force,
which was shrinking fast. Now that the battle for Guadalcanal had wound down, Nimitz had recalled most of the
fleet boats he loaned to Brisbane, and those on temporary
duty from Fremantle were sent back to the States for
overhaul. These depletions left Fife only about a dozen
submarines.

The codebreakers were still supplying the submarine
force with its most valuable intelligence on enemy ship
movements. Information from this source revealed a new
enemy supply route from the Palaus to Rabaul (and to
Wewak on the north coast of New Guinea). Fife positioned several of his submarines along the north coast of
New Guinea to interdict this flow of men and matériel.
The boat *Wahoo*, commanded by Dudley W. "Mush"
Morton, made a spectacular interception on a small convoy
and sank three ships confirmed in postwar Japanese
records. One of these was a troopship. When its hundreds
—or thousands—of survivors were in the water, Morton
surfaced and mercilessly killed them with small arms. Few,
if any, of these soldiers reached New Guinea.

The other boats did not do so well. Fife disposed too
many of them in the upper Solomons-Rabaul area, where
Japanese antisubmarine capability was strongest. Four

fleet boats were lost in the space of two months, a shattering blow to the small submarine force. Two others were very nearly lost. During five months of the lull, Fife mounted a total of twenty-five war patrols from Brisbane. The boats sank eighteen confirmed ships, including *Wahoo's* three. There were still too many cautious skippers, and after a full year of war, the torpedoes were still flawed.

Kenney's air forces, now staging from advance bases in Port Moresby, Milne Bay, and Buna in ever-growing numbers, achieved much more. Almost every night, weather permitting, the heavy bombers plastered Rabaul and other Japanese bases with scores of tons of bombs. Kenney concentrated his bombers primarily against enemy aircraft—his was a struggle to win control of the air—but on several occasions his planes destroyed ships bringing reinforcements to New Guinea. The most notable example of this occurred in early March in what MacArthur would grandly call "The Battle of the Bismarck Sea."

This incident began with an alert from the codebreakers. A big convoy was forming up in Rabaul to carry men and matériel to Lae-Salamaua. It would consist of eight transports carrying about 7,000 soldiers and marines, plus equipment. It would be escorted by eight destroyers. Willoughby passed this word to MacArthur and Kenney. MacArthur told Kenney to give the convoy highest priority. Kenney, taking personal charge of the operation, ordered a maximum search-and-destroy effort.

In the days following, Kenney massed an awesome fleet of aircraft in Papua: 207 bombers and 154 fighters. Another eighty-six bombers and ninety-five fighters were in reserve at bases in northeast Australia, ready to stage immediately to Papua if needed. Kenney and his staff selected the most likely route the convoy would follow and dispatched hordes of reconnaissance planes to look for it. The crews worked "like mad" to get every plane in shape so that when the big day came, Kenney wrote, "we could strike with everything we owned. . . ."

The convoy was detected, but bad weather plagued the airmen. Finally on the morning of March 2, it was found in clear weather in Huon Gulf. Two hours later, a fleet of twenty-nine B–17 bombers attacked. One transport went down; two were left afloat but on fire. Later that day, another flight of B–17s attacked, sinking one ship.

The following day Kenney sent a massive armada of one hundred planes against the convoy, followed during the day by scores more. (Three hundred and thirty planes were in the air that day.) These literally blew the convoy out of the water. Of the original sixteen ships, only four destroyers survived intact. The others were sunk, sinking, or badly damaged.

By this time, MacArthur had a small contingent of PT boats basing on the east coast of New Guinea at Tufi. (One squadron was commanded by John D. Bulkeley.) On the night of March 3/4, eight boats of the unit searched the Huon Gulf for cripples. They found a big abandoned ship and sank it with torpedoes. The official PT historian described what happened the next day:

> On the 4th of March our planes returned and strafed everything afloat in the Huon Gulf. Thousands of Japanese troops from the sunken transports were adrift in collapsible boats. For several days, the PTs, too, met many of these troop-filled boats and sank them. It was an unpleasant task, but there was no alternative. If the boats were permitted to reach shore, the troops, who were armed with rifles, would constitute a serious menace to our lightly held positions along the coast.

Kenney woke MacArthur in the middle of the night to report the great news. Kenney recalled: "I had never seen him so jubilant." MacArthur drafted a communiqué for the airmen:

> Please extend to all ranks my gratitude and felicitations on the magnificent victory which has been achieved. It cannot fail to go down in history as one of the most complete and annihilating combats of all times. My pride and satisfaction in you all is boundless.

Then came an unfortunate communiqué from GHQ greatly exaggerating the numbers of Japanese ships in the convoy. MacArthur flamboyantly claimed it was composed of twenty-two ships (twelve transports and ten warships) and that all were sunk or sinking, drowning 15,000 soldiers. As they were accustomed to doing for the submarine force, the codebreakers had provided fairly precise information on the actual damage, based on Japanese radio reports to Tokyo: twelve ships of sixteen sunk, about 3,000 soldiers lost. Inasmuch as the Pentagon had these same correct figures, the communiqué damaged MacArthur's—and Kenney's—credibility with the upper echelons. MacArthur further embittered King and his admirals by needlessly boasting that his land-based air power, not the U.S. Navy, could now successfully stop the Japanese from invading Australia by sea.

The controversy over the exact damage figures in the Battle of Bismarck Sea would go on for years. But there was no denying the central fact. It was a brilliant piece of work by all hands. The codebreakers had provided the information and airmen had performed with great skill and tenacity. Major Japanese reinforcements had been turned back from New Guinea.

CHAPTER
TWENTY

★ ★ ★ ★ ★

Now, AFTER AN enforced lull of six months, MacArthur launched the mighty Operation CARTWHEEL. It was one of the most intricately conceived military operations in the history of warfare. The "front" stretched across almost 1,000 miles of land and sea. It involved hundreds of thousands of soldiers, airmen, and sailors of many nations (the bulk from the United States, Australia, and New Zealand), hundreds of aircraft and hundreds of ships and submarines. These forces were organized primarily into two giant pincers, designed to close in on Rabaul; one to move up the Solomon Islands chain, one to move up the eastern coast of New Guinea.

On the right, Halsey's amphibious forces struck New Georgia on June 30, landing 6,000 men (principally the U.S. Army 43rd Division). The main goal was a new Japanese airfield at Munda. There were only about 4,500 Japanese in the area, but these were firmly entrenched in the jungles and determined to fight to the last man. Halsey's troops were soon bogged down in hideous jungle warfare, comparable to that on Guadalcanal and at Buna. He had to commit a total of 32,000 soldiers and 1,700 marines (and fire many generals and colonels) before this miserable place was finally declared secure, toward the end of July. About one thousand Americans died in the battle, almost 4,000 were wounded.

Halsey's next step up the Solomons ladder was to be the Japanese airfield on Kolombangara at Vila Plantation. But intelligence indicated (accurately) that at least 10,000 Japanese were entrenched there. Halsey recommended to MacArthur that Kolombangara be bypassed in favor of the lightly held island of Vella Lavella, letting the Japanese at Vila "wither on the vine." MacArthur approved this proposal. On August 15, Halsey landed about 6,000 men on Vella Lavella unopposed, secured the south end of the island, and built an airstrip. Later, the small Japanese force (600 men) on the north end of the island was forced to evacuate. Vella Lavella was an easy operation with almost no casualties.

The Japanese headquarters on Rabaul reacted with anger and fury to these new incursions. It launched its dwindling armada of aircraft and ships against the Allies. It tried to reinforce its garrisons with soldiers. These efforts led to several big night naval battles, with heavy losses on both sides. Rabaul ordered the evacuation of the 10,000 bypassed troops on Kolombangara by barges. In spite of the efforts of Halsey's destroyers and PT boats to prevent it (one skipper in *PT–109,* John F. Kennedy, lost his boat in the effort), most of the Japanese slipped through, going to Choiseul, then Bougainville.

By about October 1, three months into the campaign, Halsey could take satisfaction in a job well done. The casualties had been heavier than expected, the fighting on New Georgia a nightmare, but the Allies now had four advanced airfields in New Georgia and Vella Lavella, bringing the next target, Bougainville, within Allied fighter plane range.

The by-passing strategy inaugurated in the Solomons by Halsey soon came to be known as the strategy of "hitting them where they ain't"—a slogan borrowed from a famous American baseball player. This strategy was possible because of precise information provided by the codebreakers. It would save thousands of American lives. It gave the impression that the overall commanders—MacArthur and Halsey—were extraordinarily prescient. In time, Mac-Arthur and GHQ appropriated Halsey's (or the baseball player's) slogan for themselves, implying that MacArthur

himself had coined it to describe a brilliant new strategy
he had conceived.

In Brisbane during the spring, there had been a major
shake-up in the ground forces chain of command. It is
not satisfactorily explained in the MacArthur literature.
It probably took place because of GHQ's distrust of the
Australian ground force leadership. The net effect of the
shake-up was to effectively remove Blamey from direct
command of American troops. In addition, the senior
American Ground General Eichelberger, who had won
Buna for MacArthur, was once again pushed aside.

A new U.S. Army Lieutenant General Walter Krueger,
sixty-two-years-old and senior to Eichelberger, arrived in
Australia. He was appointed to command the "U.S. Sixth
Army," a paper outfit. The Sixth Army command was
then imposed over Eichelberger's I Corps, which still
consisted only of the 32nd and 41st divisions. The First
Marine Division, recouping from Guadalcanal, and other
newly arrived American units were incorporated into Sixth
Army, Krueger became Eichelberger's boss. In theory,
Krueger reported to Blamey, but owing to some leger-
demain in the command structure, he was actually responsible only to MacArthur and GHQ.

Krueger and MacArthur were old friends. Krueger was
something of a rarity in the army establishment, a general
who had not gone to West Point. Born in Prussia, he had
entered the army as a private in 1898. Self-made and self-
educated, he was commissioned in 1901. There was a
"certain hardness in him that MacArthur liked," Willoughby recalled in his memoirs. In his own memoirs, Mac-
Arthur wrote: "I do not believe that the annals of America
have shown his superiority as an Army commander." He
would remain with MacArthur all the way, a trusted associate, though, as we shall see, Krueger's innate conservatism
would cause MacArthur considerable doubt at times.

The easing aside of Blamey was further assured by
the assignment of missions for MacArthur's share of Operation CARTWHEEL. MacArthur ruled that the most difficult of his tasks—capture of Lae and Salamaua and nearby
areas—should be carried out mainly by two combat-wise
Australian outfits (plus some smaller American units),
the 7th Division and the 9th Division, recently arrived
from the Middle East, and a new Australian division, the

3rd. It was in the natural order of things to put Blamey in charge of that operation. As Dr. James observes, the effect was to reduce him to little more than a task force commander.

The lesser of the CARTWHEEL tasks—the seizure of the unoccupied outlying islands of Woodlark and Kiriwina and the landing on New Britain—was assigned to Krueger and the American ground forces. Krueger came with a good reputation, but he was green to Pacific combat. The easy amphibious operation at Woodlark and Kiriwina would give him—and the as yet unproven 32nd and 41st divisions—experience before the more difficult assault on New Britain. Krueger's group was named the Alamo Force.

Although these were Eichelberger's troops, he was again left out in the cold. And very unhappy. He wrote that three times that year Washington asked MacArthur to release him for command of a full army in the European Theater, but each time MacArthur refused the request. Eichelberger was reduced to training troops and escorting VIPs. (One of these was Eleanor Roosevelt, whom MacArthur deliberately snubbed.) All that time, Eichelberger recalled, he was a "glum fellow."

On June 30, the day Halsey's troops went ashore on New Georgia, Krueger launched two regiments of the Alamo Force against Woodlark and Kiriwina. They staged from Milne Bay, where Krueger had set up his headquarters, and from Australia. They were sealifted by an embryonic amphibious force put together and commanded by the U.S. Navy Admiral Daniel E. Barbey, another newcomer to the theater. The operation was well supported by Kenney's air force and by the handful of cruisers and destroyers under Admiral Carpender's command. The regiments landed without opposition, one on Woodlark, one on Kiriwina.

MacArthur seized these two islands mainly to use as air bases. Both were much closer to Rabaul than the most advanced fields in the Buna area, and to Halsey's next objective, Bougainville, which Kenney would help Halsey soften up. Construction of the airfields began at once. The Woodlark field received its first plane two weeks after the landing. Rain and mismanagement delayed the field on Kiriwina. It was not operational until August 18.

As an adjunct of this operation, MacArthur also decided to seize Nassau Bay, a lightly held (150 Japanese) area of the New Guinea coast about halfway between Buna and Salamaua, and only sixty miles south of Salamaua. It was deemed an ideal port to supply the troops which would assault Salamaua, and a staging base for short-legged landing craft. Units of the 41st Division (holding the Buna area) amounting to about 1,000 men staged in PT boats and landing craft, going ashore in darkness on the morning of June 30. With only slight casualties (18 killed), Nassau Bay was secured. Presently these forces linked up with the Australian 3rd Division, which was operating inland of Nassau Bay, consolidating the area. The stage was now set for the big leap to Salamaua and Lae.

Of the two objectives, Lae was by far the most important strategically. It had a fine harbor and an operational airfield. It dominated the broad Ramu Valley stretching inland, where Kenney hoped to establish a network of air bases for the later assault on Rabaul and the north coast of New Guinea. It was also less heavily defended than Salamaua. Of the 10,000 troops in the Lae-Salamaua area, the majority was at Salamaua.

For these reasons, Lae became the primary objective; Salamaua, the secondary one. In July, MacArthur ordered Allied forces at Nassau Bay (the 3rd Australian Division, units of the U.S. 41st Division) to march overland toward Salamaua, giving the impression that Salamaua was the prime objective. The Japanese commander there girded for battle, exhorting his troops to dig in and fight to the death. But Tokyo—then planning a pullback to a new defensive line—countermanded these instructions. It ordered the commander to evacuate Salamaua if the Allies posed a serious threat.

The assault on Lae, the primary objective, was a masterpiece, one of the finest military operations of World War II. The plan, largely dictated by an acute shortage of amphibious craft and naval escorts, was that one division (the Australian 9th) would hit Lae from the sea; almost simultaneously, the newly arrived U.S. 503rd Airborne Regiment would parachute onto the airfield at Nadzab, inland of Lae. When the paratroopers had secured the field, Kenney's air transports would fly in an entire division (the Australian 7th). The 7th would assault Lae from the rear, linking up with the 9th, crushing the Lae defenders between them.

During July and August, while these plans were being finalized, and Kenney's aircraft were pulverizing Japanese airfields near and far (all the way to Wewak), the force at Nassau Bay jumped off for the attack on Salamaua. Fighting through tough jungle terrain, they reached the outer perimeter of Salamaua by the first week in September, as planned. It was not an easy advance. Jungle diseases disabled about half the men (twelve hundred) of the American regiment attached to this force.

At sunrise September 4, the assault against Lae began. Five of Admiral Barbey's destroyers (entering these dangerous waters for the first time) bombarded the beaches east of Lae. Then the Australian 9th Division (plus some American support units) stormed ashore, finding no opposition other than a few sporadic and largely ineffectual air attacks. The troops moved quickly inland, advancing westward toward the Japanese fortifications at Lae. So far, so good.

On the following day, September 5, Kenney launched the airborne armada against Nadzab, in the rear of Lae. In total, there were 302 aircraft involved. Light bombers strafed the field and dropped smoke bombs. Then came ninety-six C–47 transports with the paratroopers. The men jumped at 10:20 A.M. By 10:24, seventeen hundred men were on the ground. (Three men died in the jump.) There was no Japanese resistance. The 503rd quickly secured the field. The transports went back to fly in the Australian 7th Division.

MacArthur watched the jump from a brass-hat B–17, flying high above. He and GHQ had come up to Port Moresby on August 24 for the Lae operation. Before the jump he visited the paratroopers (all green troops). He wrote: "I inspected them and found, as was only natural, a sense of nervousness among the ranks. I decided that it would be advisable for me to fly in with them. I did not want them to go through their first baptism of fire without such comfort as my presence might bring to them." Kenney, who was piloting another brass-hat B–17 in the formation, wrote that MacArthur was "jumping up and down like a kid." For this flight, MacArthur was awarded the Air Medal.

Three days after the jump, Setpember 8, the Japanese commander ordered the first of a series of withdrawals in compliance with Tokyo's instructions. That day, the troops at Salamaua were instructed to fall back to Lae. Three days later, Setpember 11, the Salamaua garrison withdrew to Lae. On the following day, the Allied force at Salamaua overran the few rear guard defenders and secured this area which had been in Japanese hands for eighteen months.

Meanwhile, on September 10, the Australian 9th Division, flown into Nadzab, began the advance by land on Lae's rear. The troops met only token resistance. The Japanese were already beginning to evacuate Lae, fleeing north into the mountains of the Huon Peninsula. By September 15, most of the nine thousand surviving Japanese, including the force from Salamaua, had withdrawn from Lae and slipped north into the mountains. The Australian 7th Division linked up with the Australian 9th and occupied Lae.

Following this spectacular victory, on September 15 MacArthur gave his commanders orders to exploit it. The Australian 7th Division wheeled around and marched (and flew) 200 miles northwestward up the Ramu Valley, capturing Kaiapit and Dumpu, then bogged down. On September 22, elements of the Australian 9th Division (staging from Lae by amphibious craft) hit the Japanese garrison (four thousand men) at Finschhafen on the eastern tip of the Huon Peninsula. After a stiff fight, Finschhafen was secured on October 2. The Japanese counterattacked, but the Australians held firm. A large chunk of New Guinea had been wrested from Japan.

CHAPTER
TWENTY-ONE

★ ★ ★ ★ ★

In August, Roosevelt and Churchill and the Combined Chiefs of Staff met again, this time in Quebec in what was known as the Quadrant Conference. By that time the U.S. Joint Chiefs of Staff, fearing a bloodbath if MacArthur made a direct assault on the bastion of Rabaul, were leaning to the idea of bypassing and neutralizing Rabaul. This concept was presented at Quadrant. It was approved by Roosevelt and Churchill. CARTWHEEL would now terminate with the invasions of Bougainville and southern New Britain. Rabaul would be left to wither on the vine.

This decision reached MacArthur on September 17, shortly after the victory at Salamaua-Lae. It was yet another blow for the general. It appeared to be a signal that King's Pacific strategy was beginning to prevail in the JCS, that the priorities would go to Nimitz's Central Pacific thrust, that the Southwest Pacific Theater operations would be throttled far back. What was probably most disturbing to MacArthur in the Quadrant decisions was the absence of long-range authorization for a push to the Philippines by Southwest Pacific forces.

Meanwhile, CARTWHEEL rolled on toward the objectives short of Rabaul. On the right flank Halsey, having secured New Georgia, bypassed Kolambangara, and occupied Vella Lavella, now faced the next major objective: Bougainville. As initially planned, the operation entailed a landing on the southern coast of Bougainville (Buin, Kahili), where there were an estimated 20,000 or more well-entrenched Japanese. Following the savage fight on New Georgia, Halsey began to mull over bypass schemes whereby he could avoid a direct frontal assault on these Japanese forces. After much discussion, MacArthur finally approved a plan for Halsey's forces to land on the lightly held west coast of Bougainville at Empress Augusta Bay on November 1. This would bypass the major Japanese garrison in the south and provide a suitable location for the airfields.

In support of the Bougainville invasion, beginning in early October, General Kenney's airmen geared up for a continuous bomber assault on Rabaul. These massive raids began on October 12, when Kenney sent 349 planes against Rabaul. His pilots, exaggerating as usual, claimed massive damage, and MacArthur (somewhat prematurely) told Kenney: "George, you broke Rabaul's back. . . ." Bad weather impeded operations for the rest of the month, but Kenney managed to stage five other big raids before the Bougainville invasion. Again, wild damage claims. But it is indisputable that these raids inflicted severe—though not decisive—damage on Rabaul.

On November 1, Halsey's troops landed at Empress Augusta Bay against a small Japanese garrison (300 men). It was a remarkably smooth operation, far different from New Georgia. By nightfall, there were 14,000 troops ashore. These established a strong beachhead, then expanded it. Soon there were 33,000 men in the perimeter—there to stay. Seabees came ashore almost immediately to begin construction of the airfields. A strong naval force (including two aircraft carriers) stood guard over the operation.

The Japanese again reacted angrily to this incursion. The Combined Fleet carriers at Truk, gathered there to blunt Nimitz's expected Central Pacific thrust, were instantly stripped of 173 aircraft. These flew to Rabaul and gave Kenney the "toughest fight" his Rabaul bombers had encountered in the whole campaign. Rabaul tried to

send to Bougainville a hastily organized cruiser-destroyer
force, carrying troop reinforcements, with the idea of
ejecting the invaders. But the codebreakers gave ample
warning of this threat, and Halsey's ships beat off the
attack.

The codebreakers now provided another valuable piece
of intelligence. The Japanese had also ordered a very large
cruiser-destroyer formation from Truk to Rabaul (further
stripping the Combined Fleet) for the purpose of ejecting
the Bougainville invaders. Following up this report, early
on the morning of November 4, reconnaissance planes
from both Kenney's and Halsey's commands found and
shadowed this force. MacArthur and Halsey decided to
let it enter Rabaul unmolested, then strike while the ships
were at anchor, as the Japanese had struck the U.S. Pacific
Fleet at Pearl Harbor. Halsey would use planes from the
two carriers supporting Bougainville, the first time any
carrier planes had flown against Rabaul.

It was an intricate operation, a fine example of the
coordination and synchronization required of CARTWHEEL
forces. At 11:30 A.M. on November 5, one hundred of
Halsey's carrier planes hit Rabaul. One hour later, while
the Japanese planes were drawn off and busy elsewhere
fighting Halsey's aircraft, Kenney put another one hundred planes over Rabaul. This combined effort heavily
damaged the newly arrived naval force, crippling six
cruisers and two destroyers. The Japanese were forced
to cancel any further naval assaults on the Bougainville
invaders. Elated by the success of his carrier planes,
Halsey assembled five carriers in the area and six days
later hit Rabaul again with 185 planes. The crippled
cruiser-destroyer force had slipped away, but the planes
raked the other shipping in the harbor, inflicting considerable damage. Truly Fortress Rabaul was being punished
hard. But it was far from being "neutralized."

Only nine days after this second carrier raid on Rabaul,
on November 20, the Nimitz forces invaded the Gilbert
Islands: Tarawa and Makin. (The same five carriers, plus
six others, supported this operation.) It was bloody going
on heavily fortified Tarawa. Before the Gilberts were
secured, Nimitz had to commit 18,000 men. They suffered
a shocking 3,000 casualties—over a thousand dead. The
Marine General Holland M. Smith thought it was too
much blood to spill for the gain, that the Central Pacific

campaign should have been launched against a more worthwhile objective. To MacArthur, it was proof positive that the Central Pacific thrust was an ill-conceived enterprise, a costly diversion from what should be the main axis of advance—his own.

During the Gilberts operations, the Japanese Combined Fleet, holed up at Truk, was unable to launch a counterattack as planned. The Japanese had stripped their carriers of airplanes and sent them to Rabaul; the cruiser-destroyer force mauled at Rabaul by Kenney and Halsey on November 5 was out of commission. Although he too opposed the Central Pacific thrust, Kenney could take some satisfaction in the knowledge that his air assaults on Rabaul, which forced the transfer of planes from Truk to Rabaul, had materially assisted Nimitz in the Gilberts operation.

Returning to MacArthur's axis of advance, it will be recalled that after Salamaua-Lae-Finschhafen, MacArthur's next CARTWHEEL objective was a landing on the southern coast of New Britain. General Krueger's Sixth Army, or Alamo, troops, mainly the U.S. First Marine Division and the Army's 112th Cavalry Regiment, had been designated for the task and had been training and planning for months. Meanwhile, the major CARTWHEEL operations in New Guinea had been carried out by Australian forces. Not since the shaky performance at Buna—almost a year past —had major American forces been committed to an important objective in MacArthur's theater.

Originally, the decision to invade southern New Britain (on which Rabaul is located) was arrived at primarily to provide a base for the land assault on Rabaul. But now that the decision had been made to bypass and neutralize Rabaul, was it necessary to proceed with the southern New Britain landing? In a book he wrote with the naval historian Elmer B. Potter, *The Great Sea War*, Nimitz, in retrospect, implies that MacArthur erred. The official Army historian writes that in the light of hindsight, the operation was probably "not essential to the reduction of Rabaul or the approach to the Philippines." The official Navy historian, Samuel Eliot Morison, wrote that "in light of the intelligence which he then had," MacArthur was justified in the operation, but it was all a "waste of time." Curiously, MacArthur does not mention the operation at all in his memoirs. Perhaps in hindsight, he too thought it was a mistake, a misguided effort to get his American forces back into action.

Krueger's overall plan for the operation apparently pleased few. Kenney objected to a not unimportant secondary feature of it and coaxed MacArthur into having it changed. The First Marine Division staff objected to the landing plan itself and, when queried by MacArthur, almost on the eve of the jump-off, bluntly told him so. The upshot was that very little of the initial Krueger plan was put into effect, including an airborne assault by the 503rd Regiment. In fact, the final invasion plan was very much like that drawn up by the First Marine Division staff.

MacArthur launched the New Britain invasion in mid-December. United States troops went ashore at two different points; a small force (112th Cavalry) at Arawe (December 15) on the southern coast, and the main force (First Marine Division) at Cape Gloucester (December 26) on the northwest tip. MacArthur probably knew in advance from the codebreakers that both places were very lightly defended and that an American victory would be cheaply bought. And so it was. Arawe was secured in a day with only a handful of casualties. Cape Gloucester was tougher. About three hundred Marines died and a thousand were wounded before it was secured. Neither place ever became an important base of operations. But at least MacArthur had got American ground troops back into the campaign in force.

All the while, Australian troops on the northern coast of New Guinea were engaged in a little known and arduous series of battles to secure the Huon Peninsula. Generally, the CARTWHEEL goal was to push as far west as Madang, killing as many Japanese as possible. The 7th Division, which had bogged down after a two-hundred-mile advance in Ramu Valley, would push on northwestward, approaching Madang from the land; elements of the 9th Division would advance along the coast (by amphibious hops) from the newly won base at Finschhafen.

Advancing through unspeakably tough terrain, the 9th Division slogged westward from Finschhafen. The Japanese 20th Division, brought east from Madang in a grueling forced march to stop the Australians, faltered and fell back to Sio, riddled by disease, hunger, and fatigue.

The Australians pushed into Sio, forcing the Japanese
20th (already down to fifty per cent strength) into another
ghastly westward retreat toward Saidor, along with the
Japanese 5th Division from Kiari. A fresh Australian
division, the 5th, relieved the 9th and began a vigorous
pursuit.

It was now evident to GHQ that if something were not
done quickly, these two Japanese divisions would reach
Madang, to fight again. Along their route lay a tiny
coastal village, Saidor. It was known from the codebreakers that Saidor had no defenses; it was a garrison
of only about fifty men. If GHQ could land an amphibious
force at Saidor before the retreating Japanese got there,
the Japanese 20th would be trapped between the advancing Australian 5th Division and American forces at Saidor.

Whereupon, with a typical flourish, MacArthur ordered
Krueger to make an amphibious landing at Saidor forthwith. He was to utilize American troops exclusively, a
departure from the policy of using only Australians to
secure the Huon Peninsula. Krueger, always cautious,
was dubious. He was then securing the beachheads at
Arawe and had yet to land at Cape Gloucester. He
dragged his feet, arguing for a postponement. But Mac-
Arthur pushed hard and got his way. In an astonishingly
brief time, the amphibious forces (mainly the 126th Regiment of the U.S. 32nd Division) were embarked. About
6,000 American soldiers landed at Saidor on January 2,
1944. The handful of Japanese there fled into the hills.

In his memoirs, MacArthur maintained that the scheme
worked. Rather colorfully, he wrote: "The Japanese
were trapped. Caught between the closing pincers of the
two advancing forces, with no source of supply, the Japanese disintegrated and scattered in chaotic flight. That
the steaming jungle finished what the Allies began was
written grimly across the thousands of emaciated Japanese
corpses our troops discovered along the hills and trails
and in the mountains." In fact, the official Army historian
wrote that the "pincers" closed on empty terrain. The
Japanese were ordered to bypass Saidor to the south,
avoid a fight, and withdraw to Madang. They did just
that, while the outwitted Americans looked on helplessly
from Saidor. Many Japanese died of starvation and exhaustion, but about 10,000 men from the two divisions
finally reached Madang—to fight again. As at Salamaua-

Lae, MacArthur had let a powerful Japanese force slip through his fingers.

The Australian 5th Division reached Saidor on February 18, and once again the Australian generals took charge. The 5th and the U.S. 126th Regiment advanced westward by land and sea toward Madang, pursuing the fleeing Japanese. The Australian 7th Division broke out of the Ramu Valley and on March 21 linked up with the 5th at Kul on the coast. Both units pressed forward along the coast, meeting resistance every yard of the way.

All this time MacArthur and GHQ had been growing more and more dissatisfied with the naval commander in the Southwest Pacific, Admiral Carpender. Both Sutherland and Kenney, and perhaps MacArthur, thought he had been overly timid in not earlier sending his combatant naval vessels into the waters along the east coast of New Guinea, and was not doing all he should in support of amphibious assaults. Also Carpender, against all orders to the contrary, continued to communicate directly with Nimitz and King, a heinous offense in Brisbane. His meddlesome and nit-picking personality antagonized GHQ. In November 1943, he was replaced.

Admiral King, perhaps realizing it was the U.S. Navy that ultimately suffered most by sending MacArthur mediocre admirals, ordered Thomas C. Kinkaid to Brisbane to command the "MacArthur Navy," or the 7th Fleet, as it was now called. He took over in late November. Kinkaid, a brother-in-law of the former Navy commander at Pearl Harbor Husband Kimmel, was a distinguished sailor who had commanded important naval units at Guadalcanal, and in Alaska, MacArthur was pleased. Here, at last, was an admiral to respect. There was also an immediate, positive reaction throughout the 7th Fleet. In Fremantle, Ralph Christie, commanding the submarine fleet there, noted in his diary: "This is a happy day for the 7th Fleet; A new, fresh, good-natured attitude has come over the staff."

MacArthur's submarine force was still restricted by an edict of Admiral King's to twenty fleet boats. (Nimitz received far more.) After the Solomons operations of CARTWHEEL were completed, these were redistributed; twelve for Fremantle, eight for Brisbane. Shortly thereafter, King pronounced that MacArthur would receive ten more fleet boats for a total of thirty. Forward refueling bases were established at Tulagi, Milne Bay, and Darwin. Utilizing these bases, the submarines were able to greatly extend time on station. In addition, that fall, Charles Lockwood, in Pearl Harbor, isolated the last two flaws in the submarine torpedo—after twenty-one months of combat. Most of the overly cautious skippers had finally been replaced by younger, more aggressive and experienced officers.

As a result of these factors, and others, the MacArthur submarine force began to show a marked improvement in "bags" as the year 1943 drew to a close. The submarine force had finally learned how to fight a strategic submarine war, and the higher-ups called on them less and less for fruitless tactical employment. In the last half of 1943, Brisbane and Fremantle submarines sank a total of seventy-two ships, many of them important oil tankers. One Fremantle submarine, *Bowfin*, with codebreaking help, was credited with sinking nine ships on a single patrol. This was reduced in postwar records to five, but it was an astonishing achievement and merely a portent of what was to come in 1944. After a desultory two years, the contribution of submarines in the following year, 1944, would be decisive to the defeat of Japan.

CHAPTER TWENTY-TWO

★ ★ ★ ★ ★

TOWARD THE END of 1943, the Big Three—Roosevelt, Churchill, and Stalin—convened a global strategy conference at Teheran known as Sextant. For the Pacific war, they reaffirmed the "dual" road concept, leading to a junction in the Luzon-Formosa area. They laid down specific goals (with timetables) to be achieved in 1944. MacArthur and Halsey would complete CARTWHEEL—the reduction of Rabaul—by seizing several other Japanese strongholds around it. These were Kavieng, New Ireland (March), Manus in the Admiralties (April). In addition, MacArthur would continue the westward push along the north coast of New Guinea: Hansa Bay (February), Humbolt Bay (June), the Vogelkop Peninsula, on the extreme western tip of New Guinea (August). In the Central Pacific, the goals and timetable for Nimitz were Marshall Islands (January), Ponape (May), Truk (July), and the Marianas (October). There was no specific directive regarding the Philippines.

General Marshall, who had attended the Big Three sessions, decided to return to the United States by way of the Pacific so that he could have a firsthand look at the situation and talk face-to-face with MacArthur. He arrived at Port Morseby on December 13. MacArthur was then on Goodenough Island, where General Krueger had established Sixth Army (and Alamo) headquarters. MacArthur and Krueger were putting the final touches on the Arawe-Cape Gloucester operation.

MacArthur's friend the journalist Frazier Hunt, and one of those who believed in the anti-MacArthur "conspiracy" in Washington, wrote that MacArthur thought about snubbing Marshall: "He was of the opinion that as a result of both the present and the past differences between himself and Marshall, their meeting might be somewhat embarrassing to his distinguished visitor. MacArthur seriously considered conducting the Gloucester operation in person, thus relieving Marshall of his presence." In fact, MacArthur did not meet Marshall when he landed at Port Moresby, a serious breach of military etiquette and custom. He sent Kenney in his place. Kenney took Marshal on a brief inspection tour of New Guinea, then delivered him to Goodenough Island on December 15.

This was the only meeting between Marshall and MacArthur during the entire war. They discussed global strategy. Later, when Kenney was present, they discussed the Pacific war. Kenney boldly took this occasion to again speak against Nimitz's Central Pacific drive and wrote in his book "General Marshall looked as though he agreed with me." MacArthur wrote in his memoirs that he and Marshall had "a long and frank discussion." MacArthur complained about the low priority granted the Pacific, the thin trickle of men and supplies. MacArthur wrote that Marshall blamed all that on King, who was doggedly determined to make the Pacific war a Navy show to help remove the "blot" of Pearl Harbor. According to MacArthur's memoir, Marshall reported King was "vehement in his personal criticism" of MacArthur and "encouraged Navy propaganda to that end." Marshall and MacArthur parted amicably.

As the New Year dawned, Nimitz's forces prepared to execute the first of the objectives decreed at Teheran: invasion of the Marshall Islands. During the planning for this endeavor, Nimitz was guided by a stream of valuable information from the codebreakers. They told him which of the Marshall Islands were heavily defended, which were lightly defended. Most important, they provided him with a detailed analysis of the Combined Fleet at Truk. Short of a suicidal foray, it would probably not challenge the invaders.

On January 31, 1944, Nimitz's forces landed on two lightly held Marshall Islands: Kwajalein and Majuro. The latter fell without a single American casualty. The fight on Kwajalein was tougher. It cost the United States 372 dead and 1,582 wounded. Within one week the island was secure and the Seabees had begun an airstrip. As the codebreakers predicted, the Japanese Combined Fleet did not strike. In fact, the codebreakers reported, most of it withdrew in haste far westward to the Palaus and Mindanao. This was a clear signal to Nimitz that the Japanese had abandoned the Marshalls—and maybe Truk —to their fate.

Rushing to capitalize on this new situation, Nimitz ordered his amphibious forces to leap ahead and seize Eniwetok, the westernmost of the Marshall Islands (scheduled for a May invasion). On February 17 the troops landed, and after a stiff fight which cost the United States 195 killed and 521 wounded, the island was secured. In support of this operation, Nimitz's carriers struck Fortress Truk (720 miles distant) for the first time in the war. Achieving total surprise, the carrier planes had a field day, sinking many Combined Fleet support ships which had not yet left: two light cruisers, four destroyers, three auxiliary cruisers, two submarine tenders, four valuable tankers, and twenty merchant ships. In all, they sank thirty-five ships which were confirmed in postwar records. In addition, they shot down or destroyed scores of Japanese aircraft.

The Central Pacific drive was supported, tactically and strategically, by the Pearl Harbor submarine force under Charles Lockwood. Now grown to about 75 boats, it operated in Japanese home waters or in direct support of amphibious operations. These boats now began to take a heavy toll of Japanese shipping. In the last three months of 1943, Lockwood's submarines sank 100 Japanese ships. In the first four months of 1944, the score was 125 ships. A great many of these were from convoys bringing reinforcements to the islands scheduled for invasion by Nimitz in 1944.

For MacArthur and Halsey, the next objectives on

the CARTWHEEL timetable were Kavieng and Manus in the Admiralties. The capture of Kavieng by Halsey's forces was first. In December, MacArthur and Halsey (with support from Nimitz) began to close the noose on Kavieng by air and naval assault. Along with Rabaul, it became a primary target for Kenney's bombers. On Christmas Day, off Truk, the submarine *Skate*, alerted by the codebreakers, intercepted the superbattleship *Yamato* (the largest warship ever built, up to that time) which was coming down to help land reinforcements on Kavieng. One of six torpedoes fired hit *Yamato's* bow. The damage was slight but sufficient to force *Yamato* to break off the mission and seek cover at Truk. That same Cristmas day, two of Nimitz's carriers, sent down to southern waters to interdict any further attempts to reinforce Kavieng by sea, raided Kavieng harbor. Two other raids were staged on the area on New Year's Day and January 4. (None did much damage.) On February 15, Halsey's forces took possession of unoccupied Green Island, bringing land-based air to within 115 miles of Rabaul and 220 miles of Kavieng. American destroyers bombarded Kavieng.

Halsey was uneasy about Kavieng. The codebreakers reported it to be heavily defended. At a conference with MacArthur in Brisbane in December, Halsey made his objections, suggesting Kavieng be bypassed in favor of Emirau, a small island about ninety miles northwest of Kavieng which the Japanese had never occupied. MacArthur replied it made no real difference to him, either place would serve equally well for the reduction of Rabaul and for covering his forthcoming operations in the Admiralties. Halsey conferred with Nimitz and King in San Francisco, but he was unable to persuade King to overturn a decision made at Teheran. Moreover, shortly after this, MacArthur changed his mind and insisted that Halsey invade Kavieng. On February 13, GHQ issued a revised CARTWHEEL timetable: both Kavieng and Manus would be invaded about the same time, April 1. The postponement was caused in large part by the unforeseen extension of Nimitz's operations in the Marshalls to Eniwetok.

MacArthur assigned the Manus invasion to General Krueger and his Alamo forces. Krueger, in turn, chose a brand-new division to spearhead the assault. This was the United States 1st Cavalry (no longer equipped with horses, hence described in official dispatches as "dismounted"). It had recently arrived in Australia and been assigned to Krueger's Sixth Army. It, and associated amphibious units, began to prepare for the Manus D–day, April 1.

Kenney's aircraft now began to focus on Manus and nearby Los Negros. The planes strafed and bombed the two places intermittently. Photo reconnaissance aircraft kept a close surveillance. On the evening of February 23, Kenney wrote, a reconnaissance report indicated "that the Jap might be withdrawing his troops from Los Negros back to Manus." A report the following evening seemed to confirm this estimate. A reconnaissance plane had flown low over Los Negroes for half an hour. There was no ack-ack, no sign of life. Observing that there had not even been any laundry hanging on the line for three days, Kenney wrote: "Los Negros was ripe for the plucking."

Kenney now conceived—and proposed to GHQ—a very bold plan: quickly seize Los Negros with a few troops, put the airfield there in shape so that, if necessary, it could be reinforced by flying in troops. Or Admiral Kinkaid could shuttle troops in at night by destroyer, as the Japanese had done in the Solomons. Kenny could provide air cover in force to beat off Japanese airplanes from Manus. "We need not take any real chances," he wrote, ". . . if the Nips did too much shooting, we could always call it an armed reconnaissance and back out."

MacArthur's intelligence chief, Charles Willoughby, looked askance at this proposal. He knew from code-breaking and other intelligence sources that in recent weeks the Japanese had been reinforcing Manus and Los Negros. Two attempts had been foiled by American submarines, which sank or turned back troopships; but in late January the Japanese had managed to sneak through a battalion. Willoughby's estimate was that there were 4,050 Japanese troops on Manus and Los Negros— with the "main strength" at Los Negros. His estimate was almost exactly correct.

But Kenney's scheme appealed to MacArthur. He was then chaffing to get on with the war. The April 1 timetable for the seizure of Manus had been dictated by the availability of Nimitz's aircraft carriers. If he could jump the gun by a whole month, literally stealing Los Negros from under the noses of the Japanese without an elaborate amphibious force (or carriers), it would be a *coup de main*. He would dramatically turn the spotlight from the Central Pacific, where it seemed fixed for the moment, back to the Southwest Pacific Theater.

So it was decided. On February 24, GHQ issued urgent orders for a "reconnaissance in force" of Los Negros, to be landed within five days! No doubt the conservative Krueger was dumbfounded. And perplexed. His intelligence officer (as he wrote) had put the Japanese strength at Manus-Los Negros at 4,500 men, close to Willoughby's estimate. Not only that, a few days later there came word from some scouts Krueger had sneaked ashore on Los Negros that the island was "lousy with Japs." But his staff and Admiral Barbey's staff went to work. Within five days the 1,000-man force, built around elements of the 1st Cavalry Division, was ready

MacArthur now decided he would personally oversee this risky operation. He flew up to Milne Bay on February 27 and joined Admiral Kinkaid on his flagship, the light cruiser *Phoenix*. Finding him there, Krueger was appalled. He urged MacArthur to return. "He had expressly forbidden me to accompany our assault landings and yet now he proposed to do so himself," Krueger wrote. "I argued that it was unnecessary and unwise to expose himself in this fashion and that it would be a calamity if anything happened to him. He listened to me attentively and thanked me, but added: 'I have to go.'" Apparently MacArthur wanted to be on the spot if a fiasco developed and it became necessary to withdraw.

The forces landed on Los Negros on the morning of February 29. Opposition was slight. Two hours later they had seized the primary objective, Momote Airfield. By early afternoon, all one thousand men were ashore and it looked like a picnic. But the Japanese were merely recovering from surprise. They were then massing for a night attack.

At about 4:00 P.M., MacArthur and Kinkaid came ashore. It had been raining hard. There was intermittent sniper fire on the small beachhead. Courtney Whitney wrote that a worried officer tried to hustle MacArthur back to the landing barge. "Excuse me, sir," he said, pointing to a place in the jungle very close by, "but we killed a

Jap sniper in there only a few minutes ago." MacArthur retorted: "Fine. That's the best thing to do with them." He went on to the airstrip, then returned to the perimeter to present an officer a medal. To the commander of the force, he said: "Hold what you have taken, no matter against what odds. You have your teeth in him—don't let go." After that, "wet, cold, and dirty with mud up to the ears," MacArthur returned to *Phoenix*. Everybody ashore was vastly relieved when he had gone.

The Japanese attacked in force that night. The perimeter held. By March 4, the Japanese were forced into defensive positions. Thereafter, large reinforcements were brought up, and Kenney delivered the promised air cover. Krueger landed forces on Manus and captured the primary objective there, the airfield. It took time to rout out and kill all the 4,000 to 4,500 Japanese, but soon all but 75 taken prisoner were dead. The Admiralties, with the magnificent Seeadler Harbor, were MacArthur's. The cost in American casualties had been small—326 dead, 1,189 wounded. The daring gamble had paid off. Even King conceded it was a "brilliant maneuver."

MacArthur's success in the Admiralties led directly to a dramatic deletion from the CARTWHEEL agenda. Clearly there was no longer any need to invade the Kavieng stronghold. In mid-March, the JCS adopted Halsey's original proposal to bypass Kavieng and seize unoccupied Emirau. Halsey carried out this operation with ease on March 20, while Krueger's troops were still mopping up on Manus.

The capture of Manus provoked yet another brouhaha between MacArthur and the U.S. Navy. One of the chief assets of the island is the magnificent Seeadler Harbor. Before the invasion, it was decided that this harbor would be utilized as a major fleet anchorage. Halsey's staff planned the layout for MacArthur and provided the Seabees to build it. After construction got underway, Nimitz, rather arrogantly—certainly undiplomatically—proposed to Admiral King and the JCS that his administrative area be extended to include Manus and Seeadler Harbor. In other words, a piece of real estate, hard won by MacArthur, would be handed over to Nimitz.

As Halsey tells the story in his memoirs, MacArthur, who had been sent a copy of the Nimitz proposal, promptly went through the ceiling. He immediately called Halsey to Brisbane. Halsey wrote:

> Before even a word of greeting was spoken, I saw that MacArthur was fighting to keep his temper. . . . I had no hand in originating the dispatch; I did not even hear of it until after it had been sent. But MacArthur lumped me, Nimitz, King, and the whole Navy in a vicious conspiracy to pare away his authority. Unlike myself, strong emotion did not make him profane. He did not need to be; profanity would have merely discolored his eloquence. It continued for about a quarter of an hour, illuminating two main themes: he had no intention of tamely submitting to such interference; and he had given orders that, until the jurisdiction of Manus was established, work should be restricted to facilities for ships under his direct command—the 7th Fleet and British units.

Bill Halsey was appalled. What it boiled down to was this: MacArthur was so furious about the Nimitz proposal, he would bar Nimitz's ships from using the harbor. He turned to Halsey for support: "Am I not right, Bill?" Halsey—and Kinkaid and other naval officers present—all "answered with one voice: 'No, Sir.'" Halsey added: "I disagree with you entirely. Not only that, but I'm going one step further and tell you that if you stick to this order of yours, you'll be hampering the war effort." Hasey went on: "His staff gasped. I imagine they never expected to hear anyone address him in those terms this side of the Judgment throne, if then."

The meeting broke up after an hour. Halsey thought he had won. But the next morning MacArthur, "mad all over again," called him back. They argued for an hour, broke up, and resumed again in the afternoon, going over the same ground a third time. Finally, MacArthur yielded. "You win, Bill," he said.

And so, at last, the big CARTWHEEL pincers from east and west had closed on Fortress Rabaul. She was now half-encircled by Allied airfields (Bougainville, Green Island, Los Negros, Manus, Emirau) and deserted by her chief source of supply, Truk. Nine months had elapsed since the simultaneous jump-offs in the Solomons and

New Guinea in July 1943. The heroic conquests bear repeating: New Georgia, Vella Lavella, Empress Augusta Bay, Salamaua-Lae, Finschhafen, Cape Gloucester, Sio, Saidor, Madang, Los Negros-Manus. Thousands of Allied soldiers, sailors, and airmen had died gallantly in the effort. The Japanese Combined Fleet had been bled white in these waters, its air forces decimated. In addition to the tens of thousands killed in return for this miserable, malarial real estate, well over 100,000 Japanese troops had been sealed off at Bougainville, Rabaul, and Kavieng, left behind as the war moved relentlessly westward. For all of this, MacArthur more than deserved the laurels showered on him from all over the world. It had been, on the whole, a splendid performance.

CHAPTER
TWENTY-THREE

★ ★ ★ ★ ★

IN EARLY 1944, following the decisive victories in the Central and Southwest Pacific and the withdrawal of the Japanese Combined Fleet from Truk to the Palaus and westward, military planners in Brisbane, Pearl Harbor, and Washington reappraised the Pacific objectives and timetable for 1944. They had two basic goals: to resolve, once and for all, the continuing conflict between MacArthur and Nimitz on the most effective road for reaching Japan; and to capitalize on what appeared to be a strategic withdrawal of Japanese forces across the whole Pacific.

In Brisbane, with CARTWHEEL succesfully closed out, MacArthur and GHQ now faced a whole new campaign: a drive across the entire northern coast of New Guinea to the Vogelkop Peninsula. It would not be an easy campaign. The terrain and climate were as bad as those in the Solomons and Huon Peninsula—or worse. The first objective was the Hansa Bay-Wewak area. It was known to be heavily fortified and garrisoned by some 50,000 troops of the 18th Japanese Army. These troops were weary and hungry from months of desperate fighting on the Huon Peninsula, but they were skillful and tenacious combatant personnel. Hansa Bay-Wewak would not be easy.

About this time, MacArthur fell heir to a valuable intelligence legacy. Some of his soldiers found a trunkful of Japanese code books buried in the sand of a north New Guinea beach. The covers had been carefully removed, perhaps sent to Tokyo as "proof of destruction," but the books were intact and—most important—the codes were still current.

GHQ contacted the codebreaking unit in Melbourne for assistance. It sent two of its best Japanese linguists to Brisbane, Thomas R. Mackie and Forrest Biard. Mackie said later, "The books were beautiful. I guess the Japanese general who had charge of them couldn't bear to see them destroyed." For twelve days and nights Mackie and Biard eavesdropped on conversations between the Japanese generals in charge of the defense of New Guinea. "They were arguing back and forth," Mackie recalled, "about which places should be heavily defended and which places they ought to ignore."

Exactly what Mackie and Biard learned is still locked up in classified files. But the situation in New Guinea at that time has been spelled out by the official Army historian from captured Japanese documents. Generally, the Japanese ground forces were in a somewhat chaotic and uncertain state. There was a command reorganization in progress, and the debate Mackie alluded to probably had to do with whether or not to keep the Eighteenth Army in the Hansa Bay-Wewak area or to withdraw it westward to a new defensive line in Dutch New Guinea. Headquarters appeared to want a withdrawal. The local commanders, expecting MacArthur to invade Hansa Bay-Wewak next, appeared to want to stand and meet the Allies on the beaches, withdrawing only if absolutely necessary.

Central to these discussions was the Japanese-occupied base at Hollandia in Dutch New Guinea. Undoubtedly this place was to become an important new bastion along the proposed new Japanese defensive line. The Japanese had already established a complex of airfields and headquarters of the New Guinea air forces. The fine harbor was now the terminus for Japanese sea resupply lines. Japanese Seabees were already embarked on a major harbor expansion program. There were plans afoot to reinforce

Hollandia and vicinity with several new divisions from China and Japan. If these forces arrived, and the Eighteenth Army were withdrawn from Hansa Bay-Wewak, Hollandia would become another Fortress Rabaul, lying directly across MacArthur's path westward.

Digesting this important intelligence, some planners at GHQ began to formulate a wild scheme: cancel Hansa Bay-Wewak and leap directly to Hollandia. The advocates of this scheme—Kenney asserts he was one— pointed to a compelling and curious fact. For some reason the Japanese had yet to fortify Hollandia or provide it with adequate ground forces. There were only about twelve thousand military personnel, and most of these were service troops. If, in a lightning stroke, the Allies could seize Hollandia before the projected reinforcements arrived, they would prevent the creation of another fortress, cut off and trap the Eighteenth Army between the Australians pressing Madang and Allied forces at Hollandia, and advance the Allied bomber line 450 miles westward.

But there was a problem. The leap was so long that it went beyond range of most of Kenney's fighter planes. He could not provide close air support for the amphibious forces. To make such a leap, MacArthur would require a substantial force of aircraft carriers, and Admiral Kinkaid still had no carriers; Nimitz controlled all the carriers in the Pacific. Could he be persuaded to interrupt his Central Pacific operations to lend MacArthur a hand?

Some at GHQ had grave reservations about the scheme, which was not inappropriately code-named RECKLESS. But when MacArthur was briefed on it, he was enthusiastic. The Nimitz thrust against the Marshalls and the raid on Truk had stolen the Pacific spotlight. A bold strike at Hollandia would not only return the beam to MacArthur's theater it would advance his new Guinea timetable by several months. Also, it would probably save many Allied lives. MacArthur sent the proposal along to the JCS with a strong endorsement. It arrived in Washington just as the JCS was completing its reappraisal of Pacific strategy and was added to the agenda at once.

A few days later, March 12, 1944, the JCS handed down the revised 1944 Pacific strategy. It reaffirmed the "dual road" concept, with a converging of the roads at

Mindanao. It left unresolved the big steps after—whether Luzon or Formosa or both would be recaptured. The decree included a specific set of objectives and a new timetable. MacArthur would take Hollandia on April 15, Nimitz would take the Marianas on June 15 and the Palaus on September 15. Both forces would converge on Mindanao for a November 15 assault. Hansa Bay-Wewak, Truk, and Ponape would be bypassed. Nimitz would provide maximum carrier support for MacArthur at Hollandia.

RECKLESS planning moved ahead swiftly. MacArthur removed General Eichelberger from the obscurity he had endured since Buna and named him task force commander of the Alamo troops or Hollandia. A smaller landing at Aitape—about halfway between Wewak and Hollandia—was added to help block a westward attack by the Japanese Eighteenth Army and gain another airfield. Kinkaid and Barbey began amassing an armada of 113 ships to lift the 52,000 assault troops and their supplies and provide naval support.

In late March, Nimitz and his staff flew to Brisbane to confer with MacArthur and his staff on the carrier support for the landings. By all accounts, this first wartime encounter between the two Pacific Theater commanders was, at least outwardly, cordial. MacArthur met Nimitz at the airport—a courtesy he had not shown Marshall. He entertained Nimitz at a lavish banquet. In a long series of meetings, Nimitz outlined his plans. His dozen fast carriers would strike the Palaus at the end of March, return to the Marshall Islands for replenishment, and then steam to Hollandia for the invasion, now postponed for one week to April 22. In addition, Nimitz would provide eight "jeep" carriers to Kinkaid for close air support. MacArthur could not have asked for more.

As D-Day approached, GHQ launched a deception scheme designed to encourage the Japanese belief that the next Allied target was Hansa Bay-Wewak. They leaked fake invasion plans. Air force planes dropped flares over the area, simulating photo reconnaissance missions. To foster the idea that area fortifications were under active scouting, the Air Force dropped dummy parachutes, and Ralph Christie's submarines left empty rubber boats along the beaches. The codebreakers provided GHQ intercepts that showed the deception was working very well. Everything was being done at Hansa Bay-Wewak to prepare for invasion; nothing, at Hollandia.

Kenney, too, engaged in an elaborate deception. His primary task was to knock out the three hundred or four hundred Japanese aircraft (sources conflict on the exact number) at the Hollandia airfield complex. By that time, he had assembled a force of P–38 fighters with range enough to escort the heavy bombers to Hollandia. He planned to decimate the Japanese aircraft in a massive knockout daylight blow while they were parked wing-tip-to-wing-tip on the fields. (Clark Field in reverse.) To lull the Japanese into believing he had no fighters capable of reaching Hollandia (which, if true, would force his bombers to operate only at night), he forbade the P–38s to fly beyond Aitape, bombed Hollandia only in a desultory way (one plane at night), and kept heavy air pressure on Hansa Bay-Wewak. The strategy worked beyond Kenney's wildest dreams. Photo reconnaissance and codebreaking reported an astonishing apathy at the Hollandia airfield complex.

Massing his air strength, Kenney struck Hollandia in three big daylight raids, March 30 and 31 and April 3. On each of those days, Kenney sent in about 65 heavy bombers escorted by about 75 P–38s, plus an additional 171 medium and light bombers and strafers on the third day. It was a devastating blow to the Japanese. As he had hoped, Kenney caught the planes on the ground. In the three raids, he destroyed the entire Japanese air force at Hollandia, some 300 to 400 planes, plus fuel and ammo dumps, repair facilities, barracks, and mess halls.

Staging from western New Guinea bases, the vast fleet —the largest amphibious operation in the Pacific up to then—moved northward on a devious course to disguise its true destination. It included the eight jeep carriers on loan from Nimitz. MacArthur was present. He had flown to Finschhafen in his private B–17—named *Bataan*—with staff and media representatives, and boarded Kinkaid's flagship, the cruiser *Nashville*. Eichelberger had established his headquarters on Barbey's command ship, the destroyer *Swanson*. Krueger rode the destroyer *Wilkes,* a radar picket ship positioned fifteen miles ahead of the convoy. Astonishingly, not a single Japanese plane detected this massive armada.

Meanwhile, Nimitz's fast carriers were at sea, as planned. They struck the Palaus on March 30–31. The Japanese received advance warning, and the Combined Fleet had steamed out in a futile effort to organize for an attack. The carriers could not find the widely dispersed Japanese fleet, but they blasted everything in sight in the Palaus and nearby islands, destroying 150 aircraft. The Palaus would be no threat to Hollandia. They returned to the Marshalls, replenished, and steamed to New Guinea. On April 21, they hit Wakde-Sarmi, a Japanese air complex about a hundred miles to the west of Hollandia, destroying 33 aircraft. Then they stood by off Hollandia where they found nothing much of value to shoot at. (On the way back to the Marshalls, they struck Truk again.)

The invasion fleet wheeled around and turned south toward Hollandia-Aitape. The Aitape force split off. On the morning of April 22, one force hit Hollandia (in two landings); the other hit Aitape. The surprise was total. The Japanese service troops jumped up from their breakfasts and fled into the hills and jungles, offering only token resistance. (Thousands perished trying to make their way west to the next Japanese garrison.) Later, a lone Japanese bomber hit an ammo dump on the Hollandia beachhead, causing a huge fire; but other than that, the operation was a brilliant success.

Four hours after the first assault wave hit the beaches, MacArthur collected Krueger, Eichelberger, Barbey, and the media representatives and went ashore in a landing craft. They toured the beachhead for two hours. MacArthur, now sixty-four years old, kept a vigorous pace. In the afternoon, MacArthur went ashore a second time for about an hour. It was hot and humid. Eichelberger then noted with "astonishment" what others had observed about MacArthur in times past: "Despite the sweltering heat and the vigorous exercise, he did not perspire at all." Back on *Nashville,* MacArthur celebrated the victory by passing out chocolate ice cream sodas. Eichelberger recalled: "There at the equator, they certainly hit the spot. When I finished mine with celerity, the Allied Commander grinned and gave me his own, untouched, frosted glass. I polished off that soda too."

On the following day, *Nashville* took MacArthur to Aitape. He went ashore there for about eight hours, touring the area in a jeep. He had reason to be pleased. Brigadier General Jens A. Doe, who commanded this force independent of Eichelberger, had performed well.

But there was a new worry. What would be the reaction of the Japanese Eighteenth Army at Wewak, only a hundred miles east? Would they march overland and attempt to recapture Aitape, and then attack Hollandia? Against this possibility, Krueger reinforced Aitape and ordered strong defensive positions placed at the Driniumor River. To avoid a Japanese bypass (as had happened at Saidor), Doe extended his lines far inland.

Before returning to Brisbane, MacArthur made a startling proposal to Eichelberger. He suggested that he immediately leap another 125 miles westward and seize Wakde-Sarmi while the Japanese were still off balance. The area was reported to be lightly held; Nimitz's carrier pilots had worked it over. Here were all these combat troops at Hollandia with nothing to do. Eichelberger was a bit staggered by this suggestion and argued against it. He felt exposed enough at Hollandia. Beside, intelligence reported Sarmi was crawling with Japs. But when MacArthur got back to Brisbane, he ordered half the project anyway: seizure of Wakde Island. Staging from Hollandia, Alamo forces invaded Wakde on May 18. The Allies met stiffer resistance then they expected. But after four days, Wakde was declared secure and turned into an air base for Kenney. Only forty American had died. An adjunct landing on the mainland opposite Wakde (to secure the island from Japanese artillery attacks) fared less well; four hundred Americans were killed.

After Eichelberger had secured Hollandia and its airfield complex, his engineers, working in feverish haste, transformed it into a massive Allied base. He wrote: "Where once I had seen only a few native villages and an expanse of primeval forest, a city of one hundred and forty thousand men took occupancy." Kenney's airmen set up operations at the refurbished airfield complex; Kinkaid's fleet moored in the huge, well-protected anchorage. MacArthur and GHQ prepared to move there, and Eichelberger's men built a command quarters of prefabricated sheet metal huts on a pleasant hillside. Kinkaid's men set up a Navy headquarters of Quonset huts lower down the hill. But the GHQ move was postponed until summer.

There was a grim aftermath to these easy operations. Units of the Japanese Eighteenth Army did, in fact, march west from Wewak to assault Alamo lines at Aitape. For months, while MacArthur moved ever westward, there was savage jungle fighting, requiring very large Alamo reinforcements. In the end, the Eighteenth Army was decimated, losing almost half of the twenty thousand men committed to the battle. The United States suffered three thousand casualties—five hundred killed or missing. Krueger finally declared the area secure on August 25. Later, Australian troops took over and launched an assault on Wewak, killing another seven thousand Japanese. Wewak did not fall until May 10, 1945—a full year after the initial Aitape landings.

CHAPTER
TWENTY-FOUR

★ ★ ★ ★ ★

IN THE FACE of the MacArthur and Nimitz victories on land and in the air, and the ever-tightening submarine blockade, Japan was reeling. Tokyo demanded prompt and vigorous action to stop the relentless Allied advance. There seemed only one solution: to assemble all the ships of the Japanese Navy for a single, all-out showdown battle with the U.S. Pacific Fleet. Accordingly, in May 1944, Tokyo promulgated what was called Operation A-Go. It would dominate all Japanese military movements in the immediate future and considerably influence Allied operations. It would lead MacArthur and his ground generals into a wholly unexpected and bloody tactical setback and near-disaster.

At that time, the Japanese Navy could muster only about nine first-line aircraft carriers. Moreover, most of the air units on these carriers were poorly trained and inexperienced. By contrast, Nimitz then had about fifteen fast carriers and the jeep carriers. Most of the air units on these carriers were seasoned combat outfits. To overcome this disparity, the Japanese planned—or hoped—to lure the U.S. Pacific Fleet into waters where Japanese land-based aircraft could be brought into play. They did not know of the forthcoming Marianas invasion. They had incorrectly assumed the Allies were only going one road to Tokyo—MacArthur's. To them, the logical area for the showdown seemed to be the waters between The Palaus and New Guinea, where Nimitz would send his carriers to support MacArthur, as he had supported him at Hollandia. Here, Japanese land-based planes at Biak, Morotai, Talaud, Mindanao, and smaller islands could attack the U.S. Fleet in unison with the Japanese carriers.

In addition, the Japanese set great store by two extraordinary ships the *Yamato* and *Musashi*. These were sixty-thousand-ton battleships, by far the largest in the world. (The third sister ship *Shinano* was being converted to an aircraft carrier.) Each had a main battery of nine 18-inch guns, more firepower than any ship in history. Each had heavy armor and was considered by the Japanese to be unsinkable, either by aircraft or submarine. It was believed that if these two behemoths could get within firing range of the American carriers at night, when the planes couldn't fly, they would provide the decisive edge in the battle.

In mid- through late-May, the Japanese began to assemble the carriers, battleships, cruisers, destroyers, and auxiliaries in the Celebes Sea. Most of these ships holed up in the anchorages at Tawi Tawi Island and Davao, Mindanao. Additional land-based planes flew to The Palaus and Biak and other bases to replace those destroyed by Nimitz and Kenney in earlier operations. The land-based naval air forces were, like the carrier air units, seriously understrength and green. Nonetheless, the Japanese were highly optimistic, foreseeing a decisive sea victory that would stop the Allied advance.

The American codebreakers were listening attentively to these new plans, and passed the information on to MacArthur and Nimitz. Nimitz welcomed the news. He was not about to be lured into a trap in waters near The Palaus. His next objective was the Marianas—Guam, Saipan, Tinian—far to the north. But he hoped that the Marianas invasion would lure the Japanese Fleet into *his* waters, where (assuming complete destruction of land-based air in the Marianas) he would have a decided edge.

By now, both MacArthur and Nimitz were being aided enormously by the submarine forces under Christie and Lockwood. In 1944, prior to the Marianas operation, they sank about three hundred Japanese ships. A great many of these were carrying reinforcements of men and supplies to New Guinea and the Marianas or to other captured possessions. When the Japanese Fleet gathered at Tawi Tawi and Davao, it was harassed so persistently by Christie's submarines it dared not put to sea for much-needed training exercises. Christie's boats picked off a cruiser, six destroyers, and many auxiliaries, including tankers. They severely damaged dozens of other ships. They kept a close watch on the Tawi Tawi and Davao anchorages, reporting the movement of every Japanese ship. These precise movement reports would prove to be priceless in forthcoming operations.

MacArthur now ordered a speedup in his New Guinea drive—seizing new places before the last had been secured. The next objective was the island of Biak, one of the Schouten Islands about 180 miles northwest of Wakde and 350 miles west of Hollandia. It is a curious piece of real estate, formed (the theory goes) by a prehistoric upheaval that pushed part of the ocean floor to the surface. It is layered and cut by coral ridges, terraces, and shelves, covered over by a thick tropical rain forest and jungle. Beneath this is a vast honeycomb of interconnected and multileveled caves. There is little fresh water. It is surrounded by rough coral reefs. There could scarcely have been a less inviting place, but Biak had three airfields that, with refurbishing, would permit Kenney's aircraft to dominate all of the Vogelkop Peninsula.

The seizure of Biak was assigned to Krueger's Alamo force. He chose units of the American 41st Division and support forces, all commanded by Major General Horace H. Fuller, a classmate of Eichelberger's at West Point and a lifelong friend. Admiral Kinkaid provided a supporting naval force of five cruisers and twenty-one destroyers, plus amphibious craft. Kenney furnished close air support from his new network of bases at Wakde Island. After air and naval units had heavily blasted Biak, Fuller's ground forces, staging from Hollandia, landed on May 27, only ten days after the landing at Wakde.

The codebreakers and other intelligence sources had provided some information on Biak. They estimated the

Japanese garrison numbered about 4,400, of which about half were combatant troops. The codebreakers intercepted messages in early May ordering the defenses of Biak strengthened. But no one was able to define the progress that had been made. The exact state of the defenses was unknown. It could be a picnic like Hollandia, or it could be another Buna.

At first it looked like a picnic. There was little opposition on the ground, only token attacks from the air, and none from the sea. Fuller's troops, "in high good humor" (as Eichelberger put it), raced for the nearest airstrip. They did not bother to bring up artillery, nor scout ahead. They ignored a towering cliff on their right flank, which was, in Krueger's words, a "tactical· imprudence." The Japanese let Fuller's troops advance, then sprang the trap. The picnic transformed instantly into a nightmare, another Buna.

The codebreakers and other intelligence sources had erred badly. Because of the impending A-Go operation, the Japanese Navy was heavily dependent on Biak for land-based air. Biak in Allied hands would not only deny them a crucial base but give the Allies an upper hand in the showdown battle area. For some weeks, the Japanese Navy had been reinforcing the Japanese Army on Biak, most recently with 1500 Marines. It had also ordered 100–150 (sources conflict) aircraft to the area. There were, in fact, almost three times as many Japanese on Biak as intelligence estimated—11,400 men. The 4,000 troops originally there were mostly combat-wise veterans of China, led by Colonel Naoyuki Kuzume. He had organized his defenses cleverly, utilizing the honeycomb of caves, and he planned to use the 7,000-odd service troops in combat.

When the Japanese Navy got word that Biak was under siege, it immediately ordered that it be reinforced. This operation was code-named Kon and was staged from Tawi Tawi and Davao. There were three sorties. Each was thwarted, in part, by precise sighting reports from Christie's submarines, which were swarming off Tawi Tawi and Davao and elsewhere in the Celebes Sea.

Kon–1 consisted of one old battleship, four cruisers, and eight destroyers. It left Tawi Tawi and embarked about 2500 troops from Mindanao. It was tracked—and repeatedly attacked—by four of Christie's submarines.

They did no noteworthy damage, but their position reports enabled GHQ to keep tabs on the Japanese ships. In spite of the fact that Willoughby erroneously discredited the threat, Kinkaid sent his entire available surface force—four cruisers, ten destroyers—to intercept. But after passing Talaud, the Japanese—now told that American carriers had appeared off Biak, and having been sighted by a fifth submarine—turned back.

Kon–2 was a lesser effort. It consisted of six destroyers towing barges. Alerted by the codebreakers who were now focused intently on the area, Kenney's aircraft found the destroyers and attacked. The Japanese cut the barges loose and fled. Typically, Kenney exaggerated the damage, claiming four destroyers sunk. Only one sank, the other five fled. Kinkaid brought up his forces in a long stern chase, but he couldn't catch up. One of Christie's submarines, *Haddo,* positioned off Davao sank one of the five destroyers as it was returning to port.

Kon–3 was a massive, determined effort. It consisted of the superbattleships *Yamato* and *Mushasi,* five cruisers, seven destroyers, and other miscellaneous craft. When it sortied from Tawi Tawi on June 10, it was sighted by famous submarine skipper Samuel D. Dealey in *Harder,* who had already sunk three destroyers off Tawi Tawi. Dealey attacked a Kon–3 destroyer but was driven off by a vicious depth charging. Later that night, he reported the sortie of this astonishing force. It went on to Batjan to pick up Japanese troops to take them to Biak.

As it turned out, before this operation could be carried further, Nimitz invaded the Marianas, forcing the Japanese to execute A-Go in the wrong place—of which more later. The Kon–3 force was halted and the ships ordered to join A-Go. That was a fortuitous turnabout for MacArthur and Kinkaid. If the Kon–3 force had gone on to Biak as scheduled, it could have easily annihilated Kinkaid's entire surface Navy, plus all the Allied amphibious and support craft at Biak, and landed its reinforcements on the island.

In addition to these efforts, the Japanese Navy ordered the newly arrived 100–150 aircraft to attack. They hit Biak repeatedly and also Wakde, where Kenney had overconfidently jammed his planes in close formation on the ground. The Japanese destroyed sixty of these planes and blew up a bomb dump. The dump explosion was so violent, it was thought an earthquake had struck Wakde. Fortunately for Kenney and Kinkaid, these Japanese Navy pilots were new to the area. The majority came down with jungle diseases and, after the first week or so, were unable to man their planes.

Meanwhile, ashore on Biak, General Fuller was in trouble. Although MacArthur had issued a communique on June 3 declaring the Japanese on Biak had collapsed and Fuller was now merely engaged in mopping up, Fuller was completely bogged down and desperate. On June 13, Fuller reported (prematurely) that the Japanese had landed reinforcements and requested additional reinforcements himself. Krueger, urged on by icy messages from MacArthur, promptly relieved him of command and ordered Eichelberger and his staff to Biak. It was with a heavy heart that Eichelberger replaced his classmate and old friend.

Now, once more into the breach, in a kind of replay of Buna, Eichelberger took tactical command of Allied Forces, which were quickly reinforced. Fearlessly exposing himself at the very front lines or in fragile Piper Cub spotting planes, Eichelberger injected an aggressive spirit into the troops. The fighting was bloody. They had to root the stubborn Japanese out of the caves with flaming gasoline and TNT. On June 23, Colonel Kuzume assembled his surviving officers in a cave and ordered a last-ditch banzai attack. Eichelberger wrote: "Then, in samurai tradition, he knelt and disembowled himself with his warrior's sword." The insane attack failed. By June 28, the situation was such that Eichelberger and his staff could leave, turning over command to General Jens A. Doe.

As a reward for this job well-done, MacArthur promoted Eichelberger to command a new army, the Eighth, then being readied for the Mindanao invasion. The formation of this new army put Krueger's nose badly out of joint. As Eichelberger wrote, Krueger "steadfastly opposed" it. When Eichelberger got back to Hollandia from Biak, Krueger was so angry about the new army, he refused to speak to Eichelberger and told him he was too busy to see him. That was Krueger's thanks to Eichelberger for pulling his chestnuts out of the fire on Biak. Eichelberger was astonished but, as he wrote, "The Army teaches men to be philosophical. I took General Krueger at his word and stayed away."

The Allies were desperately busy on Biak for weeks afterwards clearing out pockets of holed-up Japanese. The casualties on both sides were frightful. Only 220 of the original 7,400 (plus 1200 others who got in by barge) Japanese were taken alive. Some may have evacuated, but most died or committed suicide. The Allies suffered 400 dead, 2300 wounded, plus over 7,000 disabled by disease (1,000 came down with scrub typhus). A miscalculation in intelligence had caused this misery and bloodshed.

A thousand miles to the north, Nimitz's vast armada assaulted the Marianas on June 15. (Nine days earlier, Eisenhower's forces had landed in Normandy.) It was composed of Task Force 58 and 535 amphibious ships, transporting 127,000 troops, two thirds of them Marines. They went ashore first at Saipan, meeting fierce opposition. As Nimitz wrote later, the preinvasion bombardment had not been strong nor specific enough as to targets. The Japanese were well-entrenched behind strong fortifications.

When the Japanese realized (from preinvasion aerial attack) that Saipan would be invaded, they launched Operation A-Go. This was not where they had planned the showdown battle, but the time had come to strike. In Japanese minds (as in Admiral King's mind) the Marianas were the key to the vast western Pacific basin. To lose the Marianas would be a catastrophe. The orders to fight to the finish went out on June 13. That day the Japanese Fleet steamed out of Tawi Tawi under radio silence, observed and reported by one of Christie's submarines, *Redfin*. That same day, the Kon–3 force was ordered to terminate operations against Biak and join the fleet. En route to this rendezvous, the Kon–3 force was sighted by one of Lockwood's submarines, *Seahorse*. Another Lockwood submarine, *Flying Fish,* reported the main body going through San Bernardino Strait.

The two fleets met in what was called the Battle of the Philippine Sea (or more popularly, The Marianas Turkey Shoot) June 19 to 21. The Japanese had hoped to utilize land-based air from the Marianas to offset the disparity in carriers. But, as we have seen, some of that air had been stripped to help defend Biak. The rest were wiped out by Nimitz's carrier planes in the preinvasion phase, as were reinforcements en route from Japan. On the first day of the battle, the Japanese launched four separate carrier air attacks against Nimitz's forces comprising 430 planes. Each failed utterly. About 330 planes were lost. That same day, two of Lockwood's submarines, *Albacore* and *Cavalla*, sank two of the first-line Japanese carriers, *Taiho* and *Shokaku*. On the second day, Nimitz's carrier planes sank one carrier, *Hiyo*, and severely damaged two others, *Chiyoda* and *Zuikaku*. Following these disasters, the surviving ships fled toward Japan. The great show-down battle had failed.

The invasion of the Marianas continued apace. After a bloody fight, Saipan was finally declared secured. On July 21, Guam was invaded, and Tinian, three days later. After more ghastly bloodshed, those places were also declared secure. The casualties were staggering. Some sixty thousand Japanese were killed. Over five thousand Americans were killed and more than twenty thousand wounded.

The loss of the Marianas brought a tremendous shock wave to Japan. Prime Minister Tojo and his entire cabinet resigned. Tojo and company were replaced by the government of General Kuniaki Koiso. The Emperor made known to Koiso his desire for early peace negotiations. Nimitz and Potter wrote, "Yet so binding was the Japanese military code, so rigid the demands of Oriental 'face,' that for a whole year no official in Japan could bring himself to initiate steps for ending hostilities." Nor would a negotiated peace have been acceptable to the Allies. At Casablanca, Roosevelt and Churchill had declared that both Germany and Japan must submit to "unconditional surrender."

This Nimitz victory in the Marianas took much pressure off MacArthur. The Japanese Fleet was gone now— back in Japan. There was nothing at Tawi Tawi or Davao to again seriously threaten Kinkaid's Navy or the Alamo forces on Biak. One consequence was that MacArthur's Alamo forces were able to quickly leap westward to Noemfoor Island (July 2), seventy-five miles west of Biak, then to Sansapor (July 30). At neither place did Alamo forces encounter noteworthy resistance.

In a little more than five months, MacArthur had advanced 550 miles from Hollandia to Sansapor. In one year he had moved 1500 miles from Milne Bay. New Guinea was his. Mindanao lay only 500 miles to the northwest.

CHAPTER
TWENTY-FIVE

★ ★ ★ ★ ★

IN THE UNITED States, 1944 was a presidential election year. There was no doubt about the Democratic nominee; Roosevelt, despite a drastic decline in his health, would run for a fourth term. The Republican nominee was not so clear cut. Wendell Willkie, defeated by Roosevelt in 1940, was still the titular head of the party. But there was growing sentiment for New York's Governor Thomas E. Dewey. Dewey was "reluctant" and playing coy.

Enter now Douglas MacArthur.

Over the years, MacArthur had frequently been mentioned as a possibility for president. He appealed to various right-wing extremists, isolationists, American Firsters, Roosevelt-haters, and some responsible, middle-of-the-road Republicans. In 1942, when the stand at Bataan and Corregidor made him a mythic figure and a household word, the talk that he might successfully run against Roosevelt increased substantially. One of those who considered this seriously was the much-respected senator from Michigan, Arthur H. Vandenberg, a Republican. He wrote to a member of his family: "If he gets out alive, I think he will be my choice for President in 1944."

In 1943, according to his son Arthur H. Jr., editor of *The Private Papers of Senator Vandenberg,* the Senator "began searching for a candidate he could support." He was opposed to Willkie. He was impressed by Dewey but seriously doubted Dewey could pull sufficient votes to defeat Roosevelt. By that time, MacArthur was even better known and, according to various polls of Republican voters, ran fairly strong behind Willkie and Dewey, even though he was in Australia and not a candidate. The idea began to form in Vandenberg's mind that if Willkie and Dewey ran a close race and the convention deadlocked, dark horse MacArthur might well emerge as the compromise nominee.

MacArthur and most of his aides and friends have written that he had no real interest in the presidency, did not seriously consider the nomination in 1944, and did not actively seek it. However, there is strong evidence to the contrary. After a visit with MacArthur, Eichelberger noted in his diary (published in *Dear Miss Em,* edited by Jay Luvaas) on June 13, 1943: "My Chief talked of the Republican nomination for next year—I can see that he expects to get it and I sort of think so too. Maybe he could run a good race." In the added notes for this book Eichelberger said: "Before the 1944 elections, he talked to me a number of times about the Presidency, but would usually confine his desires by saying that if it were not for his hatred, or rather the extent to which he despised FDR, he would not want it." Sid Huff wrote: "The idea wasn't unpleasant to MacArthur." Dr. James, who has investigated the point exhaustively, concluded that more likely than not, at first MacArthur did want the nomination and actively encouraged certain of his aides to pursue it for him, while he, MacArthur, maintained a public attitude of indifference or unavailability.

The Vandenberg push seems to have got up a head of steam in the spring of 1943. Clare Boothe Luce, wife of the *Time-Life* press czar Henry Luce, and then a Roosevelt-hating congresswoman from Connecticut, was one of those responsible Republicans who adored MacArthur. She invited Vandenberg to her Washington apartment to meet Sutherland and Kenney, who were in Washington to appear before the JCS in MacArthur's behalf. At the meeting in Luce's apartment, Vandenberg (and maybe Luce too) made a "vigorous" statement in praise of

MacArthur. Shortly after this meeting, Vandenberg gave his first, cautious, public signal that he might be a MacArthur supporter; Secretary of War Stimson restated, publicly, a long-standing Army regulation that prohibited personnel on active duty from becoming an active candidate for any public office. Vandenberg huffed that the move was "aimed at keeping MacArthur out of the next presidential campaign."

Vandenberg had not yet communicated directly with MacArthur. To his astonishment, he received a hand-delivered cable from him that said: "I am most grateful to you for your complete attitude of friendship. I only hope that I can some day reciprocate. There is much that I would like to say to you which circumstances prevent. In the meanwhile I want you to know the absolute confidence I would feel in your experienced and wise mentorship." Delighted, Vandenberg noted in his diary that the message "*might* be supremely historic. . . . 'Mac' certainly is not 'running away' from *anything*. It is typical of his forthright courage."

Vandenberg, interpreting this as a signal that MacArthur was available, and convinced that MacArthur was the only Republican who could beat Roosevelt, now began to move quietly behind-the-scenes, recruiting responsible people to his scheme. Clare Boothe Luce apparently thought better of it and, like her husband, steered clear. But other anti-Roosevelt media czars joined in: William Randolph Hearst, Frank Gannett, Roy Howard, Colonel Robert R. McCormick, Joseph Patterson, representatives of Los Angeles newspapers, and West Pointer Frank C. Waldrop of the *Washington Times-Herald*. These men and many others put their vastly influential resources behind MacArthur, flooding the country with pro-MacArthur stories, profiles, editorials, and quickie, idolatrous campaign books. Robert E. Wood, Chairman of the Board of Sears, Roebuck and Company (then on active duty as a brigadier general in the Supply Corps), "offered to underwrite any necessary expenses," and shortly thereafter, Vandenberg wrote Willoughby, established contact with him.

Vandenberg fully recognized he was engaged in a delicate, long-shot operation. He had a candidate who could not actively campaign. He had to find some way of controlling the extremist, wildcat MacArthur-for-President groups, springing up all over the country. He did not want them to "martyrize" MacArthur into a "completely irresistible" figure, thus angering Roosevelt to the point that he would engage in "political reprisals"—such as relieving MacArthur of command. Above all, he did not want MacArthur's name entered into "ordinary precon-vention political activities" such as the primaries, where MacArthur had no organization and would surely run poorly. What he wanted was a "ground swell" that would force Republican delegates at the convention to turn to MacArthur when the hoped-for deadlock came.

In February 1944, Vandenberg publicly and unre-servedly threw his support behind MacArthur. In an arti-cle in *Collier's* magazine entitled "Why I Am For Mac-Arthur," he gave three main reasons: that MacArthur should have "total sway" over U.S. military strategy; that he would be the best man to put the country "back on its postwar feet;" and that he would bring a great mind, heart, capacity, and spiritual Christian devotion to the task.

However, Vandenberg's dark-horse strategy was dealt a fatal blow in the spring of 1944. Against Vanden-berg's wishes, wildcat groups in Wisconsin and Illinois entered MacArthur's name in the primaries in those states. In Illinois, where he was unopposed by any major candidate and strongly backed by the *Chicago Tribune,* he got over 550,000 votes. But in Wisconsin, Willkie, Dewey, and Harold E. Stassen (two-term governor of neighboring Minnesota, then on active naval service as an aide to Bull Halsey) were on the ticket. Vanden-berg feared "catastrophe." He was right. On April 4, Dewey won a smashing victory: 24 delegates (plus two leaners). Stassen got 4, MacArthur 3. Willkie, who was slipping badly in the polls, got none. There was little chance now for a convention deadlock. Even if there was, MacArthur's feeble showing had all but elimi-nated him as a dark-horse possibility. Vandenberg com-mented: "It is all over but the shouting."

Not quite. Following the Wisconsin primary, there was an embarrassing postscript. It appeared to place MacArthur in the unsoldierly role of openly and ac-tively seeking the nomination. It forced him twice to make public statements denying any such attempt. For the background on this postscript, we must backtrack seven months to September 18, 1943.

On that day, a conservative freshman congressman from Nebraska, Dr. Albert L. Miller, wrote a letter to MacArthur, the text of which is included in Frazier Hunt's biography of MacArthur (plus the follow-up correspondence). Miller told MacArthur there was a "tremendous ground swell" of anti-New Deal sentiment building. He suggested that MacArthur not be an active "candidate" for the Republican nomination but that he "permit people to draft you." He concluded: "You owe it to civilization and to the children yet unborn to accept the nomination."

On October 2, 1943, MacArthur responded with a letter that (as Hunt put it) "obviously was intended only for the Congressman's eyes." MacArthur seemed to agree with Miller's criticism of the New Deal. He wrote: "I thank you so sincerely for your fine letter . . . I do not anticipate in any way your flattering predictions, but I do undeservedly agree with the complete wisdom and statesmanship of your comments."

On January 27, 1944, Miller wrote MacArthur a second letter. Again he reported a "mass movement" against the "many domestic mistakes being made by the Administration." He ranted on: "If this system of left wingers and New Dealism is continued another four years, I am certain that this Monarchy which is being established in American will destroy the rights of the common people. . . . It is going to take an individual who is fearless and willing to make political sacrifices to cut out the underbrush and help destroy this monstrosity. . . ." That man, of course, was MacArthur.

On February 11, 1944, MacArthur responded, thanking Miller for his "scholarly letter." (It was anything but "scholarly.") Again he seemed to agree with Miller's diatribe against the Roosevelt administration: "Your description of conditions in the United States is a sobering one indeed and is calculated to arouse the thoughtful consideration of every true patriot. We must not inadvertently slip into the same condition internally as the one which we fight externally. Like Abraham Lincoln, I am a firm believer in the people, and if given the truth, they can be depended upon to meet any national crisis. The great point is to bring before them the real facts. . . ."

On April 14, after the catastrophe in the Wisconsin
primary, Miller, perhaps wishing to get the MacArthur
boomlet moving again (or to garner personal publicity),
released his two letters and MacArthur's two replies. It
caused a furor. To most journalists, MacArthur's correspondence was proof that he was a willing and eager
candidate, and that was big news. Anti-MacArthur pundits found the letter disloyal to Commander-in-Chief
Roosevelt. So intense was the media coverage that Mac-
Arthur was forced to make a public statement. On April
17, from Brisbane, he said:

> My attention has been called to the publication
> by Congressman Miller of a personal correspondence
> with him. In so far as my letters are concerned they
> were never intended for publication. Their perusal
> will show any fair-minded person that they were
> neither politically inspired nor intended to convey
> blanket approval of the Congressman's views. I en-
> tirely repudiate the sinister interpretation that they
> were intended as criticism of any political philos-
> ophy or personages in high office. They were written
> merely as amiable acknowledgmens, to a member of
> our highest law-making body, of letters containing
> flattering and friendly remarks to me personally. To
> construe them otherwise is to misrepresent my in-
> tent. I have not received Congressman Miller's third
> letter in which he is reported to advise me to an-
> nounce candidacy for the office of President of the
> U.S.
> The high Constitutional processes of our repre-
> sentative and republican form of government, in
> which there resides with the people the sacred duty
> of choosing and electing their Chief Executive, are
> of so imposing a nature as to be beyond the sphere
> of any individual's coercion or decision. I can only
> say as I have said before, I am not a candidate for
> the office nor do I seek it. I have devoted myself ex-
> clusively to the conduct of war. My sole ambition is
> to assist my beloved country to win this vital strug-
> gle by the fulfillment of such duty as has been or
> may be assigned to me.

This merely fanned the flames. The pro–New Deal

liberal pundits skewered MacArthur so thoroughly, he was forced to issue a second statement specifically denying that he was actively seeking the nomination. On April 30, from Brisbane, he said:

> Since my return from the Hollandia operation I have had brought to my attention a number of newspaper articles professing in strongest terms a widespread public opinion that it is detrimental to our war effort to have an officer in high position on active service at the front, considered for nomination for the office of President. I have on several occasions announced I was not a candidate for the position. Nevertheless, in view of these circumstances, in order to make my position entirely unequivocal, I request that no action be taken that would link my name in any way with the nomination. I do not covet it nor would I accept it.

Vandenberg was furious at Miller. He described the release of these letters a "tragic mistake" and a "magnificent boner." It made the general's position "untenable." By the time the Republican Convention convened in Chicago on June 26, MacArthur's candidacy was dead as a dodo. Dewey clearly had it in the bag. Vandenberg's final service to MacArthur was to head off a misguided effort to put the general's name in nomination. He felt it would have been an "insufferable humiliation" for MacArthur "to wind up with only one or two votes." As it happened, there was one vote cast for MacArthur, 1056 for Dewey. The lone holdout refused, as is customary, to withdraw the vote and make it unanimous.

All this generated vast publicity for MacArthur. It firmly implanted in many minds the idea of MacArthur as conservative presidential timber. This was an idea that would not go away. It would linger on to 1948 and 1952 with—as we shall see—about the same results.

CHAPTER
TWENTY-SIX

★ ★ ★ ★ ★

WITH EISENHOWER FIRMLY established on the continent in Europe, MacArthur entrenched throughout New Guinea, and Nimitz in the Marianas, the U.S. Joint Chiefs of Staff began to consider ways to greatly speed up the war in the Pacific. There was a general feeling that Nimitz's massive naval power ought to be brought more directly to bear against Japan. Admiral King proposed that MacArthur's next major target, the Philippines, be bypassed, that the preponderance of his troops be transferred to Nimitz, and that Nimitz should seize Formosa and plan for an early assault on the Japanese home islands. The other two members of the Joint Chiefs, General Marshall and Air Force General Henry H. Arnold, agreed.

Accordingly, on June 12, 1944, the J.C.S. notified MacArthur and Nimitz that they were considering the possibilities of expediting the Pacific campaign by bypassing all previously selected objectives, going directly to Formosa, and choosing new objectives "including Japan proper." Whitney wrote that MacArthur found this message "disquieting." In fact, it must have been a shatter-

174

ing bombshell. The Navy point of view had prevailed after all. The Philippines were to be bypassed.

MacArthur replied promptly—and eloquently. He told Marshall that it was not feasible to speed up operations, that it would be "utterly unsound" militarily to bypass the Philippines and go directly to Formosa. "I do not believe the campaign would succeed," he said. It was too big a bite too soon. Formosa was a heavily defended fortress, like Rabaul. The occupation of Luzon was "essential" for the establishment of air bases for an assault on Formosa. Besides that, the Philippines was United States territory. America had a moral obligation to liberate her seventeen million pro-Western people and the tens of thousands of Bataan POWs. He felt so strongly about this, he said, that he would personally proceed to Washington to fully present his views.

Marshall's rejoinder on June 24 must have been equally "disquieting." Marshall, who had steadfastly backed the "dual road" strategy, had finally caved in and gone over to the Navy. He told MacArthur that "all information we have received" (i.e., codebreaking) indicated the Japanese were greatly strengthening the present objectives (Palau, Mindanao, etc.), that in effect MacArthur would find it tough to "hit 'em where they ain't" any longer. Moreover, Marshall said, "The great Pacific Fleet with its thousands of planes should be maintained in practically continuous employment." Then a strong putdown: "With regard to the re-conquest of the Philippines we must be careful not to allow our personal feeling and the Philippine political considerations to overrule our great objective." Bypassing, he said, was not "synonymous with abandonment." The quickest way to liberate the Filipinos and POWs was to crush Japan proper. He concluded by saying that if MacArthur wanted to come to Washington to fully present his views, that was fine. He would speak to the President, who he was certain "would be agreeable to your being ordered home for that purpose."

But Roosevelt had another plan up his sleeve. He would travel to the Pacific—to Pearl Harbor—to meet with MacArthur. No one has satisfactorily explained this decision. Perhaps in view of the recent political boomlet for MacArthur, Roosevelt feared that if MacArthur came to Washington, it would touch off a political storm (con-

gressional hearings, press conferences, etc.) detrimental
to calm reasoning and decision-making and ultimately
harmful politically to Roosevelt. MacArthur might seize
a public forum like this to *demand* a return to the Philippines. If Roosevelt met with MacArthur under tight
security (and press censorship) at Pearl Harbor, none
of this would happen. Moreover, meeting MacArthur
halfway was a political gesture that would not be lost on
MacArthur's followers in the States.

Whatever the reason, on July 21, shortly after he had
been nominated for a fourth term, Roosevelt embarked
for Hawaii at San Diego on the cruiser *Baltimore*. Meanwhile, Marshall had alerted MacArthur, requesting that
he report at Pearl Harbor for an important conference.
He did not say why or who would be there. But as
MacArthur wrote in his memoirs, he was "reasonably
certain" it would be President Roosevelt and that the
conference would deal with "something closely affecting
me." Quite obviously the principal subject matter would
be Pacific strategy, with the question of bypassing the
Philippines paramount. MacArthur flew to Pearl Harbor
in his B–17, "Bataan," taking only five aides and "no
plans or maps."

Frazier Hunt wrote that MacArthur was in a towering rage by the time he reached Pearl Harbor. Mac-
Arthur, wrote Hunt, believed the conference to be a
publicity stunt. "The humiliation of forcing me to leave
my command to fly to Hawaii for a political picture
taking junket!" he quotes MacArthur as saying. This is
difficult to believe. As MacArthur well knew, the JCS
were then unanimous in their decision to bypass the
Philippines. He, almost alone among the top brass, held
the view it was necessary to return there. If the JCS
decision was to be overturned, only Roosevelt could do
it. And here was a heaven-sent opportunity for Mac-
Arthur to get the President on his side. Besides that,
MacArthur had only recently told Marshall he was willing to go all the way to Washington to present his views.

Roosevelt and MacArthur arrived in Pearl Harbor
the same day, July 26. MacArthur went immediately to
the Fort Shafter home of an old West Point friend Lieutenant General Robert C. Richardson, who commanded
Nimitz's Army forces. When the *Baltimore* docked, Roosevelt sent for Nimitz, Halsey, MacArthur, and others.

MacArthur was late arriving. This has been construed by some as a deliberate insult to the President, but it seems unlikely MacArthur would prejudice his case at so crucial a moment.

His arrival at the *Baltimore's* dock was memorably dramatic. He came in an enormous open black limousine, escorted by motorcycle police with sirens screaming. MacArthur sat majestically alone in the back seat, wearing a brown leather aviator jacket, dark glasses, and his floppy campaign hat. When the chauffeur swung the car on the dock, the Army soldiers present cheered MacArthur. When the applause died, MacArthur alighted from the limousine, strode rapidly to the gangway, paused to acknowledge another ovation, saluted the *Baltimore's* quarterdeck, then went aboard to greet Roosevelt and the very large assembly of Army and Navy officers present.

It was the first face-to-face meeting for Roosevelt and MacArthur in seven years—since 1937, when MacArthur called at the White House to urge the President to see Quezon. MacArthur, eternally young, had changed very little physically. Roosevelt looked ghastly. MacArthur was "shocked." He recalled: "I had not seen him for a number of years, and physically he was just a shell of the man I had known. It was clearly evident that his days were numbered."

After a few friendly formalities, MacArthur returned to Richardson's quarters at Fort Shafter for dinner with the general. Again Hunt depicts MacArthur in a bizarre frame of mind. He was depressed—as depressed as he was two years before on Corregidor when Roosevelt ordered him to leave and go to Australia. Pacing the floor, Hunt says, he unburdened himself on an aide, reviewing "his long years of struggle and his many defeats and frustrations." He fretted about the "inadequate leadership" of the country and the "terrible mistakes" made in the war. Hunt concluded: "He seemed to unburden himself in a way he had seldom if ever done before in all his life." It could well have been that MacArthur was exhausted, utterly drained. The flight from Australia had taken almost twenty-six hours.

The next day MacArthur joined Roosevelt and his personal chief of staff, Admiral William D. Leahy, at Roosevelt's quarters, a private home on Waikiki Beach.

Roosevelt spent that day in an open limousine, making crash visits to various Army and Navy installations to see the troops. Leahy sat up front with the chauffeur, Roosevelt, MacArthur, and Nimitz sat in the back—Nimitz between Roosevelt and MacArthur. MacArthur recalled that he and Roosevelt "talked of everything but the war—of our old carefree days when life was simpler and gentler, of many things that had disappeared in the mists of time."

That night Roosevelt was host for dinner. After dinner they retired to the living room for strategy talks. MacArthur recalled that Nimitz had a "tremendous paraphernalia of maps, plans, manuscripts, statistics of all sorts and other visual adjuncts. I began to realize I was to go it alone." He went on to say that Nimitz "with his fine sense of fair play" was "amazed and somewhat shocked" when he learned that MacArthur had not been told in advance what was to be discussed.

After Roosevelt had briefly outlined the purpose of the meeting, Nimitz spoke first. What he presented was the Admiral King plan. MacArthur should establish a strong operating base on Mindanao to neutralize Japanese air in the Philippines. But the rest of the Philippine Islands should be bypassed. Nimitz would advance on Formosa. For this purpose all of MacArthur's American forces save a "token" two divisions and a "few" air squadrons were to be transferred to Nimitz. By the summer of 1945, Nimitz would be ready to invade Formosa. MacArthur recalled: "The President apparently knew the general concept of the plan, but was evidently doubtful of it. He was entirely neutral in handling the discusion." One wonders how much heart Nimitz put into his briefing. As he said later, he, too, was doubtful about it.

Now it was MacArthur's turn. Roosevelt picked up a pointer and placed it on Mindanao. All were in agreement that Mindanao should be retaken. But Roosevelt said: "Douglas, where do we go from here?" MacArthur replied: "Leyte, Mr. President, and then Luzon." MacArthur followed up with a lengthy restatement of his case for retaking the Philippines. He particularly stressed the moral obligation to the loyal Filipinos. By all accounts, this moment, rhetorically, was one of MacArthur's finest hours. He made his points concisely and convincingly. But, as he wrote, the meeting adjourned at midnight "with the President making no final decision."

They met again the following morning at Roosevelt's quarters. Both Nimitz and MacArthur elaborated on their cases. This session, like the first, was as cordial as could be. Leahy was surprised at this, he recalled in his memoirs. He had come expecting fireworks. But he came away immensely impressed by both men, feeling they were the "two best qualified officers in our service for this tremendous task." MacArthur, perhaps sensing that Nimitz had no heart for the King plan, told Roosevelt that he should have no concern about any difference of opinion between them. "We see eye to eye, Mr. President. We understand each other perfectly."

This meeting—the last—adjourned at lunchtime. MacArthur had planned to leave that afternoon for Brisbane, but Roosevelt asked him to go along on another inspection tour in the limousine. During this tour (Nimitz did not go), MacArthur asked Roosevelt about the upcoming election. Roosevelt, MacArthur recalled, "seemed completely confident. In turn, he inquired what I thought were the chances. I told him I knew nothing of the political situation in the United States but that he, Roosevelt, was an overwhelming favorite with the troops. This seemed to please him greatly."

That night, while Roosevelt hosted a lawn party at his quarters, MacArthur departed for Brisbane in the "Bataan." Samuel Eliot Morison wrote that at that point, MacArthur told an aide: "We've sold it." He may have felt that—Admiral Leahy "seemed" to support his case during the meetings—but there had been no definite decision reached. The one solid achievement at Pearl Harbor had been the warm relations established between MacArthur and Roosevelt.

In fact, in the weeks following, the Joint Chiefs lapsed into a curious period of indecision. They left standing the original plan for Nimitz to invade the Palaus on Setpember 15 and converge with MacArthur's forces at Mindanao on November 15. But beyond that, nothing. King still clung to his Formosa plan, maintaining that, as Morison wrote, liberating the Philippines "would slow up the war for mere sentimental reasons." General Marshall, influenced by MacArthur's moral arguments, had swung around to MacArthur's point of view. But the

JCS appeared paralyzed. This so exasperated Nimitz that he sent his chief planner to Washington to demand a decision of some kind. Even a bad one would be better than none.

Meanwhile MacArthur's GHQ had been reviewing projected operations short of Mindanao. GHQ had previously decided that there should be an intervening step between western New Guinea and Mindanao, a landing on Halmahera. But when the codebreakers declared there were at least thirty thousand troops on Halmahera, GHQ shifted the objective to Morotai, an island north of Halmahera, which was only lightly defended by an estimated one thousand Japanese. It was decided to invade Morotai on Setpember 15, the same day Nimitz invaded the Palaus. The carriers supporting Palaus could also support MacArthur's forces at Morotai. Shortly afterwards, October 15, MacArthur's forces would leap to the island of Talaud, then Mindanao on November 15, as scheduled.

On Setpember 11, Roosevelt and Churchill met again, this time in Quebec at what was called the Octagon Conference. By that time the Joint Chiefs had reached some decisions about future operations. The most important of these was that following Mindanao, MacArthur should advance to Leyte on December 20. Thus the question of bypassing the Philippines for Formosa was reduced to that of bypassing Luzon for Formosa. That question still remained unresolved.

The decision to invade Leyte must have heartened MacArthur considerably. It gave him a partial political victory in the JCS, a toehold in the Philippines which could be expanded. It would partially fulfill his historic promise to return. But it did not please his engineers. They submitted discouragingly negative reports. The soil on the principal areas of Leyte to be occupied was swampy; the water table, only a few inches below the surface. It would be extremely difficult to refurbish the Japanese airfields for use by Kenney's air forces and, likewise, difficult to make the roads strong enough to support heavy military equipment. Moreover, the rainy season was due. When it came, it would flood the airfields and roads, bringing a sea of mud. These reports were waved aside by GHQ.

About this time Bull Halsey, now working for Nimitz

as boss of the carrier forces, was in Palaus, waters to soften up the Palaus for the invasion. Halsey, fearing another Tarawa, had urged King and Nimitz to bypass the Palaus and strike directly at the central Philippines. But now he was carrying out his orders. During the course of these operations, he sent his planes deep into the central Philippines to strike Japanese airfields. In two days, September 12 and 13, he mounted an astounding 2400 sorties. His planes shot down 173 Japanese aircraft and destroyed another 305 on the ground. The opposition had been amazingly slight. Halsey lost only 8 planes and ten men. As he wrote: "We had found the central Philippines a hollow shell with weak defenses and skimpy facilities."

This discovery led Halsey to recommend a drastic revision in forthcoming operations. He forthwith drafted a message to Nimitz recommending that the invasion of the Palaus (and a subsidiary operation, Yap) be cancelled, that MacArthur cancel the invasions of Talaud and Mindanao, that the Nimitz forces scheduled for the invasion of the Palaus and Yap be transferred to MacArthur, and that MacArthur invade Leyte as "soon as possible." Nimitz must have raised his eyebrows when he read this dispatch. He did not agree about the Palaus —he argued, wrongly, that it was too late to stop it— but he agreed with the other recommendations (including giving his troops to MacArthur) and immediately passed them to King, who was in Quebec with Roosevelt and Churchill.

Here was galvanizing news for the JCS, a way of attaining their long-sought goal of speeding up operations in the Pacific. Immediately Marshall, also in Quebec, relayed the recommendations to MacArthur. MacArthur was then embarked on Kinkaid's flagship, *Nashville,* to observe the Morotai landings. Since *Nashville* was under radio silence, he could not be reached. However, Sutherland assumed responsibility for the decision and, after consulting Kenney (who had already recommended bypassing Talaud and going directly to Leyte) and others at GHQ, wired Marshall (in MacArthur's name) that the Halsey recommendations were entirely acceptable.

Sutherland's message arrived at Quebec in the midst of a formal dinner, September 15, the day of the Morotai-Palaus landings. The Joint Chiefs excused themselves.

About ninety minutes later, they sent MacArthur and Nimitz an order to cancel Talaud, Yap, and Mindanao and to invade Leyte October 20, two months ahead of schedule and, hopefully, prior to the onset of the rainy season.

When MacArthur learned of this decision, he was delighted. He wired the JCS that the speedup would enable him to land on Luzon December 20, two months earlier than previously planned. Luzon had not yet been approved, of course, but this new plan and timetable was tempting. Gradually Marshall and Arnold joined Leahy in siding with MacArthur, leaving only King stubbornly holding out for Formosa. Later that month Nimitz, who was never keen on Formosa in the first place, cast his lot for Luzon.

That did it. On October 3, the Joint Chiefs issued a new strategic directive for the conduct of the Pacific war—their last important one. General MacArthur would invade Luzon on December 20 with a preliminary landing on Mindoro to establish air bases December 5. Nimitz would invade Iwo Jima in the Bonin Islands January 20, mainly to provide an emergency and support facility for the B–29 Super Fortresses to be based in the Marianas. On March 1, he would invade Okinawa. Perhaps in deference to King, Formosa was not specifically cancelled, but the decision to leap to Okinawa as much as implied so.

And so finally MacArthur had carried the day. His famous promise "I shall return" would now become a reality. That it would is due, in no small part, to the aggressive spirit of his friend Bull Halsey. This brash front line commander had provided the thrust that broke the logjam in the Joint Chiefs and finally swung the case for MacArthur. It is no wonder that MacArthur's admiration for Halsey was boundless.

CHAPTER
TWENTY-SEVEN

★ ★ ★ ★ ★

ABOARD THE *Nashville* on September 15, MacArthur watched his twenty-eight thousand Alamo troops storm ashore on Morotai. It was a picnic. The five hundred or so Japanese in the area fled. Not a shot was heard. Two hours after the landing MacArthur went ashore for a close look. He remained about three hours, then returned to the *Nashville,* which got under way and returned to Hollandia, where MacArthur had moved his headquarters in early September. Morotai was without question the easiest operation of the war in the Pacific.

That same day, Nimitz's forces landed on the Palaus. Here it was a different story. As Halsey had feared, it was another Tarawa. There were ten thousand crack Japanese soldiers dug in on the target island Peleliu. As at Buna, they had prepared clever and near-impregnable defenses, taking maximum advantage of the rugged terrain and the hundreds of natural caves. It took weeks to root out and kill the bulk of the defenders, and many more weeks to wipe out the stragglers. American casualties were staggering: almost two thousand killed, eight thousand wounded. Naval historian Morison sided with Halsey. The operation should have been countermanded. However there was an important offshoot: A small Nimitz force seized unoccu-

pied Ulithi to the northeast. Ulithi became an important
fleet anchorage.

At his new quarters on a hillside in Hollandia, Mac-
Arthur now gave his undivided attention to the forthcoming invasion of Leyte. It was not going to be easy.
Willoughby estimated there were about twenty-two thousand Japanese on Leyte, half combat troops, half service
troops. The combat troops included units of the veteran
16th Division which had fought at Bataan. Moreover, the
codebreakers reported that all the major units of the
Japanese fleet except the aircraft carriers (in Japan, training
new air groups) had gathered in Singapore and Borneo.
This force, which included the superbattleships *Yamato*
and *Musashi,* could attack the landing forces at Leyte.

The final plan for the Leyte operation, issued on September 21 by MacArthur (who returned to Brisbane after
only two days at Hollandia), was immensely complicated,
the largest operation yet in the Pacific. Krueger's Sixth
Army got the job. It consisted of four assault divisions and
supporting units, in all, about two-hundred thousand men.
To get Krueger's army there and protect it, Admiral Kinkaid assembled a massive fleet of over seven hundred ships.
Among these were eighteen jeep carriers, six old battleships, eleven heavy and light cruisers, and eighty-six
destroyers.

A key part of the plan was massive fast carrier support
from Nimitz. As at Hollandia, Bull Halsey's 3rd Fleet
would support MacArthur. The 3rd Fleet was then composed of 105 ships organized into four task groups, built
around the eighteen fast carriers. Technically Halsey reported directly to Nimitz, not MacArthur. But he established a close liaison with Kinkaid to whom MacArthur
delegated responsibility for all things naval. Halsey's main
job was to protect the landing forces. But his written
orders contained this important clause: "In case opportunity for destruction of major portion of the enemy fleet
is offered or can be created, such destruction becomes
the primary task."

As a preliminary to the invasion, the 3rd Fleet was
almost continuously at sea, pounding Japanese airfields.
On September 21 and 22, Halsey sent his planes against
Manila, destroying 405 Japanese planes and some ships.
Later he hit Coron Bay, destroying dozens of ships. After

refueling and replenishing at Ulithi, Halsey swung north and hit Okinawa, Luzon, and then Formosa, October 10 to 14. He destroyed another 520 Japanese aircraft, but planes from Formosa torpedoed two of his cruisers, *Houston* and *Canberra*. (They were towed home.) On October 17–18, Halsey struck Luzon again at Aparri and Manila.

Kenney's land-based air, staging from New Guinea, Biak, and the new fields on Morotai, joined in the preliminaries. His primary target was the nest of air bases on Mindanao, which lay between MacArthur and Leyte. In addition, he plastered Halmahera, Ambon, Ceram, the Celebes, and even the faraway Borneo oil refineries. Between these raids and Halsey's, Japanese aircraft losses were, in the word of Samuel Eliot Morison, "catastrophic."

Meanwhile, Kinkaid's vast amphibious forces assembled at Manus and Hollandia. From October 10 to October 15, they put to sea. On October 14 MacArthur bid Jean goodbye in Brisbane, saying "I won't be back." She knew what he meant, Sid Huff wrote. He would be on the front until Luzon was secured. She said, "You've got to send for me the minute you think it's safe for me to come to Manila." MacArthur flew to Hollandia, spent his fourth and final night at his new quarters on the hillside (spitefully and inaccurately described by MacArthur critics as a "million-dollar mansion"), then boarded Kinkaid's *Nashville*. Sutherland, Kenney, Whitney, and others joined MacArthur. Sergio Osmeña, who had become president of the Philippine government in exile upon the death of Quezon on August 1, 1944, boarded a transport, the *John Land*. On October 16, the *Nashville* sailed.

It was a moment of high drama and a poignant one for MacArthur. Now, after thirty-one months, the general was returning to his beloved Philippines. MacArthur and Kenney were awed by the size of the armada around *Nashville*. In fact, counting Halsey's 3rd Fleet, standing by off Leyte, it was the largest naval force ever assembled (above eight hundred ships). It was a dark and moonless night when they reached Leyte on October 19. MacArthur wrote: "The stygian waters below and the black sky above seemed to conspire in wrapping us in an invisible cloak, as we lay to and waited for dawn before entering Leyte Gulf." Airman Kenney wrote: "I wished I were on an airplane instead of a ship."

At dawn, the big guns on Kinkaid's ships cut loose at the beaches. The roar was incessant and deafening. At 10:00 A.M., the assault waves of Krueger's four divisions landed at Dulag and farther north near Tacloban. The Japanese did not fight on the beaches as usual. They let the Americans come ashore, then they opened up with savage mortar and artillery fire. Wave after wave of landing craft charged ashore through this withering fire, bringing tens of thousands of men and tons of supplies.

MacArthur spent the morning on the bridge of *Nashville*. After lunch, he, Sutherland, Kenney, Whitney, and other GHQ staffers and media representatives climbed into a small landing barge to go ashore. They picked up Osmeña and his retinue (including his aide Carlos P. Romulo) from the *John Land* and headed for Red Beach, opposite Tacloban, just north of Palo, where Krueger's 24th Division had landed. MacArthur, wearing a fresh new khaki uniform, dark glasses, and his famous campaign hat, sat on the engine housing. According to Whitney, he carried his father's small pistol in his pocket, to "insure that I am never captured alive." As they approached the beach, MacArthur said to Sutherland, "Well, believe it or not, we're here."

Not quite. The landing barge went aground in knee-deep water about ten yards off the beach and stuck fast. The bow ramp slammed down, and as the cameras clicked MacArthur stepped into the water and waded toward the beach. Kenney recalled that they came ashore near four larger landing craft that had been hit by mortar fire. One was "burning nicely." Moreover, Kenney wrote: "There seemed to be a lot of Nip snipers firing all around the place and the snap of the high-velocity small-calibre rifles sounded as though some of them were not over a hundred yards away."

This unexpected wade to the beach, MacArthur's dramatic return to the Philippines, provided one of the most famous pictures of World War II. It also gave rise to many false anti-MacArthur legends. The most infamous of these was that the wade was actually staged—or repeated several times, or done in a rear area, etc. Not so. William J. Dunn, one of the four media representatives (CBS radio) on the landing barge with MacArthur, has emphatically denied in print (*Army Magazine*, March 1973) any "staging" whatsoever.

Kenney recalled that after they landed on Red Beach—a small perimeter—MacArthur "calmly walked around," chatting with soldiers and generals. Kenney and Whitney both tell the following anecdote. One soldier nudged another and said, "Hey, there's General MacArthur." The other soldier replied: "Oh, yeah? And I suppose he's got Eleanor Roosevelt along with him."

The principal event for MacArthur and Osmeña on this visit was a radio address, designed to arouse the Filipino people and guerrilla forces against the Japanese. Dunn was in charge- -more or less the master of ceremonies—of this operation. He brought up a radio transmitter mounted on a weapons carrier. The transmitter was linked to a powerful master transmitter on *Nashville,* which broadcast on several wavelengths. He set up the mike and for the next fifteen minutes repeated again and again: "People of the Philippines! In just a few moments you will hear the voices of General Douglas MacArthur and President Sergio Osmeña over the wavelength to which you are now tuned."

At about 2:00 P.M., MacArthur stood at the mike in a light drizzle and spoke these memorable words: "People of the Philippines, I have returned. By the grace of Almighty God, our forces stand again on Philippine soil. . . . Rally to me! Let the indomitable spirit of Bataan and Corregidor lead on. As the lines of battle roll forward to bring you within the zone of operations, rise and strike. . . . For your homes and hearths, strike. In the name of your sacred dead, strike. . . . Let no heart be faint. Let every arm be steeled. The guidance of God points the way. Follow in His name to the Holy Grail of righteous victory."

MacArthur's critics pounced on him for this speech. They claimed it was "sacrilegious" and "in poor taste" and proved that he was an egomaniac. But these criticisms do not seem justified. They overlook MacArthur's long and close personal identification with the Filipinos and how emotional that moment was for him. "I have returned" was a natural thing to say after his long-ago promise "I shall return." As to his repeated references to the deity, it must be remembered that the majority of the seventeen million Filipinos were devout Catholics. In no way was the speech sacrilegious. As Kenney observed, the speech was not "meant for the people back home."

During the next several days MacArthur went ashore every day, keeping a close eye on the situation. Kenney was awed by MacArthur's seeming indifference to enemy bullets. As they jeeped around in forward areas they frequently were stopped by firefights—bullets whizzing all around them. Kenney was glad, he wrote, when they got back to the beach. Nor did MacArthur seem fazed by the intermittent (and largely ineffectual) Japanese air attacks. He never took cover.

Krueger's troops pushed out of the perimeter and quickly seized the two airfield objectives, one at Tacloban, one at Dulag. Kenney was gravely disappointed when he inspected them. Both were small; as GHQ engineers had predicted, the water table at each was very close to the surface. When the rainy season came, they were likely to turn into seas of mud. Kenney and Krueger ordered the engineers to begin laying down a foundation of coral gravel for the steel runway matting. But this work progressed too slowly for Kenney's liking. It was further delayed when the landing craft captains began unloading gear on the airfields. This was stopped but only after Kenney threatened to bulldoze it all into the sea.

The airfields were vital for a number of reasons. Halsey had his fast carriers and Kinkaid had the jeep carriers, but neither of these forces could stay indefinitely, especially the jeep carriers which had limited endurance. Kenney wanted his own air power brought up, not only to defend the beachhead and provide close air support for Krueger, but also to bomb the Japanese airfields on Luzon and other places from which a threat to Leyte could be mounted. It was the first time MacArthur had leaped beyond his own air cover and Kenney was decidedly uneasy about it. As we shall see, his worry was not unjustified. The failure to quickly establish air bases on Leyte would have a gravely adverse effect on operations in the coming days and weeks.

Krueger's troops soon seized Tacloban. MacArthur jeeped there with Osmeña and others. On October 23, in what Krueger described as "an impressive ceremony," MacArthur (perhaps prematurely) proclaimed the reestablishment of civil government in the Philippines, with Osmeña the President. He named the able guerrilla leader on Leyte governor of that island. The American and Philippine flags were raised side-by-side. After that, MacArthur chose a fine concrete house for his residence and headquarters. It had belonged to an American, Walter Price, who had been killed by the Japanese. Although the Japanese air attacks were beginning to increase in intensity, MacArthur ordered a bomb shelter in the sideyard bulldozed over because, as he told an incredulous Kenney, it marred the aesthetic beauty of the grounds.

So far, so good. The main objectives had been seized, casualties had been reasonably light. The beachhead appeared secure. But the Japanese were not done yet. They were then unfolding a counterreaction that would throw the entire Leyte operation into peril, bringing with it MacArthur's most anxious moments of World War II.

CHAPTER
TWENTY-EIGHT

★ ★ ★ ★ ★

THE STRATEGIC PLANNERS in Tokyo had determined in advance of Leyte that Japan would fight to the death in the Philippines. Losing the Philippines would mean losing the war; it would cut Japan off from the vital oil and rubber supplies to the south. Accordingly, orders went out to send massive reinforcements—planes, soldiers, supplies —to Manila. Much of this shipping was interdicted by Lockwood's and Christie's submarines (which in September, October, November, 1944, sank 204 ships), but too much got through. The effects would soon be felt on Leyte.

The Japanese naval planners still hoped for a single, annihilating victory over the U.S. Pacific Fleet. They had suspected that the next large-scale Allied offensive would be against the Philippines (Mindanao, not Leyte). Accordingly, they formulated a plan, known as Sho–1, to counteract the invasion. This was a desperate—near suicidal— scheme to destroy the Halsey and Kinkaid naval forces and drive MacArthur off the beaches. They would throw everything they could muster into the effort. Battleships. Carriers. Land-based air. And two new sinister suicide weapons: kamikaze aircraft and submarine-launched, human-guided torpedoes known as Kaitens. The resultant action, a series of battles stretching over four days, was known as the Battle for Leyte Gulf. As Nimitz and Potter wrote, for sheer size and complexity, it was without parallel in naval history.

There were five major Japanese naval units involved in the action. When it began, three were in Singapore, one in Amami in the Ryukus (slightly north of Okinawa), and one in the Inland Sea, Japan. On these fell the major burden of the assault. The plan was complex and hydra-headed, perhaps too much so. The force in the Inland Sea (built around four carriers) would put to sea with a noisy flourish. It was bait. It's purpose was to lure Halsey's 3rd Fleet away from Leyte, uncovering the beaches. That done, two of the three forces at Singapore (built around battleships) would attack Kinkaid at Leyte Gulf. The third force at Singapore (built around cruisers) would escort a troop-lift unit from Manila to Mindanao, landing reinforcements on the back side of Leyte.

When Krueger's advance forces landed on some outlying islands off Leyte on October 17–18, the Japanese executed operation Sho–1. The unit at Amami, known as the Shima Force, got under way to join the two forces that were to attack Kinkaid. These, plus the troop-lift escort, departed Singapore and put in at Brunei Bay, Borneo, to refuel. The Inland Sea "bait" force got up steam and prepared to put to sea. The codebreakers followed these movements and the messages between the five units, with no small interest. Lockwood and Christie positioned their submarines according to information provided by the codebreakers.

The Shima Force, composed of two heavy cruisers, a light cruiser, and four destroyers, steamed steadily southward. Nine of Lockwood's submarines lay along its track and made contact. Only one of these, *Blackfish*, was able to fire torpedoes. All missed. However, the continuous and accurate position reports from these nine submarines provided invaluable intelligence on the Shima Force movements. The force went south to the Sulu Sea.

The troop-lift escorts, the heavy cruiser *Aoba*, and light cruiser *Kinu* departed Brunei Bay first, on the night of October 22. By then, Christie had positioned a half-dozen submarines along its projected track to Manila. Two, *Darter* and *Dace*, picked up and reported the movement, gave chase, but could not reach firing position. Farther up the

line, two others, *Angler* and *Guitarro,* had similar bad
luck. But farther north yet, *Bream* (commanded by the
redoubtable Wreford G. Chapple) hit *Aoba* with two
torpedoes. She was so badly damaged that *Kinu* had to
tow her the rest of the way to Manila Thus the troop-
lift force lost its principal escort to Christie's submarines.

The two main attacking forces left Brunei Bay shortly
after, on October 22. The first—what the Americans would
call the Center Force—was composed of the superbattleships *Yamato* and *Musashi,* three older battleships, ten
heavy cruisers, two light cruisers, and fifteen destroyers.
Its orders were to cross the Sibuyan Sea, south of Luzon,
penetrate San Bernardino Strait, and swing south toward
Leyte Gulf at dawn on October 25. The second force,
called the Southern Force, consisted of two old battleships, a heavy cruiser, and four destroyers. Its orders were
to cross the Sulu Sea, go through Surigao Strait, and attack Leyte Gulf from the south.

The submarines *Darter* and *Dace* were still in position.
They submerged on the projected track. Near dawn on the
morning of October 23, the Center Force (*Yamato,
Musashi,* etc.) came right over them. *Dace* sank the
heavy cruiser *Maya, Darter* sank the heavy cruiser *Atago*
(the Center Force flagship) and severely damaged a second heavy cruiser *Takao.* This ship had to fall out and
limp back to Singapore, where she spent the remainder of
the war futilely waiting for spare parts to repair this damage. In an effort to catch her for another shot, *Darter* ran
aground and had to be abandoned. *Dace* rescued her
crew. The Southern Force, warned by this attack, resorted
to a circuitous route to avoid Christie's submarines, then
turned and ran east into the Sulu Sea. It was undetected.

As the Center Force moved north, it continued to be
dogged by Christie's submarines. *Angler* and *Guitarro*
picked it up about 8:30 P.M. that night south of Mindoro.
Neither boat could reach a firing position, but both continued to track, sending off a stream of valuable contact
reports, which were passed on to Halsey and Kinkaid.
When dawn came on the twenty-fourth, they were forced
for their own safety to break off the chase and submerge.
But their reports led to the inescapable conclusion that
the Center Force was headed for San Bernardino Strait.

The "bait" force in the Inland Sea, called the Northern
Force, got under way on October 20. It consisted of the

heavy carrier *Zuikaku;* three light carriers *Zuiho, Chitose,* and *Chiyoda;* two battleships *Hyuga* and *Ise;* three light cruisers, and eight destroyers. Three Lockwood submarines were guarding the exits to the Inland Sea, but they were in the wrong place. The Northern Force slipped out to sea unseen. Had this been known, the Japanese would have been disappointed. Being bait, they wanted to be seen.

After *Angler* and *Guitarro* broke off the chase of Center Force at dawn on the twenty-fourth, Halsey's planes took up the reconnaissance. A short time later, at 8:12 A.M., a plane from *Intrepid* found it and broadcast a contact. At that time, three of Halsey's four carrier task groups were in position to do battle. (The fourth was returning to Ulithi for refueling.) Halsey instantly ordered his three task groups to converge near the eastern end of San Bernardino Strait and the fourth to come back and refuel at sea.

During that day Halsey's planes attacked Center Force in the Sibuyan Sea. It was a furious, remarkable action. Halsey's planes sank the unsinkable superbattleship *Musashi* and so badly damaged the heavy cruiser *Myoko,* she had to withdraw to Brunei Bay. Land-based Japanese aircraft attacked Halsey's forces, damaging the carrier *Princeton* so severely she had to be torpedoed and sunk by an American cruiser. The cruiser *Birmingham,* attempting to aid the mortally wounded *Princeton,* was so badly damaged by an explosion on *Princeton* she had to return to the States for repairs. At the end of the day Halsey was ecstatic. Putting too much faith in the greatly exaggerated reports of his pilots, he believed the Center Force had been all but wiped out and that the surviving ships had withdrawn. In fact, Center Force (including superbattleship *Yamato*) was mostly intact. It had not withdrawn. It was bearing down on San Bernardino Strait.

That same day, far to the south, the Southern Force, closely trailed by the Shima Force, had been detected by Allied aircraft in the Sulu Sea, obviously headed for Surigao Strait. Some of Kinkaid's jeep carrier planes struck it a glancing blow, inflicting minor damage on the old battleship *Fuso* and a destroyer. As this force passed on, Kinkaid prepared to ambush it in a night battle in Surigao Strait. He deployed PT boats and destroyers ahead of his cruisers and battleships. The PTs mounted a fruitless attack. Then came the destroyers. In a brilliant salvo of forty-seven torpedoes, the destroyers hit both of the battle-ships, sinking one, *Fuso*. They also sank a destroyer and put two others out of action. More Kinkaid destroyers charged in and again hit the surviving battleship, *Yama-shiro*, and sank one of the disabled destroyers. Then the cruisers and battleships opened up, sinking *Yamashiro* and crippling the heavy cruiser *Mogami*.

The trailing Shima Force now closed up. The PTs dam-aged the cruiser *Abukuma* with a torpedo. Shima Force's flagship *Nachi* collided with the crippled *Mogami*. In the face of withering fire, the Shima Force ordered a with-drawal. The Kinkaid surface and air forces (from the jeep carriers) pursued, sinking a damaged destroyer and again damaging *Mogami*, this time so badly that she was de-stroyed by the Japanese. By dawn, all that was left of the Southern Force was one battered destroyer. But the Shima Force was still intact.

The Northern Force, or bait, had been doing everything possible to attract Halsey's attention that day. It made heavy smoke. It broke radio silence on various frequen-cies. It sent an advance guard of destroyers, hoping Halsey would see them. It sent planes to attack Halsey's ships. But Halsey had been too busy all that day with the Center Force. It was not until late in the afternoon that one of Halsey's scouts actually saw and reported the pres-ence of, the Northern Force.

Halsey now faced a fateful decision. Go after the Northern Force or stay close by Kinkaid's landing forces? Reasoning that Kinkaid could easily handle the Southern Force and Shima Force, and that the Center Force had been wiped out—a grave error—and that an offensive pos-ture was better than a defensive posture, Halsey ordered his entire force north toward the bait. In yet another mis-taken assumption that would lead to grave consequences on the morrow, Kinkaid believed that Halsey had left a strong force of battleships guarding San Bernardino Strait, thus protecting his right flank. Halsey had not. He over-estimated the size of the Northern Force and did not want to divide his own forces. In fact, he did not leave so much as a destroyer picket to guard the strait.

During that night the Center Force steamed through San Bernardino Strait undetected and turned south for Leyte Gulf. It heard that the Southern Force had been ambushed and that the Shima Force had withdrawn. That meant the southern pincer no longer existed. The Center Force would have to go it alone, a suicidal mission. Urged on by a patriotic message from Tokyo, it continued on the original plan, not knowing if Halsey had taken the bait or if he lay in wait over the horizon.

At dawn, a lookout on *Yamato* reported masts on the horizon. As they drew closer, the Japanese believed these masts to be Halsey's carriers. In fact, they were part of Kinkaid's jeep carrier force with destroyer escorts. The Japanese opened fire. The vulnerable jeep carriers, taken completely by surprise, ran for Leyte Gulf where Kinkaid's battleships had converged. The little carriers laid smoke screens, ducked into rain squalls, zigzagged, launched planes and destroyers against Center Force. It was a furious, David and Goliath battle, one of the bravest in the history of the Navy. The destroyers and planes so thoroughly harassed Center Force that it fell into confusion, circling idiotically, breaking formation and shooting wildly with the wrong kind of ammunition.

About this same time, far to the north, Halsey launched his aircraft against the Northern Force. In the midst of this operation, he received the startling news that the Center Force he thought his aviation had destroyed was attacking Kinkaid's carriers and that Kinkaid desperately needed help. Still he was not overly concerned. He thought that Kinkaid's sixteen jeep carriers plus battleships could handle whatever was left of Center Force. His orders from Nimitz contained that important clause that destruction of "a major portion of the enemy fleet" was his primary task. Not realizing the Northern Force was bait, and not knowing that it was only feebly equipped, Halsey considered it to be the graver threat of the two and that its destruction was absolutely necessary for the safety of the whole Leyte operation.

So he continued the attack on the Northern Force. His pilots did remarkably well. In repeated assaults during the day, they sank all four carriers, a destroyer, and badly damaged the cruiser *Tama*, which, that night, was polished off by Lockwood's submarine *Jallao*. The rest of the Northern Force fled under heavy air attack. A dozen of Lockwood's submarines gave chase, some firing torpedoes, but the surviving ships made it back to the Inland Sea. The Northern Force had been decimated, but it had accomplished its objective of luring Halsey away from Leyte.

Meanwhile, the Center Force, after regrouping, again pressed on toward Leyte Gulf, attacking the jeep carriers and their escorts. An American destroyer, a destroyer escort, and the jeep carrier *Gambier Bay* were sunk. Other ships were heavily damaged. Kinkaid was in near-panic. He could not bring out his battleships. They were deployed defensively at Leyte Gulf to ward off a possible attack by the Shima Force, and besides that, Kinkaid wrongly believed they were too low on ammunition. He sent off a series of messages to Halsey—one in plain language—begging for assistance.

Halsey was exasperated. Then came a message from Nimitz, inquiring as to his location. As was customary, the encoders had inserted some padding into the message, but it was a highly inappropriate group of words on this occasion. The message, as handed to Halsey, read: "The whole world wants to know where is Task Force 34." Halsey, not realizing "The whole world wants to know" was padding, mistook the message as a goading rebuke from Nimitz. He was enraged. Then, in a decision he would regret the rest of his life, he broke off the pursuit of the Northern Force and swung south to go to Kinkaid's aid.

Meantime, the aircraft from Kinkaid's jeep carriers were putting up a heroic attack on Center Force. Fortunately, the Japanese antiaircraft fire was no better than the naval gunfire. The planes bore in continuously, inflicting severe damage on two heavy cruisers and confusing and distracting others. Some jeep-carrier based planes no longer had a "home." They landed on other carriers to reload or made for Kenney's fields at Tacloban and Dulag. The fields were yet too soft, and many planes (twenty-eight) crashed on landing. But others survived, reloaded, and flew back into battle. Many pilots, out of ammunition, gallantly made diverting "dry runs" against the enemy ships to help those pilots who had bombs.

The Japanese were completely confused. Wrongly believing the jeep carriers to be Halsey's fast carriers, and the destroyers to be heavy battleships, and that other reinforcements were on the way and not having any word from the Shima or Northern Forces, they began to lose heart. Shortly after noon, to the astonishment of Kinkaid and everyone else at Leyte Gulf, the Center Force broke off the attack and turned north. It slipped through San Bernardino Strait (avoiding a direct confrontation with Halsey coming down from the north) and sped west. Halsey's planes caught up with it later, sinking a cruiser. But four battleships, three cruisers, and seven destroyers escaped.

The jeep carriers were not yet out of trouble That day Japan unleashed its Kamikaze Corps. These suicide planes, staging from Davao, attacked nine of the surviving seventeen jeep carriers. The *St. Io* went down from the attacks. The others survived, but many were severely damaged, and a Japanese submarine sank the destroyer *Eversole*, which was searching for survivors of *Gambier Bay* and *St. Io*. The battered, decimated jeep carrier force was withdrawn to Manus. Seldom had any United States naval force fought more bravely or suffered so severely.

Japan also unleashed its other sinister suicidal weapon, the *Kaiten*. Four I-class submarines, each fitted with four human-guided torpedoes, set off from Japan for the American fleet anchorages at Ulithi and in the Palaus. However, American codebreakers were especially adept at reading Japanese submarine codes. (This fact had rendered Japan's large submarine force virtually useless.) Two of the four submarines were sunk en route to station. Two reached Ulithi. Both fired their human torpedoes, blowing up the fleet tanker *Mississinewa*. Beyond this initial success, the Kaiten program, hobbled by a shortage of mother ships and torpedoes, and hounded by the codebreakers, failed to achieve much else in the war. One Kaiten sank the *Underhill* at Okinawa, and one may have been responsible for the sinking of the *Indianapolis*.

So ended the Battle for Leyte Gulf. For MacArthur—and Kinkaid—it had been a near thing. Very near. If the Center Force had pressed the attack, it could well have entered Leyte Gulf and destroyed everything in sight, stranding MacArthur as he had been stranded at Bataan. As naval historian Morison wrote, Halsey's 3rd Fleet alone could not have maintained MacArthur's communications. But the Center Force had stopped short of its goal. The price of Sho–1 had been fearful for the Japanese: four carriers, three battleships, ten cruisers, nine destroyers. The United States in total lost one carrier, two jeep carriers, two destroyers, and a destroyer escort. The Japanese Fleet would never again fight as an integrated unit.

During most of this action MacArthur followed developments from *Nashville*. Kenney wrote: "MacArthur wasn't saying much, but he didn't act too happy, either. We kept pretty close to the radio . . ." Morison reports that on October 24, Kinkaid told MacArthur *Nashville* would be needed in the Battle of Surigao Strait and that he would be well-advised to move his headquarters ashore. MacArthur demurred. He wanted to go along. He wrote: "All my life I had been reading and studying naval combat, and the glamour of a sea battle had always excited my imagination." Kinkaid was adamant, stating "I will not commit the *Nashville* as long as GHQ is aboard."

In his memoirs MacArthur wrote that with that he moved GHQ ashore on the twenty-fourth—and *Nashville* steamed into "honored position in the battleline." In fact, as Morison reported, MacArthur did *not* move that day, and Kinkaid was forced to withhold *Nashville* from combat. The next day, after the Center Force attacked the jeep carriers, Kinkaid urgently requested MacArthur to shift to Krueger's flagship, *Wasatch*, because *Nashville* was "badly needed with combatant forces." MacArthur moved to *Wasatch* at the height of the battle against Center Force. He wrote: "It was a dramatic situation fraught with disaster. . . . I could do nothing but consolidate my troops, tighten my lines, and await the impending outcome of the naval battle." The next day, October 26, after the battle, MacArthur moved ashore to his quarters in Tacloban.

Though some naval historians have faulted Halsey's action in this battle, MacArthur did not. When criticism of Halsey inevitably cropped up in GHQ, Kenney reported, MacArthur pounded the table and said: "That's enough. . . . Leave the Bull alone. He's still a fighting admiral in my book." MacArthur sent Halsey a message: "We have cooperated with you so long that we expect your brilliant success. Everyone here has a feeling of complete confidence and inspiration when you go into action in our support." Like Halsey, MacArthur laid the blame on the confusion of a divided command. MacArthur wrote:

I have never ascribed the unfortunate incidents of this naval battle to faulty judgment on the part of any of the commanders involved. The near disaster can be placed squarely at the door of Washington. In the navel action, two key American commanders were independent of each other, one under me, and the other under Admiral Nimitz 5,000 miles away, both operating in the same waters and in the same battle. The Seventh Fleet of my force performed magnificently, as they always had, and always would, and Admiral Kinkaid wrote his name in this engagement among the greatest leaders in our naval annals.

CHAPTER
TWENTY-NINE

★ ★ ★ ★ ★

FOR MACARTHUR, Leyte quickly turned into a nightmare. Sho–1 had failed, but the Japanese did not let it go at that. For them, Leyte was still do or die. They hurled every available combat aircraft and kamikaze at the Allied ships in Leyte Gulf and the forces ashore. Almost daily, they sent large convoys of troop reinforcements from Manila to Ormoc, on the back side of Leyte. The furious air attacks caused much damage to Kinkaid's ships, interfered with the unloading of critically needed supplies, and retarded work on the airfields and roads. Then the rains came in unending torrents (thirty-five inches in the next forty-five days, about double the normal rainfall for the rainy season), turning the entire zone of occupation into a vast quagmire of mud—just as the GHQ engineers had predicted.

Militarily, the overriding problem was that the Allies had not yet achieved air superiority. The battered jeep carrier force had retired. Halsey's pilots were exhausted and their supplies running low. Halsey hung around a few more days, but was forced to return to Ulithi for replenishment. It was not until October 27 (seven days after the initial landings) that Kenney could bring a limited number (thirty-four) of fighters forward to the hastily and imperfectly refurbished, small Tacloban airfield. But the operation of these aircraft (and further reinforcements on October 31) was severely limited by the poor condition of the field and facilities, and by the onset of the rainy season with its bad flying weather, and by persistent Japanese air attacks. Attempts to refurbish or build airfields at other locations had to be mostly abandoned due to impossible soil conditions.

It was for that reason that the Japanese were able to send the convoys of troop reinforcements to Ormoc, almost with impunity. (Christie's submarines attacked these heavily defended convoys, but the attacks were largely unsuccessful.) In the ten days between D-day and October 30, the Japanese sent seven convoys to Ormoc without Allied air opposition. These landed tens of thousands of troops and thousands of tons of supplies without a single battle casualty. The arrival of these reinforcements, together with the inclement weather and mud, would significantly retard Allied operations on Leyte, causing many additional thousands of Allied casualties and, ultimately, a postponement of the assault on Luzon.

At Tacloban airfield, General Kenney was a man beset and frustrated. All day and night Japanese aircraft strafed and bombed the field, forcing Kenney repeatedly to dive for slit trenches. He was desperately trying to get the steel mat runway built. And now the inadequate Leyte roads were being churned to pieces by Allied military vehicles; many engineers were pulled off the airfield work to build equally desperately needed roads. "There weren't enough engineers," Kenney complained in his memoirs.

By November 1, however, the Tacloban field was in good enough shape and had enough planes to begin operations against the Japanese reinforcement operation at Ormoc. That day, a large (fourteen-ship) Japanese convoy arrived with eleven thousand troops and supplies. Kenney's planes hit the convoy at dawn and kept attacking all day. The planes sank one merchant ship which was ninety percent unloaded and inflicted personnel casualties by strafing, but most of the troops and supplies were unloaded. In the following days, the Japanese landed more troops and supplies. By November 12, the official Army historian reports, the Japanese had landed an estimated forty-five thousand troops—a two hundred percent reinforcement—and ten thousand tons of supplies. In sum, Kenney's few planes could do little or nothing to stop the Ormoc operation.

Naval historian Morison described the situation as "serious." If the reinforcement operation were not stopped quickly, Leyte might turn into another Guadalcanal, a prolonged and bloody battle in the swamps and jungles. MacArthur urgently requested that Halsey's 3rd Fleet return and provide air support. Halsey was then preparing a project dear to his heart: a massive carrier assault on the Japanese home islands. Nimitz ordered this plan abandoned and the 3rd Fleet back to Leyte. Disappointed, Halsey led three of his four carrier task groups to Leyte waters in early November. He conducted a two-day strike on Luzon, destroying 439 Japanese aircraft and attacked shipping in the bays and harbors, sinking the heavy cruiser *Nachi*, among other vessels.

On the night of November 10–11, the codebreakers detected yet another large (fifteen-ship) convoy embarked from Manila to Ormoc. MacArthur requested Halsey to interdict this convoy with all possible air strength. Halsey launched 347 planes at dawn on November 11. They found the convoy about one mile off Ormoc. In this attack, and follow up attacks, every ship of the convoy was destroyed, a remarkable achievement. Morison reported that "of the about 10,000 troops embarked in this convoy, all save a few who swam ashore were drowned . . ." Two weeks went by before the Japanese were able to collect enough ships to mount another effort, although other reinforcements continued to arrive by barges and lighters.

Halsey now redirected his attention to Luzon, the source of Japanese reinforcements and air attacks. In repeated strikes during the remainder of November, his aircraft again inflicted severe damage on airfields and harbors. They sank the previously damaged heavy cruiser *Kumano*, light cruiser *Kiso*, five destroyers, and about ten merchant ships, all of which could have been utilized in the Ormoc resupply operation. Japanese aircraft and kamikazes attacked Halsey's ships, badly damaging *Intrepid*, *Cabot*, and *Essex*. (Three other carriers, *Lexington*, *Franklin*, and *Belleau Wood*, had been damaged earlier.) At the end of November, Halsey withdrew most of his war-weary ships to Ulithi for repairs and replenishment. The November 3rd Fleet operations, Morison wrote, significantly impaired the

Japanese ability to reinforce Leyte: far more so, at any rate, than Kenney's efforts.

Meanwhile, Kenney still only had two airfields in operation, Tacloban and Dulag, both small. The rainy season was in full sway. The city of Tacloban, Kenney recalled, was "knee deep" in mud. It took three hours to travel the mud bog called a road between Tacloban and Dulag airfields. The engineers worked feverishly to keep the roads and airfields open. But everything slowed to a crawl, including air sorties. With his limited aircraft, Kenney concentrated against Ormoc, achieving limited success. But he was not able to provide close air support for Krueger's ground forces, a major shortcoming.

The air situation was partially remedied at the end of November. MacArthur requested that Nimitz send several squadrons of highly skilled Marine Corps fighters from the Solomons and the Palaus. Nimitz promptly sent eighty-seven Marine aircraft and support units. These planes provided limited close air support for Krueger's ground troops and defended Tacloban and Dulag airfields against the persisting and damaging night air attacks. But the air situation was still considered critical and would remain critical throughout the costly Leyte campaign. Never again would MacArthur attempt an invasion without adequate land-based air support.

All things considered, it is not surprising that after the successful landing operation, Krueger's ground troops began to bog down. Bog is the word, both figuratively and literally. With the onset of the rainy season, the primary objective, Leyte Valley, became a sea of mud. The battle plan had been designed to utilize the few roads through the swamps and rice paddies. But under continuous hard use, these roads crumbled so badly they had to be restricted largely to emergency traffic. The Japanese had prepared defenses skillfully utilizing the swampy terrain. Allied casualties began to mount at an alarming rate.

MacArthur, established ashore in Tacloban, was, by all accounts, a model of the brave and unflappable general. The Walter Price house became a main target for Japanese bombers and strafers. The memoirs of this period are redolent with awestruck tales of MacArthur conducting meetings and briefings with his staff in the midst of a bombing attack without so much as batting an eyelash.

On several occasions MacArthur narrowly missed being killed. The house was pockmarked with bullet and shell holes, but fortunately, no one at GHQ (nor any visitor) was ever so much as scratched.

The official Army historian wrote that MacArthur left the conduct of the land battle entirely in the hands of General Krueger and his Sixth Army. MacArthur, as he wrote, merely "closely" followed the unfolding situation. Dr. James rightly finds this a little hard to believe, considering MacArthur's personality and the gravely unfavorable situation on Leyte during the early weeks. In fact, James reported, MacArthur became dissatisfied with Krueger's slow progress and considered relieving him of command. From this, it is not unreasonable to infer that MacArthur played a far larger role than mere observer. No doubt he, in effect, assumed tactical command.

There was other trouble in the high command, James reported. Against all common sense (and official policy), General Sutherland brought his secretary, an Australian woman, to Tacloban and had her commissioned as an officer in the Women's Army Corps. Furious—and fearing a GHQ scandal—MacArthur royally chewed out Sutherland and promptly had the woman shipped home. From that point onward, James said, Sutherland fell from favor at GHQ. Courtney Whitney, a "pompous, opportunistic officer who was probably the most despised by other members of the GHQ" would rise to become MacArthur's alter ego. Wrote James: "It would develop into the strangest relationship of MacArthur's entire career—and undoubtedly the most damaging to his reputation."

By early November Krueger had got about 100,000 combat troops ashore, plus thousands of supporting personnel. These were organized into two corps (X Corps with the 1st Cavalry and 24th Infantry divisions, XXIV Corps with the 7th and 96th Infantry divisions plus other units). All of these outfits, save the 96th Infantry Division, had previously served in combat. The X Corps had landed near Tacloban and pushed northwestward to Carigara. The XXIV Corps had landed near Dulag and pushed westward toward Ormoc. But both corps, facing about 70,000 Japanese (many of them skilled veterans of the China campaign) determined to fight to the death, found the fighting on Leyte more savage and difficult than any previous campaign. All too soon, MacArthur faced a stalemate. The ground troops could not achieve their planned objectives.

By mid-November Krueger's troops were in a bad way. They had been fighting in the mud for three intense weeks. They were exhausted and dispirited. They were short of everything but especially ammunition, food, and hospital facilities. Because of an inexplicable accounting system at GHQ, many commanders were unable to obtain adequate replacements for the many casualties from combat and jungle diseases. For all these reasons, it became necessary to bring in three more Army divisions: the 32nd, the 77th, and the 11th Airborne. By the end of November, MacArthur had about 180,000 soldiers on Leyte. Still victory was not in sight by a long shot.

What was needed was a bold, imaginative stroke. MacArthur provided it: a daring plan to make a surprise subsidiary amphibious landing at Ormoc, coordinated with a major frontal assault by both the X and XXIV Corps. This would deny that major staging and resupply base to the Japanese and split the Japanese forces already entrenched on Leyte from the rear while they were being asaulted from the front.

When the plan was approved, Krueger selected the newly arrived 77th Division for the amphibious assault. It landed at Ormoc with complete surprise on Pearl Harbor Day, December 7. It met little resistance on the beaches, but kamikazes and fighters inflicted severe damage on five ships of the amphibious force. Recovering from the surprise, the Japanese ground forces put up a stiff fight for Ormoc, but by December 10 the port was secure. The 77th pushed beyond and on December 21, linked up with elements of the X Corps, which (with XXIV Corps) was assaulting Ormoc frontally. The result was total success for the Americans. The Japanese were now denied Ormoc, had been divided from the rear and thrown into confusion, forced to entrench in the mountains in suicidal units.

All the while MacArthur, GHQ, and Krueger and his 6th Army staff had been devoting much time and work to the forthcoming invasion of Mindoro and Luzon, scheduled for December 5 and 20, respectively. Mindoro was lightly held. At first it was thought it would be a picnic. But now Kenney, perhaps grown more cautious after his failure on Leyte, began to hedge. It was about 260 miles from his Leyte airfields to Mindoro, a long round trip for fighters. To maintain continuous air cover over the beaches, many planes would have to take off or land in the dark at Leyte. Many of Kenney's pilots lacked night flying experience. Besides that, the crowded conditions of the fields on Leyte would severely limit the number of planes he could send. And then there was the weather. If it was bad, he could not provide much help. In sum, Kenney could not absolutely guarantee air superiority over Mindoro.

This was a blow. Mindoro was necessary for Luzon—to provide air strips for land-based planes. It could not be cancelled. MacArthur had sworn never to make another invasion beyond range of his land-based air, as he had done at Leyte. But now there was no alternative. Once again he would have to depend entirely on Navy carriers for air support—until fields could be built on Mindoro. That meant again calling on the jeep carriers as well as Halsey's fast carriers. Kinkaid was violently opposed. To send the frail jeeps 260 miles into Japanese territory, where kamikazes could take off from any one of the seventy known airfields, could be suicidal. But in the end, he yielded.

This change in plan, plus the slow progress on Leyte and a temporary lack of shipping, forced a postponement in the Mindoro and Luzon operations to December 15 and January 9, respectively. MacArthur was sorely disappointed, but GHQ and Krueger were delighted. They felt that MacArthur was rushing things. Inasmuch as Nimitz's fast carriers had been committed to help MacArthur, the postponement caused a postponement in Nimitz's plans as well. Iwo Jima was put off from January 20 to February 19; Okinawa, from March 1 to April 1. So, miserable Leyte cut into everyone's plans.

The grim, dirty task of rooting out the fanatical Japanese holdouts on Leyte fell to General Eichelberger. On Christmas Day he relieved Krueger (substituting his Eighth Army command for Krueger's Sixth Army command but keeping the same troops) so that Krueger could organize for the January 9 assault on Luzon. To Eichelberger's dismay, that same day MacArthur declared that all organized resistance on Leyte had ceased and that Eichelberger's troops would merely carry out the mopping up.

That description, Eichelberger wrote bitterly, was demeaning, inaccurate, and "not a good enough phrase to die for." It took his troops another four months to liquidate the Japanese on Leyte. When all was said and done, there were only 828 prisoners taken out of the estimated 70,000 Japanese defenders. Some (no more than a thousand) slipped out in canoes, but most were killed—or died of starvation or disease—at least one third during the so-called mopping up. Allied casualties, too, had been severe: 15,500, of which 3,500 were dead.

Coincidental with the premature announcement of victory on Leyte, MacArthur received another star. Congress had created a new super-rank known as General of the Army. Marshall, MacArthur, Eisenhower, and the Air Corps' Hap Arnold were promoted to five stars. (At the same time Leahy, King, and Nimitz were promoted to the five-star rank of "Fleet Admiral.") MacArthur's chief engineer, L. Jack Sverdrup, had a Tacloban native fashion the new collar insignia from melted-down coins of the six nations which then had military forces serving under MacArthur's command: United States, Australia, New Zealand, the Netherlands East Indies, Holland and the Philippines. In a little ceremony at headquarters on the day after Christmas, GHQ staffers pinned the new insignia on the general's collar tabs. MacArthur radioed President Roosevelt his thanks.

CHAPTER
THIRTY

★ ★ ★ ★ ★

THE INVASION OF Luzon, the last campaign of World War II that MacArthur would directly command, and by far his largest and most complex, began with the Mindoro sideshow. Neither MacArthur, Kenney, Kinkaid, nor Krueger were on the scene. Busy at their respective Leyte headquarters with the fighting on Leyte and the final planning for Luzon itself, they gave the responsibility to subordinates and watched from a distance.

The Mindoro invasion force was rather small, comparatively. Kinkaid sent a covering and bombardment task group of six jeep carriers, three battleships, three heavy cruisers, and eighteen destroyers. The assault force, which would land about 30,000 men, including service troops and airmen, was made up of about 135 ships plus 23 PT boats and a miscellaneous collection of auxiliary craft. Kinkaid's *Nashville* was the flagship. These units got under way from Leyte Gulf and the Palaus. Admiral Halsey's vast 3rd Fleet left from Ulithi about the same time to pound the airfields on Luzon again.

En route to Mindoro, the assault force was detected by a Japanese plane on December 13. That day and the following, as it steamed toward its objective, it was attacked brutally by kamikazes. The flagship, *Nashville*, and a destroyer were so badly damaged they had to return to Leyte Gulf. On D-day, December 15, more waves of kamikazes struck the fleet off the Mindoro beaches. The ships threw up a wall of antiaircraft fire, destroying many of the suicide planes. Kenney's fighters from Leyte got others. But some kamikazes got through, utterly destroying two LSTs.

The assault troops met no opposition whatsoever. There were only five hundred Japanese garrison troops on Mindoro. As at Hollandia and Aitape, these fled for the hills in fright By noon all primary objectives had been seized. By nightfall, Kenney reported, the engineers were already at work on two airstrips. Here the soil was blessedly firm and dry, ideal for the purpose. Five days later, Kenney wrote, he moved fighters to Mindoro. More followed rapidly, as the facilities were completed in record-breaking time It was a far cry from Leyte.

Supporting the Mindoro landings, Halsey's thirteen fast carriers attacked Luzon December 14–16. His planes flew 1671 sorties, mostly against Luzon airfields, where they established a continuous patrol known as the Big Blue Blanket This blocked any chance the Japanese had for sending aircraft or kamikazes from Luzon to Mindoro. During these operations, Halsey's planes claimed to have destroyed 270 Japanese planes, about 208 on the ground. After the air blockade was established, not one Japanese plane from Luzon got through to Mindoro. No doubt MacArthur and Kinkaid were thankful for that.

Following this, on December 18, Halsey's fleet was dealt a devastating blow—by Mother Nature. A small but vicious typhoon, undetected by the Navy's legions of weather forecasters, struck virtually without warning. Three destroyers which had failed to take on saltwater ballast capsized and sank. Seven other ships were badly damaged. About 186 aircraft were blown overboard or jettisoned. In all, eight hundred officers and men were lost. For the next four days, Halsey's ships were busy searching the rolling seas for survivors. After that, the typhoon passed over Luzon, preventing further air attacks. Halsey limped back to Ulithi, his fleet looking as though it had fought a major sea battle. A Court of Inquiry later rapped his knuckles for this fiasco; but Nimitz, in his endorsement, rightly took much of the onus off Halsey, blaming the debacle on "insufficient information."

During the Mindoro invasion the Japanese had positioned the remnants of their naval fleet in three areas: the Inland Sea (home waters), Singapore, and Camranh Bay, Indochina. These consisted of the superbattleship *Yamato*, five other battleships, four carriers (mostly lacking air groups), ten cruisers, about forty destroyers, and forty-three submarines. Had these ships put to sea as an organized entity, they might well have been more than a match for the Mindoro invasion fleet. But the Japanese Navy was now completely disorganized and dispirited, no longer able to mount any kind of effective action. Every time a ship moved, even in what was supposed to be Japanese-controlled waters, it was hounded by United States submarines, which in 1944 alone sank seven Japanese carriers, one battleship, nine cruisers, scores of destroyers, and dozens of important fleet tankers and auxiliaries.

Even so, the Japanese Navy did not let Mindoro go without a gesture. On Christmas Eve, a force of one heavy and one light cruiser and six destroyers (originally the Shima Force) steamed out of Camranh Bay to attack the assault forces at Mindoro. Skillfully eluding a half-dozen American submarines, it raced across the South China Sea, concealed by dirty weather kicked up by the typhoon. Approaching Mindoro, it was spotted by a U.S. Navy plane which gave the alarm, mistaking the heavy cruiser for the battleship *Yamato*.

By that time Kinkaid had withdrawn the main support force of jeep carriers and battleships (needed for Luzon), leaving the Mindoro landing craft almost defenseless. *Yamato* could make mincemeat of what was left. It could be Leyte Gulf all over again. Gravely concerned, Kinkaid ordered a task force of four jeep carriers and eight destroyers from his command to the rescue. But he need not have bothered. By that time Kenney had more than a hundred planes on his two Mindoro strips. They swarmed into the air while the twenty-odd PT boats at Mindoro put to sea. After a brief ineffectual half-hour bombardment, the Japanese ships were driven off by the planes and PT boats. Remarkably, one PT boat sank one of the Japanese destroyers. That was the end of the naval threat to Mindoro.

Meanwhile the main Luzon invasion force had been gathering in various ports. The ground troops, commanded by Krueger, numbered some 200.000 men, of which 130,000 were combat soldiers, the rest service troops. (Another 80,000 men would land later, bringing the total troop commitment to more than 280,000 men.) The Sixth Army shock troops were organized into two main units, I Corps (6th and 43rd Infantry divisions), and XIV Corps (37th and 40th Infantry divisions), with countless support units. It was by far the largest operation in the Pacific to date. There were so many ships involved, no one ever bothered to count them—probably upwards of a thousand.

MacArthur's final plan for the reconquest of Luzon was remarkably similar to the Japanese plan three years earlier. The main assault forces, I and XIV corps, would land on the shores of Lingayen Gulf and drive down the broad, open plain toward Manila. Lesser forces would land on the coast northwest of Subic Bay and at Nasugbu, south of Manila Bay. These lesser forces were designed to seal off the Bataan Peninsula and Corregidor (so the Japanese could not withdraw there as MacArthur had) and to—hopefully-—seize Manila from the rear, or south, in a lightning dash. The primary objective was to destroy the Japanese military. But an important secondary objective was to rescue Allied POWs before the Japanese murdered them.

The Japanese high command had shrewdly anticipated all of this, including the timing of D-day. There were about 275,000 troops in the defense garrison. The high command might well have organized defensive positions at the beaches for a "decisive battle," but the decisive battle had been fought, and lost, on Leyte. The Japanese troops on Luzon, the official Army historian wrote, were a bedraggled lot. United States submarines, operating in wolf packs in the Formosa and Luzon Straits, and Halsey's carrier strikes had virtually isolated them. They had no air power. They were critically short of food, ammunition, medicine, gasoline, even artillery. They were ill-trained, poorly led, and grown soft from the long years of garrison duty. After the disaster of Leyte, where the best units had been decimated or cut off, the Philippine garrison had no stomach for a showdown battle at the beaches.

Accordingly, the Japanese plan for the defense of Luzon was fundamentally static, designed not to win but to oc-

cupy MacArthur, delaying the inevitable assault on Japan
for as long as possible. They considered holing up on
Bataan, as MacArthur had done, but rejected that scheme.
Bataan was too confined for 270,000 men. Instead they
resorted to a strategy some military analysts believe Mac-
Arthur should have adopted in 1941. They retreated to
three separate, strongly defended, mountain redoubts. One
to the northeast in the Caraballo range (152,000 men),
one in the western Zambales range (30,000 men) dominating Clark Field, and the third in the Sierra Madre range
(80,000 men) east of Manila. Manila itself would be left
undefended—but as we shall see, this part of the plan
went awry.

As a preliminary to the invasion, Halsey again went
to sea with his 3rd Fleet, now patched up from the typhoon. Leaving Ulithi December 30, Halsey swung north
to hit Formosa January 3–4, to prevent those forces from
sending air support to Luzon. But again Mother Nature
dealt Halsey a setback. Formosa was socked in by thick
weather—a solid overcast. Halsey sent off his planes
(twenty-two were lost), but the results were inconclusive
and Halsey claimed no damage. He retired to refuel and
to prepare a second strike against Formosa.

Meanwhile the Air Corps was doing its share—or more.
Kenney's heavy and light bombers, basing from the Palaus
or Mindoro, and fighters from Mindoro swept over Luzon
in ever-increasing numbers, smashing Japanese airfields or
shooting down kamikazes and fighters. From bases in
China and the Marianas, B–29 Super Fortresses conducted
high altitude bombing attacks against Formosa, the Ryukyus and southern Japan, concentrating on air bases.
These continuous air attacks destroyed many Japanese
aircraft and seriously impeded efforts to send aircraft to
Luzon.

Kinkaid's covering and preinvasion bombardment force
had now set sail for Lingayen Gulf. This was a mighty
armada of 164 bristling warships—twelve jeep carriers,
six battleships, six cruisers, thirty-nine destroyers, and destroyer escorts, and a host of minesweepers and other
auxiliaries. As this armada approached Luzon the kamikaze pounced on it in force, causing fearful damage. From
January 3 to January 8 inclusive, they made thirty-six hits
or very near misses on Kinkaid's ships, four on the jeep
carriers, one of which had to be sunk (*Ommaney Bay*).

In addition, two destroyers were sunk, three cruisers, and many other vessels were severely damaged. Hundreds of sailors were killed or wounded.

This was the worst blow the U.S. Navy had suffered, since the grim days of 1942 in the Solomons. The Navy was jarred. It appeared that the Japanese had at last come up with a weapon that could neutralize (temporarily, at least) American naval power, perhaps prolonging the war beyond even the most pessimistic estimates. Those on the spot at Luzon, Morison wrote, radioed Kinkaid urgently requesting additional air support and even suggesting a reconsideration of the Lingayen landing. It was pointed out that the invasion troops might be "slaughtered" before they even reached the beaches.

MacArthur was with those invasion troops, coming up behind in another vast armada. He and others at GHQ (Sutherland, Whitney, etc.) had boarded the cruiser *Boise* at Leyte Gulf on January 4, maintaining strict radio silence. Kinkaid had established his flag and staff on *Wasatch*. There could be no turning back now, no matter how severe the kamikaze threat. To retire now, Morison wrote, "Would crown the efforts of the suicide plane with success." Kinkaid relayed the request for urgent air support to Halsey and Kenney. Halsey postponed his second strike on Formosa and struck Luzon again. Kenney sent every available plane.

As the invasion force approached Luzon, it was another poignant moment for MacArthur. He took a position on the bridge of *Boise* with his corncob pipe, staring at familiar landmarks. "My own thoughts," he wrote with feeling, "went back to that black night three years gone, when I churned through these same waters with only the determination to return . . . At the sight of those never-to-be-forgotten scenes of my family's past, I felt an indescribable sense of loss, sorrow, of loneliness and of solemn consecration."

Now the Japanese directed their efforts against the invasion force itself. On the afternoon of January 5, midget submarines attacked *Boise*, at least one firing a torpedo at the ship. *Boise*, alerted by *Phoenix*, took evasive action, dodging the torpedo. One midget got away but a combined aircraft and destroyer attack destroyed the others. MacArthur watched from the bridge, Whitney wrote, "still calmly puffing on his corncob." On January 7 and 8, kamikazes struck the force, hitting several ships. But on the whole, kamikaze damage to the invasion force was fortunately slight.

The invasion force arrived off the beaches of Lingayen Gulf at dawn January 9. It was an unforgettable naval spectacle. As far as the eye could see there were ships, ships and more ships. Then came the kamikazes. That day they hit four important targets: a battleship, two cruisers and a destroyer. Amid this tumult, at 9:30 A.M., the assault forces churned toward the beach in hundreds of landing craft. MacArthur watched this massive operation from the bridge of *Boise*. "It warmed my heart to finally see the weight on my side," he wrote.

The troops went ashore against little or no opposition. There was to be no savage fight on the beaches; the Japanese were holed up far away in the three mountain redoubts. The I and XIV corps soldiers pushed rapidly inland, widening the beachhead. About five hours later, MacArthur, Sutherland and other staffers went ashore in a landing craft. By then the Seabees had bulldozed a dirt pier into the water, suitable for docking VIPs. But, as Dr. James reported, MacArthur spurned this convenience and, as at Leyte, waded ashore in shallow water. James wrote: "His Leyte wading scene was unintentional, but this one seems to have been a deliberate act of showmanship. With the worldwide attention that his Leyte walk through the water received, apparently the Barrymore side of MacArthur's personality could not resist another big splash of publicity and surf. Surely enough, his act got both."

There remained the possibility that Japanese naval forces believed to be in Camranh Bay, Indochina, might launch an attack on the Lingayen forces as they had done at Mindoro. In actuality, no such attack was planned. The Japanese naval forces at Camranh Bay had retreated to Singapore. Unaware of this, Halsey received permission from Nimitz to slip his vast 3rd Fleet into the South China Sea to block a possible move against the Lingayen forces. On the night of January 9–10, the fleet steamed boldly into these enemy waters and remained there for a total of eleven days.

Halsey did not find the major Japanese naval units he expected, but his pilots had a field day in this virgin territory. His aviators sank forty-four ships, including the light cruiser *Kashii* and a dozen important tankers, and destroyed a hundred aircraft. Swinging about, the fleet hit Hainan, Hong Kong, and then on the way out, Formosa. Halsey wrote: "It was one of the heaviest blows that Jap shipping ever sustained. It was also a strongly-worded notice that control of the South China Sea had changed hands." Indeed it had.

At Lingayen Gulf, kamikazes continued to harass the invaders during January 10–13. They struck fourteen more ships, severely damaging ten, including a jeep carrier. But after the thirteenth, the kamikaze attacks dwindled to zero. The beachhead was safe. For the Navy, it had been a costly landing. In total, kamikazes had hit forty-three ships: four were sunk, eighteen were severely damaged. About 738 soldiers, airmen, and sailors had been killed; another 1400 wounded. But now the threat from the sky was over. MacArthur had complete air superiority over Luzon. It was now a question of destroying the Japanese Army, rescuing the POWs, and liberating Manila.

CHAPTER
THIRTY-ONE

★ ★ ★ ★ ★

FOUR DAYS AFTER the Luzon landing, January 13, Mac-Arthur left *Boise* and moved his headquarters ashore to the town of Dagupan. Where at Leyte he had remained largely in the background, now he emerged full-bore in the role of field commander. He made no bones about it. He was everywhere at once, fearlessly exposing himself to snipers on the front lines in an open jeep, cheering the men on, emersing himself in the smallest tactical details.

For one thing, he was not satisfied with Krueger's progress. In four days, against slight resistance, I Corps (on the left) and XIV Corps (on the right) had advanced only about 10 miles. This would never do. In his arguments for the invasion of Luzon, MacArthur had assured Washington that Manila would be liberated within two weeks of the initial landing. Manila was still 115 miles away. At the rate Krueger was moving, it would take two months to get there. By then, surely, the Japanese would have murdered the POWs. What MacArthur wanted was a decisive breakout and a "dash" to Manila.

There was another reason for urgency. Nimitz had demanded the ships he had loaned Kinkaid be returned for the Iwo Jima operation, a month hence. MacArthur, fearing a Japanese naval attack on his beachhead, was reluctant to release these ships until Kenney had sufficient planes based at the big Clark Field complex to deal with a Japanese naval threat. Nimitz was pressuring MacArthur, implying that unless the ships were returned promptly, he might have to delay Iwo Jima again. MacArthur did not want the blame for another delay in Central Pacific operations. It became imperative that Krueger seize Clark Field as quickly as possible.

Krueger, always cautious, was understandably concerned about the large Japanese force (125,000 men, according to his intelligence chief) holed up in the Caraballo redoubt on his left (I Corps) flank. Some of these troops had been probing his lines and setting up stiff delaying actions. But the overriding danger was that at any time they could launch an all-out attack, possibly wedging behind Krueger, cutting him off from his supply base at Lingayen Gulf. Moreover, Krueger argued, his troops had been trained for slow, cautious jungle warfare, not Patton-like mechanized advances of ten, twenty, or fifty miles a day. Besides all that, the Japanese (as well as Kenney's aircraft) had been destroying bridges. Unaccountably Krueger had not enough pontoon bridges to replace them, nor nearly enough transport.

Krueger's plan was, like the man himself, ultraconservative. Before pushing on to Manila, he would consolidate his beachhead, then await the arrival of two more infantry divisions from Leyte (the 32nd and 1st Cavalry) in late January. Half of these would be deployed to reinforce his left flank and rear against a possible Japanese attack from Caraballo. Then—and only then—would he make the all-out push for Clark Field and Manila. But MacArthur, who had been wildly misled by his intelligence chief, Willoughby, on the number of troops in the Caraballo (only 75,000 said Willoughby) was adamant. Wrote Krueger: "General MacArthur did not seem to be impressed by my arguments. He did not appear to take very seriously the danger that the enemy might well take advantage of any overextension of our forces to attack them in the flank as we moved south."

Here, then, was a serious command crisis, the thorniest MacArthur had faced in the Pacific war. There is not much on the record about it—nothing at all from MacArthur himself. But MacArthur's friend Frazier Hunt,

and Dr. James (quoting Eichelberger), say that Mac-
Arthur very seriously considered the drastic step of relieving Krueger as commander, Sixth Army. Hunt writes that
MacArthur sent an emissary to Krueger (probably Sutherland). This emissary told Krueger that if MacArthur had
to personally come to Krueger's headquarters again to
urge action, "he was certain he would finally lose his
temper and relieve his old comrade. . . ."

That, apparently, did it. On January 18 Krueger reluctantly issued new orders. XIV Corps would get moving
and seize Clark Field, I Corps would protect its rear and
left flank. The plan worked. By January 21, Krueger's
troops had seized Tarlac, fifty miles south of Lingayen
Gulf, and by January 24, they had advanced another ten
miles to Bamban River, overlooking Clark Field. Here, in
the face of increasing Japanese resistance, Krueger temporarily halted the advance, so that supplies could be
brought up, the troops rested, and regrouped.

Meanwhile I Corps moved east and southeast against
the Japanese in the Caraballo to secure the rear. The
Japanese were dug in strongly, utilizing caves, tunnels,
and buried tanks. "There was no surrendering," Mac-
Arthur wrote. "Every Japanese soldier fought to the death.
You had to blow his head off or thrust him through with
a bayonet." At San Manuel, the Japanese launched a small
but fierce counterattack. "Our lines reeled," MacArthur
wrote, "and I became so concerned over a possible pene-
tration that I personally hastened to the scene." The infantry commander in this area, James Dalton II, MacArthur
wrote, "was one of my finest field commanders. I joined
him in steadying the ranks. The enemy was finally stopped."
For his own personal front line bravery in this incident,
MacArthur was awarded a third Distinguished Service
Cross. Dalton was later killed.

Krueger's XIV Corps now launched the attack on
Clark Field. Elements of the 40th Division bore the
brunt of this fighting, which was tough. But within four
days, Clark Field (and Fort Stotsenburg) was once again
in American hands, though the Japanese had been driven
only two miles west of it—back into the foothills of the
Zambales redoubt. Urged on by MacArthur in no uncertain
language, other XIV Corps troops pushed south another
twenty-five miles, reaching Calumpit on January 30, about
twenty-five miles from the outskirts of Manila. Thus in

the space of twelve days, MacArthur had personally pushed Sixth Army very close to its final objective, Manila. Although Krueger's lines were now greatly extended, no serious enemy threat developed from the Caraballo.

Soon after Clark Field was secured, Kenney drove there for an inspection. His men found over six hundred Japanese planes in the complex. About fifty, which had been cleverly concealed in the woods, were untouched; fifty, slightly damaged; but the other five hundred were shot-up "junk." The runways were pockmarked with bomb craters. The engineers set to work at once filling in the holes. By February 10, Kenney wrote, the complex was refurbished sufficiently to receive his C–47 troop carriers. Not long after that, the heavy bombers arrived. Clark Field became Kenney's principal command headquarters for the remainder of the war.

Now, with elements of the XIV Corps poised just outside Manila, it was time to execute the other two major facets of the Luzon plan. These were the lesser amphibious landings on the coast northwest of Subic Bay and south of Manila at Nasugbu. Elements of Eichelberger's Eighth Army, XI Corps (38th Infantry Division plus the 34th Infantry Regiment), and the 11th Airborne Division were designated for these operations. Eichelberger himself came from Leyte and, as it developed, personally led the 11th Airborne in one of the most spectacular operations of the Luzon campaign.

The landing northwest of Subic Bay took place first, January 29. Eichelberger's 30,000-man XI Corps (which immediately fell under Krueger's command) came ashore near San Antonio, to the west of Calumpit and to the rear of the 30,000-man Japanese redoubt in the Zambales. It's primary mission was to dash eastward to prevent the Japanese in the Zambales from slipping down to the Bataan Peninsula, and to capture an airfield at San Marcelino. This force quickly seized Olongapo on the north shore of Subic Bay (in prewar years an auxiliary U.S. Naval base); but on January 31, it bogged down against strong Japanese resistance in Zigzag Pass on northern Bataan.

Sixty miles to the south of Zigzag Pass, at Nasugbu, the 11th Airborne Division (less one regiment) landed on January 31. At MacArthur's personal request, Eichel-

berger himself was on hand with extraordinary orders. He
was to lead this small unit on a dash to undefended (or so
it was believed) Manila—about fifty miles north on Route
17. In handing Eichelberger this assignment, MacArthur
had said it would be a venture that "would have delighted
Jeb Stuart," the famous Confederate hit-and-run raider of
the Civil War. Although Eichelberger was still busy mopping up on Leyte and preparing for Eighth Army campaigns in the southern Philippines, the chance to liberate
Manila with a small, elite force appealed greatly to this
front line fighter of the Buna and Biak jungles.

Eichelberger landed the 11th Airborne virtually unopposed. By 9:45 A.M., Nasugbu and its airstrip were his.
Amid cheering Filipinos, the 11th Airborne moved on
quickly, capturing a miniature railroad at a sugar depot,
which was ingeniously utilized to haul up supplies and
move troops inland. They advanced so quickly that the
confused Japanese had no time to destroy the bridges.
They did not pause at nightfall. They pushed on, making
a lot of noise, trying to convince the Japanese that (as
publicly announced) the whole Eighth Army had landed.
When they met strong resistance at 2400-foot Tagatay
Ridge, Eichelberger called for the 3rd Regiment of the
division to make an air drop. Kenney's planes airlifted
the paratroopers from Mindoro. They floated down on
February 3 and linked up with Eichelberger's other forces.
A furious fight ensued, with Eichelberger leading the
front line troops through whizzing bullets, as he had at
Buna and Biak. From the top of the ridge Eichelberger
could see "the city of Manila gleaming whitely in the
sunshine." It was only twenty-five miles away.

The next day, February 4, Eichelberger's troops roared
north on Route 17, advancing almost twenty miles. They
reached Imus, three miles south of Nichols Field and the
Manila city limits. Here they had a shock. They encountered a large, tough force of Japanese Marines, skillfully dug in at a wall-enclosed Spanish barracks. It was
soon apparent that Manila was not "undefended" as
advertised by MacArthur and GHQ; Eichelberger was to
be denied his easy, triumphant entry. The 11th Airborne
was soon bogged down in savage combat, suffering heavy
casualties.

The Japanese Army had decided to leave Manila undefended, but not so the Japanese Navy. A Japanese ad-

miral took charge, commanding about 20,000 men. These were mostly Marines and naval personnel, but the force also included a sizable contingent of Army personnel who had not yet, as ordered, slipped into the Sierra Madre redoubt east of Manila. The admiral and his men were grimly determined to deny MacArthur Manila for as long as possible. They would fight to the death and, in the process, cause the complete destruction of this beautiful city, "The Pearl of the Orient."

By February 1, the stage was set for the final drive on Manila. The 1st Cavalry and 32nd divisions had landed at Lingayen Gulf. Both veteran outfits were sent directly into action; the 1st Cavalry attached to XIV Corps, the 32nd to I Corps to help protect the rear. The 1st Cavalry and 37th divisions of XIV Corps would spearhead the drive, pushing down from the north while Eichelberger's 11th Airborne (as we have seen) pushed up from the south. MacArthur, personally launching the envelopment, told the able commander of the 1st Cavalry, Verne D. Mudge: "Go to Manila. Go around the Nips, bounce off the Nips, but go to Manila."

Now it was evident that the Japanese were going to fight for Manila, MacArthur was gravely concerned about the fate of the POWs imprisoned there, especially a group of about 3,700 Allied civilians held at Santo Tomas University. Accordingly, he devised a daring plan to rescue them. Mudge would form two special motorized task forces, "flying columns," from 1st Cavalry (to be supported by Marine Corps fighter aircraft) that would dash ahead of the division, go directly to the university, and free the POWs.

It was done as ordered. Roaring down the highway, seizing bridges before they were blown, these special forces, commanded by Brigadier General William C. Chase, crossed into the Manila city limits at 7:00 P.M. on February 3. They were the first Allied troops to enter the city. Boldly speeding down the streets, scattering amazed knots of Japanese, the force, aided by Filipino guerrillas, reached the university. A tank crashed through the front gate of the campus wall and liberated the prisoners. Another element of this force seized Malacanan Palace. The following day, February 4, an advance unit of the 37th Division freed 1,500 POWs from Old Bilibid Prison. About

800 of them were Battling Bastards of Bataan; the others were civilians.

The liberation of these 5,000 POWs was surely one of the most moving moments of the Pacific War. They were emaciated, hollow-eyed. They wore rags. MacArthur, who first entered the city limits with the 37th Division, visited Santo Tomas and Old Bilibid on February 7. "I cannot recall," he wrote, "even in a life filled with emotional scenes, a more moving spectacle . . . When I arrived, the pitiful, half-starved inmates broke out in excited yells. I entered the building and was immediately pressed back against the wall by thousands of emotionally charged people. In their ragged filthy clothes, with tears streaming down their faces, they seemed to be using their last strength to fight their way close enough to grasp my hand . . . One man threw his arms around me, and put his head on my chest and cried unashamedly . . . I was grabbed by the jacket. I was kissed. I was hugged. It was a wonderful and never-to-be-forgotten moment—to be a lifesaver, not a lifetaker." When one POW gasped "You're back!", MacArthur replied: "I'm a little late, but we finally came."

CHAPTER
THIRTY-TWO

★ ★ ★ ★ ★

MacArthur had returned to Manila, at last. The world was galvanized. Messages of congratulations flowed in from Roosevelt, Churchill, Chiang Kai-shek—even George Patton. The liberated portion of Manila "was in a frenzy," MacArthur wrote. "Men, women and children literally danced in the streets." Everywhere he went the people shouted "Mabuhay," Tagalog for "Hurray!" MacArthur ordered up a triumphant parade, but when it became obvious that Manila was far from won, it had to be cancelled.

In truth, before Luzon could be declared militarily secure, there would be months of grim and bloody fighting. The principal tasks were three: to clear the Japanese from Manila, to recapture Bataan and Fortress Corregidor, and to root the remaining 170,000 Japanese out of their three mountain redoubts.

By February 12, the twenty thousand Japanese in Manila had consolidated into an area on the south waterfront docks and below. They were holed up in hospitals, government buildings, the U.S. Army-Navy Club, LaSalle University (and its stadium), the Manila Hotel, and in Intramoros, the famous old "Walled City" with its fortress,

Fort Santiago. They had plenty of weapons, ammunition, food, and water. They were fiercely determined to fight to the last man.

From the north, the 1st Cavalry and 37th divisions swung through the lightly defended sections of the city, encircling the Japanese, backing them against Manila Bay. Eichelberger had now relinquished command of the 11th Airborne, still bogged down at Nichols Field. Krueger, taking command, sent in heavy artillery and extricated the unit. Within a couple of days, the 11th captured Nichols Field, wiped out the Japanese Marines there, linked up with the 1st Cavalry and came north to help in Manila.

The battle for Manila was brutal. The Japanese refused to yield an inch without a vicious fight. MacArthur made it harder for his troops by refusing close air support—to spare the lives of the civilians. But thousands of civilians, caught in the murderous crossfire of the opposing forces, died anyway.

MacArthur had hoped that his beloved Manila Hotel penthouse, with his furniture and library, would survive intact. No such luck. The fight for the hotel began on February 21. On the following day, MacArthur came to watch. By then, the west wing of the hotel had been almost demolished. MacArthur did not wait for the fighting to stop before he took a look at his quarters.

He wrote: "Flanked by submachinegun men, I climbed the stairs to the top. Every landing was a fight. Of the penthouse, nothing was left but ashes. It had evidently been the command post of a rearguard action. We left its colonel dead on the smouldering threshold, the remains of the broken vases of the emperor [given to his father in 1905 when he was an envoy to Japan] at his head and feet—a grim shroud for his bloody bier. The young lieutenant commanding the patrol, his smoking gun in his hand and his face wreathed in the grin of victory, sang out to me, 'Nice going, Chief.' But there was nothing nice about the victory to me. I was tasting to the last acid dregs the bitterness of a devastated and beloved home."

A few of MacArthur's personal possessions turned up, from time to time, sometimes in curious ways. Sid Huff reported that a Filipino gardener who had squirreled away a mahogany box containing the flat silver turned it over to a GHQ staffer. United States soldiers found a box in a warehouse labeled *Medical Supplies—For Shipment to Tokyo.* Actually, Huff wrote, it contained "a rich assortment of tea sets, candelabra, serving bowls and other silver articles that had belonged to the families of both Jean and the General." His black 1941 Cadillac limousine was found in good shape at Santo Tomas University. Soldiers, poking through the ruins of the Manila Hotel, found his set of *Cambridge Modern History* books. And much, much later in Tokyo, Huff wrote, Jean, tipped off, recovered "a few hundred books with the MacArthur bookmark" from the home of a Japanese general who was then in prison awaiting trial for war crimes. He told Jean that all the rest of MacArthur's personal belongings had been "distributed" among the Japanese conquerors of Manila.

By the twenty-seventh of February, three weeks and two days after the first U.S. soldiers had entered Manila, the Japanese were wiped out. The battle for Manila was over. United States forces counted almost 17,000 dead Japanese (about 3,000 had escaped). In the fight for the city alone, the United States suffered 6,575 casualties— 1,010 killed. But the greatest casualties were suffered by the civilians. An estimated 100,000 were killed. Worse, Manila, spared air attack but not heavy artillery, was a wretched shambles.

That day, February 27, 1945, MacArthur drove to the magnificent Malacanan Palace, which, miraculously, had survived intact. There, before President Osmeña, his cabinet, and a large delegation from GHQ, MacArthur pronounced the reestablishment of the Philippine government in Manila. As he spoke eloquently of democracy and sacrifice and freedom, Whitney reported, his "voice broke." For a moment he could not go on. And no wonder. As MacArthur wrote, "In this city my mother had died, my wife had been courted, my son had been born." He did not say so, but he must have also remembered that almost half a century earlier his father had also presided over the formation of a new Philippine government.

For his new quarters, MacArthur chose a mansion with a swimming pool in north Manila near the palace, the property of the immensely wealthy Bachrach family. (Actually, as Kenney related humorously, he (Kenney) had picked that mansion for himself, but MacArthur took it away from him. Kenney wound up with another Bachrach mansion that was even more imposing and comfortable.) Jean, Arthur, and Ah Cheu left Brisbane on a ship, the *Columbia Express,* on February 21 and arrived in Manila on March 6, only three days after Krueger pronounced the city secure. It had been almost five months since MacArthur had left Jean in Brisbane. It was a happy reunion—but her presence at the war front gave MacArthur's critics more poison for their darts. GHQ diluted the sting somewhat by announcing that Jean would devote herself to caring for the POWs, a task she carried out with compassion and deep dedication.

While Manila was being cleaned out, MacArthur had turned his attention to the second large task he faced: recapturing Bataan and Corregidor. The latter's massive batteries were still in Japanese hands. Corregidor dominated Manila Bay. Until it was recaptured, MacArthur's forces could not safely utilize Manila Bay nor the port facilities at Cavite and Manila. Besides that, for MacArthur and the men at GHQ, Bataan and Corregidor had deep symbolic value. Until the American flag again flew over those places, the Luzon job was far from complete.

Intelligence on Japanese forces holding Bataan and Corregidor was hard to come by. The upshot was a gross miscalculation. It was believed that there were about six thousand to eight thousand Japanese on Bataan in well-fortified positions and only about nine hundred on Corregidor. Hence Bataan would be tough; Corregidor, after a merciless air bombardment, easy. In fact, it would be the other way around. There were only a handful of Japanese on Bataan, but there were over five thousand on Corregidor. Bataan would be easy; Corregidor, tough.

A variety of forces were assigned to the Bataan-Corregidor operation. Elements of I Corps—the outfit that landed on the west coast, captured Olongapo, then bogged down in Zigzag Pass—would bear the largest responsibility on Bataan. One of its regiments, joined by a regiment from XIV Corps near Clark Field, would push down the east coast road. Another regiment of XI Corps, staging from Olongapo, would make an amphibious landing at Marivales on the southern tip and push north, thus encircling the Japanese. The independent 503rd Airborne Regiment, then on Mindoro, would be dropped on Corregidor, while XI Corps troops came from Marivales in an amphibious assault.

Execution of this plan was delayed somewhat by the XI Corps bogdown in Zigzag Pass. The United States troops there (elements of the 38th Division) were green. The jungle terrain was formidable and the Japanese (from the force holed up in the Zambales redoubt) tenacious. It became necessary to relieve a division commander and a regimental commander. William Chase, the general who led the 1st Cavalry dash to free the Santo Tomas POWs, was put in command of the division. After that, the troops broke through Zigzag Pass and reached Orani, the staging point for the drive down Bataan's east coast.

On February 14, the campaign to liberate Bataan and Corregidor commenced in earnest. The two regiments pushed rapidly down the east coast, meeting surprisingly light resistance. The regiment from Olongapo embarked and landed at Marivales on February 15 against virtually no opposition. It immediately swung northward to link up with the southward-moving regiments. Meanwhile, at dawn the next day, February 16, the paratroopers on Mindoro boarded transports for the drop on Corregidor, and the Corregidor amphibious support force at Marivales made ready to embark. All the while, Kenney's aircraft and Kinkaid's naval vessels pounded Corregidor with bombs and shells.

This was a campaign dear to MacArthur. That same day, February 16, he and some GHQ staffers jeeped to Bataan to join the regiments driving down the east coast road. This front line visit very nearly cost MacArthur his life. Apparently anxious to watch the paratrooper assault on Corregidor. MacArthur's party (in two jeeps), according to the official Army historian, "proceeded south along the coastal road to a point nearly five miles beyond the . . . front lines." He might have gone further but the jeeps were stopped by a demolished bridge. A flight of Kenney's P–38 fighters spotted the two jeeps. Thinking they must be Japanese the airmen prepared to strafe. Luckily the flight leader decided to check with General Chase by radio. Chase, knowing MacArthur was somewhere down the road, denied permission. But for that, MacArthur would surely have been killed by his own airmen.

MacArthur left no personal remarks on his reentry of Bataan. No doubt he was surprised and gratified by the absence of Japanese and the easy victory. That day the peninsula was declared secure. Japanese casualties were about two hundred killed. Casualties of XI Corps were fifty killed, one hundred wounded. About a thousand Japanese holed up near Mount Natib, but they presented no threat. Eventually they were killed or died of starvation.

That same day, February 16, the assault on Corregidor began. At 8:30 A.M., about one thousand men of the 503rd Airborne Regiment dropped on an overgrown parade ground and golf course Topside. The Japanese, taken by surprise, inflicted no casualties on the jumpers, but a whopping twenty five percent were injured when they landed. Two hours later, the one-thousand-man amphibious force from Marivales landed. Also achieving complete surprise, the first four waves of landing craft met no opposition. But the fifth and subsequent waves were raked by machine gun fire. Casualties were light. By 11:00 A.M., these amphibious forces had a firm hold on Malinta Hill. At 12:40, a second wave of paratroopers, another one thousand men, dropped. Now there were three thousand U.S. soldiers on Corregidor to face the Japanese, who numbered not nine hundred, as estimated, but five thousand.

For the next ten days the fighting on Corregidor was ghastly. The Japanese troops composed of disorganized bands rather than coordinated military units, were determined to fight to the death. They made piecemeal suicidal banzai charges, blew up tunnels and hilltops, killing both themselves and U.S. troops. But by February 26, most resistance had ceased. The Americans counted 4,500 dead Japanese. The other 500 had escaped or were buried in the tunnels. The United States had suffered 1,000 casualties —210 dead.

On March 2, MacArthur and "The Bataan Gang" embarked for Corregidor. They went back the same way they had left it—in four PT boats. It was, MacArthur wrote, a moment of "drama and romance." He inspected the grisly ruins of Malinta Tunnel and other familiar landmarks, then proceeded Topside for a ceremony. There, before the old wrecked stone barracks, the 503rd commander, Colonel George M. Jones, stepped forward, saluted, and said: "Sir, I present to you Fortress Corregidor." Decorating Jones with a Distinguished Service Cross, MacArthur said with feeling: "I see the old flagpole still stands. Have your troops hoist the colors to its peak, and let no enemy ever haul them down."

MacArthur now turned to the third and final Luzon task: clearing the remaining 170,000-odd Japanese out of the three mountain redoubts. Krueger had counted on eleven divisions for this onerous job, but MacArthur had other plans. He had directed Eichelberger and his Eighth Army on Leyte to invade and reconquer the remaining southern Philippine Islands: Palawan, Panay, Bohol, Negros, Cebu, Mindanao, etc. As Morison points out, this extended operation was never officially authorized by the Joint Chiefs of Staff, who had assumed it would be done by Filipinos. MacArthur gave two of Krueger's eleven divisions to Eichelberger, leaving Krueger only nine tired and, in some cases, severely depleted divisions for the Luzon operations. Krueger's job would be all the more difficult.

It would be tedious to follow this large, complicated yet important campaign in detail. It took about six months. The Japanese fought desperately, even suicidally. Krueger, facing the largest Japanese Army anyone would fight in the Pacific War, and operating on a shoestring, did the best he could with what he had. At great cost he succeeded in killing over one hundred thousand Japanese, but he never did wipe them all out. At the end of the war, there were still about sixty thousand dug in the mountain redoubts. (They surrendered.) Some historians have faulted MacArthur's decision to strip Krueger's forces and launch the southern Philippines operation. Certainly the decision caused bitterness in Sixth Army headquarters.

Eichelberger's campaign proceeded in tandem with Krueger's Luzon operations. It was extraordinary for its speed and efficiency. In all, he made fifty-two landings. In one furiously busy forty-four-day period, Eichelberger recalled, he made fourteen major, and twenty-four minor, invasions. Most of these were easy, but others—notably Cebu and Mindanao—were tough. Mindanao, which had originally been the first target for the Philippine invasion, turned out to be the last island to be liberated. MacArthur was unreservedly pleased by Eichelberger's operation.

MacArthur, meanwhile, had submitted plans to the Joint Chiefs of Staff for further conquests in the south by Eichelberger's Eighth Army, principally Borneo and Java. The Chiefs somewhat reluctantly approved Borneo, but they vetoed Java, which was very strongly held. The

Borneo job was assigned to the Australians, who until then, had been stuck with mopping up operations in the backwaters of New Guinea and Bougainville, and who were demanding a more active role in the war. After beating off an attempt by MacArthur to name Eichelberger's Eighth Army as overall commander of the Borneo operation, General Blamey led his all-Australian force ashore at Tarakan on May 1 and Brunei Bay on June 10.

Now that these southern operations were drawing to a close, MacArthur embarked on what Eichelberger called a grand tour of the battlefields. On June 3, he, Eichelberger, and others boarded the cruiser *Boise* at Manila. They stopped briefly at Mindoro, then went on to Mindanao, approximating the route MacArthur had followed when he escaped from Corregidor in the PT boats. On June 5, he went ashore on Mindanao to visit old haunts (notably the Del Monte Country Club, where he and the Bataan Gang had awaited the B–17s to take them to Australia) and soldiers of the 31st Division. It was an eight-hour jeep ride of 120 miles over a hideously rough road in the rain. Eichelberger recalled: "My own teeth were clicking like castanets, and my sacroiliac was in painful revolt . . . but General MacArthur never once acknowledged physical discomfort."

On went the grand tour. MacArthur visited Cebu and Negros. From Negros, he took a side excursion to Iloilo, Panay, by PT boat. There, Eichelberger dropped off the tour to resume directing the campaign on Mindanao. Then on to Palawan, where Kenney joined the party. *Boise* departed there on the afternoon of June 8 and joined the attack force steaming for Brunei Bay, Borneo. (Next day, Kenney wrote, he and MacArthur had four ice cream sodas apiece.) On June 10, from the bridge of *Boise,* MacArthur and Kenney watched the Australians go ashore against light resistance.

Two hours after the Aussies landed, MacArthur, Kenney, and others went ashore. Hearing Japanese rifle and machine gun fire nearby, Kenney was nervous. He wrote: "I began to feel all over again as I had at the Leyte landing. MacArthur kept walking along, enjoying himself hugely, chatting with a patrol along the road every once in a while and asking the men what they were shooting at." A little later a photographer who was standing close to MacArthur was hit in the shoulder by a sniper. At that, Kenney insisted the party return to *Boise*. It did.

Next day, June 11, MacArthur went ashore a second time. After wading through a half mile of swamp, the party climbed into a jeep and "headed off for more trouble," as Kenney put it. They traveled deep into the jungle until they were halted by an Australian colonel. Whitney recalled that MacArthur protested, saying he saw some Australians "fully five hundred yards ahead." The colonel, undaunted by MacArthur's five stars, replied: "General, that is only a forward patrol, and even now it is under enemy fire." Moving on, MacArthur said: "You can't fight 'em . . . if you can't see 'em." The colonel turned to Whitney, grinned, and said: "This is the first time I have ever heard of a commander-in-chief acting as the point." Finally, much to everybody's relief, they ran out of things to see and returned to *Boise*.

Next day, June 12, *Boise* moved to Jolo, where Eichelberger rejoined the tour. Then *Boise* steamed to Davao, Mindanao, where Kenney departed the group. After a day ashore visiting soldiers in the jungles behind Davao, MacArthur returned to *Boise* and went on to Zamboanga, Mindanao, where he spent the day, June 14, ashore. *Boise* returned to Manila, but on June 27 MacArthur reembarked to watch the third and final Australian landing on Borneo at Balikpapan, July 1. *Boise* stopped at Tawi Tawi, then joined the invasion group on the eve of the landing, which was the last amphibious operation of World War II.

On July 1, shortly after the Australians got ashore, MacArthur followed, with his nervous retinue. He took position on a hill dotted with Australian foxholes, only two hundred yards from the Japanese positions. Suddenly a Japanese machine gun opened up. Everyone in the MacArthur party save MacArthur hit the dirt. He stood there, boldly erect, holding a map, apparently completely unperturbed. To one witness in the party, MacArthur "gave the impression that no Japanese bullet had been made that could bring him down."

That night *Boise* got under way again. After another stop at Tawi Tawi, she reached Manila July 3. By that time, the Australian operations on Borneo were considered a complete success, and Eichelberger had control of the key territory on Mindanao. For all practical purposes (except mopping up) the Southern Philippine and Borneo campaigns were over.

The Philippines (plus Borneo) had been liberated, as MacArthur had demanded all along. It was a uniquely personal victory for the general. He had engineered it against relentless opposition in Washington. After Leyte and Luzon, he had brazenly enlarged it without advance approval of Washington. He earned the undying gratitude and loyalty of the Filipinos. In the coming years of political turmoil in Southeast Asia, the Philippine Islands would, for the most part, remain pro-American, a strategic base of vital importance. Had King's strategy prevailed, had the Philippines been bypassed, the story might have been far different.

Contrary to the impressions left by GHQ communiqués and the memoirs of MacArthur's aides, the cost of liberating the Philippines was high. Including Leyte, Luzon, and Eichelberger's southern campaign, the Sixth and Eighth Armies had suffered a total of 62,000 casualties—14,000 dead. Japanese casualties were far higher, of course. The official Army historians estimated that in these same three campaigns the Japanese lost 450,000 killed, including about 24,000 civilians. For every American killed, thirty-two Japanese died.

CHAPTER
THIRTY-THREE

★ ★ ★ ★ ★

IN EARLY 1945, when MacArthur was fighting his way into Manila, the Joint Chiefs of Staff were intensely debating the best method of administering the *coup de grace* to Japan. That is, the steps to take after the Iwo Jima and Okinawa invasions. Among the various proposals, three were favored: a landing on the coast of China near Shanghai; a direct thrust at the southernmost Japanese home island Kyushu, to be followed within several months by the invasion of Honshu; and an air bombardment by B–29s basing from the Marianas and Okinawa so massive it would compel surrender without a landing.

On one point, there was almost unanimous agreement: landings on Japanese home islands would lead to huge casualties. For this reason, and others, most planners held the view that Russia should be encouraged to come into the war in the Pacific about three months after the defeat of Germany. She should be encouraged to attack Japan in Manchuria, the Kurile Islands, and perhaps Hokkaido, the northernmost of the home islands. This would have the effect of encircling the home islands in giant pincers and would take pressure off invading United

States forces. It was recognized that if Russia did come into the war, certain concessions would have to be granted. But at that stage it was believed the concessions would be worth the help.

In later years MacArthur (and his aides) would say that he opposed the entry of Russia into the Pacific War. Japan was already beaten, why give Russia concessions that would enhance Communist power and prestige in the Far East in the postwar world? But Dr. James proves conclusively that in this later version of his position, MacArthur, to use James's word, was "lying." James quotes three written military sources (including a note in the diary of Navy Secretary James Forrestal) who interviewed MacArthur on this question at about this time. All report MacArthur as not only favoring but insisting that Russia come into the war. And on June 18, James wrote, MacArthur radioed the JCS that in the proposed Allied landings on Japan, "the hazard and loss will be greatly lessened if an attack is launched from Siberia sufficiently ahead of our target date to commit the enemy to major combat."

On February 4, 1945, the Big Three—Roosevelt, Churchill, Stalin—met again, this time at Yalta in the Crimea. In later years, conservatives would argue that a "sick" Roosevelt, unable to cope with the cunning Stalin, made concessions that were severely damaging to the United States in the postwar world. One of these was to encourage Stalin to enter the Pacific war, a proposition Stalin agreed to. But, as we have seen, Roosevelt was merely carrying out the wishes of the majority of his top generals—including MacArthur.

The military plan for the final defeat of Japan agreed upon was the one most favored by MacArthur. Following Russia's entry into the war three months after the defeat of Germany, United States forces would land first on Kyushu, then Honshu. The Kyushu landing (Operation Olympic) was originally set for September 1, 1945. It would be spearheaded by Krueger's Sixth Army. The Honshu landing (Operation Coronet) was set for December 1, 1945. It would be spearheaded by Eichelberger's Eighth Army.

There was, finally, the ticklish question of who would command the invasion of Japan, MacArthur or Nimitz? In one of his last acts before his death on April 12,

Roosevelt provided the answer: neither. The Pacific command was split three ways. Nimitz would command all naval forces, including Kinkaid's 7th Fleet; MacArthur would command all land and tactical air forces; a crusty Air Corps general named Carl "Tooey" Spaatz would command the strategic air power, i.e., the B–29 Super Fortresses basing in the Marianas, Okinawa, and China. Like MacArthur and Nimitz, Spaatz reported directly to the JCS. Since Japan proper was technically in Nimitz's Central Pacific zone of responsibility, GHQ believed the appointment of MacArthur to command the ground forces was a political victory. But it could hardly have been otherwise.

The invasions of Iwo Jima and Okinawa proceeded on the delayed schedule forced by the setbacks on Leyte. Both operations were supported by the massive fast carrier forces under command of Admiral Raymond A. Spruance, who had relieved Halsey for a well-earned rest. (When Spruance commanded, the name was changed from 3rd to 5th Fleet.) Both operations proved to be very, very tough.

For months the Japanese had been reinforcing Iwo Jima and building an intricate network of defensive positions in the volcanic soil. Likewise for months, Nimitz's aircraft, surface ships, and submarines had been interdicting the reinforcements and bombarding the island. By February, when the invasion force set sail, it was believed that Iwo Jima would not be an unusually difficult operation. Nimitz was sadly mistaken. There were 19,000 fanatical Japanese dug in on Iwo.

As a preliminary, Spruance conducted an operation Halsey had long cherished: the first carrier attack on Japan proper since the hit-and-run Doolittle raid in April 1942. Leaving Ulithi on February 10, Spruance reached Japanese waters on February 16 in heavy weather, which helped conceal his mighty armada but interfered with air operations. Soon the first U.S. Navy planes of the war were over Tokyo. Spruance conducted a second raid the next day, February 17, then swung south to support Iwo Jima. These two historic raids on Japan, Morison wrote, were "substantial but not spectacular." Another, on February 25–26, was even "less effective."

The preliminary bombardment of Iwo Jima com-

menced on February 16. Six battleships, five cruisers,
and numerous destroyers pounded the island relentlessly
for three days. On D–day, February 19, there was another furious bombardment, then the Marines stormed
the beaches. Because the Japanese defenses were so
strong and deep, all this bombardment had done but
slight damage. Later the Marine commander, Holland M.
Smith, would partly blame MacArthur for this. As will
be recalled, MacArthur had been reluctant to release
the ships Nimitz loaned to Kinkaid during Luzon. Had
these ships been available, Smith maintained, and had
the Navy bombarded Iwo for ten days instead of three,
the destruction might have been more complete. But
Morison doubts this. The Japanese were dug in so
deeply, all the explosives in the world would not have
reached them.

Iwo Jima was brutal; the toughest battle in the history
of the Marine Corps. The fighting went on for a full
month before the island was finally and completely seized.
Of the 19,000 Japanese, only 200 were taken prisoner.
The Marines and Navy suffered hideous casualties: 26,000,
of whom 7,000 were killed. Kamikazes crashed into five
ships including the luckless carrier *Saratoga* and the
jeep *Bismarck Sea*. The latter sank. Even so, the campaign was considered worth it. Iwo Jima provided a base
from which fighters could escort B–29s to Japan. And,
Morison reports, about 2400 B–29s carrying crews of
some 27,000 men made emergency landings on the
island.

Next, Okinawa.

Spruance's 5th Fleet, now reinforced by the British
Fleet (four carriers, two battleships, six cruisers, ten
destroyers), departed Ulithi on March 14. On March 18,
this large force arrived off Japan and launched planes
that day and the next against targets in the Inland Sea.
This time the Japanese were waiting. Their aircraft
bombed the carriers *Enterprise, Yorktown, Wasp,* and
Franklin. Franklin lost eight hundred men and nearly
sank; but thanks to extraordinary damage control, she
was saved. Following these raids, which destroyed about
160 Japanese planes, Spruance turned south to soften up
Okinawa. These operations were coordinated with B–29
strikes against airfields on Kyushu. When it was all done,

there were few Japanese planes available for the defense of Okinawa.

Following a six-day bombardment of the landing area, two Marine and two Army divisions (50,000 men) went ashore on Okinawa April 1. The 100,000 Japanese defenders had reverted to the strategy of Luzon, abandoning the beaches and holing up in the southern mountains. The Marines and soldiers met little or no opposition. By April 18, they had captured all of northern Okinawa. On April 19, Army troops attacked the Japanese in the southern mountains. They were savagely repulsed. After bringing up reinforcements, U.S. forces attacked again. But the Japanese were dug in strongly; it would take weeks of bloody fighting to destroy them. The island was not secured until June 21, and mopping up continued to the end of the war. About 90,000 Japanese were killed, about 10,000 surrendered. Some 25,000 civilians were killed. The U.S. ground forces suffered almost 40,000 casualties, nearly 8,000 killed, plus an additional 26,000 nonbattle casualties.

MacArthur was openly critical of the Okinawa ground operation. According to James, he criticized it as "expensive" and "wasteful." He thought that rather than trying to uproot the Japanese by frontal assault, American generals should have established defensive positions and let the Japanese destroy themselves in piecemeal assaults. Inasmuch as MacArthur had directed Krueger to uproot the Japanese dug into Luzon redoubts at considerable cost in casualties, it seems a strange criticism. Whatever the case, MacArthur's carping inevitably reached Nimitz, James reported, and "contributed toward making the final weeks of the war the most tense period in their relations."

Japanese aircraft and kamikazes basing from Formosa assaulted the Navy at Okinawa in full fury. They sank fifteen ships—none larger than a destroyer—and damaged another two hundred, some beyond salvage. In these attacks, the Navy suffered its greatest casualties of the war, greater than the Pearl Harbor disaster. (One of those ships damaged was Spruance's flagship, *Indianapolis*.) Some five thousand sailors were killed, another five thousand wounded. The severity of the attacks quite rightly caused Nimitz grave concern about the forthcoming invasion of Japan. Obviously, his naval forces were going to get an even rougher pasting.

The Japanese Navy made one final spasm-reaction to break up the Okinawa landings, a suicidal assault. On April 6, the mighty battleship *Yamato*, light cruiser *Yahagi*, and eight destroyers charged out of the Inland Sea. They had just enough fuel oil for a one-way trip. The insane plan called for the ships to beach themselves in the landing area at Okinawa and shoot at American vessels until all the Japanese ships had run out of ammunition or been destroyed. But two of Lockwood's submarines, *Threadfin* and *Hackleback*, alerted by codebreakers, spotted the force and gave position reports. Next day, April 7, in a remarkable action, Spruance's aircraft sank *Yamato*, *Yahagi*, two destroyers and so damaged two more destroyers they had to be sunk. The remaining four destroyers fled back to the Inland Sea.

While these two operations were in progress, airman Tooey Spaatz was sending his Marianas-based B–29 Super Fortresses against Japanese cities almost nightly. At first these raids were largely ineffectual. It was a 3,000-mile round trip from Guam to Tokyo In order to make it, the bomb loads had to be restricted to three tons, one-third the maximum load. Until fighter escorts were based on Iwo Jima, the B–29s had to fly at 28,000 feet in order to protect themselves. That was too high for precision bombing.

In late February, Spaatz changed his bombing tactics. He decided to burn down Japanese cities with new incendiary bombs dropped from low level at night. In a first test of the bomb, on the night of February 25–26 (when Spruance was conducting his second raid on Japan), some 200 B–29s burned down two square miles of Tokyo. These raids were stepped up in intensity. For example, on the night of March 9–10, some 334 B–29s hit Tokyo, burning down fifteen square miles of the city. About 84,000 people were killed, 40,000 wounded, and a million left homeless in this one raid alone. In subsequent firebomb raids, Spaatz hit Nagoya, Kobe, Osaka, Yokohama, and Kawasaki, killing and wounding hundreds of thousands more. Later, Kenney's aircraft, basing from Okinawa, joined the air assault. He recalled that on any given day, upwards of 600 of his bombers, fighters, and strafers would be attacking Japan.

The Navy rejoined the air assaults on Japan. On May 27, Halsey relieved Spruance and the 5th Fleet once again became the 3rd Fleet. On June 2 and 3 Halsey (in his flagship *Missouri*, a new battleship) raided airfields on Kyushu. Then, for the second time in the war, another small, tight, undetected typhoon struck the 3rd Fleet. It was an episode remarkably similar to the storm of December 1944. The eye passed right through the Fleet. Almost every ship was damaged, some severely, but none sank. The cruiser *Pittsburgh* lost her bow, but she limped to Guam. About 142 planes were destroyed. Again, a Court of Inquiry laid the "primary responsibility" on Halsey. The court went so far as to recommend that "serious consideration" be given to assigning Halsey "to other duty." Navy Secretary Forrestal agreed with this recommendation but was dissuaded. Halsey was too much the popular hero. After another swipe at Kyushu, Halsey retired the fleet to Leyte for rest and replenishment.

From Leyte, Halsey flew to Manila to have lunch with MacArthur. It was their first meeting in a year. In his memoirs, Halsey recalled that he found MacArthur "in spirits as high as my own." No doubt they spent some time discussing the Okinawa operation. The Navy was angrily dissatisfied with Kenney's air operations over Formosa, the source of many of the kamikazes that hit the fleet at Okinawa. As we saw, MacArthur was dissatisfied with ground operations on Okinawa. Halsey was critical of Spruance's handling of the fleet, utilizing it for "static defense" of the island, rather than strategically against Japanese home islands. Worse, the protracted and expensive operation on Okinawa had forced a drastic postponement of the invasion of Kyushu, from September 1 to December 1.

On July 1, Halsey and the Third Fleet put to sea again. Operating against the Japanese home islands that month, he struck Tokyo three times, Hokkaido twice, and the Inland Sea three times. These eight massive air attacks wiped out whatever was left of the Japanese Navy and inflicted much damage on Japanese airfields and defense factories. The destruction of enemy aircraft was light. Few planes rose to meet Halsey's fighters. The Japanese were holding back, waiting for the invasion of the home islands.

At last, the Japanese high command began to yield. On June 22, after Okinawa fell, Emperor Hirohito called his Supreme War Council together and said a way must be found to end the war. This was more complicated to do than it may seem. Among the Japanese Army leaders there were many diehard fanatics who believed "face" required a fight to the death. There was real danger that these fanatics might depose the emperor and seize the government. (Indeed, they tried to.) There was another problem. Some means had to be found to convince the Allies to allow Hirohito to remain on the throne after the war was over, to keep the imperial system intact. Thus everything had to be done in secrecy and terms short of the Allies' avowed "unconditional surrender" arranged.

The Japanese negotiators decided to use the Russians as an intermediary, partly to keep Russia from entering the war against Japan. However, Stalin was playing his own tightfisted game, waiting for the moment to attack Japan when his risk would be least and his gain the greatest. The Japanese ambassador in Moscow met a cold reception; the Russian ambassador to Tokyo refused to negotiate. Hirohito proposed that a special envoy be sent to Moscow to carry a personal message to Stalin. But Stalin refused permission for the envoy to enter Russia.

These peace feelers were known to Washington. The codebreakers were reading the dispatches betwen Tokyo and the Japanese ambassador in Moscow. It fell to Harry Truman, in office a scant seventy days, to set a course of action. The crux of the matter was whether or not to keep the emperor on the throne. It was a difficult decision for the new president to make, both morally and politically. Almost every American had been brainwashed to loathe Hirohito; it was generally assumed (as Chiang Kai-shek was demanding) that Hirohito would be tried as a common war criminal and executed. After much conferring with the top leaders of government, Truman decided to put the matter to Churchill, Stalin, and Chiang Kai-shek, with whom he would meet for the first time at Potsdam, Germany, July 16.

MacArthur, of course, was not solicited for his views

on the question. Nor was Nimitz. Although they were the senior military men in the Pacific, and had a vital interest in the decision, this was not a military matter. It was purely political. Moreover, Truman, a former artillery captain in the AEF in France during the First World War, had, as he said many times in later years, an innate distrust of generals and was not about to seek their advice, especially that of MacArthur whom he had never met. MacArthur wrote that had he been solicited, he would have advised retaining the emperor on the throne.

When the Big Four met at Potsdam (Churchill was voted out of office in mid-conference, replaced by the Labor Party's Clement Attlee), Stalin still playing his tightfisted game, at first said nothing about the Japanese peace feelers. The other three drafted and issued a declaration on the Japanese surrender terms, somewhat ambiguous about the emperor. The declaration said that occupation forces "shall be withdrawn from Japan as soon as these objectives (total demilitarization of Japan, etc.) have been accomplished and there has been established a peacefully inclined and responsible government." Some Japanese leaders interpreted this to mean that after a decent interval, they would be permitted to determine their own form of government, including the fate of the imperial system. Others, notably Prime Minister Suzuki, thought not. At a press conference on July 28, Suzuki stated the Potsdam Declaration was merely a rehash of previous declarations and was not worth official notice. That same day Stalin finally conceded to Truman and others at Potsdam that the Japanese had tried to extend peace feelers through him. But by then, Suzuki had spoken, "disheartening" Truman and his advisers.

Meanwhile, United States scientists had exploded the first test atomic bomb at Alamogordo, New Mexico, July 16. Word of this successful test was relayed, in code, to Truman at Potsdam. There were two more bombs en route to the Pacific, one on the cruiser *Indianapolis* (later sunk by a Japanese submarine, probably utilizing human-guided Kaiten torpedoes). From Potsdam on July 24, Truman approved a provisional order to General Spaatz to drop two A–bombs on Japan as soon after August 3 as weather permitted visual bombing. On the

way home from Potsdam on the cruiser *Augusta*, Truman
gave the final order to go ahead. As the world knows,
these bombs were dropped from the B–29s on Hiroshima
August 6, and Nagasaki August 9. The Hiroshima bomb
killed 72,000 and wounded 68,000. The Nagasaki bomb
killed about 40,000 people and injured 60,000.

MacArthur had been briefed in advance on the atomic
bomb—but not much in advance. As Dr. James reported,
a War Department representative called at Manila to
reveal the existence of the bomb in "late July," only a
couple of weeks before the first one was dropped. He was
more fully briefed on August 7 by Dr. Karl T. Compton,
one of Truman's key scientific advisers. James reported
that MacArthur felt the use of the bomb was "completely unnecessary from a military point of view" for
compelling Japan to capitulate. This may well have been
true. By then, Japan was certainly on the point of total
collapse. But the bomb was welcome news to every soldier, sailor, and airman who faced the murderous invasion of the home islands.

On August 8, between the A–bomb drops, Stalin entered the war against Japan. The Red Army moved into
Manchuria. James wrote that two days before, Mac-
Arthur held an off-the-record press conference. He quoted
one reporter's notes: "Russian participation in the war
was welcome. . . . Every Russian killed was one less
American who had to be. If he were running their war,
he would pull a double envelopment Cannae-style and
commit all the Japanese in Manchuria by running one
force straight down the railway to Port Arthur while
another came through Chahar and Mongolia . . ." On
August 10, Russian forces entered Korea.

That same day, Emperor Hirohito again summoned his
Supreme Council. He advised immediate acceptance of
the Potsdam Declaration. Shortly afterward Japan sent
word (via Swiss and Swedish diplomatic channels) to
Washington, London, Moscow, and Chungking that it
would accept the Potsdam Declaration—provided the
imperial system were kept intact. Truman's Secretary of
State James F. Byrnes drafted the Allied reply which
contained two stipulations: the emperor must submit to
the authority of a Supreme Allied Commander; and the
Japanese people would ultimately determine the emperor's status through free elections.

The United States, meanwhile, maintained unremitting pressure on Japan. Hundreds of bombers from the Marianas and Okinawa pasted Japanese cities every day and night Halsey, having prudently withdrawn at the end of July to escape another typhoon. returned to hit northern Honshu August 9, the day the second A–bomb was dropped Alerted by the codebreakers his planes destroyed two hundred Japanese bombers which were preparing to crash-land (with two thousand suicide troops) at the B–29 base in the Marianas. On August 13 and 14, Halsey again hit Tokyo with one-thousand-plane raids.

On August 15, Japan accepted the Allied terms for surrender. From Washington, Truman announced the cessation of hostilities and a two-day holiday to celebrate. At GHQ in Manila, Sid Huff reported, there was "jubilation but no great amazement." Kenney reported simply, "We celebrated a little that night."

CHAPTER
THIRTY-FOUR

★ ★ ★ ★ ★

HOSTILITIES WERE OVER in the Pacific, but there remained several important, immediate problems: arranging the surrender of the millions of Japanese military personnel, landing U.S. troops in the home islands, and the creation of a military occupation government to carry out the terms of the Potsdam Declaration. In a singular vote of confidence, President Truman assigned all these tasks to Douglas MacArthur, whom he named (on August 15) Supreme Commander for Allied Powers in Japan (SCAP). James writes that MacArthur promptly cabled Truman: "I am deeply grateful for the confidence you have so generously bestowed upon me . . . The entire eastern world is inexpressibly thrilled and stirred by the termination of the war. I shall do everything possible to capitalize [upon] this situation among the magnificently constructive lines you have conceived for the peace of the world." And so the postwar relationship between Truman and MacArthur began on a cordial note.

For the next two weeks, MacArthur and GHQ were frenetically busy in Manila, laying the groundwork for these three tasks. MacArthur, drawing on his occupational experience in the Rhine sector following the

armistice in World War I, and his father's experience as
military governor of the Philippines, set the general tone.
The Allies would not swagger or provoke the Japanese,
nor demean the emperor. Everything would be low, low
key, firm but cool. Everyone would be alert for trickery;
the Japanese military were fanatical. The "peace" could
be a hoax.

As a first step, MacArthur radioed orders to Tokyo
to send a delegation of high-ranking military men to
Manila. A party of sixteen, led by Lieutenant General
Toroshiro Kawabe, Vice Chief of the Imperial General
Staff, departed Tokyo. They flew in two aircraft painted
white and bearing green crosses. At MacArthur's in-
sistence the radio recognition signal for the planes was
"Bataan." When this group reached Manila August 19,
they were escorted to GHQ. MacArthur watched them
arrive from a distance, but did not meet with them. After
they had deposited their swords in an anteroom, Sutherland, Whitney reported, received them with "chilly
formality," refusing handshakes. The talks went on all
night. The Japanese, as instructed, turned over documents and maps describing the location of POW camps
and Japanese military and naval installations.

The principal subjects discussed during the night were
the texts of the capitulation papers and a plan for the
initial landing of U.S. troops by aircraft. The former
included actual drafts of the surrender document to be
signed, a speech the emperor was to make to the Japanese
people accepting the terms of the Potsdam Declaration,
and a general order for the Japanese Imperial General
Headquarters, directing arrangements for the physical
surrender of its far-flung units. The plan for the airlift of
U.S. troops called for a landing at Atsugi, twenty miles
west of Yokohama, on August 23. The Japanese would
clear the general area of all troops, take the propellers
off all aircraft, and arrange billeting for officers and men
at the New Grand Hotel in Yokohama. The Japanese
asked for a three-day delay to accomplish all this—to
August 26. When all was agreed, the Japanese delegation
returned to Tokyo.

MacArthur chose Eichelberger's Eighth Army to spearhead the U.S. troop landings on Japan, a singular honor
for this loyal and devoted subordinate, and something of
an insult to Krueger, the senior ground general. Eichel-

berger in turn picked the 11th Airborne and 27th Infantry divisions, both on Okinawa, to go in first. General Arnold loaned Kenney three hundred big four-engine C-54 transports to lift the troops from Okinawa to Japan. MacArthur stunned Eichelberger (and all at GHQ) with the news that he would go in with the first regular troops. Eichelberger, and others, attempted in vain to dissuade MacArthur from this risky move. Finally, Eichelberger pleaded for two day's time—to make sure that the situation was in hand. Wrote Eichelberger: "He gave me two hours."

Nature intruded into these complicated plans. A typhoon swept the Japanese home islands, forcing a delay in the landings from August 26 to 28. Then, as it turned out, these were not the first Americans to land at Atsugi after all. On August 27, Halsey reported, a "brash young," Navy pilot from the *Yorktown,* "wholly against orders," landed alone at Atsugi, the first American to set foot on Japanese soil. He forced the startled Japanese to paint and hang a sign: "Welcome to the U.S. Army from the 3rd Fleet." The story has an improbable ring—but naval historian Morison has made it official. Unfortunately the Navy pilot's name is not known.

Meanwhile all the big names who were to participate in the surrender ceremony were gathering. On August 28 Halsey's massive 3rd Fleet—258 ships—moved into Tokyo Bay. *Missouri* was still his flagship, but since she had been designated as the platform for the surrender ceremony, he shifted his flag to *Iowa.* The following day, Nimitz flew up from Guam in a seaplane and raised his flag on the battleship *South Dakota.* That same day— August 29—MacArthur (and most of the senior GHQ generals) boarded a C-54 transport "Bataan" at Manila and flew to Okinawa, where Kenney and Eichelberger were overseeing the details of the airlift. Tooey Spaatz was also there. Krueger arrived two days later—August 31—from Manila.

August 30 dawned fair. The sky, Eichelberger wrote, was "a gay and unbelievable blue." By that time, advance elements of the 11th Airborne had already landed at Atsugi, but this was the day of the big, regular troop lift. Eichelberger departed Okinawa at 6:30 A.M. on his own plane. It was a five-hour flight, he remembered. He was "worried" all the way. MacArthur was not far behind. There would not be many U.S. soldiers at Atsugi. Anything could happen. It was up to Eichelberger to insure that this triumphant moment would not end in tragedy.

MacArthur and his GHQ retinue came along shortly in the C–54, "Bataan." Outwardly MacArthur was calm, preoccupied not with the danger of the landing (as was everyone else) but with the long-term goals for Japan. Pacing up and down the aisle, puffing on his corncob pipe, he dictated random notes to Whitney. Whitney recalled these were "First destroy the military power . . . Then build the structure of representative government . . . Enfranchise the women . . . Free the political prisoners . . . Liberate the farmers . . . Establish a free labor movement . . . Encourage a free economy . . . Abolish police oppression . . . Develop a free and responsible press . . . Decentralize the political power . . . Could he, for the first time in modern history, accomplish that miraculous phenomenon: a successful occupation of a defeated nation?"

MacArthur, Whitney wrote, "quietly slept" for the last thirty minutes of the flight. When Mount Fujiyama (bare of snow this time of year) loomed into view, Whitney woke him. MacArthur gazed down on this majestic symbol of Japan and said: "Fuji—how beautiful." Then the plane banked for the landing at Atsugi. Here, finally, was the moment of truth. Would fanatical diehards make a suicidal attempt to assassinate MacArthur? Whitney wrote: "I held my breath."

He needn't have. A nervous, meticulous Eichelberger had everything under control. There were present about five hundred 11th Airborne troops (including the band), very much on the alert for trouble. A C–54 landed every three minutes, disgorging more troops. When MacArthur's plane landed at about 2:00 P.M., the band played and Eichelberger, together with a handful of officers, stepped up to the boarding ladder to greet the boss, saluting. MacArthur, smoking his corncob pipe, returned the salute, paused a second or two to look around, descended the ladder, and, as Whitney recalled, said: "Bob, this seems to be the end of the road. As they say in the movies, this is the big 'payoff.'" Then for the first time in eight years—since his 1937 visit with Quezon—MacArthur set foot on the soil of Honshu.

The Japanese had arranged transportation to Yokohama: a comical caravan of decrepit jalopies, plus one
Lincoln Continental of "uncertain vintage" for Mac-
Arthur. By that time, Kenney and his top staff had arrived in another aircraft and joined the party. They
were wearing pistols, as they customarily did. Kenney
recalled that MacArthur ordered them to take off their
weapons and leave them on the plane. A good idea,
Kenney thought with hindsight: "It was excellent psychology and made a tremendous impression on the
Japanese to see us walking around in their country
unarmed . . . To them it meant that there was no doubt
about it. They had lost." Nonetheless, "twenty good-
looking tall Yank soldiers," all armed, climbed into a
truck and joined the caravan to guard MacArthur.

It was about twenty miles to Yokohama—a memorable
journey. To Eichelberger, still nervous, it was like a
"sequence in a dream fantasy." On both sides of the
road there were hundreds of armed Japanese soldiers,
most of them with their backs to the procession. "It was
partly a token of submission," Kenney wrote, "but was
also meant to insure against any possibility of sniping
by any Jap who didn't agree with the imperial edict
calling off the war." Eichelberger "did not draw an easy
breath until that journey ended." Because the Japanese
cars were so slow, and repeatedly broke down, it took
two long hours to drive the twenty miles.

The final destination was the New Grand Hotel, where
the Japanese had arranged billeting for VIPs. It was a
magnificent structure that had survived the bombing
raids with slight damage. When the caravan arrived,
Eichelberger established a "perimeter defense" around
the hotel, manned by "five hundred veterans" of the 11th
Airborne. But there were no untoward events: no suicidal
attempts on MacArthur or anyone in the party. Standing
amid the desolate ruins of Yokohama, once a thriving
city of a million people, the starving, haggard, benumbed
Japanese civilians were docile. The Emperor had spoken:
Japan was defeated. Yet the Americans were still edgy.
That night when they sat down to a steak dinner in the
hotel dining room, Whitney could hardly resist an im-
pulse to snatch MacArthur's food away: it might be
poisoned.

MacArthur's entry into Japan that day in this simple

fashion was a magnificent display of courage and psychology. Some years later, Churchill wrote: "Of all the amazing deeds of bravery of the war, I regard MacArthur's personal landing at Atsugi as the greatest of the lot." The Japanese scholar Kazuo Kawai, wrote in his brilliant book, *Japan's American Interlude:* "It was an exhibition of cool personal courage; it was even more a gesture of trust in the good faith of the Japanese. It was a masterpiece of psychology which completely disarmed Japanese apprehensions. From that moment, whatever danger there might have been of a fanatic attack on the Americans vanished in a wave of Japanese admiration and gratitude."

For the next two days MacArthur remained closeted in the New Grand Hotel. Meanwhile U.S. soldiers and Marines were pouring into Japan by aircraft and ship. Uppermost in the minds of all hands was the fate of the Allied POWs, and the desire to free them as rapidly as possible. There were some 35,000 in the Japanese home islands. Many had already been released and "had roamed all over the country" and were "hard to locate," Krueger recalled. But within two weeks most had been rounded up, processed, and sent off on ships or aircraft to the United States.

Among the POWs, the most senior, and most famous, were two generals, one American, one British. They were Jonathan "Skinny" Wainwright, who surrendered Corregidor, and Arthur E. Percival, who surrendered Singapore. They had been incarcerated in Mukden, Manchuria. On the night of August 31, after a long plane flight via Chungking, both men arrived in Tokyo at the specific invitation of MacArthur, who wanted them to attend the surrender ceremony on the *Missouri* on September 2.

MacArthur's critics have fabricated many unkind stories about the reunion of these old veterans of the dark days on Bataan and Corregidor. The most infamous and dishonest was that told by Harry Truman on a retrospective broadcast of his presidential years. Truman said that when Wainwright walked in and started to salute, MacArthur, who was having lunch, arrogantly said: "General, I told you I'd see you at three o'clock. I'll see you at that time."

What really happened was far, far different. William
Dunn, the CBS correspondent attached to MacArthur's
headquarters, witnessed the reunion. He described it in his
Army Magazine article. He said he had stopped at the
New Grand Hotel about 7:00 P.M., looking for possible
news. About then, someone came running from the
lobby to announce that Wainwright's car had just arrived. Dunn rushed for the lobby. Then, he wrote: "General MacArthur dashed out of his office and across the
lobby to greet the emaciated, hungry-looking scarecrow
who was approaching. Without waiting for the formality
of a salute, General MacArthur grabbed Wainwright's
hand and put his arm around his shoulder in a half
embrace . . . General MacArthur was marked with more
emotion than I ever saw the general display . . ."

MacArthur invited Wainwright to join him for dinner
right then. MacArthur recalled: "He was haggard and
aged. His uniform hung in folds on his fleshless form.
He walked with difficulty and with the help of a cane.
His eyes were sunken, and there were pits in his cheeks.
His hair was snow-white and his skin looked like old
shoe leather. He made a brave effort to smile as I took
him in my arms; but when he tried to talk, his voice
wouldn't come. For three years he had imagined himself
in disgrace for having surrendered Corregidor. He believed he would never again be given an active command.
This shocked me. 'Why Jim,' I said. 'Your old corps is
yours when you want it.' "

On the morning of September 2, a Sunday, the Allied
dignitaries who would be present at the surrender, including Wainwright and Percival, began making their
way to the *Missouri,* anchored in Tokyo Bay. It was a
cloudy, overcast morning. Nimitz and his large party
arrived at 8:05 A.M. MacArthur and his party arrived at
8:43 on the destroyer *Nicholas.* Halsey was on the quarterdeck. When he saw Wainwright, he recalled, "I could
not trust my voice; I just leaned over the rail and grabbed
his hand." Nimitz and Halsey greeted MacArthur, then
escorted him to Halsey's cabin. Halsey offered coffee, but
MacArthur declined: "No thanks, Bill, I'll wait till
afterwards."

Now the curtain rose on this historic ceremony. At
8:56 A.M. the Japanese delegation arrived on the U.S.

destroyer *Lansdowne*. They were Foreign Minister Mamoru Shigemitsu (who had one artificial leg), General Yoshijiro Umezu, chief of the Army general staff, and nine others from the Foreign Office, Army, and Navy. The civilians wore formal morning dress and top hats; the military men "ill-fitting" uniforms. The Japanese were stiff, silent, somber. They were led to an open area near No. 2 turret, where dozens of top Allied military men (including Lieutenant General Kuzma N. Derovyanko of Russia) were standing, three deep by rank, around an enlisted men's mess table covered with green felt cloth from *Missouri*'s wardroom. On the table were the surrender documents and a fountain-pen stand. The Japanese, told where to stand, remained rigidly immobile while a chaplain gave an invocation over the PA system followed by a recording of "The Star Spangled Banner." There was a special flag flying on the flag staff: the one that had flown over the Capitol on December 7, 1941. The decks and superstructure were crowded with gawking officers and enlisted men, many with cameras.

Now the last delegates to the ceremony came on deck: MacArthur, Nimitz, Halsey, Wainwright and Percival. MacArthur, looking grave, walked directly to a small battery of microphones by the tables and opened the ceremony. Wainwright and Percival stood behind him in a position of honor. MacArthur said in part:

> It is my earnest hope, and indeed the hope of all mankind, that from this solemn occasion a better world shall emerge out of the blood and carnage of the past—a world dedicated to the dignity of man and the fulfillment of his most cherished wish for freedom, tolerance, and justice.

MacArthur now summoned the Japanese to sign the document. Foreign Minister Shigemitsu came first. There was an awkward, even tense moment. He fumbled his hat, gloves, and cane and appeared not to know where to sign. Was he deliberately stalling? (Halsey wanted to slap him and say "Sign, damn you, sign.") MacArthur boomed out: "Sutherland, show him where to sign." (Morison wrote that Shigemitsu's bumbling was caused by intense pain from his ill-fitting artificial wooden leg.) Sutherland indicated the proper place, and Shigemitsu signed at 9:04. Officially that ended the war. He was followed by General Umezu, then MacArthur (signing for the United Nations), Nimitz (signing for the United States), Halsey, and the representatives of the United Kingdom, China, Russia, Australia (General Blamey), Canada, France, Netherlands, and New Zealand.

When MacArthur signed the document, he used five or six pens (accounts vary). Kenney says he gave one to Wainwright, one to Percival, one to West Point, and one to the Naval Academy. Willoughby says one went to *Missouri,* another to Truman. Whitney claims MacArthur gave *him* one—one of his own that MacArthur had borrowed. All accounts agree that MacArthur kept one for himself—a red fountain pen that Kenney said he recognized as Jean's. When all had signed, MacArthur spoke a final word: "Let us pray that peace be now restored to the world and that God will preserve it always. These proceedings are now closed."

The Japanese, given a copy of the document (in Japanese), bowed stiffly and left *Missouri* as they had come. They were saluted at the quarterdeck by the victors. About then the clouds parted, the sun shone through, and nearly two thousand Army and Navy aircraft flew overhead in close, thunderous formation. After the noise died, MacArthur moved to another microphone and made an eloquent broadcast to the world. He said in part:

Today the guns are silent. A great tragedy has ended. A great victory has been won . . .

As I look back upon the long, tortuous trail from those grim days of Bataan and Corregidor, when an entire world lived in fear, when democracy was on the defensive everywhere, when modern civilization trembled in the balance, I thank a merciful God that he has given us the faith, the courage, and the power from which to mold victory. We have known the bitterness of defeat and the exultation of triumph, and from both we have learned there can be no turning back. We must go forward to preserve in peace what we won in war.

A new era is upon us. Even the lesson of victory itself brings with it profound concern, both for our future security and the survival of civilization. The destructiveness of the war potential, through progres-

sive advances in scientific discovery, has in fact now
reached a point which revises the traditional con-
cepts of war.

Men since the beginning of time have sought
peace . . . Military alliances, balances of power,
leagues of nations, all in turn failed, leaving the
only path to be by way of the crucible of war. We
have had our last chance. If we do not now devise
some greater and more equitable system, Armaged-
don will be at our door. The problem basically is
theological and involves a spiritual recrudescence
and improvement of human character that will syn-
chronize with our almost matchless advances in
science, art, literature, and all material and cultural
developments of the past two thousand years. It
must be of the spirit if we are to save the flesh.

Not long after this ceremony, President Truman suggested to General Marshall that he invite MacArthur
back to the States so the nation could express its gratitude with ticker-tape parades and the like. The invitation
went out on September 17. But MacArthur declined
owing to the "delicate and difficult situation" in Japan.
Truman was miffed. The invitation was repeated on
October 19, this time beginning "The President has asked
me. . . ." Again MacArthur declined, because of the
"extraordinarily dangerous and inherently inflammable
situation" in Japan. And again Truman was miffed. A
suggestion from the President was tantamount to an
order. Although MacArthur had not technically violated
an order, his response was insulting. He further angered
Truman by announcing from Tokyo on September 17,
without clearance from Washington, that the 400,000-
man occupation force could be pared in half. This,
Truman wrote in his *Memoirs*, was "embarrassing." And
so the cordial note on which the Truman-MacArthur
relationship began quickly turned acrimonious. That would
prove to be unfortunate for MacArthur. Had he accepted
Truman's invitation, gone home, and got to know the
President, his postwar life might have turned out far
differently.

CHAPTER
THIRTY-FIVE

★ ★ ★ ★ ★

NEVER IN THE history of the United States had one man been handed so much responsibility and so great a challenge as that thrust upon MacArthur in postwar Japan. Germany had been split up into four occupation zones; Japan was not. As Supreme Commander for the Allied powers, MacArthur, at age sixty-five, was absolute ruler of a nation of seventy-five million people. He was dictator, proconsul, shogun, czar. He would retain that position for five years and seven months—until April 11, 1951. His influence on postwar Japan was profound. His tour there —his final career assignment—would be the high point of a long and distinguished life in war and peace.

After the surrender ceremony, MacArthur and GHQ remained in Yokohama at the New Grand Hotel a week or so longer. But all hands were anxious to move to Tokyo and establish a permanent headquarters from which to supervise the horrendous tasks which lay immediately ahead. On September 8, MacArthur and his party traveled through twenty-two miles of rubble from Yokohama to Tokyo by automobile caravan. Bull Halsey and Eichelberger were in the party. It proceeded to the vast, luxurious American Embassy compound (built in

President Hoover's day), which, except for damage to the Chancery building, had survived the bombing of Tokyo.

There was an honor guard from the 11th Airborne in parade formation on the Embassy grounds. Taking position on the terrace facing the bombed Chancery, MacArthur said to Eichelberger: "Have our country's flag unfurled, and in Tokyo's sun, let it wave in its full glory as a symbol of hope for the oppressed and as a harbinger of victory for the right." The flag was the same that had flown over the Capitol on December 7, 1941, and on the *Missouri* during the surrender ceremony. As it rose, bugles sounded and, Eichelberger recalled, "there were many wet eyes in that martial assembly." The long road to Tokyo had at last come to an end. Curiously, Nimitz did not attend this final ceremony. Perhaps he thought it anticlimactic.

MacArthur had chosen the Embassy for his personal quarters. It had not been occupied during the war. It was a mess inside. The furniture was ruined; there was ankle-deep water on the floor in places. Sloshing through the mess, MacArthur found an undamaged portrait of George Washington. Later he wrote: "It moved me more than I can say. It seemed peculiarly appropriate that he should be there calmly awaiting the arrival of Americans arms."

Eichelberger's troops set to work immediately to make the Embassy habitable. Meanwhile, MacArthur lived in temporary quarters in Yokohama and Tokyo. Little by little, the prewar Embassy servants and gardeners drifted back to their old jobs, timidly going in the back way. Whitney wrote that they went to the attic, dug into some trunks, and reappeared in Embassy staff kimonos. By mid-September the Embassy was ready, and MacArthur sent for his family.

The family party arrived by aircraft at Atsugi on September 19. It included Jean, Arthur, Ah Cheu, and a new addition, Arthur's private tutor, Mrs. Phyllis Gibbons. Mrs. Gibbons, or, "Gibby," was an English schoolteacher who had been interned by the Japanese in Manila on December 28, 1941, and liberated by MacArthur's forces in February 1945. By now, she was an integral part of the family and would remain so until 1951. The ever-present Sid Huff was not in the group.

He was escorting Wainwright back to the States. He would shortly rejoin the MacArthur family in Tokyo.

MacArthur, unarmed and escorted by a single unarmed aide, met the plane. One aide wrote that on the trip to Tokyo, Jean saw the Japanese soldiers along the road and asked her husband: "It it safe?" MacArthur replied: "Perfectly safe."

For his SCAP headquarters, MacArthur chose the Dai-Ichi "Number One" building, formerly the offices of a large Japanese insurance firm. It faced the moat of the emperor's burned-out palace. Considering MacArthur's station, his personal office was austere, a small, walnut-paneled, air-conditioned room on the sixth floor with a single window looking on a blank wall. It had formerly been a storage room. It was furnished with "crumpled, leather-covered, and overstuffed furniture" and a plain desk covered with green baize. There was a glass-front bookcase containing books of Army Regulations and a pipe table with fifty pipes and a tobacco bowl. But no telephone. On the wall were portraits of Washington and Lincoln. Beneath the portrait of Lincoln was a lettered card:

> If I were to try to read, much less answer, all the attacks made on me, this shop might as well be closed for any other business. I do the very best I know how, the very best I can, and I mean to keep doing so until the end. If the end brings me out all right, what is said against me won't amount to anything. If the end brings me out wrong, ten angels swearing I was right would make no difference.

Once he had moved to his embassy home and Dai-Ichi office, MacArthur settled into a remarkably fixed existence. His entire world became home and office. He worked seven days a week, keeping late hours. He observed no holiday—not even Christmas or Easter. Except for occasional trips to the Tokyo airport to greet arriving VIPs, he never traveled about Japan. He did not attend parties or receptions. Only twice in almost five years did he leave Japan: On July 4, 1946, to fly to Manila for the celebration of Filipino Independence Day, and to Seoul, Korea, on August 15, 1948, to attend cere-

monies proclaiming the creation of the Republic of Korea.
Both of these trips were one day affairs.

The day began in the MacArthur household at seven
or seven-thirty in a second-floor eating area. Most morn-
ings were like a "mild touch of madness" says Huff, or
"near bedlam," says Whitney. The MacArthurs now had
four dogs: a cocker spaniel named Blackie, the general's
favorite; a white akita called Uki; a Japanese shiba ter-
rier, Brownie; and another cocker, Koko. At about eight
o'clock, these four yapping, frisky dogs would be allowed
into the house. Invariably they made a beeline for the
eating area. At about that time, the general would take
his place at the breakfast table, wearing his grey West
Point bath robe with a black *A* over the heart. About
that same time, Mrs. Gibbons would arrive.

Then, with the dogs skittering around, the family had
breakfast. This was preceded by prayer. Mrs. Gibbons
read from the Anglican Book of Prayer. MacArthur read
a passage from the Bible. Then they ate. MacArthur
always had a hearty breakfast: fruit, cereal, eggs, toast,
coffee. Afterwards Mrs. Gibbons escorted Arthur, now
seven years old, to a room in the embassy which she
utilized for her tutoring.

MacArthur returned to his bedroom for his daily
calisthenics, the only exercise, other than pacing, he
indulged in. The four dogs followed him into the bedroom. Huff wrote: "He had a regular routine of simple
exercises, always ending up with the same bending exercise
and the dogs knew perfectly when he came to the last
one. After he had finished, Uki and Brownie and Koko.
. . . left the room, but Blackie was permitted to remain
while the general washed and shaved . . . Blackie lived
the life of Riley, acting as if he owned the place."

Now the work day began—about nine o'clock. Mac-
Arthur read the newspapers, then he tackled his mail. He
opened all his own personal mail, both at home and at
the office. He usually wrote a reply on the opposite side
of the letter in longhand or else directed it by initials to
the proper subordinate for reply. Very occasionally he
would dictate a letter to Jean that would later be typed
at the office. During this time, Courtney Whitney would
telephone from the Dai-Ichi Building to brief the general
on "important" wire-service stories. During football season,
these included the scores of every major college game.

Since his days as superintendent at West Point, MacArthur had been a football fanatic. He remained so until his death.

About ten-thirty or eleven o'clock, sometimes later, MacArthur left for his office. He rode alone in the back seat of his black 1941 Cadillac, liberated in Manila. At first he had an escort—two soldiers in a jeep. MacArthur disliked the escort and had it curtailed It was later reinstated when his car broke down and he had to hitch a ride from an astonished soldier in a jeep.

It was a five-and-a-half-minute drive from the embassy to the Dai-Ichi Building. Along the way Japanese policemen, signalling to one another down the street, turned the traffic lights green for the Cadillac, stopping cross traffic. On arrival at the Dai-Ichi, MacArthur alighted, saluted the spit-and-polished sentries on duty, strode to the elevator (held for his sole use at that time), and went up to the sixth floor.

Over the years, this ritualized trip became somewhat of a tourist attraction—for Japanese and Americans alike. Crowds, mostly Japanese, gathered at both the embassy and the Dai-Ichi Building to get a fleeting glimpse of the Supreme Commander. It would have been the simplest matter in the world for an assassin to mingle in these crowds and kill MacArthur. GHQ constantly fretted over this danger But MacArthur apparently never did. He was still the fatalist. When his time came, it would come.

Many of the Bataan Gang were still on hand, but there had been a significant shift in the inner power structure. Sutherland had now fallen from favor. He would shortly leave for home. After that the chief of staff job became a revolving door. Following Sutherland came Richard J. Marshall, another from Battan days. Then Stephen J. Chamberlain, who had joined MacArthur in Australia; and Paul J. Mueller, who served Nimitz in the war; and then Major General Edward M. Almond, from the European Theater.

The real second-echelon power at SCAP, rested no longer with the chief of staff but with Courtney Whitney, who was now head of the Government Section, and to a lesser extent with Charles Willoughby, still the intelligence chief. Wrote Frazier Hunt of Whitney: "He had to a most unusual degree a talent for translating to paper

MacArthur's wishes and thoughts, and he became extremely valuable in the important task of writing out statements and announcements that gave the exact shade of meaning the General desired." Whitney's office was immediately adjacent to MacArthur's. He was the first man MacArthur talked to in the morning (by telephone) and the first man he saw at the Dai-Ichi Building. Whitney allegedly was the only man at SCAP who could knock on MacArthur's door without a prior appointment. It was natural that others at SCAP were jealous of Whitney's role as *eminence grise*.

Now, settled in his phoneless office, MacArthur, with Whitney present, tackled the accumulated paperwork. This usually fell into two categories: dispatches and personal mail. The envelopes of the latter were half slit by a clerk—but not opened. As at home, MacArthur usually replied to his personal mail in longhand on the reverse side of the letter. (Everyone who wrote MacArthur received a personal reply.) He seldom used a stenographer—although he sometimes dictated to Whitney, who "invariably had difficulty keeping abreast of his flow of words." He wrote as he talked, Whitney said, "in fully composed sentences." He did practically no revising.

It is perhaps unfortunate that MacArthur, or Whitney, or whoever was doing the writing of the moment did not take time to revise. MacArthur's prose had always been ornate in the extreme. The florid war communiqués were bad enough, but in Tokyo the written output diminished ever further in conciseness and objectivity. A visitor to SCAP a few years later, the writer John Gunther (author of the best-selling *Inside* series) observed in his book *The Riddle of MacArthur*: "It is astonishing that anybody who talks as well as MacArthur should write so badly. . . . It is not merely that his style is pompous. It is worse than that."

After MacArthur cleared his desk, he was ready for appointments. This schedule, as Whitney explained, often turned into something of a problem. As we have seen, MacArthur was a talker, a monologist. Once he began talking to a visitor, pacing on the gray Army-issue carpet, lighting one of his pipes, he was difficult to stop, "as if he had nothing to do for the rest of the day," Whitney reported. For this reason, appointments with MacArthur were severely restricted. Few Japanese, other than the prime minister, ever saw him.

MacArthur had lunch at the embassy with Jean—or with guests. Lunchtime was the only occasion they entertained. He usually left the Dai-Ichi about 2 P.M., returning home in the Cadillac by the same route, with the same gawking-tourist crowds and the same rigid traffic rituals. If there were guests, Jean and Sid Huff would have them assembled in the drawing room, waiting. When MacArthur came into the room, Jean (already alerted by phone of his arrival time) would look up, feign surprise, and say: "Oh, here's the general!" Mac-Arthur would walk over and kiss her. She would beam and say: "Hello, Sir Boss," or "Hello, General." (She never called him Douglas or Doug in public.) No cock-tails were served; the guests were ushered into the dining room with polite chitchat. The MacArthurs did not observe protocol—seating people by military or diplo-matic rank. For those who set much store by these formalities—many diplomats did—this was disconcerting.

Gunther and his wife attended one of those luncheons. He wrote of MacArthur: "What struck me most was his lightness, humor, and give-and-take. The *mystique* of the great commander so surrounds MacArthur that one is apt to forget how human he is. I expected him to be oracular, volcanic, and unceasing. He was all of that, but some-thing else too; he laughed a good deal, enjoyed jokes, told some pretty good ones, permitted interruptions, and listened well . . . MacArthur ate almost nothing, but drank several cups of coffee with heaping spoonsful of sugar. Part of the time he looked directly at us or his wife; part of the time he talked with his face gazing steadily, fixedly, out of the window to his right. What was he looking for, looking at?"

There was one notable exception to the guests-only-at-lunch rule. That was when the Japanese Emperor Hirohito came to call, usually twice a year. He did *not* come for lunch. These visits were coldly formal affairs. MacArthur described the first visit in his memoirs.

Immediately upon arrival in Japan, some of Mac-Arthur's staffers insisted that he summon the forty-four-year-old Emperor to SCAP as a "show of power." MacArthur, who understood the Japanese far better than any of his staff, "brushed the suggestion aside," explaining that "to do so would be to outrage the feelings of the Japanese people and make a martyr of the emperor in their eyes." Above all, MacArthur did not wish to demean the emperor. He was counting on the emperor's mystical hold over the Japanese to further his own grand design for rebuilding the country. He would wait; the emperor would voluntarily come to see him.

Indeed, shortly thereafter, the emperor requested an interview with MacArthur. On September 27, four weeks after the formal surrender and eight days after Jean arrived, the emperor, wearing a cutaway, striped trousers, and top hat, arrived with an aide in his Daimler. MacArthur cordially met him at the door and escorted him to a seat before the fire at the end of the long reception hall. There was only one other person present: the emperor's interpreter. MacArthur thought Hirohito was nervous; the stress of war plainly showed. He offered Hirohito an American cigarette; the emperor accepted with thanks. As MacArthur lit the cigarette he noticed the emperor's hands were shaking.

By this time the British and Russians—particularly the Russians—and not a few Americans were clamoring for Hirohito's head. But MacArthur thought that would be "tragic," leading to widespread rioting and insurrection in Japan. MacArthur had told Washington that if Hirohito were arrested and tried as a war criminal, he, SCAP, would need "a million reinforcements." Now, facing the man he had saved, MacArthur "had an uneasy feeling he might plead his own cause against indictment as a war criminal." But he did the opposite. He assumed the entire blame. As MacArthur recalled, the emperor said: "I come to you, General MacArthur, to offer myself to the judgment of the powers you represent as the one to bear sole responsibility for every political and military decision made and action taken by my people in the conduct of the war." MacArthur was moved to "the very marrow" of his bones.

After the emperor had departed—not much else was said in this first ceremonial meeting—MacArthur immediately sought out Jean to tell her how the emperor looked. But she was far ahead of him. As MacArthur told it, she laughed and said: "Oh I saw him. Arthur and I were peeking behind the red curtains." Added

MacArthur: "It's a funny world, but delightful, no matter how you figure it."

After lunch, after the guests had departed, MacArthur invariably went to his bedroom, took off his clothes, and had a solid one-hour nap. Afterwards he would read the evening paper, talk with Jean about Arthur, still the apple of his eye. Then, about five o'clock, MacArthur would return to the Dai-Ichi Building for a second stint in the office following the same route in the Cadillac.

By now, of course, the general was refreshed and ready to put in long hours. The staff, which had already worked a full, normal day, would now gear up for three or four hours of overtime. This second stint made normal social life for the staffers impossible. Gunther, who spent several weeks at SCAP, wrote: "This is hard on the staff. In fact it is murderous." But, wrote Gunther, when someone complained to the general that he was "killing" his staff with work, MacArthur replied: "What better fate for a man than to die in performance of his duty?"

The evenings were also rigidly programmed. MacArthur usually left the office about 8:30 or 9:00 P.M., returning by the same route. The MacArthurs almost never entertained at dinner. MacArthur had a very light snack, then he and Jean proceeded at once to the larger dining room for the evening movie. All embassy staffers, including soldiers on sentry duty, were invited to the movies; usually about fifty people attended. MacArthur sat in a red-painted bedroom wicker rocking chair with cushions which he had had since Australia days. He lit up a cigar, leaned back, and stretched out his legs. Jean, who usually chose the movie fare, gave him newsreels, light comedies, or westerns—nothing heavy or depressing because the point was "relaxation." Arthur was permitted to attend on Saturday nights. There was no movie Sunday night.

After the movie, Huff wrote, MacArthur would feel the need to talk again. As usual, he paced. The embassy first floor was an idea place for that—125 linear feet of unobstructed walkway. He would pace up and down, hands clasped behind his back, pouring out his problems to Jean, "thinking out loud." Sometimes he paced until one o'clock in the morning, talking, talking. "By then Jean could hardly keep her eyes open," Huff wrote. Then, finally, to bed.

That, then, with few deflections, was the MacArthur life in Japan, day after day, week after week, month after month, year after year. It was a spartan life, almost monastic. It was self-imposed, designed to enable MacArthur to focus his enormous energies on the problems at hand. These were truly astounding in scope and complexity.

CHAPTER
THIRTY-SIX

★ ★ ★ ★ ★

IT IS UNIVERSALLY agreed by journalists and scholars who have studied the postwar period in Japanese history that MacArthur and the officers and soldiers under his command did an excellent job of demilitarizing and democratizing the nation. It was probably the most successful occupation of a major defeated power by its victors in the entire history of the world. The success was due partly to the restraint, the austerity, the goodwill, idealism, and dedication projected by MacArthur, his staff, and the first occupying troops; partly to the peculiar nature of the Japanese people; partly to the absolute thoroughness of the defeat.

Japan was physically and morally devastated. When the war ended, the people were uprooted, starving, disillusioned with their way of life, demoralized, paralyzed. But they were by nature and custom a peculiarly adaptable race with a strong sense of hierarchy and obedience, combined with an historical desire to please and be accepted. The emperor, who held a mystical power over these people, had set the tone: repent, redeem ourselves, play by the new rules. By and large, the people did. Most wanted to build a new way of life. Another factor was the absence of any personal animosity on the part of the Japanese. Since the days of Commodore Perry, the Japanese had sincerely liked and looked up to Americans. The vicious wartime anti-American propaganda had not taken root.

Yet another factor, often overlooked, was MacArthur's decision to retain not only the emperor but the Japanese government. In Germany, which had been invaded and overrun, the Nazi government had been completely destroyed. It was replaced, temporarily, by a four-power government of occupation officers, all too many unqualified for the jobs. But the Japanese government was intact at the surrender and remained so. Thus, MacArthur ruled Japan symbolically through the emperor and practically through existing government machinery, from the prime minister down. From the start he adopted the practice of having SCAP suggest rather than order, and while the Japanese understood well that a SCAP suggestion had the force of an order, this wrapping of the iron fist in velvet made things more palatable. The Japanese developed a tremendous respect for MacArthur.

On his part, MacArthur brought to his job and position a long-held respect for the Japanese. This respect dated back to 1905, when he joined his father in Tokyo. It had not been diminished by wartime atrocities. These had been committed by a relatively small handful of Japanese soldiers, not the populace, who were generally shocked dumb when they learned of them. MacArthur considered the Japanese thrifty and industrious. In the entire Far East, they alone had industrial know-how. His goal was to demilitarize the nation, then rebuild it industrially and economically, and turn it into an ally of the United States, again dominating the Far East. Always the optimist, he thought this could be done in three years, by which time, historically, occupiers even under the most favorable of circumstances usually lost the respect and cooperation of the occupied. After that time, American troops would go home.

The first of his tasks, demilitarization of Japan, embraced six major programs. These were the demobilization of military personnel, destruction of military equipment, the breakup of the military-industrial establishment (Zaibatsu), the purging of militarists (or ultranationalists) from public office or key jobs in industry, the trial of war criminals, the abolishment of State Shinto, and a sweeping reform in Japan's police system. Each of these programs is worth a brief look.

Demobilization

When the war ended, there were nearly seven million Japanese men in the uniform of the armed forces. About half of these were in Japan proper, the rest overseas, as were three million Japanese civilians. The immense task of demobilizing these men and returning those overseas to Japan was carried out by the Japanese Army and Navy headquarters, renamed Demobilization Bureaus. Owing to an acute shortage of shipping it took more than a year to complete this job. Some of the civilians overseas had been there most of their lives and did not want to go home. They lost their accumulated possessions and businesses and came home to become a burden on the economy, like the demobilized military. The Russians had captured about 470,000 Japanese in Korea, Manchuria, and elsewhere. Most were sent to slave labor camps. Only 90,000 were returned to Japan, and many of these had been converted to Communism. In addition to the foregoing, the Demobilization Bureaus freed about a million and a half Chinese and Koreans who had been enslaved by the Japanese. About a million elected to go home and were sent. But half a million remained in Japan.

Destruction of Military Equipment

Throughout Japan, and in other places, such as Formosa, there were mountains of military equipment and supplies. In Japan, for example, there were twelve thousand aircraft of various kinds—four thousand operable. There were countless tanks, rifles, and other tools of war. For months, Eichelberger's and Krueger's troops scoured Japan, blowing ammunition dumps, burning aircraft, or dumping weapons into the ocean. Arsenals and factories producing war matériel were padlocked. Naval bases and shipbuilding yards were destroyed, airfields ploughed up—though many airfields were refurbished for the occupying Allied air forces. Inasmuch as it became necessary to rearm Japan five years later (at American expense) the destruction of these billions of dollars worth of war matériel has been criticized in some quarters. But that is a criticism with the benefit of hindsight. In the fall of 1945, no one would have voted for stockpiling and saving Japan's munitions.

The Breakup of Zaibatsu

For decades, about eighty percent of Japan's industrial and financial wealth had been closely held by a very few extraordinarily rich families, such as the Mitsubishis and Mitsuis. These cartels were known collectively as Zaibatsu. MacArthur, and others, believed them to be undemocratic, militaristic, and imperialistic, like the German Krupp cartel. He ordered that this vast and complex corporate structure be dissolved. Originally twelve hundred companies were destined for dissolution. But this program was hugely unpopular both in the United States and Japan. The Japanese economy could not function without the Zaibatsu—or some benevolent form of it. When it was realized that economic recovery might be delayed indefinitely, with the United States taxpayers footing the bill through foreign aid programs, the breakup of the Zaibatsu was curtailed. In the end, only nine of the twelve hundred corporations were dissolved. However, these initial efforts, plus other steps, greatly diminished the power of the Zaibatsu families. The surviving corporations were prohibited from manufacturing anything remotely useful in war, such as aircraft, synthetic oil, and rubber—even bearings.

The Purge

In January 1946, SCAP began a so-called purge program aimed at barring militarists and imperialists, or ultranationalists, from public office or key jobs in industry. The purge idea had originated at Potsdam. MacArthur "doubted its wisdom" and put it in effect "with as little harshness as possible." It turned Willoughby's intelligence office into a Gestapolike operation, probing into people's past lives, and it caused widespread grief among the Japanese. Generally, anybody who had served as a commissioned officer in the military, or held important posts in certain ultranationalistic political associations or in occupied countries, or in the military-industrial complex, were purged. A total of about 200,000 persons were barred from public office (including all of the Zaibatsu) and some 1300 political or quasipolitical, ultranationalistic organizations disbanded. The purge effectively broke the hold of the old-line executives and politicians in the power centers, allowing new, untainted leadership to emerge. However, the purge was not entirely successful, and occasionally it was unfair. It was not punitive, as was the "de-Nazification" program in Germany. None of the 200,000 purgees went to jail or paid fines, but many had a hard time finding new jobs. After the Occupation terminated, some people were "de-purged." But by that time, the senior citizens were too old to regain control of the power structure.

War Crimes Trials

These trials, as in Germany, were meant to serve two purposes; punish those responsible for starting the war and allowing or committing atrocities, and to drive home to the Japanese the message that war does not pay. There were three classes of war criminal: A, B, C. The "A" criminals were big shots, such as Tojo. Twenty-five of these (mostly generals) were tried in Tokyo by an International Military Tribunal, which was staffed with judges from eleven nations. Six generals and one civilian were hanged, sixteen got life sentences, two received lesser sentences. The "B" offenders were twenty-odd high-ranking generals whose troops had committed atrocities (Homma's Bataan Death March, for example). They were tried by SCAP military courts. Two (including Homma) were executed; all others were acquitted. The 4,200 "C" offenders were those accused of minor atrocities or mistreatment of POWs. (Tokyo Rose was one.) They were tried by various Allied military courts. Seven hundred were sentenced to death, four hundred were acquitted, and the rest sent to jail for various terms. The Japanese scholar Kazuo Kawai wrote that these trials "did not have a major impact on the Japanese people." The trials dragged on interminably (to November 1948), people got bored, or irritated, by the constant reminder of their guilt. This finally turned into "mild pity" for these old, broken men.

Abolishing State Shintoism

Long before the war, the Japanese militarists had seized on Shinto as a means of hyping nationalistic fervor. Shinto was a highly complicated religion that combined ancestor worship, patriotism, and a conviction that the emperor and the people (even the soil) were divine. (The emperor is said to be a descendent of the sun goddess.) It's chief features were emperor worship and self-sacrifice.

In time Shinto became the official state religion—State Shinto—and it served the armed forces well in wartime. Shinto held that a man killed in battle became a god himself.

Almost immediately SCAP took steps to wipe out State Shinto. On December 15, 1945, it was disestablished as a state religion. The Japanese government was prohibited from supporting it—or any other religion. All mention of it was deleted from school textbooks. All symbols of it were removed from public buildings. Shinto holidays were abolished. Some 8,000 Shinto monuments were torn down. The emperor's portrait was removed from the schools, and students were prohibited from bowing toward the Imperial Palace, as was the custom. On January 1, 1946, Hirohito (no doubt encouraged by MacArthur) told the Japanese people that he was not divine, had never been divine, and it was all a regrettable "myth." To further humanize himself, the emperor was encouraged to go about Japan like a European monarch, attending sporting events, concerts, and other public functions. Thus was the emperor turned into a more conventional sovereign.

Police Reform

The police force in Japan was a national organization, controlled by bureaucrats in Tokyo. During the war it had become very much like the Nazi Gestapo. It was used to suppress—and oppress—the people and to encourage warlike sentiment. In the early days of the Occupation, MacArthur demanded the police force be decentralized. Every town of more than five thousand population would be responsible for maintaining its own local police force, which would be answerable only to local authority. This measure effectively destroyed the hated national police force but led to many problems. Some communities could not afford adequate police protection, and the quality of career policemen fell dramatically, leading to widespread police corruption. After the Occupation the Japanese reinstituted the national police force—with more effective controls.

While these programs were under way, MacArthur and SCAP were also engaged in positive programs to democratize Japan. It is often said that SCAP started from scratch. Not so. As Kazuo Kawai, Edwin O. Reischauer, and other Japanese scholars point out, there had been democratic sentiment building in Japan for some time— even before the war. A large proportion of the Japanese were now ready for a more democratic system. What SCAP did was to skillfully utilize these sentiments, hurrying along a process that might well have taken decades. The principal steps were five: a new constitution; buildup of local political autonomy; land, labor, and educational reform. Each of these, too, deserves a brief look.

New Constitution

SCAP and Japanese authorities, after much internal debate, produced a new constitution for Japan. The end result (actually an amendment to the existing constitution) was somewhat like a cross between the British and American constitutions. It reduced the emperor to the status of a "symbol" of Japan, granting the real sovereignty to the people. It established a three-part national government, like that in the United States: legislative, judicial, executive. The legislature, the Diet, would be the "highest organ of state power," the "sole law-making organ of the State." The Diet's two bodies were called the House of Councillors (somewhat like the U.S. Senate) and the House of Representatives. All members of each body would be popularly elected to terms of six and four years, respectively. (Heretofore, many legislators had been appointed or had inherited seats.) The Diet's House elected the prime minister, who (as in Britain) was responsible directly to the Diet. The majority of the prime minister's cabinet would also be members of the Diet. The constitution also contained no less than thirty-one articles guaranteeing the rights of the people: freedom of religion, assembly, speech, press, etc.

It also contained the famous no-war clause: "The people forever renounce war as a sovereign right of the Nation and the threat or use of force as a means of settling international disputes." There would never again be an army, navy, or air force.

The constitution was announced by the emperor and MacArthur on March 6, 1946. At MacArthur's specific request, it was put to the people for a vote in the first general election (in which women, for the first time, were permitted to vote) on April 10, 1946. It was widely de-

bated and overwhelmingly approved. It took effect on
May 3, 1947.

Buildup of Local Political Autonomy

The local governments in Japan (state, city, etc.) were
rigidly controlled by the Tokyo bureaucracy; the power
centered in the infamous Home Ministry. Local executives
were appointed by Tokyo, not elected. The people were
required to belong to "neighborhood associations" through
which Tokyo's orders were passed. MacArthur ordered
that the Home Ministry and the neighborhood associations
be abolished outright, that local authorities be chosen by
popular elections, and that local legislative bodies —also
popularly elected -pass or revoke the laws dealing with
their areas. The American scholar (and one time ambassador to Japan), Edwin O. Reischauer, believes this
program was something of a failure, like the decentraliza-
tion of the police. He wrote: "The Japanese, unfamiliar
with the concept of broad local self-government, have
shown little interest in the increased powers of their local
assemblies and have continued to look to Tokyo for leadership even in matters on which local bodies are now em-
powered to take independent action."

Land Reform

Japan had a feudalistic agrarian economy. Half of the
arable land was, as Whitney put it, "worked by tenants
under exorbitant sharecropper arrangement and in some
areas even under near-slavery conditions imposed by
dictatorial landlords." At MacArthur's suggestion, the
Diet passed a series of sweeping new laws designed to
correct this inequity. The most important of these directed
that the federal government buy about five million acres
of farm land and then resell it to the tenants on a very
long term arrangement. By 1950, eighty-nine percent of
the arable land of Japan was owned by free, independent
farmers who worked their own property. MacArthur
described this program as "the most successful experiment
of its kind in history."

Labor and Economic Reform

The war had completely destroyed Japan's economic
base. Most of the people had no food, no money, no
clothes, no shelter, no jobs. To survive, city folk went

to the countryside and traded heirlooms to farmers for scraps of food. Inflation was rampant; a large black market sprang into being. SCAP distributed whatever food it could round up from American bases and doled out confiscated Japanese military clothing: twenty-one million pairs of socks, seven million wool blankets, five million pairs of shoes, and so on. Later MacArthur received authorization to import three and a half million tons of food from the United States. This food kept hundreds of thousands of Japanese from starving. In addition, MacArthur gave firm orders that no occupation troops would ever take—or even buy—food from the Japanese.

Rebuilding Japan's economic base was naturally the most challenging job of the Occupation. It was complicated by the plan to dissolve the Zaibatsu and the purging of skilled business executives. The goal was to establish a new system of private competitive enterprise which was more widely owned and from which the workers would derive a greater share of the profits. The new constitution specified that all people (male and female) had "the right and obligation" to work and that "the right of workers to organize and to bargain and act collectively is guaranteed."

Labor unions were not new to Japan. Before the war, some half-million workers had been organized, but in postwar Japan the growth of unions was phenomenal, nearly uncontrollable. By 1949 almost half of the fifteen million workers were members of some thirty-five thousand unions. The Diet passed a liberal labor law not unlike the Wagner Act, with provisions for protecting workers' rights and granting them the right to strike. Labor immediately ran amuk with this new freedom, creating widespread unrest (strikes, riots) and forcing some corporations, barely limping along, to close down. Labor's excessive demands were severely retarding economic recovery. MacArthur had to swing the pendulum the other way. In 1949 he pressured the Diet to pass a more restrictive labor law, one which was more like the Taft-Hartley Act. The workers were unhappy with this— and other restrictions—but ultimately the pendulum swung back to the middle of the road. The overall goal was achieved. Wrote Kazuo Kawai: "The Japanese labor movement must be regarded in its overall effects as one of the most significant forces for democracy set in motion by the Occupation."

Economic recovery was slow at first. It became necessary for the United States to give Japan economic assistance —some two billion dollars in all. This pump-priming, together with the energy, diligence, ambition, and skill of the Japanese people (and a fortuitous series of unprecedented large bumper crops on the farms) did the trick. By 1950, Japan was well on the road to economic recovery. In later years she would boom spectacularly. The workers enjoyed a much higher standard of living than they had ever known.

Educational Reforms

The Japanese school system was somewhat like the European system: rigid and discriminatory. There was a six-year compulsory coeducational elementary school, separate five-year middle schools for boys and girls, and finally, for boys only, a higher school of three years, and three or four years at a university. Only about 3.5 percent of the students went beyond eleventh grade, and only 1 percent went on to universities. The system was rigidly controlled by the Ministry of Education in Tokyo. SCAP completely scrapped the school system, building in its place a liberal, American-type system. It extended the compulsory phase; introduced new teaching methods designed to encourage independent thinking; issued new textbooks from which false propaganda, emperor worship, and militarism had been weeded; encouraged local control of schools; and "de-purged" many teachers who had been barred from their jobs. Japanese educators were thoroughly baffled by these sweeping changes, but the students profited. They emerged better educated and more independent-minded. A far higher percentage went on to junior colleges and universities.

To all of this must be added a final note: the contribution of the G.I. as ambassador. Over 400,000 soldiers, sailors, and marines poured into Japan after the surrender. They bivouacked all over the home islands, even in the remotest hamlets. The Japanese, expecting raping and plundering (young girls were hidden away), were astonished to find the G.I.s big, friendly, honorable, helpful. They gave children food and clothing. They provided some jobs. The G.I.s in turn discovered the Japanese people were not the sinister, treacherous animals they had been briefed to find. They were charming, docile, eager to learn, to be friends. So, as Whitney observed, "Kipling erred; the twain *did* meet." There is nothing more demorcatic than the average G.I. The contribution of these men to the democratization of Japan was immeasurable and profound.

CHAPTER
THIRTY-SEVEN

★ ★ ★ ★ ★

IN THE POSTWAR years, Communism in its various guises became a potent force in the Far East. In return for entering the war, Russia had occupied the Kurile Islands, Southern Sakhalin, North Korea down to the 38th parallel, and parts of Manchuria. On the Chinese mainland, the army of the Communist Mao Tse-tung, locked in battle with the Nationalist army of Chiang Kai-shek, was growing ever more powerful and effective. MacArthur viewed these developments uneasily. On Communism he had been a hawk for years. It will be recalled that after the Bonus March episode he believed he had been personally marked for destruction by the Kremlin.

The Russians soon sought to expand their influence in Japan by various means. The first step was an astonishing proposal from the Russian liaison officer in Japan, Lieutenant General Kusma Derevyanko, that Soviet troops occupy Hokkaido, the northernmost of the Japanese home islands. These troops would not be under MacArthur's command. MacArthur refused point blank Derevyanko became "abusive," MacArthur wrote, threatening that Stalin would have MacArthur dismissed. Then he said the troops would come whether MacArthur approved or not. MacArthur told Derevyanko that if a single Russian soldier entered Japan without his permission, he would throw the entire Russian Mission, including Derevyanko, in jail. Derevyanko considered this and said, "By God, I believe you would." In the face of this firm stand, the Russians backed down, and Japan was not divided.

The Russians did not stop there. They turned next to political harassment. With the assistance of the British, in December, 1945, in Moscow, they succeeded in creating a so-called Far East Commission which would meet in Washington and give MacArthur orders through a Tokyo agency, the Allied Council for Japan. MacArthur was not consulted. When he learned of these two bodies, he was furious. He was further enraged when an American State Department spokesman told the media that MacArthur had been consulted throughout the proceedings in Moscow and "did not object" to the plan. In Tokyo, MacArthur released a public statement saying he had "no iota of responsibility" for the Moscow proceeding, and it was "incorrect" to say that he did not object to it.

In reality, these two bodies were to have little or no effect on MacArthur or his Occuation policies. They turned into debating societies, useful mainly as a platform for Moscow's anti-SCAP propaganda. But the fact that Washington had yielded to the Russians in creating them, and then told the media MacArthur did not object, caused profound distress and renewed paranoia at SCAP and GHQ. In essence, the view from the Dai-Ichi Building was that Washington was soft on Communism. This was a view that increased in intensity over the years. Whitney wrote: "It seemed to us on MacArthur's staff that at every crisis with the Communists in Japan, the failure of Washington support seemed to reflect almost studied indifference. We constantly received reports of underground opposition to MacArthur and his occupation policies, with the focus of the opposition seeming to be in the State Department. . . . he found it difficult to believe that there actually were people in Washington conspiring against him. There were those of us on his staff, however, who were not so charitable, and we viewed the situation with a growing uneasiness that gradually increased to actual alarm."

As time went on, SCAP staffers identified specific targets within the State Department. As Frazier Hunt wrote, it was a "tight little group" led by the newly appointed Undersecretary (later Secretary) of State Dean Acheson. It included John Carter Vincent, John Paton Davis (head of the China division), John Stewart Service, Lauchlin Currie, Owen Lattimore, and Alger Hiss. All these people would later be viciously attacked by Senators Richard Nixon and Joseph McCarthy, and other Republican conservatives who sought to create the impression that they were a pro-Communist clique or even Communist secret agents, bending American policies to the benefit of the Kremlin.

The feud between SCAP and the State Department—Dean Acheson in particular—began very early in the Occupation. As reported, on September 17, before the Occupation had much begun, MacArthur made a public statement to the effect that it would be possible to cut the 400,000-man occupation force by half within six months. Both Truman and Acheson were shocked by this statement from the field. As Acheson wrote in his memoirs, only thirty days before MacArthur had told Washington he would need a half-million men (subsequently reduced to 400,000). The Administration had fought hard for that force level in the Congress. MacArthur's statement, not cleared with Washington, seemed to bespeak a significant change in policy toward Japan, perhaps not the all-out occupation called for in the Potsdam Declaration.

Within the next two days, both Truman and Acheson were queried on the matter by the media. The President said—pointedly—that MacArthur had not consulted him. Acheson went much farther. Declining to comment on the technicality of troop levels, he said: "The important thing is that the policy in regard to Japan is the same policy which has always been held by this government and still is so far as I know, and I think I know. In carrying out that policy, the occupation forces are the instruments of the policy and not the determinants of policy. . ."

This comment from Acheson was considered a sharp rebuke to General MacArthur, a warning that Washington and not MacArthur made policy. Navy Secretary James Forrestal, in a note in his diary, considered MacArthur had been publically "censored." MacArthur's conservative supporters in the Senate rose to his defense. Senator

Kenneth Wherry of Nebraska insisted Acheson had "blighted the name" of MacArthur. He and others began an abortive movement to withhold Acheson's confirmation to office, then pending in the Senate. Acheson reflected: "If we could have seen into the future, we might have recognized this skirmish as the beginning of a struggle leading to the relief of General MacArthur from his command on April 11, 1951."

Thereafter, MacArthur, ever sensitive to criticism, regarded the State Department—Acheson in particular—as the enemy. William Sebald, the senior State Department officer at SCAP (he had rank of minister), in his memoir *With MacArthur in Japan*, wrote that MacArthur often considered State "foreign and hostile." He recounted numerous examples of what MacArthur considered the State Department "crowd" or "clique" trying to "undermine his position." After one such incident, Sebald wrote, MacArthur launched into a "pillorying of the State Department which, he said, he would one of these days 'blast wide open.'"

What was happening to MacArthur? The available evidence seems to indicate not only extreme paranoia but (a frequently related symptom) illusions of grandeur. He had stripped the emperor of his divinity, but now MacArthur, replacing the emperor as absolute ruler of Japan, appeared to be assuming a godlike posture himself. He was aloof, withdrawn, monastic. Other than Whitney, few men saw him. He refused to hold press conferences. American or foreign reporters who criticized a SCAP policy were harassed or evicted from Japan. The press was absolutely forbidden to publish anything other than favorable stories on SCAP. When he or SCAP were criticized in United States newspapers, he (or Whitney) would draft and send verbose and baroque replies—even to the smallest and least significant journals—often unwisely adding fuel to a fire that would have died of its own accord. The staff treated MacArthur with awed reverence. To visting journalists (John Gunther, for one), MacArthur was "the greatest man alive" or "too enormous, too unpredictable," the greatest general in history or the greatest man since Christ. MacArthur himself would say that "My major advisers now have boiled down to two men—George Washington and Abraham Lincoln."

This unhealthy state of mind, together with the unwise

counsel of a zealous and protective staff and the dissatisfaction with the Washington "crowd," may have led MacArthur into yet another bumbling political fiasco. As the presidential elections loomed in 1948, MacArthur was again being talked of as a possible Republican candidate. Although he had failed in 1944 to attract any substantial political base and had been humiliated in the Wisconsin primary, he decided to go for it. This time he was not coy. From his spartan office in the Dai-Ichi Building in Tokyo, he openly sought the nomination, within the legal restrictions imposed on an officer on active duty.

It was almost an exact replay of the 1944 fiasco. Fanned by the stridently anti-Truman Hearst press, MacArthur-for-President Clubs sprang up all over the country. In mid-March, MacArthur, vastly overestimating his political power base, threw his hat into the ring with this rococo press release:

> I have been informed that petitions have been filed in Madison, signed by many of my fellow citizens of Wisconsin, presenting my name to the electorate for consideration at the primary on April 6th. I am deeply grateful for this spontaneous display of friendly confidence. No man could fail to be profoundly stirred by such a public movement in this hour of momentous import, national and international, temporal and spiritual. While it seems unnecessary for me to repeat that I do not actively seek or covet any office and have no plans for leaving my post in Japan, I can say, and with due humility, that I would be recreant to all my concepts of good citizenship were I to shrink because of the hazards and responsibilities involved from accepting any public duty to which I might be called by the American people.

As in 1944, his supporters entered him in the Wisconsin primary as a "favorite son." Once again he faced opposition from Tom Dewey, the leading national Republican candidate, and Harold Stassen, no more than an outside hopeful, but an energetic campaigner who had support from Wisconsin's Senator Joe McCarthy. During the campaign, Dewey said of MacArthur: "This is not a war crisis—it is a peace crisis. Military genius, no matter

how excellent, is not the answer." Joe McCarthy ruth-
lessly attacked MacArthur, comparing him to two "physically weak presidents" (Wilson and Roosevelt), and made
repeated references to his divorce. MacArthur's opponents
also brought up the court-martial of Milwaukee's hero
Billy Mitchell, charging that MacArthur had voted for
his conviction. Wisely, MacArthur did not respond directly
to these charges; he maintained a Joblike silence.

When the votes were counted, the hard-slugging Stassen
had swept the field. He won nineteen delegates to Mac-
Arthur's eight. (Dewey had not campaigned much in
Wisconsin in the belief that MacArthur had sewn up the
state.) As in 1944, defeat in Wisconsin spelled the end
of MacArthur's chances. Wrote pro-Dewey *Time* magazine: "MacArthur's poor showing let the air out of the
MacArthur balloon with a sudden, dismal whoosh." So
far not a single important Republican had come out for
him.

It was not yet over. In late May, Republican Senator
Styles Bridges wrote MacArthur inviting him to appear
before a Senate committee to testify on Far East problems.
SCAP staffers, still overestimating MacArthur's presidential strength, urged MacArthur to accept the invitation—
to go home and take the country by storm. But after due
and careful reflection, MacArthur declined the invitation,
pleading "heavy pressure" in Tokyo and the fact that the
visit would be characterized by his critics as "politically
inspired." This was the final blow to his candidacy.

When the Republicans convened in Philadelphia in late
June, the leading contenders were Dewey, Stassen, Robert
A. Taft, and MacArthur's 1944 backer Arthur Vandenberg, a reluctant candidate who had said he would accept
a draft in the event of a deadlock. Dewey's forces soon
captured the convention. The Republicans permitted Mac-
Arthur's name to be placed in nomination in a deliberately
demeaning way—at about 4:00 A.M., when the hall was
all but deserted. He was nominated by blind Wisconsin
war veteran and attorney Harlan Kelley. Pitiful "Skinny"
Wainwright followed with a reedy seconding speech—to
empty chairs. On the first ballot MacArthur received 11
out of 1,094 votes. On the second, he got 7. Tom Dewey
was chosen unanimously on the third.

This final pathetic scene was a blow to MacArthur. His
journalist friend Clark Lee wrote that when Whitney de-

livered the news to MacArthur, the general "hung his head in deep emotional stress." Lee added: "The defeat was something of a shock also to the Japanese people, who could not understand how America could turn its back on this great leader." It may also have been a shock to Jean and little Arthur, now ten years old. Some of the memoirs suggest they were looking forward to going to the States, where Jean had not been in eleven years and Arthur never.

MacArthur later commented that those efforts of his supporters further angered Truman who, of course, beat Tom Dewey in a famous squeaker. MacArthur wrote, somewhat dishonestly and paranoicly: "I had not the slightest desire to become the head of state, having had more than enough of such an office in the administration of Japan. It was a great mistake on my part not to have been more positive in refusing to enter into the political picture. As might have been expected, the attempt was abortive, and its only tangible result was to bring down on my head an avalanche of political abuse from the party in power . . . From that moment on it only became a question of time until retaliation would be visited on me."

While the 1948 election was in progress, the civil war in China raged on toward a momentous climax. At Truman's request, General Marshall had gone to China to try to structure a coalition government between the Nationalists and Communists. When that failed, Mao Tse-tung's army went on full offensive again. Despite the fact that the United States had given Chiang Kai-shek one billion dollars in military aid and a similar amount in economic aid (through 1948), the generalissimo was steadily losing. By the end of 1948 Mao had control of all of Manchuria and most of China north of the Yangtze River. Chiang and his corrupt, inept staff were reeling; his army had lost the will to fight. On January 7, 1949, Chiang resigned as president of the Republic of China, turning the job over to his second in command, and fled to Formosa, which had been granted to Nationalist China after the war. He had already sent China's foreign exchange and monetary reserves there. The civil war was over; within a few months all of China was Mao's.

Few events in American foreign relations have inspired so much emotionalism and hokum as the so-called "loss of China." Republicans and Democrats unfriendly to Truman (such as young Congressman John F. Kennedy) heaped abuse on the President and Acheson, now Secretary of State. The United States had long had sentimental ties to the Chinese. They had been allies in the war. They had suffered unspeakably in decades of civil war. The Republicans desperately wanted to oust the Democrats from the White House. The loss of China was a heavensent issue, and they made the most of it. Acheson, in reality one of the shrewdest and most hawkish Secretaries of State in United States history, was painted in countless histrionic speeches as a bumbling idiot, a Communist party-liner, even a traitor.

MacArthur wisely withheld public comment on Chiang's defeat, but in his memoirs and in the memoirs of his aides, it is clear that his sympathy lay with Chiang Kai-shek. He took the highly questionable and hardly insightful or new position that had Truman and Acheson given Chiang more military aid, Chiang's collapse could have been avoided. He wrote: "At one blow, everything that had been so laboriously built up since the days of John Hay was lost. It was the beginning of the crumbling of our power in continental Asia—the birth of the taunt 'Paper Tiger.' Its consequences will be felt for centuries, and its ultimate disastrous effects on the fortunes of the free world are still to be unfolded."

China, then, was far from MacArthur's bailiwick. As Richard H. Rovere and Arthur Schlesinger, Jr. have written in their book *The MacArthur Controversy*, the general was not much of an expert on China. He had not been to China since 1905—when he visited briefly with his father. He had declared himself in favor of the coalition government. In March 1948, he had declined to respond to a House Committee seeking information on China because his information was too meager. ("With this background," he wrote, "you will readily perceive I am not in a position to render authoritative advice.") He had not smelled the corruption in Chiang's headquarters or seen his soldiers throwing down their rifles, fleeing by the thousands, or defecting to Mao. A new idea had taken hold in China. It could not have been snuffed out with ten billions in military aid.

CHAPTER
THIRTY-EIGHT

★ ★ ★ ★ ★

WHEN THE BIG Four were carving up the postwar world into spheres of influence at Yalta and Postdam, Korea received scant attention. The United States had little interest in this poor, wretched nation of thirty million peasants that had been enslaved by the Japanese in 1905. Stalin showed more interest. From his point of view Korea was strategic real estate: a buffer between Japanese and Russian soil. In the end the Big Four agreed somewhat vaguely that in the postwar era Korea would become, for twenty-five years or so, a "trusteeship" controlled by the United States, Russia, Great Britain, and China.

As the Pacific War drew to a close and Russia entered that war, the United States and U.S.S.R. hastily agreed to a joint occupation of Korea. An Army colonel in the Pentagon, Charles H. Bonesteel, arbitrarily selected the 38th parallel as a dividing line. It was not a natural boundary, but on the maps Bonesteel had available, it seemed to cut the nation in two quite nicely. The Russians never officially accepted this division. But in practice they abided by it. Thus, in this offhand way, Korea was partitioned and the stage was set for endless strife and conflict, and ultimately war.

MacArthur ordered the XXIV Corps, commanded by
Lieutenant General John R. Hodge, to occupy Korea
south of the 38th parallel. An advance party arrived by
air on September 4, two days after the Japanese surrender.
They landed at Kimpo Airport, which served the large city
of Seoul on Korea's west coast. Four days later, the bulk
of the XXIV Corps arrived by ship at Inchon, Seoul's
small seaport. By this time Russian soldiers had overrun
North Korea in force, sealing off the 38th parallel border.
There was little contact between the north and south, no
victorious meeting of American and Red soldiers, as in
Europe The Russians accepted the surrender of the Japanese armies in the north and sent them to slave labor
camps from which most never returned. Hodge's troops
accepted the surrender of the Japanese in the south, eventually sending them back to Japan.

MacArthur, busy in Japan, delegated to Hodge all the
problems of South Korea. They were considerable. Industry and commerce had come to a standstill The economy
was near collapse. Few Koreans were qualified to take over
the government or the railroads or utilities. Hodge's men,
trained for combat, had no experience or background in
civil government, nor could they speak Korean. Meanwhile
there was political turmoil. Over seventy political parties
sprang up within a month, all vying for control and demanding complete independence at once. Other than to
prepare for the vague Four-Power trusteeship over Korea,
Hodge had no guidance from Washington on what to do
in his area. And could not get any. Hodge found the situation so complex and frustrating he urged Washington to
propose to Moscow that both powers pull out immediately
and leave Korea to its own fate.

This idea was rejected. In December 1945, in Moscow,
the United States and Russia formally agreed to a five-
year trusteeship for Korea, after which free elections would
be held to determine the nation's future. The United States
brought in a Korean expatriate, Dr. Syngman Rhee, to try
to bring order out of the political chaos in South Korea.
The Russians installed a Moscow-trained Korean expatriate, Kim Il Sung, as head of the government machinery in
North Korea. Operating under Hodge's control, Rhee made
slow progress. Kim Il Sung, controlled by the Soviet occupiers, took a firm hold on North Korea and began to build
a nation very much along the pattern of the Soviet Union,

reinforced by the creation of a large and well-equipped army.

In the postwar years, Washington continued to evince little interest in the Korean problem. In the general demobilization and defense economy waves that followed VJ-Day, Hodge's troops were gradually withdrawn (as were the Soviet troops). In April 1948, President Truman, determined to further reduce defense spending and to avoid an inflammatory incident in Korea, directed that every effort be made to withdraw all U.S. troops from Korea by the end of that year. He approved a policy which stated: "The United States should not become so irrevocably involved in the Korean situation that an action taken by any faction in Korea or by any other power in Korea could be considered a '*casus belli*' for the United States." General Omar Bradley, chairman of the Joint Chiefs of Staff, opposed the withdrawal of all U.S. troops—and the writing off of South Korea—but the other three chiefs declared that "Korea is of little strategic value" and that any commitment of U.S. troops to Korea would be "ill-advised and impractical." Thus it was decided to abandon South Korea militarily and turn the thorny problems there over to the State Department.

It was recognized from the outset that South Korea must have some type of police force to replace the withdrawing U.S. troops. Accordingly, the Joint Chiefs ordered MacArthur to form a national police force and equip it with surplus heavy infantry weapons. The general envisioned a force of 25,000 regular police, 25,000 state police, and a "coast guard inshore patrol." This project got off to a very slow start, but by the end of 1947 there were a total of 20,000 men in the South Korean constabulary.

Beyond that lay a larger problem: Should not South Korea have an army to counterbalance the large, Soviet-trained army in North Korea? The official Korean War Army historian James F. Schnabel wrote that in October 1947, Washington asked MacArthur's views on this matter. MacArthur bucked it down to Hodge. Hodge thought that within one year a South Korean Army of 100,000 men could be fielded. He urged that this be done in "secrecy." At the very least, Hodge said, the national constabulary should be brought to its 25,000-man authorized strength and at once equipped with field artillary.

By that time the Korean problem had been dumped

into the lap of the United Nations. Interestingly, when MacArthur received Hodge's proposal for a South Korean Army, he, in Schnabel's words, "threw cold water" on it. MacArthur told Washington: "I believe no definite decisions can be made until action is reached by the United Nations. Unilateral action by the United States at this time would be inconsistent with the proposal submitted by it to the United Nations. If the United Nations accepts the problem, decisions, such as the one under discussion, will pass to it." The compromise finally reached was to increase the constabulary to 50,000 men without fanfare and equip it with heavy infantry weapons. Thus the formation of a regular South Korean Army to offset the North Korean Army was postponed indefinitely—on MacArthur's recommendation.

All this time, American diplomats had been pressing the Russians in various commissions and forums (United Nations included) for an overall, long-term settlement of the Korean problem. But the Russians sabotaged every one of these attempts. Finally, in October 1947, the United States recommended that in the following spring, elections be held in Korea (North and South), supervised by the United Nations, and that a unified government be thereafter established, reflecting the voters' choice. The U.N. General Assembly approved the plan, but Russia refused to cooperate. They barred the United Nations Commission from North Korea.

The South Koreans went ahead anyway. On May 10, 1948, they voted in a new National Assembly. When the Assembly convened on May 31, it elected Dr Rhee (then seventy-three) its chairman. The Assembly drew up a new constitution and elected Rhee president of what was now called the Republic of Korea (ROK). On August 15, 1948, Rhee was inaugurated. MacArthur was present—one of his two trips away from Tokyo between September 1945 and June 1950. With this ceremony, Hodge's military government folded its tent, and by the end of the year, all of his troops, save a small military "advisory" staff, left Korea.

Now, finally, it was done. American troops were gone; Korea was written off—at least in Washington. Apparently not so in Tokyo. A few months after Rhee's inauguration (October 22, 1948), the *New York Times* carried an interview with Rhee in which Rhee quoted MacArthur as saying: "Personally, I will do anything I can to help the

Korean people and to protect them. I would protect them as I would protect the United States or California against aggression." This astonishing pronouncement may have been fabricated by Rhee or issued by MacArthur merely to chill the North Koreans. Whatever the case, it was directly contrary to Washington's policy, and it must have dismayed Truman, Acheson, and the Joint Chiefs. In fact, MacArthur's responsibility for Korea in event of trouble had been specifically delimited by Washington to evacuation of American civilians and military personnel.

Among the many problems confronting President Rhee, none was more pressing than that of providing his embryonic nation with an army. In late November 1948, the Assembly passed the Armed Forces Organization Act, creating a department of defense. The 50,000-man police force became the nucleus of the army. By mid-1949, the army had increased to 100,000 men, organized into eight divisions. It was supplied with more than a hundred million dollars worth of surplus American equipment and "advised" by the U.S. Army.

Curiously, MacArthur was still not enthusiastic about building up the South Korean armed forces. According to Schnabel, MacArthur was fearful of provoking the North Koreans and perhaps fearful Rhee might invade North Korea. He insisted the ROK Army be strong enough to maintain internal security—but no stronger—and that it "be so organized as to indicate clearly its peaceful purpose and to provide no plausible basis for allegations of being a threat to North Korea." Because an ROK air force or navy had no conceivable "internal security" role, MacArthur ruled there should be neither.

The North Korean Army was still growing in size and effectiveness. It was soon a highly professional army, manned by many veterans of Mao's Communist Army in China and the Soviet Army in Europe and "advised" by Russian soldiers. By 1950, it was composed of 135,000 men organized into eight infantry divisions, an armored brigade, two half-strength divisions, and other units. Significantly, it possessed one hundred fifty T–34 Russian-made tanks, large amounts of heavy artillery, and at least 180 high performance aircraft.

By June 1950, the ROK Army was good, but not good enough. It had about 95,000 men, organized into eight divisions. But only four of these divisions were near full strength. The United States had been niggardly in providing equipment. The ROK Army had no tanks (for fear Rhee might invade North Korea). Its heavy artillery was markedly inferior to the heavy artillery of the North Koreans. It was woefully short of ammunition. An air force had been belatedly founded. But it was composed of only two dozen aircraft—all liaison planes or trainers.

By the beginning of 1950, the North Koreans were ready to seize South Korea by force. The main deterrent was this question: Would the United States come to South Korea's defense? If the North Koreans consulted American policy statements on the public record, there were two of significance. The first was by General MacArthur in an interview with British journalist G. Ward Price. The interview took place in Tokyo on March 1, 1949. In it, he reversed his previous assurance to Rhee that he would "personally" come to South Korea's aid. In describing the United States' "line of defense" in the Far East, he said: "It starts from the Philippines and continues through the Ryukyu Archipelago, which includes its main bastion, Okinawa. Then it bends back through Japan and the Aleutian Island chain to Alaska." The "bends back" clearly excluded Korea. The State Department officer at SCAP, William Sebald, wrote that MacArthur told him he considered Korea "militarily indefensible."

The second policy statement was made by Dean Acheson on January 12, 1950, at the National Press Club in Washington, D.C. Acheson also described the United States' defense line in the Far East. His words were almost exactly those of MacArthur except he reversed the description of the line. He said: "This defensive perimeter runs along the Aleutians to Japan and then goes to the Ryukyus. We hold important defensive positions in the Ryukyu Islands, and these we continue to hold. . . . The defensive perimeter runs from the Ryukyus to the Philippine Islands. . . . So far as the military security of other areas in the Pacific is concerned, it must be clear that no person can guarantee these areas against military attack." Acheson, too, had clearly excluded Korea.

In the months and years ahead, Acheson would be roundly pilloried for his statement. His legions of critics would argue that it "gave the green light" to the North Koreans to invade South Korea. The almost identical statement from MacArthur would not be recalled. Acheson professed to be amazed. In his memoir *Present At The Creation,* he wrote: "With the authority of the Joint Chiefs of Staff and General MacArthur behind me, it did not occur to me that I should be charged with innovating policy or political heresy."

During the spring of 1950, a steady stream of reports from American intelligence sources in Korea (Army, C.I.A., and a special unit Willoughly had established there) warned that the North Korean Army was preparing to invade South Korea. But such reports from Korea by now were almost routine. SCAP and the C.I.A. officer in Tokyo passed them on to Washington with no special flags. On the contrary, many were discounted altogether. Twice that spring Willoughby told Washington there would be no war in Korea. The official Army historian quotes these dispatches to Washington. In part: "It is believed that there will be no civil war in Korea this spring or summer . . . The most probable cause of North Korean action this spring and summer is furtherance of attempts to overthrow South Korean government by creation of chaotic conditions in the Republic of Korea through guerrillas and psychological warfare." The second dispatch read in part: "Apparently Soviet advisers believe that now is the opportune time to attempt to subjugate the South Korean government by political means, especially since the guerrilla campaign in South Korea recently has met with serious reverses."

CHAPTER
THIRTY-NINE

★ ★ ★ ★ ★

AT 4:00 A.M., June 25, 1950 (Tokyo time), the North Korean Army crossed the 38th parallel in all its formidable strength. After massed heavy-artillery barrages, Russian-made tanks and Russian-trained infantry poured south. Opposing this army were four ROK divisions. Only one-third of the ROK troops was dug into defensive positions. The other two-thirds were in rear areas, ten to thirty miles from the border. The North Koreans achieved complete surprise, overwhelming the thinly held ROK positions. Some ROK units fought bravely, but others broke and ran, leaving all their equipment, except rifles and carbines.

Word of this attack reached Tokyo six and a half hours after the first North Korean crossed the border. It was a Sunday. State Department officer William Sebald, who saw MacArthur that day, wrote that the general was not "unduly concerned." He went on: "Instead, speaking with the contagious enthusiasm which he so often showed, MacArthur expressed confidence in the ability of the South Korean Army to brace itself and hold, once the initial shock of the Communist attack had worn off." There had been border "incidents" in the past; MacArthur wrongly assumed this was merely another. MacArthur had no legal responsibility for Korea. His only standing orders were to evacuate Americans, should that become necessary.

It was soon apparent from a steady flow of reports from Korea that this was a more serious situation. The American Ambassador in Seoul, John J. Muccio, sent an urgent plea for ammunition; the reeling ROK Army had only a ten-day supply. Entirely on his own initiative, MacArthur ordered a massive supply of ammunition to be sent immediately to South Korea and told the U.S. Navy and Air Force under his command to protect the ship carrying it. He notified Washington: "Enemy effort serious in strength and strategic intent, and is undisguised act of war subject to United Nations censure."

In Washington, after consultation with President Truman, Secretary of State Dean Acheson had the matter placed before the United Nations Security Council. The Russian delegate was then boycotting the Council. The others, by a vote of nine to zero (with one abstention), passed a resolution calling for a ceasefire and a withdrawal of North Korean forces back to the 38th parallel, and asking "all members to render every assistance to the United Nations in the execution of this resolution and to refrain from giving assistance to the North Korean authorities." The words "render every assistance" would become the legal authorization and rallying cry that shortly led to full-scale American intervention.

As the situation worsened in Korea, Truman got his back up. There had now been almost five years of agonizing "cold war" with the Soviets all around the world. But this was raw military aggression, a "hot war" or "shooting war," in the phrases of the time. Truman wrote in his memoirs: "I felt certain that if South Korea was allowed to fall, Communist leaders would be emboldened to override nations closer to our own shores. If the Communists were permitted to force their way into the Republic of Korea without opposition from the free world, no small nation would have the courage to resist threats and aggression by stronger Communist neighbors. If this was allowed to go unchallenged, it would mean a third world war. It was also clear to me that the foundations and the principles of the United Nations were at stake unless this unprovoked attack on Korea could be

stopped." Dean Acheson and the Joint Chiefs of Staff
felt the same way. For these reasons—not strategic military considerations—the decision to "write off" Korea
was abruptly reversed.

Shortly thereafter orders went out from the Pentagon
to MacArthur. He was named to head all American military operations in Korea. He would continue to send ammunition to South Korea, post a sizable military survey
group with South Korean forces to show they had not
been abandoned, and evacuate the 1,500 Americans in
Seoul. He was authorized to utilize U.S. Air and Navy
forces to ensure that the evacuation was successful. The
latter authorization—not cleared with the United Nations—was the first commitment of American combat
forces to Korea.

So now, at age seventy, after fifty years of Army service, Douglas MacArthur, for the fourth time in his
life, confronted a shooting war. Truman would euphemistically call it a "police action," but it was a war.
MacArthur's nose was out of joint again. He had not
been consulted. He was amazed, he wrote, by the way
the momentous decisions on Korea had been reached.
"With no submission to Congress, whose duty it is to
declare war, and without even consulting the field commander involved, the members of the executive branch of
the government agreed to enter the Korean War. All the
risks inherent in this decision—including the possibility
of Chinese and Russian involvement—applied then just
as much as they applied later."

Nevertheless, he had a new assignment, and he turned
to it with typical energy and dedication. He decided to
fly to Korea for a firsthand look at the situation. That
day, June 29, the weather was terrible. MacArthur's personal pilot, Lieutenant Colonel Anthony Story, refused
to make the trip without a direct order. MacArthur gave
it. The famous "Bataan" once again flew MacArthur to
war.

Colonel Story chose to land at a field at Suwon, twenty
miles south of Seoul, which had already fallen to the
North Koreans. As "Bataan" was preparing to land, two
Russian-built YAK fighters of the North Korean Air
Force appeared over Suwon and dropped a bomb on
the air field. "Bataan" landed at 11:15 A.M. MacArthur
went immediately to a small schoolhouse, where Presi-

dent Rhee, Ambassador Muccio, and the senior U.S. military advisers were waiting. Colonel Story, fearful that the YAKs would return and destroy "Bataan," flew back to Japan.

After a brief conference, MacArthur, wearing his floppy campaign hat and a brown leather flying jacket, and carrying his corncob pipe, amazed everyone by announcing he would visit the "front." The group climbed into three broken-down cars and drove thirty miles north to the Han River, one mile below North Korean-held Seoul. They passed through throngs of fleeing refugees and confused, bewildered, and disorganized units of the ROK Army. MacArthur took position atop a hill, where he could see and hear enemy mortar fire. He remained there about an hour, watching the wavering lines of the ROK Army. (Only 16,000 men of the 100,000-man ROK Army could be found.) Then he returned to the Suwon air field, where "Bataan" was waiting. At 4:00 P.M., four hours and forty-five minutes after landing, "Bataan" returned to Japan without further incident.

The next day, June 30, MacArthur sent off a gloomy report to Washington. He concluded by making what would be a historic recommendation: "The only assurance for the holding of the present line, and the ability to regain later the lost ground, is through the introduction of U.S. Ground Combat Forces into the Korean battle area. . . . If authorized, it is my intention to immediately move a United States Regimental Combat Team [RCT] to the reinforcement of the vital area discussed and to provide for a possible build-up to a two-division strength from the troops in Japan for an early counter-offensive."

Washington was hesitant. Many did not want to go that far. But after considerable debate, Washington responded: "Your recommendation to move one RCT to combat area is approved. You will be advised later as to further build-up." And so American ground forces were committed to the Korean War. The official Army historian wrote: "General MacArthur quite clearly had tipped the balance of favor of troop commitment."

There were, at that time, a mere 108,500 U.S. soldiers on occupation duty in Japan. These were organized, principally, into what was grandiosely called the Eighth Army. It was commanded by General Walton Walker, who had been one of Patton's corps commanders in

Europe. The Army was composed of four under-strength divisions (1st Cavalry, 7th, 24th, and 25th Infantry divisions) and seven anti-aircraft battalions. Most of these troops were green, ill-trained, and, Schnabel wrote, a "very high percentage" were of "low intelligence." Japan was too crowded for military maneuvers; none of the divisions had conducted exercises above battalion level.

MacArthur chose the 24th Division, commanded by Major General William F. Dean, to go first. Advance elements of this division were flown to Korea, landing at Pusan, a city on the southern tip of the peninsula, on July 1 and 2. This force hurried immediately to the "front" near Taejon, about 120 miles northwest of Pusan. On the morning of July 5, North Koreans, backed by Russian-built T-34 tanks, attacked the American positions. The U.S. troops fought bravely, but they were vastly outnumbered, had no tanks or heavy weapons, and little ammunition. They suffered heavy losses and fell back.

The situation forced MacArthur to resort to that most dangerous and ineffective of military tactics: piecemeal commitment of troops. Day by day, as additional elements of the 24th Division arrived, they were thrown into combat in small units—without heavy artillery and tanks. At every hand the Americans were overwhelmed and thrown back, suffering ghastly casualties in savage hand-to-hand fighting. General Dean, a fearless front-line fighter like Eichelberger, was captured. To all intents and purposes, the U.S. 24th Division was wiped out.

The enemy objective was to reach Pusan before MacArthur could land enough troops there to form a strong perimeter defense. Here, MacArthur had one element in his favor. The farther the North Koreans advanced, the thinner they stretched their supply lines. They had no Navy to bring supplies forward. Everything had to be shipped down the roads of Korea in trucks. Inevitably, the advance slowed, then bogged down. This gave MacArthur time to rush the 25th Infantry Division and the 1st Cavalry Division (reinforced by cannibalizing men from the 7th Infantry Division) to Pusan. These, plus some surviving ROK troops integrated into American divisions, formed the perimeter. With the majority of his Army troops now committed to Korea, General Walker flew there to take personal command of the bloody and savage fighting.

MacArthur—and everyone else at SCAP—was astonished at the professionalism of the North Korean Army. In truth, he and his staff had vastly underestimated it. MacArthur told Washington the North Korean Army was as good "as any seen at any time in the last war." It was going to be tough—very, very tough—to hold the Pusan perimeter. To ultimately win the war in Korea would require a great many more U.S. soldiers. Accordingly, MacArthur began bombarding Washington with strongly worded requests for additional planes, ships, and soldiers— another army of four field-strength divisions with equipment. He wanted these urgently. In one cable he said: "Business as usual—to hell with that concept. . . . grab every ship in the Pacific and pour the support into the Far East."

Washington was unwilling to make such a full-scale commitment to the Korean War. Many planners believed that Korea might well be a Stalin "feint," designed to draw in U.S. troops there, denuding whatever little strength the United States had in Europe and elsewhere. In fact, most eyes in Washington were glued on Europe. It was just like World War II. If there was to be a general war with Russia, Europe would take first priority, the Pacific second. For these reasons, Washington parried most of MacArthur's larger requests but worked unstintingly on fulfilling his lesser requests.

MacArthur was understandably furious, and he did not conceal his anger in his messages. It was Bataan and Australia all over again. Schnabel wrote that MacArthur concocted a "colorful analogy" to describe the fallacy of this strategy. He wrote: "Assuming the world to be a metropolis of four districts, of which District No. 1 was the most important and District No. 4 the least so, General MacArthur asked his visitors to consider whether a fire in No. 4 should be allowed to burn uncontrolled because city officials were saving their fire equipment for District No. 1. As he concluded: 'You may,' he said, 'find the fire out of control by the time your equipment is sent to No. 4. . . .' General MacArthur felt that the United States would win in Korea or lose everywhere." To the leaders in Washington, then gravely concerned over the possibility of war with the Soviet Union, these views were considered parochial.

Meanwhile, intelligence sources indicated that Mao, who had now consolidated his hold on mainland China, was preparing to invade Formosa and annihilate the remnants of Chiang's Nationalist Army. Given the delicate situation in the Far East, a fight over Formosa was a headache no one wanted. Accordingly, on July 27, Truman ordered MacArthur to deploy his Seventh Fleet into the Formosa Straits. Its mission was twofold: to prevent a Chinese Communist attack on the island, and to prevent Chiang from attacking the mainland.

This new policy, known as "neutralizing" Formosa, was extremely controversial. Those Republicans (and Democrats) in Congress who had heaped abuse on Truman and Acheson for the "loss" of China now attacked them for "leashing" Chiang Kai-shek. The impression was fostered that Chiang had a strong, effective army that, with American help (notably air power and amphibious craft) could "return to the mainland" and destroy Mao's army and regain China. All Communist aggression was controlled from the Kremlin. If the Kremlin had dictated the invasion of South Korea, why not "unleash" Chiang to attack Mao, thus weakening the overall Communist position in the Far East?

Having been handed this hot potato, MacArthur decided to fly to Formosa to confer with Chiang on purely military matters. He informed the Joint Chiefs of his plans. The Chiefs, acutely aware of the sensitivity of the Formosa issue, suggested that at this time MacArthur might well send someone else—a senior officer. However, they added a postscript. If MacArthur felt it necessary, he should feel free to go to Formosa, since the responsibility for neutralizing the island militarily was his. MacArthur stuck to his original plan. He would go.

It was no low-profile visit. MacArthur took along a party of sixteen SCAP officers in two aircraft, one of them the "Bataan." Bad weather delayed the landing at Taipei for an hour and a half. Chiang waited patiently at the airport. When the plans finally landed, Whitney reported, MacArthur shook hands with Chiang for the first time and said (rather prosaically, for MacArthur):

"How do you do, Generalissimo. It was nice of you to come down and meet me."

There followed two full days of military conferences and a formal state dinner hosted by the Generalissimo and his wife. Of the latter, Whitney wrote: "The Generalissimo's natural handicap in his ability to speak English on such social occasions was more than made up by his wife's charm as a hostess. She personally greeted by name every guest as he arrived, though she had never met most of us and probably had only heard of us through an official briefing for the occasion; how she did it I do not know. She made everyone at once feel the warmth of the hospitality of this great leader and his wife, who for so long have symbolized implacable resistance to the advance of Communism in the Far East."

This two-day visit to Formosa—the first and last time MacArthur saw Chiang Kai-shek—created an absolute furor all over the world. Neither Truman nor Acheson had been informed of the visit in advance. They were, as Acheson put it in his memoirs, "startled to read in the press on August 1 that General MacArthur had arrived in Formosa, kissed Madam Chiang's hand, and gone into conference with her husband." The media reports on the visit, encouraged by Chiang's aides, gave the impression that MacArthur had reversed the "neutralization" policy and had given all kinds of secret assurances of military support to Chiang. As Acheson put it: "The Generalissimo crowed happily from Formosa that 'now that we can again work closely together with our old comrade in arms,' victory was assured."

Truman wrote: "The implication was—and quite a few of our newspapers said so—that MacArthur rejected my policy of neutralizing Formosa and that he favored a more aggressive method."

Truman was boiling mad, and no wonder. The Formosa "question" had been laid before the United Nations. The Communists had taken the propaganda position that neutralization meant, in actuality, that the United States would convert Formosa into a powerful military base. Washington was walking on egg shells, denying this and worrying that the issue would become so heated that it might provoke the Chinese Communists—or the Kremlin—into a rash move that would widen the war: Chinese intervention in Korea, for example.

As the controversy raged on, MacArthur issued one of those unfortunate statements that added fuel to the fire. He proclaimed: "This visit has been maliciously misrepresented to the public by those who invariably in the past have propagandized a policy of defeatism and appeasement in the Pacific. I hope the American people will not be misled by sly insinuations, brash speculations, and bold misstatements invariably attributed to anonymous sources, so insidiously fed them both nationally and internationally by persons 10,000 miles away from the actual events, if they are not, indeed, designed, to promote disunity and destroy faith and confidence in American purposes and institutions and American representatives at this time of great world peril."

Throughout the furor, Truman showed admirable restraint. He might well have fired MacArthur right then. Instead, he sent roving Ambassador Averell Harriman to Tokyo to explain American policy to MacArthur and to solicit MacArthur's views on a variety of problems in the Far East. As reported by Harriman in a memorandum to Truman, MacArthur's views on Chiang and Formosa were unequivocally strong: "MacArthur feels that we have not improved our position by kicking Chiang around. . . . I do not feel that we came to a full agreement on the way we believed things should be handled on Formosa and with the Generalissimo. He accepted the President's position and will act accordingly, but without full conviction . . . he would, as a soldier, obey any orders that he received from the President." Harriman's visit cooled the matter—for a time.

MacArthur, meanwhile, had lit the fuse on another bomb. The fifty-first Encampment of the Veterans of Foreign Wars was to be held in Chicago. MacArthur was invited to be its speaker. He declined, of course. However, he sent a letter, through official Army communications facilities in Japan, to be read at the convention. The subject could not have been more sensitive: Formosa. After a description of the strategic importance of Formosa, MacArthur wrote:

Formosa in the hands of such a hostile power could be compared to an unsinkable aircraft carrier and submarine tender ideally located to accomplish offensive strategy and at the same time checkmate

defensive or counter-offensive operations by friendly
forces based on Okinawa and the Philippines. . . .

Nothing could be more fallacious than the thread-
bare argument by those who advocate appeasement
and defeatism in the Pacific that if we defend Formosa we alienate continental Asia. Those who speak
thus do not understand the Orient. They do not
grant that it is in the pattern of Oriental psychology
to respect and follow aggressive, resolute, and dynamic leadership—to quickly turn on a leadership
characterized by timidity or vacillation—and they
underestimate the Oriental mentality.

This document, intended for release on August 28,
was leaked to the press on August 26. Truman and
Acheson were naturally astounded. Truman wrote: "He
called for a military policy of aggression, based on Formosa's position. The whole tenor of the message was
critical of the very policy which he had so recently told
Harriman he would support. There was no doubt in my
mind that the world would read it that way and that
it must have been intended that way."

Truman convened his chief advisers. Acheson wrote:
"When we filed into the Oval Office, the President, with
lips white and compressed, dispensed with the usual
greetings."

Truman wrote: "I gave serious thought to relieving
General MacArthur as our military field commander in
the Far East and replacing him with General Bradley. I
would keep MacArthur in command of the Japanese
occupation, taking Korea and Formosa out of his hands.
But after weighing it carefully, I decided against such a
step. It would have been difficult to avoid the appearance of a demotion, and I had no desire to hurt General MacArthur personally."

Again, Truman was restrained. This drastic course was
not discussed at this meeting. Truman's primary concern
was to let the world know that MacArthur's message to
the V.F.W. "was not official policy." The confreres decided, finally, that the best way to accomplish this would
be to order MacArthur to officially "withdraw" the statement. That would not stop its dissemination. Indeed, its
highlights were moving on wire-service tickers the world
over, and the full text was already on the presses of the

newsmagazine *U.S. News & World Report*. But an official withdrawal would be a slap on the wrist—dramatic proof that Washington disagreed with the context of the message.

On August 26, Washington time, the extraordinary order went out to MacArthur: "The President of the United States directs that you withdraw your message for the National Encampment of Veterans of Foreign Wars, because various features with respect to Formosa are in conflict with the policy of the United States and its position in the United Nations."

MacArthur's response was astonishing. He protested to Secretary of Defense Louis Johnson, stating it would be a grave mistake to withdraw the statement in this manner and that the views expressed in the message were "purely my personal ones." Washington was unyielding. MacArthur was forced to officially withdraw the letter.

In his memoirs, MacArthur insists that throughout this Formosa furor his position was consistently misrepresented, that he engaged in no political skulduggery, and that he was steadfastly loyal to the President and his Formosa policy. The truth would appear to be the opposite. MacArthur sincerely believed, as did many conservatives, that the decision to neutralize Formosa was either madness or traitorous, or both. He must have decided that it was his duty to try to reverse the policy through whatever means were available to him—even if it meant dismissal. Wittingly or unwittingly, he had embarked on the course chosen by his old friend Billy Mitchell.

CHAPTER
FORTY

★ ★ ★ ★ ★

THE MILITARY SITUATION in Korea was still desperate. The North Korean Army hammered mercilessly at General Walker's Pusan Perimeter, determined to throw the Eighth Army out of Korea. MacArthur sent Walker all available reinforcements: the Army's 2nd Infantry Division, shipped from the States; an Army Regimental Combat Team: a Marine brigade; thousands of individual replacements. Navy carrier and land-based Air Force planes, easily winning air superiority over South Korea, hammered at the long and vulnerable North Korean supply line. But with all of this, Walker was just barely hanging on, suffering heavy casualties, making do on a shoestring. Given his limited resources, the tactical disadvantages, and the fierce determination of the North Korean Army, there was little or no possibility that Walker could mount a decisive attack and break out of the Perimeter.

What to do? MacArthur personally provided the answer: a daring coordinated amphibious-airborne landing deep behind enemy lines. This would cut the North Korean supply line and trap the North Korean Army between the amphibious-airborne forces and Walker's Eighth Army in the Pusan Perimeter. With a strong U.S. force at its

rear, the North Koreans would be forced into a turnabout. sufficiently reducing pressure on the Pusan Perimeter for Walker to break out. The North Korean Army
would be crushed between these two giant pincers. It
was a plan reminiscent of the Ormoc landing on Leyte.

It was a brilliant scheme, but there was one large
obstacle. The Korean War had caught the United States
at a time of military retrenchment. The Army, Navy, and
Marine Corps had very few combat units; all that could
be spared had already been rushed to the Far East. The
United States was now remobilizing. National Guard
and Reserve units were being called to active duty, and
the draft had been reinstated, but it would take time—
much time—to train and equip these forces for duty in
Korea. There simply was not enough trained manpower
for an amphibious-airborne assault behind the North
Korean lines.

MacArthur was unfazed by these realities. Through
sheer force of will, he got the Joint Chiefs of Staff to
send him the First Marine Division, based in California.
(The Chiefs would not release U.S.-based paratroopers,
so the airborne phase of the landing was scrubbed.)
In addition, MacArthur ordered the rebuilding of the
Japan-based 7th Infantry Division, which had been can-
nibalized to provide replacements for the Pusan Perimeter.
This division was brought up to strength by transferring
about 8,000 ROK Army troops from Korea to Japan. In
this manner, MacArthur pieced together a force sufficient
for an amphibious landing.

Where to land? From the outset, MacArthur had
chosen Inchon, Seoul's seaport, known to be very lightly
held. He reasoned that a surprise stab there would quickly
yield Seoul, the communications and rail center of
South Korea. But MacArthur's naval planners objected
strongly to Inchon. It was a notoriously poor port, the
worst in Korea, with narrow channels and extreme tidal
swings (thirty feet). Men could be landed only during
the three hours of high tide. Between high tides, the men
on the beach would be stranded; they could not be reinforced. Moreover, in order to land, the men would have
to scale seawalls twelve to fourteen feet high. The assault
would land troops in the heart of Inchon, where every
structure could be utilized for defense.

MacArthur brushed aside these objections with this

statement: "The very arguments you have made as to the impracticabilities involved will tend to ensure for me the element of surprise. For the enemy commander will reason that no one would be so brash as to make such an attempt. Surprise is the most vital element for success in modern war."

The planning for this risky enterprise proceeded with the greatest secrecy. MacArthur furnished the Joint Chiefs one slim outline of the plan but no specific details. One reason, Whitney and MacArthur wrote, is that the Chairman of the Joint Chiefs, Omar Bradley, was on record as saying amphibious landings were obsolete. MacArthur was afraid that if Bradley and the Chiefs were told too much, they might veto the plan.

In fact, as Schnabel wrote, the silence caused the Chiefs to become "increasingly worried." They wondered "if MacArthur was not getting ready to bite off more than the United States could chew." Accordingly, on August 19, two of the Chiefs, Admiral Forrest Sherman of the Navy and General J. Lawton Collins of the Army, flew to Tokyo to confer with MacArthur. They were joined by Major General Oliver P. Smith, who commanded the First Marine Division, MacArthur's naval chief, C. Turner Joy, his air chief, George E. Stratemeyer, and other brass.

Whitney described this meeting as "one of the most important strategy debates in American military history." It was not that, but it was a tense moment for MacArthur. The Admirals, General Collins, and General Smith—indeed, almost everyone except MacArthur— were strongly opposed to the Inchon landing. If the two Chiefs returned to Washington and recommended Inchon be cancelled, there was no doubt their recommendations would be followed. For that reason, the meeting was crucial—reminiscent of MacArthur's meeting with Roosevelt in Hawaii in 1944.

The Navy contingent led off the "debate." For an hour and a half they spelled out the difficulties and risks involved. "Their remarks were decidedly pessimistic," Schnabel wrote. The two Chiefs, General Collins and Admiral Sherman, recommended an alternate landing site: Kunsan, a hundred miles south of Inchon. Then MacArthur, pipe in hand, defended his plan eloquently for a full hour. He concluded, according to Whitney: "If my estimate is inaccurate and I should run into a defense with which I cannot cope, I will be there personally and will immediately withdraw our forces before they are committed to a bloody setback. The only loss then will be my professional reputation."

The two chiefs flew back to Washington. They unveiled the plan to Bradley and to the Air Force's Chief of Staff, General Hoyt S. Vandenberg. The Chiefs, Schnabel wrote, "found no real disagreement with what MacArthur intended to do." They briefed Truman on the plan, giving their full approval to it. Truman wrote: "It was a daring strategic conception. I had the greatest confidence that it would succeed." On August 28, the Chiefs notified MacArthur that they "approved" the plan, but they urged him to provide them with "timely information" as the final plans firmed up.

The Joint Chiefs later had second thoughts. On September 7, with the landing scheduled for September 15, they asked MacArthur for a "new estimate and a reconsideration of Inchon." This message infuriated MacArthur. As Whitney put it: "Had someone in authority in Washington lost his nerve?" Would the Chiefs now about-face and cancel the operation? MacArthur immediately fired off a strongly worded defense of his plan, pointing out that the only alternative was a prolonged and costly holding action in the Pusan Perimeter, followed by a bloody frontal assault that would cost thousands of lives. That message did the trick. On September 8, the Joint Chiefs gave the final approval.

The force for the Inchon landing was designated X Corps. It was commanded by MacArthur's Chief of Staff, Edward M. Almond. In all, there were 70,000 men. The First Marine Division (25,000 men) would spearhead the assault. The Army's hastily reorganized and trained 7th Division (with its 8,000 ROKs) would follow. The First Marine Brigade was secretly withdrawn from the Pusan Perimeter to serve as a floating reserve, either for Inchon or for the Pusan Perimeter, should Walker encounter renewed pressure. The transports loaded at Pusan and the Japanese ports of Sasebo and Kobe.

MacArthur chose the *Mount McKinley* for his flagship. He boarded her on the night of September 12 in Sasebo. The weather was foul, churned up by a typhoon. The seas were mountainous. The *McKinley* rolled and pitched violently. ("The less said about that first night out, the better," Whitney wrote.) The storm raged all day, but by September 14 the seas had calmed considerably. *McKinley* joined the main invasion force in the Yellow Sea and proceeded toward Inchon.

On the eve of the invasion, MacArthur was a bundle of nerves. He awoke Whitney and invited him to his cabin. MacArthur, Whitney wrote, "was a lonely man." Pacing up and down, he launched into a prolonged monologue, reviewing the entire Inchon plan in minute detail. Everyone had opposed the plan. Had he, MacArthur, made some dreadful miscalculation? He fretted about the secrecy. The success of the operation hinged on secrecy Had it been broken? What, then? If they met a strong defense at Inchon, it could be a debacle, "one of the great military disasters." Whitney wrote: "No, there was no doubt about the risk. It was a tremendous gamble." Finally, at 2:30 A.M., MacArthur ran out of steam and went to sleep. The armada bore down on Inchon.

By this time the United States had unquestioned air superiority over South Korea. There would be no danger of air attack and, of course, no suicidal kamikazes. When dawn broke and the heavy ships began bombarding Wolmi-do, a fort guarding the narrow Inchon Channel, the skies were black with Navy and Air Force props and jets. Two YAKs showed up, but these were instantly shot down. There was no answering fire of any kind from Wolmi-do or Inchon. So far, so good.

The Marines swarmed ashore at about 7:00 A.M., landing on Wolmi-do and scaling the seawalls at Inchon with special ladders. MacArthur had achieved complete surprise. There was no opposition worth describing. The stunned Communists fled. The Marines secured their beachheads without suffering a single casualty. That afternoon (on the next high tide) MacArthur went ashore on Wolmi-do. The next morning at high tide he went ashore at Inchon, which by then had been captured by the fast-moving Marines. He jeeped three miles to the front lines, inspected a Russian tank, some North Korean POWs, then with a hearty "well done" to the Navy and Marines, he returned to the *McKinley*. In every respect, the landing operation had been brilliantly executed. MacArthur's judgment had been sound.

In the next few days, the Marines and soldiers rapidly expanded the beachhead. One thrust ran north to the gates of Seoul, recapturing Kimpo airfield. Another ran south toward Osan. In spite of the tides, the Navy unloaded supplies at the rate of 4,000 tons a day. Kimpo was utilized for an airlift. A plane landed every eight minutes. By September 21, there were 50,000 Marines and soldiers ashore, together with 25,000 tons of supplies and 6,000 vehicles. American casualties had been extremely light. North Korean casualties were heavy.

Far to the south—180 miles by air—General Walker's Eighth Army was to have attacked out of the Pusan Perimeter on the day after the Inchon landing. However, the North Koreans, evidently not yet aware of the Inchon landing—or ignoring it—fought with fierce determination. For nearly a full week they held the Eighth Army in check. For a time MacArthur began to doubt that General Walker *could* break out. But by September 22, Walker began to feel a softening along the North Korean front. Indeed, on the next day, the North Koreans, realizing they were in a trap, began to withdraw hastily.

The withdrawal—a difficult military maneuver—failed. Shortly it turned into a rout. Eighth Army poured out of the Perimeter in pursuit, racing northwest to Taejon, then Osan. On the morning of September 26—eleven days after Inchon—advance elements of the northward-moving Eighth Army linked up with southward-moving advance elements of the 7th Division near Osan. That same day, after a stiff week-long fight, the Marines recaptured Seoul. Much of the North Korean Army had been destroyed or captured within the space of two weeks; what remained fled north in panic.

Three days later, September 29, MacArthur and President Rhee flew to Seoul to re-establish the ROK government. In a brief, simple ceremony, MacArthur said:

In behalf of the United Nations I am happy to restore to you, Mr. President, the seat of your Government, that from it you may better fulfill your constitutional responsibility. It is my fervent hope that a beneficent providence will give you and all of your public officials the wisdom and strength to meet your perplexing problems in a spirit of benevolence and justice, that from the travail of the past there may emerge a new and hopeful dawn for the people of Korea.

This was MacArthur's finest hour, a fitting climax to fifty-five years of military service. Messages of congratulation poured in from all over the world. On September 30, Truman said in part: "No operations in military history can match either the delaying action where you traded space for time in which to build up your forces, or the brilliant maneuver which has now resulted in the liberation of Seoul. . . . I salute you all, and say to all, from all of us at home, 'Well and nobly done.' "

CHAPTER
FORTY-ONE

★ ★ ★ ★ ★

MacArthur and Washington now faced a delicate question: Should United Nations forces cross north of the 38th parallel? MacArthur's position was an unequivocal yes. He wanted to pursue the remnants of the North Korean Army and restore "peace and order" in the northern half of the peninsula. The Joint Chiefs and the newly appointed Secretary of Defense General George Marshall shared his view. But others in Washington—and London—disagreed. They feared that if MacArthur crossed the 38th parallel, the Russians or Chinese Communists might enter the war.

There was reason to fear Chinese Communist intervention. According to Schnabel, on August 31, Willoughby reported to MacArthur and Washington that ". . . sources have reported troop movements from Central China to Manchuria for sometime which suggest movements preliminary to entering the Korean Theater." Willoughby described these Chinese troops as about 246,000 men, organized into nine armies totaling thirty-seven divisions. Through diplomatic channels, China's Foreign Minister Chou En-lai had let it be known that if United Nations forces crossed the 38th parallel, Chinese troops would be sent to help the North Koreans.

Despite these ominous portents, the decision was made to cross the 38th parallel. On September 27, the Joint Chiefs (with the approval of the President) sent Mac-Arthur specific and detailed and restrictive orders governing these operations. He was to cross the parallel and destroy the North Korean Armed Forces, provided that the Russians or Chinese had not announced the intention of intervening or had not actually intervened. Under no circumstances would he cross the Russian or Manchurian border or conduct air or naval operations against those areas. Only ROK troops would enter the areas near the borders. In case of Soviet intervention south of the 38th parallel, open or covert, he was to go on the defensive, make no move to "aggravate" the situation and await further orders from Washington. In the event of open or covert Chinese intervention south of the 38th parallel, he would continue the action as long as there was a reasonable chance of "successful resistance."

Much to his irritation, MacArthur was required to submit his tactical plans to Washington for approval. The plan was this. Walker's Eighth Army would advance up the west coast of Korea and capture the North Korean capitol, Pyongyang. Almond's X Corps, operating as a separate force responsible to MacArthur, would make an amphibious landing at Wonsan on the east coast of Korea, opposite Pyongyang. The Eighth Army and X Corps would link up and then move north across the narrow waist of the peninsula, stopping at a line: Chongju-Yongwon-Hamhung. Beyond that, ROK forces only would conduct operations in the northern border provinces.

Washington approved this plan. Perhaps to soothe Mac-Arthur's feelings, on September 30 Secretary of Defense George Marshall sent a personal "eyes only" message to MacArthur that could—and would—be construed by some, including MacArthur, as broadening the plan. "We want you to feel unhampered tactically and strategically to proceed north of the 38th parallel." MacArthur replied: "Unless and until enemy capitulates, I regard all Korea as open for our military operations."

General Walker and many of MacArthur's staff officers did not approve of the plan in its entirety. Everyone had assumed that after Seoul was secured, Almond's X Corps would be integrated into Eighth Army under Walker's overall command, to be directed in its operations solely by Walker. All agreed Wonsan was necessary as a supply post, but Walker had a different plan for seizing it. Rather than an amphibious landing, he would send X Corps laterally, overland to Wonson, joining the ROK I Corps moving up the east coast. But for reasons never fully explained, MacArthur, against all advice, retained personal control of X Corps, treating it, in effect, as a separate army, on a par, in a command sense, with Eighth Army. In doing so, he violated one of the fundamental tenets of Clausewitz: he divided his forces.

By early October, Willoughby was receiving harder intelligence on the Chinese Communist forces massing in Manchuria. He now speculated there were as many as 450,000. On October 3, there were reports that "twenty" Chinese divisions were in North Korea and they had been there since September 10. Two days later GHQ reported "nine" Chinese divisions in North Korea and said the potential "exists for Chinese Communist forces to openly intervene in the Korean War if United Nations Forces cross the 38th parallel." Willoughby later reported that between nine and eighteen of the thirty-eight divisions believed to be in Manchuria were massed at the border crossings along the Yalu River. But, as Schnabel wrote, GHQ discounted all these reports of border crossings and labeled Chou's threat to intervene "political blackmail." Schnabel wrote that Willoughby "did not, so far as is known, attempt to dissuade General MacArthur from crossing the parallel."

United Nations forces now advanced northward over the parallel. The first to cross was the ROK I Corps on the east coast. It raced along spectacularly and by October 11, it had captured Wonsan. However, Mac-Arthur did not fully trust the ROKs, so the plan for the X Corps amphibious landing there was not cancelled. Walker's Eighth Army (which now included units from other nations, such as the British 27th Brigade) drove across the parallel on October 9. Walker encountered strong resistance at Kumchon on the Yesong River banks, but by October 15 the North Koreans collapsed and the way was open to Pyongyang.

Truman was increasingly worried about the possibility

of Chinese intervention in North Korea. Accordingly, on October 9, the Joint Chiefs sent a message to Mac-Arthur modifying his original orders. The first order had said that if the Chinese intervened in *South* Korea, Mac-Arthur was to continue operations as long as he saw a reasonable chance of success. The new order specified he was to do that in the event the Chinese intervened *any-where* in Korea. There was a postscript: MacArthur was not to take any military action against objectives in Chinese territory without "authorization" from Washington.

Truman then decided, rather abruptly, that he should like to confer face-to-face with MacArthur. Why? He wrote: "The first and simplest reason. . . . was that we had never had any personal contacts at all, and I thought he ought to know his Commander in Chief and that I ought to know the senior field commander in the Far East. . . . MacArthur had lost some of his contacts with the country and its people in the many years of his absence. He had been in the Orient for nearly fourteen years then, and all his thoughts were wrapped up in the East. I had made efforts through Harriman and others to let him see the world-wide picture as we saw it in Washington, but I felt that we had had little success. I thought he might adjust more easily if he heard it from me directly. The Peiping reports of threatened intervention in Korea by the Chinese Communists were another reason for my desire to confer with General MacArthur. I wanted to get the benefit of his firsthand information and judgment."

Marshall informed MacArthur that the President would like to meet with MacArthur either at Hawaii or Wake Island on October 15. MacArthur chose Wake, thus forcing Truman to fly thousands of miles farther. Truman announced this forthcoming meeting to the media. Dozens of reporters and photographers applied for permission to go along. In the end, Truman's contingent, which included Omar Bradley, Secretary of the Army Frank Pace, Averell Harriman and others, required four aircraft. (Truman had invited Secretary of State Dean Acheson to go along, but he declined. He wrote: "While General Mac-Arthur had many attributes of a foreign sovereign, I said, and was quite as difficult as any, it did not seem wise to recognize him as one.") MacArthur had intended to bring the Tokyo press corps, but the Pentagon denied permission. He and Courtney Whitney flew to Wake in MacArthur's plane SCAP. During most of the eight-hour flight from Tokyo to Wake, Whitney wrote, MacArthur restlessly paced up and down.

MacArthur arrived at Wake Island the night before Truman. The Navy provided quarters in a Quonset hut. Still on Tokyo time (three hours earlier), MacArthur did not want to go to bed, Whitney wrote. However, Whitney insisted that he do so. He turned in at 2:00 A.M. (Wake time) and slept for an hour and a half, until 3:30 A.M. He arose, shaved, and put on his usual uniform: khaki trousers, open-neck khaki shirt, floppy hat. As was his custom, he wore no "fruit salad," only the five-star insignias on his collar. Whitney wrote: "He looked as chipper as if he had slept twelve hours. . . ."

The President was scheduled to land at 6:00 A.M., October 15. His plane was a half-hour late. The three planes carrying Truman's advisers and the press arrived ahead of Truman's plane Independence. Reporters and photographers swarmed all over the airfield, preparing to record this historic moment. (To one reporter, it was like a meeting of heads of states of different governments.) Then, finally, Independence touched down and taxied to a designated area.

MacArthur was there to meet Truman. When the President came down the boarding ladder, he said: "I've been a long time meeting you, General." They shook hands and MacArthur said: "I hope it won't be so long next time."

For the next hour Truman and MacArthur were alone. They climbed into a 1948 Chevrolet sedan and were driven to a Quonset hut reserved for Truman. What they discussed has never been revealed in full. Truman wrote:

> We discussed the Japanese and Korean situations.
> The General assured me that the victory was won in Korea. He also informed me that the Chinese Communists would not attack and that Japan was ready for a peace treaty.
> Then he brought up the subject of his statement about Formosa to the Veterans of Foreign Wars. He said that he was sorry if he had caused any

embarrassment. I told him I considered the incident closed. He said he wanted me to understand that he was not in politics in any way—that he had allowed the politicians to make a "chump" (his word) of him in 1948 and that it would not happen again.

I told him something of our plans for the strengthening of Europe, and he said he understood and that he was sure it would be possible to send one division from Korea to Europe in January 1951. He repeated that the Korean conflict was won and that there was little possibility of the Chinese Communists coming in.

The General seemed genuinely pleased at this opportunity to talk with me, and I found him a most stimulating and interesting person. Our conversation was very friendly—I might say much more than I had expected.

MacArthur wrote:

I had been worried about Mr. Truman's quick and violent tempers and prejudices, but he radiated nothing but courtesy and good humor during our meeting. He had an engaging personality, a quick and witty tongue, and I liked him from the start. . . . He seemed to take great pride in his historical knowledge, but, it seemed to me that in spite of his having read much, it was of a superficial character, encompassing facts without the logic and reasoning dictated by those facts. Of the Far East he knew little, presenting a strange combination of distorted history and vague hopes that somehow, some way, we could do something to help those struggling against Communism.

At about 7:30 A.M., Truman and MacArthur were joined by Bradley, Pace, Harriman, and others for a formal conference. Most of the discussion focused on the economic and military rehabilitation of postwar Korea, the Japanese peace treaty, and a Pacific pact similar to N.A.T.O. in Europe. However, during the course of the conference, MacArthur made two off-quoted statements: "I believe that formal resistance will end throughout

North and South Korea by Thanksgiving" and "It is my hope to be able to withdraw the Eighth Army to Japan by Christmas."

Truman put the key question to MacArthur. What were the chances of Chinese interference? MacArthur replied:

> Very little. Had they interfered in the first or second months it would have been decisive. We are no longer fearful of their intervention. We no longer stand hat in hand. The Chinese have 300,000 men in Manchuria. Of these probably not more than 100/125,000 are distributed along the Yalu River. Only 50/60,000 could be gotten across the Yalu River. They have no air force. Now that we have bases for our Air Force in Korea, if the Chinese tried to get down to Pyongyang there would be the greatest slaughter.

This historic meeting lasted one hour and thirty-six minutes. Afterward, Truman and MacArthur went to Truman's Quonset hut for "small talk." MacArthur inquired if Truman intended to again seek the presidential nomination in 1952. Truman ducked this by asking MacArthur if *he* intended to run. MacArthur replied: "If you have any general running against you, his name will be Eisenhower, not MacArthur." Truman chuckled and said: "He doesn't know the first thing about politics. . . . Why, if Eisenhower should become President, his administration would make Grant's look like a model of perfection."

Now it was time to leave. MacArthur and Whitney accompanied Truman to the Independence. Truman surprised MacArthur with the presentation of the Distinguished Service Medal (MacArthur's fifth). As Truman boarded his plane, he said: "I've never had a more satisfactory conference since I've been President." Then he was gone. MacArthur left in SCAP five minutes later.

Most of MacArthur's aides have written that the Wake Island meeting was purely a political gimmick. The Congressional elections were a little more than two weeks away. Truman wished to identify himself and the Democratic Party with the victorious Inchon landing and the rout of the North Korean Army. But MacArthur wrote:

"Such reasoning, I am sure, does Mr. Truman an injustice. I believe nothing of the sort animated him, and that the sole purpose was to create good will and beneficial results to the country."

CHAPTER
FORTY-TWO

★ ★ ★ ★ ★

BACK IN TOKYO, MacArthur resumed personal direction of the war in Korea. The goal now was to destroy what remained of the North Korean Army—the remnants that had escaped from the Pusan Perimeter, the rear area service units, and thousands of hastily recruited, ill-trained "replacements." MacArthur demanded speedy, vigorous operations. At the Wake Island conference he had brashly predicted an end to "formal" resistance by Thanksgiving, the return of the Eighth Army to Japan by Christmas.

His master plan was unfolding nicely. In the western sector, Walker's Eighth Army took Pyongyang on October 19. The next day, Ned Almond's X Corps should have landed at the east coast port of Wonsan, now held by the ROK I Corps. But the Wonsan harbor had to be swept of mines and the landing was delayed nearly a week—to October 26. By then it had been decided to land only Oliver Smith's First Marine Division at Wonsan; the 7th Army Infantry Division landed at Iwon, one hundred fifty miles farther up the coast.

On October 20 MacArthur uncorked yet another surprise. He ordered the 187th Airborne RCT (a unit of the

11th Airborne Division), which had only recently arrived from the States, to jump at Sukchon and Sunchon, about thirty miles north of Pyongyang. The purpose of this jump was to trap North Korean soldiers and government officials fleeing north from Pyongyang. As at Nadzab seven years before, MacArthur was overhead in his personal plane when the paratroopers jumped. Afterward MacArthur landed at Pyongyang's airport and proclaimed that the jump "closes the trap on the enemy." He boasted that half the surviving soldiers of the North Korean Army had been caught. In fact, the paratroopers had jumped too late; the North Koreans slipped through to safety.

The escape of these large numbers of North Koreans may have influenced MacArthur's next order, issued on October 24. It was extraordinary. According to the official Army historian, MacArthur instructed Walker and Almond "to drive forward with all possible speed using all forces at their command." This was a direct violation of the JCS instructions of September 27, prohibiting the use of other than ROK forces in the northern border provinces. It was clear insubordination. Upon learning of the order, the Joint Chiefs objected timorously with a query: "While the Joint Chiefs realize that you undoubtedly had sound reasons for issuing these instructions they would like to be informed of them, as your action is a matter of concern here." Acheson wrote that this message was "magnificent understatement." Indeed, official Washington was stunned.

MacArthur responded with a typically long and convoluted message. Gist: He had lifted the restriction on the use of United States forces in the border areas "as a matter of military necessity." The ROKS, he argued, had neither the experience nor the leadership to successfully carry out the mission. As for the legal justification, he said the September 27 JCS directive was not "final." Besides that, Marshall's "eyes only" message of September 30 (which seemed to broaden the directive) gave him authority. On top of that, MacArthur said, "this entire subject was covered at my conference at Wake Island." (Actually, it was not touched on in the official meeting.)

Here was a crucial moment in the Korean War. In the face of increasing reports that the Chinese had entered North Korea in strength, Walker's Eight Army and Almonds X Corps were racing northward willy-nilly with no contact between them. Walker's right flank and Almond's left flank were completely exposed. The idea of a defensive line across the narrow waist of Korea had been abandoned. The instructions to use only ROK forces in the border provinces had been violated.

Washington was concerned but continued to be timorous. Apparently no one had the gumption to stand up to the military genius who had just pulled off the miracle of Inchon and captured Pyongyang. They allowed MacArthur's plan to stand, hoping for another military miracle and, as Collins said later, hoping that MacArthur would not violate any more orders.

As MacArthur's forces raced north, the Chinese Communists issued new warnings from Red China: "Now that the American forces are attempting to cross the thirty-eighth parallel on a large scale, the Chinese people cannot stand idly by with regard to such a serious situation created by the invasion of Korea. . . ." MacArthur's operations were "a serious menace to the security of China. . . ." Between October 14 and November 1, the Army historian wrote, it appeared that some 180,000 troops of the Chinese Fourth Field Army crossed the Yalu River border into North Korea.

On October 25—only one day following MacArthur's order for all forces to rush north—a ROK outfit in northwest Korea ran head on into a Chinese outfit near Onjong. The ROKs killed many Chinese and took some POWs. The latter reported they were serving in organized Chinese Army units. But no one at GHQ put any credence in the reports. On the contrary, Willoughby told Washington that the "auspicious time for intervention had long since passed." If the Chinese intended to intervene, they most certainly would have intervened when Eighth Army was squeezed into the Pusan Perimeter. GHQ indulged in various speculations: the Chinese were bluffing, saving face, or merely trying to protect the many hydro-electric plants along the Yalu. There was as yet no hard evidence from intelligence sources that they were in North Korea in strength.

The next day, October 26, one ROK outfit, the 6th Division, pushed all the way to the Yalu River, near the village of Chosan. That same day, organized Chinese forces struck the ROK 1st Division, badly mauling it. One regiment of the ROK 6th Division, returning from the

Yalu River, was surrounded by Chinese troops and nearly destroyed. Within a day or two the entire ROK II Corps' (three divisions) was in full flight, leaving equipment behind and further exposing Walker's right flank. On the night of November 1–2, the Chinese, blowing whistles and bugles and firing Russian rockets, hit the U.S. 8th Cavalry Regiment, inflicting crippling damage. With that, Walker halted the offense, pulling back to the Chongchon River. He reported to MacArthur that he had been ambushed by "fresh, well-organized and well-trained units, some of which were Chinese Communist Forces." He was short of food, ammunition, everything—a shortage caused in large part by the diversion of ships to land X Corps at Wonsan and Iwan.

On the east coast of Korea, Oliver Smith cautiously advanced his First Marines from Wonsan toward his first objective, the Chosin Reservoir. (A new American infantry division, the 3rd, was landed at Wonsan to occupy that port area.) He was not pushing with all possible speed as MacArthur had demanded. Smith was out there in rugged mountains completely exposed. He very carefully took the high ground as he moved along. On October 26, the same day the Chinese hit the 1st ROK Division, Smith's Marines ran into Chinese troops. They took eighteen POWs from the Chinese 124th Division. A few day later, they encountered Chinese tanks and captured soldiers from two other Chinese divisions.

Still MacArthur would not believe. His eyes, his heart, were fixed on a single objective: destroying the North Korean Army, pacifying all of Korea, getting his boys home for Christmas. On November 4, in response to a query from the JCS about Chinese intervention, he responded that full intervention would be a "momentous decision of the gravest international importance." While it was always possible, he said reassuringly, "there are many fundamental logical reasons against it and sufficient evidence has not yet come to hand to warrant its immediate acceptance." He concluded: "I recommend against hasty conclusions which might be premature and believe that a final appraisment should await a more complete accumulation of military facts."

Only two days later, MacArthur made an abrupt turnabout. In a public communiqué, he now stressed the gravity of the Chinese threat. He said, in part: "While the North Korean forces with which we were originally engaged have been destroyed or rendered impotent . . . a new, fresh army now faces us, backed up by a possibility of large alien reserves and adequate supply within easy reach to the enemy but beyond the limits of our present sphere of military action." Fortunately his Eighth Army had withdrawn in time to escape "a possible trap . . . surreptitiously laid," and there was now no chance of a "military reverse." He labeled the Chinese intervention "one of the most offensive acts of international lawlessness of historic record." He concluded: "Whether and to what extent these reserves will be moved forward to reinforce units now committed remains to be seen and is a matter of gravest significance."

MacArthur now made one of the worst tactical errors of his military career. Vastly underestimating the Chinese already in North Korea and vastly overestimating the ability of aircraft to interdict, he ordered his air chief, Stratemeyer, to wipe out the Chinese interveners. Stratemeyer was to throw the full weight of the air power under his command at the enemy for two full weeks. "Combat crews," MacArthur ordered, "are to be flown to exhaustion if necessary . . . destroy every means of communication and every installation, factory, city, village."

Ever since the United Nations forces had moved into North Korea, Stratemeyer's aircraft had operated under careful restrictions, designed to avoid provoking the Chinese or Russians. They were never to cross the borders of either country; they were not to bomb anything within five miles of the border. If they encountered enemy aircraft, they could fire on them over North Korea, but could not engage in "hot pursuit" across the border. They were not to bomb the hydro-electric plants or dams along the Yalu River.

Among other instructions MacArthur gave Stratemeyer, was one to bomb the highway and rail bridges across the Yalu River between Sinuiju and Antung—the main route of the Chinese into Korea. MacArthur routinely informed the Pentagon of this plan on November 6. Stratemeyer, recognizing the delicacy and danger of the order, took the trouble to notify Air Force Chief of Staff Hoyt Vandenberg in Washington—a mere three hours before his planes were to take off.

This news again stood official Washington on its ear.

Here was another act of insubordination: violation of the rule of bombing within five miles of the border. The high-level phones burned. Acheson reached Truman in Independence, Missouri, where the President had gone to vote. Truman agreed the bombing should be postponed, unless to do so would jeopardize American forces. The JCS hastily sent MacArthur a message reaffirming the five-mile restriction and asking his reasons for bombing the bridges. MacArthur, reversing his heretofore reassuring view of Chinese intervention, replied with extraordinary heat:

> Men and material in large force are pouring across all bridges over the Yalu from Manchuria. This movement not only jeopardizes but threatens the ultimate destruction of the forces under my command. . . . The only way to stop this reinforcement of the enemy is the destruction of these bridges and the subjection of all installations in the north area supporting the enemy advance to the maximum of our air destruction. . . . Under the gravest protest that I can made, I am suspending this strike [at Sinuiju] and carrying out your instructions. . . . I trust that the matter be immediately brought to the attention of the President as I believe your instructions may well result in a calamity of major proportion.

In the face of this withering blast, the Joint Chiefs caved in again. MacArthur was authorized to bomb only the "Korean end" of the bridges (leading an Air Force wag to crack: "How do you bomb one end of a bridge?"). Stratemeyer's planes commenced the bombing on November 8, joined later by Navy planes. It was a difficult, nearly hopeless task. In order not to violate the border, the planes could approach from only one direction. The Chinese set up anti-aircraft batteries along this route, forcing the planes to fly high—20,000 feet or more. In addition, they patrolled the area with Russian-made MIG-15 jets which attacked the bombers, then retreated to safety across the border. As a result, the bombing of the bridges was a slow, costly process. By the time Stratemeyer knocked them out, the Yalu River was frozen over, making the whole effort academic.

Stratemeyer and his pilots were understandably enraged at the "privileged sanctuary" the Chinese MIG-15s enjoyed. He complained to MacArthur, who in turn told the Pentagon: "Present restrictions imposed on my area of operation provide a complete sanctuary for hostile air immediately upon their crossing the Manchuria-North Korean border. The effect of this abnormal condition upon the morale and combat efficiency of both air and ground troops is major." He did not, however, specifically request the restriction be lifted. Truman, Acheson, and the Joint Chiefs of Staff agreed the restrictions were unfair, but beyond considering and rejecting a six or eight mile "hot pursuit" doctrine, they did nothing. The restriction remained in force. Other U.N. nations with troops in Korea opposed "hot pursuit" and declared they would disassociate from it. If they did, it would leave the United States in the highly undesirable moral position of going one-on-one with Red China.

Stratemeyer's two-week air offensive was impressive to behold. The North Korean skies were black with fighters, bombers, strafers. On November 9, MacArthur optimistically told Washington he could "deny reinforcements coming across the Yalu in sufficient strength" to pose any real threats to his forces. Later he issued statements praising the air assault, claiming that it had "isolated the battlefield"—cut off enemy supplies and reinforcements. But what he did not know was that the Chinese were already in North Korea in vast strength, with supplies. Moreover, Stratemeyer's air offensive had barely fazed them. These skilled soldiers traveled light, moved at night, and carefully concealed themselves in daytime. Stratemeyer had ravaged North Korea, killed untold numbers of civilians, but he had inflicted no noteworthy damage on the Chinese forces. Most of them had melted into the frozen mountains where they awaited orders to strike United Nations forces a decisive blow.

All this time Walker and Almond had been preparing to go on the offensive. The offensive had to be postponed time and again because Walker was still short of everything. This time both men were more cautious. The days of willy-nilly running all over North Korea by exposed units were over. Both forces would move northward in slow, conventional stages. There was still one glaring weakness in the plan. Although various schemes had been proposed, there was still no satisfactory coordination between Eighth Army and X Corps. There was a forty-mile gap between them. The hope was that the rugged terrain in the gap would deter the enemy and thus protect their flanks. But this was only a hope.

Washington, meanwhile, was deeply apprehensive about the proposed offensive. The British, key partners in the European defense alliance N.A.T.O., were bringing heavy pressure on the United States to go slow. Through their outpost Hong Kong, the British, who had officially recognized the Mao regime, conducted a lucrative trade with Red China. If there were an open clash between United Nations forces (including British units) and Red China in North Korea, the Chinese might retaliate by seizing Hong Kong. The British had proposed, at the very least, a "buffer zone" between U.N. forces and the border. For these and many other reasons, the JCS timidly informed MacArthur that his original mission—destroying the North Korean Army—"may have to be reexamined." Perhaps the offensive should be abandoned.

MacArthur responded with another intemperate blast: "In my opinion it would be fatal to weaken the fundamental and basic policy of the United Nations to destroy all resisting armed forces in Korea and bring that country into a united and free nation. . . ." He insisted on the offensive. "Any program short of this would completely destroy the morale of my forces and its psychological consequences would be inestimable. It would condemn us to an indefinite retention of our military forces along difficult defense lines in North Korea and would unquestionably arouse such resentment among the South Koreans that their forces would collapse or might even turn against us." As for the British, he scathingly reminded the JCS of Munich, and vehemently denounced the proposed "buffer zone" in these words: "To give up any portion of North Korea to the aggression of the Chinese Communists would be the greatest defeat of the free world in recent times. Indeed, to yield to so immoral a proposition would bankrupt our leadership and influence in Asia and render untenable our position both politically and militarily." He concluded by saying that complete victory could be achieved if "our determination and indomitable will do not desert us."

Again, no one in Washington had the nerve to take on MacArthur. Despite all the misgivings, the offensive was approved. Acheson reflected: "Here, I believe, the Government missed its last chance to halt the march of disaster in Korea. All the President's advisers in this matter, civilian and military, knew that something was badly wrong, though what it was, how to find out, and what to do about it they muffed. . . . I have an unhappy conviction that none of us, myself prominently included, served him [Truman] as he was entitled to be served."

MacArthur, confident that the all-out air offensive had achieved its goal, fixed the date for the jump-off on the day after Thanksgiving, November 24. He had Thanksgiving dinner with the family at the American Embassy in Tokyo. The troops in Korea ate a luxurious Thanksgiving dinner in the field. Next day MacArthur flew to Eighth Army headquarters on the Chongchon River near Sinanju. Walker was still chronically short of supplies, but there was no postponing the offensive. Washington might again be stricken with faint-heartedness, the bitter Korean winter was coming on fast, the Yalu would freeze over. Besides that, the Chinese appeared to be withdrawing all along the line, a baffling development but perhaps a hopeful one. To one of Walker's corps commanders, MacArthur made what would become a famous public comment: "If this operation is successful, I hope we can get the boys home by Christmas." Later that day he issued an optimistic communique: "If successful, this should for all practical purposes end the war."

After the troops jumped off, MacArthur and his party boarded SCAP for the return flight to Tokyo, escorted by several fighters. When they were airborne MacArthur astounded everyone by ordering the pilot to head for the mouth of the Yalu River. Whitney and others protested. It was an extremely hazardous proposal. But the order stuck. MacArthur wanted to make a "personal reconnaissance" of the terrain and look for signs of enemy activity. When they reached the Yalu, MacArthur ordered the pilot to turn east and fly all the way to the Russian border at an altitude of 5,000 feet. Fortunately no MIGs jumped the formation. They did not see much. Whitney wrote: "All that spread before our eyes was an endless expanse of utterly barren countryside, its jagged hills, yawning crevices, and all but the black waters of the Yalu locked in the silent death-grip of snow and ice." For this reconnaissance, MacArthur received the Distinguished Flying Cross.

CHAPTER
FORTY-THREE

★ ★ ★ ★ ★

THE UNITED NATIONS forces moved northward with speed and confidence. Walker's Eighth Army gained twelve miles in the first thirty-six hours against almost no resistance. But shortly after dark on November 25, disaster struck. The Chinese, 200,00 strong, slipped into the gap between Walker's Eighth Army and Almond's X Corps and hit the right flank of Eighth Army—the ROK II Corps. The ROKs broke and ran in panic, leaving the U.S. IX Corps in the center exposed. The IX Corps reeled, held, then retreated. On the left, I Corps fell back with IX Corps. Two days later, November 27, in the east sector, another Chinese Army struck X Corps—Oliver Smith's First Marines—slipping behind, trapping the Leathernecks in the Chosin Reservoir area.

It was soon apparent that U.N. forces had run headlong into a first-class military force. The Chinese were astonishingly well-disciplined and well-led. Completely surprised and overwhelmed, Walker's Eighth Army was soon in full retreat. MacArthur informed Washington that his troops must now "pass from the offensive to the defensive." He added these soon-to-be-famous sentences: "The Chinese forces are committed to North Korea in great and ever increasing strength. No pretext of minor support under guise of volunteerism or other subterfuge now has the slightest validity. We face an entirely new war."

MacArthur called an emergency meeting of his troop commanders on November 28. Walker and Almond flew to Tokyo and conferred with MacArthur until a late hour at the American Embassy. There were two fundamental options. They could close the ever-widening gap between Eighth Army and X Corps, falling back to a consolidated defensive position across the narrow waist of the peninsula (Pyongyang-Wonsan, for example) or, secondly, each outfit could withdraw to an independent beachhead, Walker to wherever he could best protect his troops (Inchon or Pusan, etc.), Almond to the Hamhung-Hungnam area.

When informed of this decision, the Joint Chiefs were distressed. They agreed that the Marines and the Army's 7th Division should be extricated from the Chosin Reservoir area as quickly as possible. But once that was done, they wanted the first option: the Eighth Army and X Corps to link up in a defensive position across the narrow waist of the peninsula. They did not order that this be done; they merely "sugested" it in discreet language. But MacArthur refused the suggestion, arguing that the defensive line would be too thin and the supply problems too complex. He concluded with an urgent plea for reinforcements, since "this small command . . . is facing the entire Chinese nation in an undeclared war."

MacArthur's response evoked yet another high level meeting in the Pentagon with George Marshall, Dean Acheson, the Joint Chiefs, and others present. Among them was Lieutenant General Matthew B. Ridgway, a tough-minded, savvy paratrooper who had won fame and distinction in the European Theater in World War II. Exasperated by the shilly-shallying, Ridgway asked for permission to speak. In his memoir, he recalled: "I blurted out—perhaps too bluntly but with deep feelings—that I felt we had already spent too damn much time on debate and that immediate action was needed. We owed it, I insisted, to the men in the field and to the God to whom we must answer for those men's lives to stop talking and act. My only answer, from the twenty men who sat around the wide table, and the twenty others who sat around the walls in the rear was complete silence." After the meeting,

Ridgway asked Hoyt Vandenberg why the Chiefs wouldn't send MacArthur orders telling him what to do. Vandenberg replied: "What good would that do? He wouldn't obey the order. What can we do?" Ridgway exploded: "You can relieve any commander who won't obey orders, can't you?" Ridgway recalled Vandenberg's response: "The look on Van's face was one I shall never forget. His lips parted and he looked at me with an expression both puzzled and amazed." Such was the hold MacArthur had on Washington.

Once again the Chiefs yielded to MacArthur. Their message: "We consider that the preservation of your forces is now the primary consideration. Consolidation of forces into beachheads is concurred in." But these men, and others in Washington, had now lost faith in Douglas MacArthur. In a singular vote of no-confidence, the Chiefs sent General Collins to Korea as an "observer."

As we have seen, it was difficult for MacArthur to concede personal error. Now in this dark hour in the Korean War, when silence might have been appropriate, there came a steady stream of purple communiqués and petulant press interviews from the Dai-Ichi Building. There were two underlying themes. First, MacArthur had not blundered into a Chinese ambush; fully aware of the Chinese presence, he had merely sent out a "reconnaissance in force" and shrewdly "sprung the Red trap and escaped it." Second, the reason why the U.N. forces were now in a tight spot could be blamed on the "extraordinary inhibitions" imposed on him by those in Washington. In a published interview in *U.S. News & World Report*, he charged that the restrictions on "hot pursuit" and bombing Manchurian bases was "an enormous handicap, without precedent in military history."

This latest salvo, clearly aimed at the Truman administration, again enraged the President. Here was MacArthur (like Billy Mitchell) publicly taking issue with the policy of his superiors. But again, Truman showed remarkable restraint. He wrote: "I should have relieved General MacArthur then and there. The reason I did not was that I did wish to have it appear as if he were being relieved because the offensive failed. I have never believed in going back on people when luck is against them, and I did not intend to do it now."

Instead the President issued, on December 6, through

the Joint Chiefs, an order requiring all senior military commanders to clear with the Pentagon in advance any proposed public statement on foreign policy. This order, of course, was aimed directly at MacArthur. Astonishingly, MacArthur challenged it at once with a proposed communiqué clearly arrogant and condemnatory of Washington. It said, in part, that his forces had now successfully completed a tactical withdrawal and were waiting for "political decisions and policies demanded by the entry of Communist China into the war." He went on to say "the suggestion widely broadcast that the command has suffered a rout or debacle is pure nonsense." He blamed the intelligence failure on the C.I.A. and on the Washington-imposed restrictions on overflights of Manchuria: "Advance notice of the Chinese decision to attack was a matter for political intelligence which failed. . . . Field intelligence was so handicapped that once the decision to commit was made, this new enemy could move forward . . . without fear of detection. . . ." The Joint Chiefs, standing toe-to-toe with MacArthur for the very first time—reflecting the growing disenchantment with MacArthur in Washington—killed the communiqué and told MacArthur to henceforth confine his public comments to completed military operations.

These operations, after the initial panic subsided, were being conducted with unusual military efficiency. Walker withdrew his badly mauled Eighth Army south to the Imjin River (abandoning Pyongyang) and dug in across a ninety-mile front along the 38th parallel, with the reorganized ROKs on his right in the rugged mountains. On December 23, after setting up this line, Walker was killed in a jeep accident. Washington, on MacArthur's recommendation, named Ridgway to succeed him. In the east sector, the First Marines, in a heroic and justly famous and tortuous retrograde movement, fought its way out of the Chosin Reservoir with all of its major equipment and wounded. The 7th Division, facing less formidable opposition, likewise withdrew to Hungnam. By Christmas Eve, all of X Corps (including the ROKs), a total of 105,000 fighting men, had evacuated Hungnam and destroyed the port facilities. Later, the X Corps was brought around to Pusan and integrated into Eighth Army on the right flank.

Matt Ridgway arrived at the Dai-Ichi Building on the day after Christmas. He had known MacArthur since West

Point days, when MacArthur was superintendent and Ridgway was a young athletic coach. He wrote that he had "profound respect for his leadership, his quick mind and his unusual skill at going straight to the main point of any subject and illuminating it so swiftly that the slowest mind could not fail to grasp it. He was, despite any weakness he may have shown, a truly great military man, a great statesman and a gallant leader. . . . I welcomed the chance to associate once again with one of the few geniuses it has been my privilege to know."

The meeting was far-ranging. MacArthur complained that he was operating in a "mission vacuum"—there were no specific directives about what to do. Hold Seoul, if possible, he told Ridgway. "A military success will strengthen our diplomacy." He wished that Chiang Kai-shek could be unleashed against mainland China; that would greatly relieve pressure on U.N. forces in Korea. He warned Ridgway not to underestimate the Chinese; they were a "dangerous foe." Or to depend on U.S. air power to "isolate the battlefield." As in Australia in 1942, MacArthur denounced the failure of air power in Korea. In conclusion, Ridgway asked if MacArthur had any objections to his attacking. MacArthur, who seemed "discouraged," said: "The Eighth Army is yours, Matt. Do what you think best." And MacArthur was as good as his word. Whereas he had dictated almost every move to Walker and Almond, MacArthur gave Ridgeway a completely free hand.

Ridgway, like the MacArthur of World War I, was a striking figure on the battlefield. He wore a chest harness with hand grenades attached to it, a pistol and a distinctive fur-lined cap—with his three stars and paratrooper insignia on the turned-up bill. He inspired confidence. He took over a dispirited, disillusioned Army afflicted with "bug-out fever." He wrote: "Their courage was still high and they were ready to take on any mission I might have assigned. But there was too much of a looking-over-your-shoulder attitude, a lack of that special verve, that extra alertness and vigor that seems to exude from an army that is sure of itself and bent on winning." It was not long before Matt Ridgway had the Eighth Army on its toes, eager to fight.

They did not have long to wait. On New Year's Eve, the Chinese attacked en masse along a forty-four-mile front. Under the weight of this awesome manpower, skillfully utilizing artillery. Ridgway was forced to fall back, first to a line north of Seoul, then below Seoul, abandoning the capitol. On January 14, Ridgway, against all staff advice, ordered an attack. It achieved little tactically, but it dramatically notified the world that a new spirit had flamed in Eighth Army. Shortly thereafter, the Chinese mounted another savage attack. Ridgway's men fought with new spirit, but the massive weight of the Chinese armies forced Eighth Army to fall back yet another thirty-five miles to Ansong. For a time, further withdrawals appeared necessary, perhaps total evacuation from Korea. Then the line held—barely.

What to do now? That was the question debated the world over. In attempting to answer it, to find a policy, Truman, Acheson, and the Joint Chiefs were governed by the following almost universally held assumptions. The Kremlin controlled the world Communist movement. The Communist governments in Europe and the Far East were merely "puppets," dancing to the Kremlin's tune. The overall objective of the Kremlin was "world domination" or the "enslavement" of all free or Western nations. The greatest danger still lay in Western Europe. There, the United States must place the major portion of its military muscle and encourage its N.A.T.O. Allies to do likewise. Above all, the United States must not get bogged down in a prolonged war in Asia, draining off military strength that ought to be in Europe. That was probably exactly what the Kremlin wanted, why it started the Korean War in the first place.

The policy that began to take shape in the State Department in Washington, governed by the aforementioned assumptions, was roughly the following: Contain the war in Korea. Maintain the restrictions on air and naval power. Send no more troop reinforcements. Stabilize the military line near the 38th parallel. Order Ridgway to hold if possible, dig in strongly, and conduct a "war of attrition"—mercilessly chewing up Chinese troops until they grew exhausted and gave up. If this failed, withdraw Eighth Army to protect Japan. If it succeeded, seek a cease-fire and then an armistice, returning Korea to the status quo of June 1950. Anything more might bring the Russians into the war.

MacArthur held almost diametrically opposed views.

The showdown with Communism was here in Asia, not Europe. "In war," he said, "there can be no substitute for victory." He believed that Red China should be destroyed. His strategy was all-out. He would impose an economic embargo on China—stop British and other trade through Hong Kong. He would impose a naval blockade of China's coast. He would revoke the "neutralization" of Formosa and "unleash" Chiang Kai-shek against the mainland. He would wipe out the "privileged sanctuaries—lift the restrictions on "hot pursuit" and bombing Chinese military installations in Manchuria, indeed, in all of China. He would heavily reinforce the U.N. Eighth Army with additional units from U.N. nations committed to Korea and with some 33,000 troops Chiang had offered—a total of 75,000 additional men. He would drive the Chinese back across the Yalu River and pacify and unite Korea. Anything less was "appeasement" or "surrender." The Russians would not go to war until such a war appeared in their own best interests.

The Joint Chiefs, urged on by Admiral Sherman, came down in favor of some of MacArthur's views. On January 12, 1951, they issued a memorandum in which they recommended that the United States send two more divisions to Japan; intensify the economic blockade of China; prepare immediately for a naval blockade of China; lift the restrictions on "air reconnaissance" over Manchuria and the China coast; unleash Chiang Kai-shek and furnish him logistical support; bomb Chinese military installations and factories *if* China attacked U.S. forces *outside* Korea. However, most of these recommendations were contingent on a worsening situation in Korea. They did not recommend the kind of immediate all-out effort MacArthur wanted, or the use of Chiang's troops in Korea.

While Ridgway was rallying his Eighth Army, MacArthur was bombarding Washington with gloomy estimates of its ability to hold on, implying that unless his policies were adopted, evacuation was almost a certainty. He pointedly said that the morale of the troops "will become a serious threat to their battle efficiency unless the political basis upon which they are asked to trade life for time is clearly delineated, fully understood and so impelling that the hazards of battle are cheerfully accepted."

This gloomy report on morale in Eighth Army caused profound concern in Washington. Forthwith two of the

Joint Chiefs, Collins and Vandenberg, flew to Tokyo, then Korea. They went to the front lines. After a thorough inspection of ground and air forces, Collins and Vandenberg turned in a report completely opposite to that of MacArthur. Morale under Ridgway was excellent; the Eighth Army could hold and kill a lot of Chinese.

This new report caused jubilation in Washington; the recommendations of the Joint Chiefs of January 12 for widening the war against China were left to die on the vine. The war in Korea became a war of "attrition," an indecisive killing of Chinese. Eighth Army under Ridgway became very good at the job. It killed tens of thousands of Chinese. In the process, it inched its way back up the peninsula. By the end of February, Eighth Army once again held a line along the Han River. By the end of March, it had recaptured Seoul and dug in behind the Imjin River, approximately along the 38th parallel. There was no longer any talk of evacuation.

MacArthur continued to visit the front in Korea, bringing along some staffers and the Tokyo press corps. On one such visit, after Ridgway and his commanders had conceived and meticulously planned a limited attack, MacArthur arrived and grandiosely pronounced before Ridgway and assembled war correspondents: "I have just ordered a resumption of the offensive." Ridgway, who had a considerable ego of his own, was dismayed that MacArthur would in this way focus the limelight on himself, claiming credit for Ridgway's work. He wrote MacArthur a discreet letter, suggesting that the general's visits to the front were so ceremonious and well-publicized that there was real danger they tipped the enemy off in advance to impending offensives and were thus a security risk. From then on, MacArthur waited until the offenses had already begun to visit the front. This was probably the only instance in MacArthur's career in which a subordinate stood up to him and put him in his place.

CHAPTER
FORTY-FOUR

★ ★ ★ ★ ★

IN WASHINGTON, PRESIDENT TRUMAN, Dean Acheson, and others now gave full effort to the cause MacArthur considered "appeasement" or "surrender"—a Korean cease-fire and armistice, more or less restoring the *status quo ante bellum*. It seemed a reasonable solution to a complicated situation. The Chinese were no longer able to eject Eighth Army from Korea; they were suffering terrible casualties and might be looking for a face-saving device to end the shooting. From the U.N. point of view, it seemed unlikely the Chinese could be ejected from North Korea without a dangerous widening of the war. The invaders had once again been ejected from South Korea; why not leave it at that?

Accordingly, Acheson and his advisers, coordinating with other United Nations countries with troops in Korea, drew up a proposed statement to be issued by the President, calling for a cease-fire to open the way for a broader settlement of the Korean question. On March 20, the Joint Chiefs informed MacArthur of what was in the wind: "State Department planning a Presidential announcement shortly that, with the clearing of bulk of South Korea of aggressors, United Nations now preparing to discuss conditions of settlement in Korea."

For Douglas MacArthur, this was evidently the last straw. He now undertook a frontal assault on the Truman Administration, a course of action apparently designed to pull the rug from under Truman, sabotage any attempt to achieve a cease-fire, and throw the whole question before the world, regardless of the cost to him personally. On March 24, Tokyo date (March 23 in Washington), he issued this extraordinary statement:

Operations continue according to schedule and plan. We have now substantially cleared South Korea of organized Communist forces. It is becoming increasingly evident that the heavy destruction along the enemy's lines of supply, caused by our round-the-clock massive air and naval bombardment, has left his troops in the forward battle area deficient in requirements to sustain his operations. This weakness is being brilliantly exploited by our ground forces. The enemy's human wave tactics have definitely failed him as our own forces have become seasoned to this form of warfare; his tactics of infiltration are but contributing to his piecemeal losses, and he is showing less stamina than our own troops under the rigors of climate, terrain and battle.

Of even greater significance than our tactical successes has been the clear revelation that this new enemy, Red China, of such exaggerated and vaunted military power, lacks the industrial capacity to provide adequately many critical items necessary to the conduct of modern war. He lacks the manufacturing base and those raw materials needed to produce, maintain and operate even moderate air and naval power, and he cannot provide the essentials for successful ground operations, such as tanks, heavy artillery and other refinements science has introduced into the conduct of military campaigns. Formerly his great numerical potential might well have filled this gap but with the development of existing methods of mass destruction, numbers alone do not offset the vulnerability inherent in such deficiencies. Control of the seas and the air, which in turn means control over supplies, communications, and transportation, are no less essential and decisive now than in the past. When this control exists as in our case, and is coupled with an inferiority of ground fire power as in the enemy's case, the resulting disparity is such that it cannot be overcome by bravery, however fanatical, or the most gross indifference to human loss.

These military weaknesses have been clearly and definitely revealed since Red China entered upon its undeclared war in Korea. Even under the inhibitions which now restrict the activity of the United Nations forces and the corresponding military advantages which accrue to Red China, it has been shown its complete inability to accomplish by force of arms the conquest of Korea. The enemy, therefore, must by now be painfully aware that a decision of the United Nations to depart from its tolerant effort to contain the war to the area of Korea, through an expansion of our military operations to its coastal areas and interior bases, would doom Red China to the risk of imminent military collapse. These basic facts being established, there would be no insuperable difficulty in arriving at decisions on the Korean problem if the issues are resolved on their own merits, without being burdened by extraneous matters not directly related to Korea, such as Formosa or China's seat in the United Nations.

The Korean nation and people, which have been so cruelly ravaged, must not be sacrificed. This is a paramount concern. Apart from the military area of the problem where issues are resolved in the course of combat, the fundamental questions continue to be political in nature and must find their answer in the diplomatic sphere. Within the area of my authority as the military commander, however, it would be needless to say that I stand ready at any time to confer in the field with the commander-in-chief of the enemy forces in the earnest effort to find any military means whereby realization of the political objectives of the United Nations in Korea, to which no nation may justly take exceptions, might be accomplished without further bloodshed.

This statement stunned official Washington. It was a direct violation of the Joint Chiefs' December 6 directive to abstain from public statements on foreign policy without prior clearance with the Pentagon, hence it was flagrantly insubordinate. In that respect, it was (as Truman wrote) a challenge to the authority of the President and the Constitution—the traditional concept of civilian supremacy over the military. Moreover, its belligerent tone implied a change in policy—that the war might be widened. It was an arrogant slap in the face to the Chinese, a highly inappropriate and tactless posture to assume for negotiating a cease-fire. Finally it was a personal insult to Truman. In the worldwide diplomatic uproar that ensued, it became impossible for him to proceed with his own statement seeking a cease-fire. Truman wrote: "By this act, MacArthur left me no choice—I could not longer tolerate his insubordination."

The next morning, Truman summoned Acheson, Deputy Secretary of Defense Robert A. Lovett, Dean Rusk, and others to the White House. When MacArthur's message had been received the previous day, Acheson wrote, Lovett was "angrier that I had ever seen him" and said MacArthur "must be removed and removed at once." Acheson "shared his sense of outrage." The message, Acheson wrote, "can be described only as defiance of the Chiefs of Staff, sabotage of an operation of which he had been informed, and insubordination of the grossest sort to his Commander in Chief." But now, Lovett "had simmered down." Truman, Acheson wrote, "although perfectly calm, appeared to be in a state of mind that combined disbelief with controlled fury." Truman wrote: "I can only say on that day I was deeply shocked. I had never underestimated my difficulties with MacArthur, but after the Wake Island meeting I had hoped that he would respect the authority of the President. . . . I realized that I would have no other choice myself than to relieve the nation's top field commander. . . ."

But not this day. The relief of MacArthur was bound to pull the roof down on an administration already hugely unpopular with the American people. Truman approached this thankless task with extraordinary caution. This day he did not raise the question of dismissal, nor reveal his own thoughts; he merely dictated the following message to MacArthur:

The President has directed that your attention be

called to his order as transmitted 6 December 1950.
In view of the information given you 20 March
1951 any further statements by you must be coordinated as prescribed in the order of 6 December.

The President has also directed that in the event
Communist military leaders request an armistice in
the field, you immediately report that fact to the
JCS for instructions.

Meanwhile, MacArthur had lit the fuse on yet another bomb. Earlier in March, Congressman Joseph W.
Martin (Republican, Massachusetts), a conservative and
Minority Leader of the House, had written MacArthur a
letter:

In the current discussions on foreign policy and
overall strategy many of us have been distressed that
although the European aspects have been heavily
emphasized we have been without the views of yourself as Commander-in-Chief of the Far Eastern Command.

I think it is imperative to the security of our nation and for the safety of the world that policies of
the United States embrace the broadest possible
strategy and in our earnest desire to protect Europe
we not weaken our position in Asia.

Enclosed is a copy of address I delivered in Brook-
lyn, N.Y., February 12, stressing this vital point and
suggesting that the forces of Generalissimo Chiang
Kai-shek on Formosa might be employed in the open-
ing of a second Asiatic front to relieve the pressure
on our forces in Korea.

I have since repeated the essence of this thesis in
other speeches and intend to do so again on March
28 when I will be on a radio hook-up.

I would deem it a great help if I could have your
views on this point, either on a confidential basis or
otherwise. Your admirers are legion and the respect
you command is enormous. May success be yours
in the gigantic undertaking which you direct.

MacArthur, who wrote that he had always felt "duty-
bound to reply frankly to every Congressional inquiry,"

replied to the Martin letter on March 20. He did not label his letter confidential:

I am most grateful for your note of the eighth forwarding me a copy of your address of February 12. The latter I have read with much interest, and find that with the passage of years you have certainly lost none of your old-time punch.

My views and recommendations with respect to the situation created by Red China's entry into war against us in Korea have been submitted to Washington in most complete detail. Generally these views are well known and generally understood, as they follow the conventional pattern of meeting force with maximum counterforce as we have never failed to do in the past. Your view with respect to the utilization of the Chinese forces on Formosa is in conflict with neither logic nor this tradition.

It seems strangely difficult for some to realize that here in Asia is where the Communist conspirators have elected to make their play for global conquest, and that we have joined the issue thus raised on the battlefield; that here we fight Europe's war with arms while the diplomats there still fight it with words; that if we lose this war to Communism in Asia the fall of Europe is inevitable, win it and Europe most probably would avoid war and yet preserve freedom. As you point out, we must win. There is no substitute for victory.

Martin read this letter on the floor of the House on April 5, saying that he "owed it to the American people to tell them the information I had from a great and reliable source." It caused yet another worldwide uproar. Although MacArthur wrote that Martin had released the letter "for some unexplained reason and without consulting me," it seems apparent that MacArthur wished the letter to be made public, that he had now decided to meet the Truman Administration head-on in public debate.

The following day, April 6, Truman again summoned his top advisers: Marshall, Acheson, Averell Harriman, and Omar Bradley. They discussed what to do about MacArthur—how and when he should be relieved—for an hour. Acheson wrote: "There was no doubt what General MacArthur deserved; the sole issue was the wisest way to administer it." Harriman expressed the view that MacArthur should have been fired two years back, when he encouraged the Diet to pass a law contrary to Washington's economic policy for Japan. Marshall and Acheson advised caution, and consultation with the Joint Chiefs of Staff. Truman adjourned the meeting by asking Marshall to read all the messages in the Pentagon files between MacArthur and Washington for the last two years. The President was still noncommittal. He had made up his mind but did not want to influence the others.

This same group met again, briefly, the next day, Saturday, April 7. Marshall had read all the messages. He expressed the view (according to Truman) that "MacArthur should have been fired two years ago." But the Joint Chiefs were out of town; he had not yet consulted with them. The final decision was put over to Monday.

That day, April 9, the group met again at the Oval Office. Acheson wrote: "General Marshall announced that the Chiefs of Staff, meeting under the chairmanship of General Bradley, unanimously recommended that General MacArthur be relieved of all his commands and that both he and General Bradley concurred in the recommendation." Acheson and Harriman also concurred. Finally Truman revealed his own opinion: he had made up his mind that MacArthur had to go when he released his March 24 statement. The decision of this group was, then, unanimous. Truman directed Bradley to draw up orders relieving MacArthur. He would be replaced in all his commands by Matthew Ridgway.

Who would deliver the word to MacArthur? It was decided that this onerous chore should be performed by Secretary of the Army Frank Pace, then in the Far East. To avoid using Army communications, which might embarrass MacArthur, Truman asked Acheson to forward the orders via encoded State Department communications to Ambassador Muccio in Pusan, Korea, with instructions to relay them to Pace, who would go in person to give the news to MacArthur. But this plan went awry. The State Department radio line delayed the message; Pace was on the front lines with Ridgway.

Inevitably there was a leak to the press. Omar Bradley

rushed to the White House to report the story was going to be published the following morning, April 11, by the *Chicago Tribune*, a paper unfriendly to the Administration. Truman decided he could "no longer afford the courtesy of Secretary Pace's personal delivery of the order." He directed his Press Secretary, Joseph Short, to call in the White House Press Corps at the extraordinary hour of 1:00 A.M., April 11. Short handed out several documents. The first was an electrifying general announcement of the President's decision:

With deep regret I have concluded that General of the Army Douglas MacArthur is unable to give his whole-hearted support to the policies of the United States government and of the United Nations in matters pertaining to his official duties. In view of the specific responsibilities imposed upon me by the Constitution of the United States and the added responsibility which has been entrusted to me by the United Nations, I have decided that I must make a change of command in the Far East. I have, therefore, relieved General MacArthur of his commands and have designated Lieutenant General Matthew B. Ridgway as his successor.

Full and vigorous debate on matters of national policy is a vital element in the constitutional system of our free democracy. It is fundamental, however, that military commanders must be governed by the policies and directives issued to them in the manner provided by our laws and Constitution. In time of crisis, this consideration is particularly compelling.

General MacArthur's place in history is fully established. The Nation owes him a debt of gratitude for the distinguished and exceptional service which he has rendered his country in posts of great responsibility. For that reason I repeat my regret at the necessity for the action I feel compelled to take in his case.

The second was a message from Truman to MacArthur:

I deeply regret that it becomes my duty as President and Commander-in-Chief of the United States military forces to replace you as Supreme Commander, Allied Powers; Commander-in-Chief, United Nations command; Commander-in-Chief, Far East; and Commanding General, U.S. Army, Far East.

You will turn over your commands, effective at once, to Lieutenant General Matthew B. Ridgway. You are authorized to have issued such orders as are necessary to complete desired travel to such place as you select.

My reasons for your replacement will be made public concurrently with the delivery to you of the foregoing order.

CHAPTER
FORTY-FIVE

★ ★ ★ ★ ★

THE NEWS REACHED Tokyo first by commercial radio broadcast; urgent bulletins were broadcast all over Japan. When these bulletins arrived, MacArthur was entertaining luncheon guests, Senator Warren Magnuson of Washington State and William Sterns of Northwest Airlines, at his embassy residence. Sid Huff brought the word to the Embassy. He appeared at the dining room door, face in anguish, tears in his eyes. Seeing him at at the door, Jean quietly left the table to receive the shattering news. She then tapped her husband on the shoulder, bent down, and whispered.

Whitney wrote: "MacArthur's face froze. Not a flicker of emotion crossed it. For a moment, while his luncheon guests puzzled on what was happening, he was stonily silent. Then he looked up at his wife, who still stood with her hand on his shoulder. In a gentle voice, audible to all present, he said: 'Jeannie, we're going home at last.' " The luncheon continued, MacArthur maintaining "a mask of calm throughout." The official orders came over Army communication facilities a short while later. It fell to Huff to hand-carry the documents to his general.

There was profound shock at SCAP. The State Department officer William Sebald wrote that "the extent and seriousness of the controversy were fully recognized, of course, but in SCAP Headquarters there was little tendency to believe that MacArthur would be punished, let alone dismissed, for his action. Instead, there were many who thought, or hoped, that Washington could be converted to MacArthur's view." But now it was over; MacArthur had lost.

Many, including MacArthur, were angered by the abrupt method of the dismissal, caused in part by the communications foul-up. The orders read that his relief was immediate. There could be no usual change-of-command ceremony, no usual farewell speech to the troops. Ridgway spoke for many—military and civilian alike— when he wrote that the "crude" way it was handled was a "needless affront to the General's pride."

That afternoon MacArthur went to the Dai-Ichi Building. Sebald paid a call. He wrote:

I walked directly into the General's plain office without formality. The General rose and met me with a smile. I was so keyed that I was unable to speak. A tear rolled down my cheek. MacArthur offered me a cigarette and lighted it for me, as we sat down at our usual places in the worn leather furniture at the far end of the room. For a moment the silence was oppressive, then, with some difficulty, I remarked: "General, you are a much better soldier in this business than I am." While not a profound remark, it broke the tension.

MacArthur replied in his most earnest and telling manner. He expressed irony and bitterness over the *method* that had been used to send him home. "Publicly humiliated after fifty-two years of service in the Army," he said somberly. As a soldier, he added, he would have retired without protest, if the President had given the slightest intimation that he wished him to do so. This proud, sensitive, and determined man, who had followed a destiny which now had evaporated, was deeply hurt and, perhaps, momentarily defeated. Watching and listening to him was the most painful interview I have had.

Later that day Ridgway flew from Korea and saw Mac-Arthur at the American Embassy. He wrote:

I went directly to his office from Haneda Airport, and he received me at once, with the greatest courtesy. I had a natural human curiosity to see how he had been affected by his peremptory removal from his high post. He was entirely himself—composed, quiet, temperate, friendly, and helpful to the man who was to succeed him. He made some allusions to the fact that he had been summarily relieved, but there was no trace of bitterness or anger in his tone. I thought it was a fine tribute to the resilience of this great man that he could accept so calmly, with no outward sign of shock, what must have been a devastating blow to a professional soldier standing at the peak of his career.

Sid Huff wrote:

Watching him and listening to him, I tried to figure out how he was feeling underneath his tense but quiet manner. I got the impression that he was aggrieved; that he had suffered a bit of heartbreak. But he never said a word to indicate his attitude, and all of us realized that it would be a grave error to make any sympathetic noises in his presence. Ordinarily, there is a lot of warm friendliness about MacArthur, but in times of crisis he seems to prefer to be alone, to fight it out by himself or with only Jean's comfort and help.

Going home now, after fourteen years in the Far East, was a massively complex task. Describing this "mad scramble" Huff wrote: "Someway we got packed. Someway we said goodbye to our friends. Someway we sympathized with our Japanese acquaintances who were saddened as well as worried by the General's recall." The most touching of these encounters occurred when Emperor Hirohito came to the Embassy to pay a final call. Whitney wrote that the Emperor took MacArthur's hands in both of his and "tears streamed unchecked down his cheeks."

By April 16, everybody was packed and ready. Mac-

Arthur's personal plane, named changed from SCAP back to Bataan, was waiting at Atsugi Airport. The motorcade to the airport was like a state funeral. Every available American soldier, sailor, and airman had been posted along the streets, together with Tokyo and rural police. Behind the honor guard, tens of thousands of Japanese stood four and five deep for a last glimpse of this historic general who had helped defeat, then rebuild, Japan and who now, like their own Emperor, had been humbled. When he drove by in the 1941 Cadillac, they shouted "Makassa Gensui!" (Field Marshall!).

There was a brief, military-like farewell ceremony at the airport. A band and an honor guard—a platoon of select troops—stood in silent formation. Overhead, Air Force and Navy jets prepared for a fly-by. MacArthur's top military commanders—Matt Ridgway, Vice Admiral C. Turner Joy, General George Stratemeyer—and wives clustered to one side with members of the Diplomatic Corps and Diet. William Sebald recalled:

Promptly at 7 A.M., a limousine drew up and the MacArthurs alighted. While Jean, smiling, walked toward the wives of Occupation officials, General MacArthur reviewed the guard of honor, striding purposefully and with set face past the young men who had served under him. As customary, he ended the brief and ritualized review by shaking hands with the guard's commander. Then he walked quickly to the senior officers and shook hands with each of us, always with a smile, a penetrating glance, and frequently, a word of personal intimacy. The farewells were an ordeal. Many of the women were sobbing openly, and a number of the battle-hardened men had difficulty in suppressing tears.

Ridgway recalled:

He shook my hand and without dramatics said: "I hope when you leave Tokyo you will be Chief of Staff [of the U.S. Army]. If I had been permitted to choose my own successor [at SCAP] I'd have selected you." This simple statement, which could hardly have been other than completely sincere, was a most

generous act on the part of a great soldier-statesman.
It meant a great deal to me. . . .

One by one the MacArthur party boarded Bataan:
Arthur, Ah Cheu—she waved, bowed, and shouted
"Good-bye, everybody . . . good-bye."—Courtney Whit-
ney, Sid Huff, another aide Laurence Bunker, Mac-
Arthur's personal physician C. C. Canada and
MacArthur's personal pilot, Anthony Story. The band
played "Auld Lang Syne;" the jets thundered overhead.
Sebald wrote:

> Finally, Jean pulled herself away and, assisted by
> the General, climbed the ramp and turned for a
> final wave. The couple stood immobile, but visibly
> saddened, as a 19-gun salute rolled across the air-
> field. Then, with a quick gesture, MacArthur guided
> his wife into the plane, the door was shut, and the
> aircraft taxied away. Soon it was airborne, and the
> chilling moment was over.

The final destination for Bataan was Washington, D.C.,
where MacArthur had been invited to address a joint
session of Congress on April 19. The plane stopped overnight at Hickham Air Force Base, Honolulu, where the
MacArthurs were guests of the Navy's Pacific Commander Admiral Arthur Radford. Then on to San Francisco, where the landing was deliberately scheduled at
night to avoid a mob scene at the airport. Approaching
brightly lit San Francisco, the MacArthurs stared down
through the windows. The general said to his son, now
thirteen, with deep feeling: "Well, Arthur, my boy, here
we are home at last."
The plan to slip into San Francisco unnoticed failed.
San Francisco was waiting in force. When the plane
landed, the three MacArthurs, Whitney wrote, "were
caught up in an indescribable scene of pandemonium."
Thousands of greeters rushed from parked cars, crushing
around the airplane (among the official greeters: Governor of California Earl Warren). They lined the highway into the city to watch the slow-moving motorcade
and were "packed block-deep" around his hotel, the St.
Francis. It was a demonstration of unbridled hero-worship

that MacArthur would encounter again and again in the next few weeks.

Inevitably, the return took on a political cast. Everybody assumed MacArthur would get revenge on Truman by running against him—and defeating him—in the 1952 presidential elections. But MacArthur immediately scotched that idea. During a ceremony the following day at San Francisco's City Hall, where tens of thousands more turned out to hail him, MacArthur said: "I was just asked if I intended to enter politics. My reply was no. I have no political aspirations whatsoever. I do not intend to run for political office, and I hope that my name will never be used in a political way. The only politics I have is contained in a single phrase known well to all of you—'God Bless America.'"

On to Washington—an all-day ride on April 18. MacArthur had roughed out his speech to Congress on the flight from Tokyo to San Francisco. Now he went over a final draft, polishing, editing. Bataan reached Washington after midnight. There was another mob scene, perhaps fifteen to twenty thousand people. The official greeters were the men who had recommended his dismissal: Secretary of Defense George Marshall, Omar Bradley, Collins, Vandenberg, Sherman. Whitney wrote: "MacArthur greeted them courteously, but the irony of the situation did not escape him." From the tumultuous— even scary—scene at the airport, the MacArthurs were driven to the Statler Hotel in downtown Washington, where the presidential suite, banked with flowers, awaited them.

The next day, April 19, the general and his family rode to Capitol Hill in a motorcade—like a President-elect on inaugural day. Tens of thousands of cheering people lined the sidewalks. A committee of senators and congressmen met him and ushered him to the floor of the House. By special rule, television cameras had been permitted in the House. Television had been employed spottily at the 1948 political conventions, but this was the first major Washington "event" to fall under the all-seeing electronic eye. The largest TV audience of that day watched and waited.

The House erupted into thunderous applause as MacArthur mounted the rostrum at 12:31 P.M. and laid his speech on the lectern. He wore his Army uniform—shirt, tie, battle jacket with five-star insignia on the shoulders

—but no "fruit salad." He was grave and solemn, dignified, dedicated, completely in command of the situation.

As noted, MacArthur was not an electrifying public speaker. His speeches were often long and windy; his style of delivery cold and uninspiring. But this speech—a review of conditions in the Far East and his well-known, aggressive policies for dealing with those conditions—was among his best. Because of the dramatic circumstances, the audience, both live and on radio and TV, hung on every word. His famous conclusion evoked tears across the land:

> I am closing my fifty-two years of military service. When I joined the Army even before the turn of the century, it was the fulfillment of all my boyish hopes and dreams. The world has turned over many times since I took the oath on the plain at West Point, and the hopes and dreams have long since vanished. But I still remember the refrain of one of the most popular barrack ballads of that day which proclaimed most proudly that—
>
> "Old soldiers never die; they just fade away."
>
> And like the old soldier of that ballad, I now close my military career and just fade away—an old soldier who tried to do his duty as God gave him the light to see that duty.
>
> Good-bye.

CHAPTER
FORTY-SIX

★ ★ ★ ★ ★

MacArthur, of course, did not fade away—at least not for a while. That very afternoon, Washington staged a tumultuous motorcade and official greeting ceremony on the Washington Monument grounds. The next day New York honored MacArthur with a six and a half hour ticker-tape parade, watched by an estimated seven and a half million near-hysterical people, who dumped 2,850 tons of tape, confetti, and streamers into the air. For the next fifteen months MacArthur remained very much in the public forefront, an unprecedented public hero and martyr, an outspoken critic of the Truman Administration, a political power to reckon with.

As a five-star General of the Army, MacArthur could not by law be retired. Until his death, he would remain on "active" duty, subject to recall at any time. He received a salary of $18,761.00 per year and the special perquisites of that rank: aides, clerks, government transportation, an office in the Pentagon. MacArthur disdained most of these. He returned Bataan to the government. Courtney Whitney and Charles Willoughby retired and remained by his side as civilian aides. The MacArthurs established living and working quarters in a large and luxurious apartment in the Tower of the Waldorf Astoria Hotel in New York.

During the next fifteen months his public activities fell into three broad categories: a Congressional hearing into his dismissal, public speaking throughout the United States, and a prominent role in Republican presidential politics. Each of these is worth a brief glimpse.

Congressional Investigation

Republican members of Congress, and some anti-Truman Democrats, insisted on a thorough investigation of MacArthur's dismissal. This was carried out by a joint committee composed of members of the Senate Armed Services and Senate Foreign Relations Committees. The inquiry was conducted behind closed doors, but at the end of each day, censored transcripts were released to the media. The inquiry, which went on from May 3 to June 25, 1951, had produced over two million words of testimony, soon broadened to include a complete airing of the Administration's Far East policy. Labeled by the media "The Great Debate," the investigation dominated the news for weeks. The Senators took testimony from MacArthur (some twenty-two hours of it), Marshall, Acheson, the Joint Chiefs of Staff and many others.

What emerged from these complicated and prolonged sessions principally were the diametrically opposing views of the Truman Administration and MacArthur. The Administration continued to seek a compromise solution to the war in Korea. MacArthur, asserting that this was "no policy" or "appeasement," and "there is no substitute for victory," still wanted an all-out stand against Communism, not merely in the Far East, but the world over. He attempted to prove that the Joint Chiefs were on his side (mainly on the basis of the provisional January 12, 1951, JCS memo), that they favored widening the war in Asia. But each Chief denied it—Bradley with his famous assertion that war with China was the "wrong war in the wrong place at the wrong time." In the end, MacArthur failed to overturn the Administration's Far East policy. The disheartening war in Korea continued to yo-yo indecisively back and forth approximately along the 38th parallel while the diplomats sought a ceasefire and settlement.

The Truman Administration might well have indicted

and tried General MacArthur for insubordination in a military court. Clearly the President and Dean Acheson and some military men believed MacArthur had been insubordinate on several, if not many, occasions. But this was not done. The dismissal was considered punishment enough. The "MacArthur Hearings," as they came to be called, would remain the official record of events. In a strict legal sense, MacArthur was not ever officially found to be "insubordinate," a precious point but one ardently clung to by his legions of admirers and by the military historians who dote on such niceties.

Public Speaking

After the hearings, MacArthur, basing at the Waldorf Astoria in New York, embarked on a nationwide speaking tour. It was, Whitney wrote, "a crusade to revitalize the nation. It was a blunt-spoken, hard-hitting crusade." Mostly it was a crusade against the Truman Administration. Like other Republicans in this period, he painted a picture of complete moral decay and Communist infiltration at the highest levels of government. "It is not from the threat of external attack that we have reason for fear," he said in Houston, "it is from these insidious forces working from within." The United States foreign policies, he said, were confused, vacillating, and overly subject to foreign pressures—namely the mealy-mouth British. Everywhere he spoke, throngs of people gathered to cheer him and the media gave him saturation coverage, almost invariably sympathetic.

Presidential Politics

The leading contender for the 1952 Republican presidential nomination was for a long time Robert A. Taft. But the liberal element of the Republican Party, led by Senator Henry Cabot Lodge of Massachusetts, did not think Taft could win. Accordingly, Lodge began wooing five-star General Dwight D. Eisenhower, whom Truman had sent to Europe to help build the N.A.T.O. alliance. Shortly thereafter, Ike let it be known that he would accept a convention draft and Lodge began building a national organization. This move seriously jeopardized Taft's plans—and hopes.

To offset the Lodge campaign for Ike, Taft came to the Waldorf Astoria to solicit MacArthur's support in late 1951. According to Whitney, MacArthur greeted Taft warmly and made the following jaw-breaking pronouncement: "You have given the Republican Party during its past lean years such a dynamic leadership that you have become known to the country as 'Mr. Republican' and I feel that for the party to fail to rally to you now for the coming crucial test would be like changing a general when all the preparations for combat have been made under his guidance and the battle is just about to be joined. It would be an inconceivable betrayal." Thereafter, Taft had MacArthur's support; and MacArthur, Whitney said, "did everything in his power to discourage the rising pressures put upon him to declare himself a candidate."

As convention time approached and Ike's strength was multiplying at Taft's expense, Taft again approached MacArthur, through Whitney. Would he consider a Taft-MacArthur ticket? Whitney was sure MacArthur would not. Taft then dictated a memorandum in which he said that if MacArthur would accept the second place on the ticket, he, Taft, if elected, would designate MacArthur "Deputy-Commander-in-Chief of the Armed Forces" and give him a "voice" in the formulation of all foreign policy. When MacArthur learned of this, he was at first "horrified" but Whitney persuaded him to make "no decision" for the time being. Later, thinking on it, MacArthur liked the idea.

Meanwhile, Guy Gabrielson, Chairman of the Republican National Committee, invited MacArthur to make the "keynote" address at the Republican convention. At first MacArthur demurred, but when Taft called to twist his arm, he agreed. Wearing civilian clothes, he slipped into Chicago on the evening of July 7, 1952, went to the hall and received an awesome ovation and demonstration. The televised speech was a notable bomb, a cliche-ridden, turgid, final indictment of the Truman Administration, which could not have helped Taft. Afterward, MacArthur slipped away and flew back to New York.

The Lodge forces dominated the convention floor, skillfully manipulating delegates to Ike. Just before the first ballot, a movement was launched for Taft to withdraw and place MacArthur's name in nomination. Taft telephoned MacArthur to explain the situation, stating he would withdraw if MacArthur so desired. According to

Whitney, MacArthur replied: "Bob, you're the leader. You make any decision you think proper and I will support it. I am behind your banner to the end. Win or lose I am with you. If you think you have a chance, stand by your own nomination." Taft, "deeply moved," thought he owed it to his supporters to stay in for at least one ballot. If he did not get the nomination, he would telephone to discuss strategy on the second ballot. There was no second ballot. Ike won it on the first.

After that, MacArthur did slowly fade away from the public view. An old friend, James H. Rand, persuaded him to accept a largely ceremonial, high-paying post as Chairman of the Board of his company, Remington Rand. MacArthur entered upon these duties August 1, 1952. When Remington Rand was later merged into the Sperry-Rand Corporation, MacArthur became Chairman of the Sperry-Rand board. The MacArthurs continued to live a very private life at the Waldorf Astoria.

There was one notable interruption to this private life. In July 1961, MacArthur was invited by the Philippine government to attend the celebration of the fifteenth anniversary of independence. He appeared in the familiar khaki uniform, floppy hat and aviator sunglasses—only the famous corncob pipe was missing. A million people —the largest gathering in the history of the Philippines— turned out for the main ceremony at Luneta Park in Manila. After addressing the legislature, MacArthur toured old battlefields: Bataan, Corregidor, Lingayen Gulf, Leyte. A Manila journalist wrote that MacArthur, now eighty-one, faltered occasionally during the visit.

In the following year, May 1962, MacArthur traveled to West Point to receive its most coveted accolade: the Sylvanus Thayer Award for distinguished service to the nation. He reviewed the Corps of Cadets, then gave what was to be his final, and most moving public address. He concluded:

The shadows are lengthening for me. The twilight is here. My days of old have vanished—tone and tint. They have gone glimmering through the dreams of things that were. Their memory is one of wondrous beauty, watered by tears and coaxed and caressed by the smiles of yesterday. I listen vainly, but with thirsty ears, for the witching melody of faint bugles blowing reveille, of far drums beating the long roll.

In my dreams I hear again the crash of guns, the rattle of musketry, the strange, mournful mutter of the battlefield. But in the evening of my memory always I come back to West Point. Always there echoes and reechoes: Duty, honor, country.

Today marks my final roll call with you. But I want you to know that when I cross the river, my last conscious thoughts will be of the corps, and the corps. and the corps.

I bid you farewell.

During his private years, MacArthur had enjoyed relatively good health. But in 1960, aged eighty, he had a severe attack of prostatitis, which nearly killed him. After that, he never seemed to fully recover his strength. From 1960 to 1964, age eighty to eighty-four, his vitality ebbed, though he somehow found the power to write his long memoirs in 1963. In early 1964 he began to fail. On March 2, Jean escorted him to the Army's Walter Reed Hospital in Washington, D.C. Photographers who were waiting confronted a gaunt, emaciated shell of a man in civilian clothes wearing a gray felt hat. After several operations, including the removal of his gall bladder, MacArthur died at 2:30 P.M., April 5, 1964.

The administration of Lyndon B. Johnson accorded MacArthur the funeral he deserved. His body lay in state with full military honors in New York (at the 7th Regiment Armory), Washington (at the Capitol Rotunda), and Norfolk, where friends had built a large, magnificent marble memorial inside the former city hall building. On Saturday, April 11, while a bugler sounded taps, the body of this famous old soldier was placed in its crypt, a remarkable life consigned to history.

SOURCES

THIS BOOK IS based, for the most part, on the published books listed below, newspaper and periodical references too numerous to list, and my own personal recollections as *Time-Life*'s Pentagon correspondent during the Korean War and the "MacArthur Hearings." Of the many biographies of MacArthur to date, one towers above all others: that of *The Years of MacArthur* by D. Clayton James. It is vast in scope, meticulously researched, and scholarly. Two volumes have thus far been published, taking MacArthur's life from birth to the Japanese surrender in September 1945. A third volume (and perhaps a fourth) will deal with the Occupation, the Korean War, and the private years, 1951 to 1964. In the preparation of this biography, I frequently consulted James's thorough and excellent works.

It is also my pleasure, once again, to tip my hat to those gifted yet often unsung official military historians of World War II and the Korean War. The Army series is magnificent. I attempted no battle account without first consulting the series. Special thanks for the splendid work of Army historians Roy E. Appleman, Hamlin M. Cannon, John Miller, Jr., Samuel Milner, Louis Morton, James F. Schnabel, and Robert Ross Smith. Likewise, thanks to the Navy's official World War II historian, the incomparable Samuel Eliot Morison. I gratefully consulted seven volumes of the fifteen-volume series for this book.

Lastly, a word about Japanese codebreaking, that secret enterprise which so profoundly influenced the course of the war in the Pacific (as well as in Europe). To date, anything having to do with Japanese codebreaking is considered classified by the United States government; official documents are not available to historians. However, in a previous book, *Silent Victory: The U.S. Submarine War Against Japan,* I described the enterprise and most of its notable achievements in the Pacific. In this book, I have borrowed freely of my own previous research in this area: exhaustive interviews with nine Japanese codebreakers who were willing to talk off the record.

BIBLIOGRAPHY

Acheson, Dean. *Present at the Creation*. New York: W. W. Norton and Company, Inc., 1969.

Appleman, Roy E. *South to the Naktong: North to the Yalu (The United States Army in the Korean War)*. Washington, D.C.: Office of the Chief of Military History, 1961.

Army Times eds. *The Banners and the Glory: The Story of General Douglas MacArthur*. New York: G. P. Putnam's Sons, 1965.

Arnold, Henry H. *Global Mission*. New York: Harper & Brothers, 1949.

Beck, John Jacob. *MacArthur and Wainwright: Sacrifice of the Philippines*. Albuquerque: University of New Mexico Press, 1974.

Belote, James H., and William M. Belote. *Corregidor: The Saga of a Fortress*. New York: Harper and Row Publishers, 1967.

Blair, Clay, Jr. *Silent Victory: The U.S. Submarine War Against Japan*. Philadelphia and New York: J. B. Lippincott Company, 1975.

Bulkeley, Robert J., Jr., *At Close Quarters: PT Boats in the United States Navy*. Washington, D.C.: U.S. Government Printing Office, 1962.

Cannon, M. Hamlin. *Leyte: The Return to the Philippines (The United States Army in World War II, The War in the Pacific)*. Washington, D.C.: Office of the Chief of Military History, 1954.

Craven, Wesley F., and James L. Cate, eds. *The Army Air Forces in World War II*. Vols. 1, 4, 5. Chicago: The University of Chicago Press. 1948–1958.

Davis, Burke. *The Billy Mitchell Affair*. New York: Random House, 1967.

Eichelberger, Robert L. *Our Jungle Road to Tokyo*. New York: The Viking Press, 1950.

Eisenhower, Dwight D. *At Ease: Stories I Tell to Friends*. Garden City, N.Y.: Doubleday and Company, 1967.

————. *Crusade in Europe*. New York: Doubleday and Company, 1948.

Gunther, John. *The Riddle of MacArthur*. New York: Harper and Brothers, 1950.

Halsey, William F., and Bryan, J., III. *Admiral Halsey's Story*. New York: Whittlesey House, 1947.

Hersey, John. *Men on Bataan*. New York: Alfred A. Knopf, 1942.

Hunt, Frazier. *The Untold Story of Douglas MacArthur*. New York: The Devin-Adair Company, 1954.

James, D. Clayton. *The Years of MacArthur*, Vols I & II. Boston: Houghton Mifflin Company, 1970, 1975.

Kawai, Kazuo. *Japan's American Interlude*. Chicago and London: The University of Chicago Press, 1960.

Kelley, Frank R., and Ryan, Cornelius. *MacArthur: Man of Action*. Garden City, N.Y.: Doubleday and Company, 1950.

Kenney, George C. *General Kenney Reports*. New York: Duell, Sloan and Pearce, 1949.

————. *The MacArthur I Know*. New York: Duell, Sloan and Pearce, 1951.

Krueger, Walter. *From Down Under to Nippon: The Story of the Sixth Army in World War II*. Washington, D.C.: Combat Forces Press, 1953.

Leahy, William D. *I Was There: The Personal Story of the Chief of Staff to Presidents Roosevelt and Truman Based on His Notes and Diaries Made at the Time*. New York: Whittlesey House, 1950.

Long, Gavin. *MacArthur as Military Commander*. Princeton, N.J.: 1969.

MacArthur, Douglas. *Reminiscences*. New York: McGraw-Hill Book Company, 1964.

Mayer, Sydney L. *MacArthur in Japan*. New York: Ballantine Books, Inc., 1973.

Luvaas, Jay, ed. *Dear Miss Em: General Eichelberger's*

War in the Pacific, 1942–1945. Westport, Conn.: Greenwood Press, Inc., 1972.

Miller, Francis Trevelyan. *General Douglas MacArthur: Soldier-Statesman*. Philadelphia: The John C. Winston Company, 1951.

Miller, John, Jr. *Cartwheel: The Reduction of Rabaul*. The United States Army in World War II. Washington, D.C.: Office of the Chief of Military History, 1959.

Mills, Walter, ed. *The Forrestal Diaries*. New York: The Viking Press, 1951.

Milner, Samuel. *Victory in Papua (The United States Army in World War II)*. Washington, D.C.: Office of the Chief of Military History, 1957.

Morison, Samuel Eliot. *The History of United States Naval Operations in World War II*. Vols. III, IV, V, VI, VIII, XII, XIII, XIV. Boston: Little, Brown and Company, 1948–1960.

Morton, Louis. *The Fall of the Philippines (The United States Army in World II)*. Washington, D.C.: Office of the Chief of Military History, 1953.

Potter, Elmer B., and Nimitz, Chester. *The Great Sea War*. New York: Bramhall House, 1960.

Reischauer, Edwin O. *The United States and Japan*. Cambridge, Mass.: Harvard University Press, 1957.

Ridgway, Matthew B. *The Korean War*. Garden City, N.Y.: Doubleday and Company, 1967.

"The Role Played by the American Political Scientists in the Supreme Command for the Allied Powers. The Purge Program." (Monograph) Sixth U.S. Army, Presidio of San Francisco, 1973.

Rovere, Richard H., and Schlesinger, Arthur, Jr. *The MacArthur Controversy and American Foreign Policy*. New York: Farrar, Straus and Giroux, 1951 and 1965.

Schnable, James F. *Policy and Direction: The First Year (The United States Army in the Korean War)*. Washington, D.C.: Office of the Chief of Military History, 1972.

Sebald, William. *With MacArthur in Japan*. New York: W. W. Norton and Company, Inc., 1965.

Shaw, Henry I., Jr. "The United States Marines in the Occupation of Japan." (Pamphlet) Historical Branch, G-3 Division, H.Q. U.S.M.C. Washington, D.C. 1969.

Sheldon, Walt. *The Honorable Conquerors*. New York: The Macmillan Company, 1965.

Smith, Robert Ross. *The Approach to the Philippines (The United States Army in World War II, The War in the Pacific)*. Washington, D.C.: Office of the Chief of Military History, 1953.

————. *Triumph in the Philippines (The United States Army in World War II, The War in the Pacific)*. Washington, D.C.: Office of the Chief of Military History, 1963.

Spanier, John W. *The Truman-MacArthur Controversy and the Korean War*. Cambridge, Mass: The Belknap Press of Harvard University Press, 1959.

Stimson, Henry L., and Bundy, McGeorge. *On Active Service in Peace and War*. New York: Harper and Brothers, 1948.

Textor, Robert B. *Failure in Japan*. New York: The John Day Company, 1951.

Toland, John. *But Not in Shame*. New York: Random House, Inc., 1961.

Truman, Harry S. *Memoirs*. Vols. I and II. Garden City, N.Y.: Doubleday and Company, Inc., 1955, 1956.

Vandenberg, Arthur H., ed. *The Private Papers of Senator Vandenberg*. Boston: Houghton Mifflin Company, 1952.

Wainwright, Jonathan M., and Considine, Robert, ed. *General Wainwright's Story: The Account of Four Years of Humiliating Defeat, Surrender, and Captivity*. Garden City, N.Y.: Doubleday and Company, Inc., 1946.

Whan, Vorin E., Jr., ed. *A Soldier Speaks: Public Papers of General of the Army Douglas MacArthur*. New York: Frederick A. Praeger, 1965.

White, William L. *They Were Expendable*. New York: Harcourt, Brace and Company, 1942.

Whitney, Courtney. *MacArthur: His Rendezvous with History*. New York: Alfred A. Knopf, 1956.

Willoughby, Charles A., and Chamberlain, John. *MacArthur 1941–1951*. New York: McGraw-Hill Book Company, Inc., 1954.

Wittner, Lawrence S., ed. *MacArthur*. Englewood Cliffs, N.J.: Prentice-Hall, Inc., 1971.

Yoshida, Shigeru. *The Yoshida Memoirs*. Boston: Houghton Mifflin Company, 1962.

INDEX

369